Pam Rodges.

Judy Dinwiddie

Mary
Goo...

Diana Dean

property of

MARY MEREDITH COOK BOOK

Chicken a la Kiev

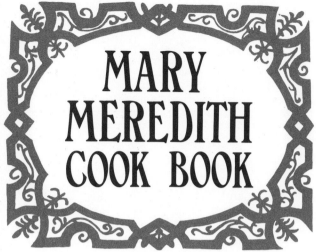

MARY MEREDITH COOK BOOK

HAMLYN
LONDON · NEW YORK · SYDNEY · TORONTO

Shown in photograph on front cover: traditional
roast beef and Yorkshire puddings (recipes
on pages 37-38), selection of hors d'oeuvre (recipes on
pages 13-15), lemon meringue pie (recipe
on page 101).

Shown in photographs on back cover, from top to
bottom: peach paradise pudding (recipe on
page 114), selection of fresh fruit and vegetables
(see chapter beginning on page 75), dressed crab
(recipe on page 32).

Published by

THE HAMLYN PUBLISHING GROUP LTD
LONDON · NEW YORK · SYDNEY · TORONTO
Hamlyn House, Feltham, Middlesex, England.

ISBN 0 600 35916 6

Printed in England by
Cox & Wyman Limited, Fakenham
Photoset by The Birmingham Typesetters Limited

CONTENTS

INTRODUCTION

Every month during the past twenty years, I have had the pleasure of presenting recipes to you through the pages of *Woman and Home*. So many of you have written to me during this time, praising the recipes you've liked, offering suggestions for new ones, requesting repeats of old ones, that I felt it was high time I combined all the best recipes—the ones I know from your letters you have enjoyed most, and found of the greatest value—into one book which you can keep by you on the kitchen shelf. So here it is—a complete reference guide to your favourite recipes, and many others too.

It is an exciting business devising new recipes, and I and my team of Cordon Bleu cooks are lucky for we have the perfect place to do this in—a beautiful, fully equipped test kitchen, which looks out over St. Paul's Cathedral and the Old Bailey, in the city of London. When we settle down to plan each month's recipes—in the way you might plan the week's menus for your family—the creative ideas, which are the essence of imaginative cooking, just fly about. Perhaps it is the view that gives us inspiration!

The task of compiling this book has been a pleasant one, for each recipe I've chosen has brought a host of happy memories back to me, of the time I and my team of cooks first planned it, tried out new methods, discussed exactly the way it should be. Of course, there are the funny memories too—like the time we were photographing a freshly-cooked salmon trout. To me, born and brought up on the banks of the River Tay, a salmon trout could only be photographed one way—on a bed of bracken. But we hadn't any bracken in the kitchen, and there the fish was under the camera looking very naked indeed. I had a sudden idea and goaded one of the photographer's assistants into climbing over a wall into a nearby bomb site car park—he came back triumphantly with a sheaf of bracken, and the salmon trout was photographed in style!

I have tried to include in this book something for everyone, for every day of the year and every possible occasion, from a simple family supper to a full-scale wedding buffet. The letters you have sent to me have given enormous help in planning and choosing the recipes. Without this guidance I would never have known exactly what you want, and which dishes appeal most. So really this book is as much yours as mine. Thank you for your help—I hope you will find your favourite recipes here, and many more dishes, too, that you've perhaps not met before.

Happy cooking to you all!

Mary Meredith

GUIDE TO GOOD COOKING

WEIGHTS AND MEASURES

English weights and measures have been used throughout this book.

The average English teacup holds $\frac{1}{4}$ pint or 1 gill. The average English breakfast cup holds $\frac{1}{2}$ pint or 2 gills. Eight tablespoon liquid measures equal $\frac{1}{4}$ pint. In case it is wished to translate any of the weights and measures into their American or metric counterparts, the following notes and table give a comparison.

LIQUID MEASURE

The most important difference to be noted is that the American (U.S.) pint is 16 fluid ounces, as opposed to the British Imperial pint, and Australian and Canadian pints which are 20 fluid ounces. The U.S. $\frac{1}{2}$-pint measuring cup (8 fluid ounces) is equivalent to two-fifths of a British pint. A British $\frac{1}{2}$-pint measuring cup (10 fluid ounces) is equal to $1\frac{1}{4}$ U.S. cups.

METRIC WEIGHTS AND MEASURES

It is difficult to convert to metric measures with absolute accuracy, but 1 oz. is equal to approximately 30 grammes, 1 lb. is equal to approximately 450 grammes, 2 lb. 3 oz. to 1 kilogramme. For liquid measure $1\frac{3}{4}$ British pints (35 fluid ounces) equals approximately 1 litre; 1 demilitre is half a litre ($17\frac{1}{2}$ fluid ounces), and 1 decilitre is one-tenth of a litre ($3\frac{1}{2}$ fluid ounces).

SOLID MEASURE

British	American
1 lb. butter or other fat	2 cups
1 lb. flour	4 cups
1 lb. granulated or castor sugar	2 cups
1 lb. icing or confectioners' sugar	3 cups
1 lb. brown (moist) sugar	$2\frac{1}{2}$ cups
1 lb. golden syrup or treacle	1 cup
1 lb. rice	2 cups
1 lb. dried fruit	2 cups
1 lb. chopped meat (finely packed)	2 cups
1 lb. lentils or split peas	2 cups
1 lb. coffee (unground)	$2\frac{1}{4}$ cups
1 lb. soft breadcrumbs	4 cups
$\frac{1}{2}$ oz. flour	1 level tablespoon
1 oz. flour	1 heaped tablespoons
1 oz. sugar	1 level tablespoons
$\frac{1}{2}$ oz. butter	1 level tablespoon smoothed off
1 oz. golden syrup or treacle	1 level tablespoon
1 oz. jam or jelly	1 level tablespoon

All U.S. standard measuring tablespoons

BRITISH TABLESPOON (LEVEL) AND OUNCE EQUIVALENTS

Commodity	Tablespoons	Ounces
Sugars		
castor sugar	2	1 oz.
demerara sugar	2	1 oz.
granulated sugar	2	1 oz.
icing sugar	4	1 oz.
soft brown sugar	3	1 oz.
Syrups		
golden syrup	1	1 oz.
honey	1	1 oz.
treacle	1	$\frac{3}{4}$ oz.
Nuts		
ground almonds	3	1 oz.
18 whole almonds	–	1 oz.
chopped hazelnuts	3	1 oz.
whole hazelnuts	2	1 oz.
whole pistachios	2	1 oz.
chopped walnuts	3	1 oz.
8 walnut halves	–	1 oz.
Crumbs		
dried breadcrumbs	6	1 oz.
fresh breadcrumbs	7	1 oz.
packet crumbs	4	1 oz.
Dried fruit		
currants	2	1 oz.
8 glacé cherries	–	1 oz.
cut peel	1	1 oz.
seedless raisins	2	1 oz.
sultanas	2	1 oz.
Miscellaneous		
arrowroot	2	1 oz.
cocoa powder	3	1 oz.
desiccated coconut	4	1 oz.
ground coffee	4	1 oz.
instant coffee	7	1 oz.
cornflour	2	1 oz.
curry powder	4	1 oz.
custard powder	2	1 oz.
flour	3	1 oz.
rolled oats	4	1 oz.
instant potato powder	2	1 oz.
rice	2	1 oz.
ground rice	3	1 oz.
semolina	2	1 oz.

NOTE: These measurements are approximate, and therefore must not be used for larger quantities than 2 oz. The tablespoon measures are level.

OVEN TEMPERATURES

Description	Electric Setting	Gas Mark
very cool	225 degrees F.	$\frac{1}{4}$
	250 degrees F.	$\frac{1}{2}$
cool	275 degrees F.	1
	300 degrees F.	2
warm	325 degrees F.	3
moderate	350 degrees F.	4
moderately or fairly hot	375 degrees F.	5
	400 degrees F.	6
hot	425 degrees F.	7
	450 degrees F.	8
very hot	475 degrees F.	9

THE FIRST COURSE

In this chapter I have included all the starter dishes other than soup which merits a chapter on its own, and I have tried to give as varied and exciting a choice as possible, for I know this is the course which often presents the greatest problems when you're menu-planning.

The important thing to remember is to give as much contrast as possible between starter and main course in flavour, texture and colour. For instance, if you're planning to have a fairly substantial main course, like a beef stew, joint or game pie, then the first course should be as light as possible—perhaps with a fruit base. Similarly if your main course is light, perhaps a fish dish, then you can choose a more filling first course, like a pâté or selection of hors d'oeuvre. Of course you would not in this case have a starter which included fish.

It's fun to experiment with starters—try combining lots of different hors d'oeuvre, or several fruits in a cocktail. If you are making a selection of hors d'oeuvre, and don't have enough dishes of the same size to serve them in, use foil containers, lined with lettuce leaves, instead.

MINTED GRAPEFRUIT

FOR 4 PEOPLE

2 large grapefruit   4 small sprigs of mint
4 white peppermint
   creams

Cut the grapefruit in half. Cut round the centre of one half with a very sharp knife and remove the core, then cut round the edges with a curved grapefruit knife. Finally, cut down both sides of each piece of skin which divides the sections of the grapefruit and lift the skin out leaving the grapefruit segments in place. Prepare the other grapefruit halves in

the same way. Great care must be taken not to pierce the rind or the juice will drip through. Put the prepared grapefruit into dishes, then crush the peppermint creams into small pieces and sprinkle them over the grapefruit halves. Leave the grapefruit in the refrigerator, or in a cold place, for at least an hour for the flavours to blend.
Place a sprig of fresh mint in the centre of each half before serving.

AVOCADO PEARS

These make a simple first course to prepare and taste best if they are really ripe. The tips should be slightly soft to the touch, though the skins should not be black or bruised.

FOR 6 PEOPLE

3 avocado pears   French dressing (see
6 lettuce leaves   page 86)

Cut the avocado pears in half and remove the large stones from their centres. Place each half on a lettuce leaf on an individual serving dish. Fill the centre of each half with French dressing.

TOMATO JUICE COCKTAIL

FOR 4 PEOPLE

a large tin of tomato   salt if necessary
  juice (1 lb. 3 oz.)   a pinch of sugar
a good dash of   4 slices of lemon for
  Worcester sauce   the garnish
a few drops of lemon   cheese straws or
  juice   cheese biscuits to
a pinch of cayenne   serve with the
  pepper   cocktail

Mix all the ingredients—except the lemon and the cheese straws—very thoroughly together, seasoning carefully. Pour the tomato cocktail into four individual glasses and garnish with lemon slices, cutting halfway through each slice so it will fit on the rim of each glass.
Serve cheese straws or cheese biscuits separately.

*Top: potato and radish salad; centre: tomato and orange
salad; bottom: eggs with horseradish dressing
(see pages 13–14)*

Top: Spanish rice; centre: cucumber refresher;
bottom: salami slices (see page 14)

Fritto misto (see page 14)

Minestrone soup (see page 19)

ORANGE AND MELON COCKTAIL

FOR 6 PEOPLE

1 medium sized ripe melon	the juice of 1 lemon
2 large oranges	sugar to sweeten

Choose the melon carefully. It is best to buy it several days beforehand and ripen it in a warm place in the house. To be sure it is ripe, press the tip gently; it should be slightly soft under the pressure. As melons ripen their scent develops, and this also helps to show when it is ready.
Cut the melon in slices an inch wide across the widest part; cut off the skin and remove the pips. Keep a piece of skin to garnish each glass. Cut the melon in chunks and put it in a mixing bowl. Cut the oranges in half, scoop out the flesh with a teaspoon and add it to the melon. Cut six triangles from the orange skin to use as garnish. Add the lemon juice to the fruit and sweeten the mixture with sugar. Put it into glasses and garnish each with melon and orange skin.

FINGER FIRST COURSE

FOR 6 PEOPLE

SMOKED SALMON CURLS

4 slices of brown bread and butter, not too thinly cut	freshly ground black pepper
4 oz. smoked salmon	1 lemon

Cut the crusts off the bread and butter and cut each slice into four. Top each piece with a curl of smoked salmon, sprinkle it lightly with freshly ground black pepper. Cut slices of lemon, quarter them and split each piece up the centre to the rind. Lay one over each piece of salmon.
These can be made early in the day and covered with polythene to keep the salmon moist.

BACON BITES

8 oz. streaky bacon, cut fairly thin	3 oz. freshly made white breadcrumbs
ready-made English or French mustard	3 oz. finely grated cheese

Cut the rind off the bacon with a pair of kitchen scissors. Spread the top side of each rasher with English or French mustard. Mix the crumbs and grated cheese together. Lay the bacon rashers closely together on a board and sprinkle them thickly with the crumb mixture. Press very firmly to the surface. Lay the rashers crumbed side upwards on the grill and grill this side to brown it and crisp it; turn the rashers and grill the undersides without crumbs. Cut each in two or three bite-sized pieces. Arrange them on the same dish as the salmon curls.

HORS D'OEUVRE

Here are some suggestions for hors d'oeuvre dishes. For 4 people you will need to prepare three or four dishes; add more for a larger party. Try to get a variety of flavours, textures and colours, and remember that neatness and freshness are more important than elaborate decoration.

EGG MAYONNAISE

3 hard-boiled eggs	3 tablespoons mayon-
2 level teaspoons capers	naise (see page 85)

Slice the hard-boiled eggs into a dish. Mix the capers into the mayonnaise and spoon over the eggs.

ROLL-MOP HERRINGS

2 roll-mop herrings
a small onion cut into thin rings

Slice the herrings, arrange in a dish and scatter onion rings over the surface.

ANCHOVY & CELERY CORK-SCREWS

2 crisp stalks of celery
1 tin anchovy fillets (14 fillets)

Cut the celery into pieces 3 inches long and not more than $\frac{1}{4}$ inch wide. Wrap an anchovy fillet round each celery piece, and arrange in a dish.

PRAWNS WITH SEAFOOD DRESSING

2 oz. frozen prawns	1 level dessertspoon
2 level tablespoons mayonnaise (see page 85)	concentrated tomato purée
1 tablespoon double cream or natural yoghourt	1 teaspoon sherry (optional)
$\frac{1}{4}$ level teaspoon paprika pepper	a few drops of Tabasco sauce

Put the prawns in a dish and leave them to thaw at room temperature. Mix all the remaining ingredients together for the dressing and pour over the thawed prawns.

POTATO AND RADISH SALAD

Slice freshly cooked new potatoes into a dish. Chop a bunch of radishes, keeping a few whole slices for the decoration. Stir the chopped radishes into enough mayonnaise (see page 85) to heap down the centre of the dish. Cross this with anchovies and put a slice of radish between each. If you prefer, the mayonnaise can be thinned with a little milk and the potatoes mixed with this before they are put in the dish.

TOMATO AND ORANGE SALAD

Skin and slice firm, good-flavoured tomatoes and lay them down one side of a dish. Peel a little rind off an orange and shred it. Cut the peel spirally off two or three oranges, removing the white inner skin as well. Slice the oranges and arrange the slices beside the tomato. Sprinkle the shredded rind down the centre of the dish.

EGGS WITH HORSERADISH DRESSING

Slice 4 hard-boiled eggs in halves lengthwise. Mix a 3½-oz. jar of horseradish sauce with 3 dessertspoons of mayonnaise (see page 85), 3 teaspoons of capers, and a teaspoon of chopped chives. Arrange 4 half eggs face downwards in a dish, coat with dressing and top with remaining eggs cut side up; sprinkle chopped chives between.

SPANISH RICE

Boil 4 oz. of Patna rice, drain it and run some cold water (as the rice is served cold) through it to separate the grains. Stir in 2 oz. seedless raisins and 1 oz. shelled and chopped peanuts. Shred 2 tinned red pimentos and add to the rice mixture. Moisten with French dressing (see page 86).

CUCUMBER REFRESHER

Dice a cucumber and heap it into the dish with a little chopped mint. Spoon natural yoghourt over it and decorate with mint sprigs.

SALAMI SLICES

Fill the dish with salami slices. Cut three slices to their centres and curl into cone shapes. Pipe a star of cream cheese in each cone. Arrange the cones on the slices, using cream cheese stars to keep them upright. Scatter over a few stuffed olives. Top each cone with a halved olive.

NORWEGIAN BRISLING IN OIL AND TOMATO

Arrange the little fish at either end of the dish. Lay two, criss-crossed, on a whole slice of lemon.

FISH AS A STARTER

SMOKED SALMON

This is sold very thinly sliced, so that it goes quite a long way with bread and butter. Serve the slices loosely curled with some pats of butter, freshly ground pepper and lemon wedges.

SMOKED TROUT

As smoked trout dry easily, make sure they are nicely moist when you buy them. Skin and fillet the trout as seen in the foreground of the photograph on page 14, and assemble again without the bone. Serve with brown bread and butter, freshly ground pepper and lemon juice. Horseradish sauce is an alternative to lemon juice.

SMOKED COD'S ROE

Cut the roe in fairly thick slices; serve one for each person with brown bread and butter. Sharpen the taste with lemon juice.

Smoked fish

SMOKED EEL

Skin the eel, take it off the bone and cut it into thin slices. Serve with brown bread and butter and lemon juice. The flesh has an oily, close texture and, like smoked salmon, it goes a long way.

SMOKED MACKEREL

This can be eaten in fillets, like smoked trout, or made into the following pâté to eat with bread and butter:

1 smoked mackerel	1 level teaspoon
3 oz. cream cheese	chopped parsley
salt and freshly ground	a pinch of ground mace
black pepper	1 oz. butter.

Remove all the skin and bones from the mackerel and flake the fish. Beat the cream cheese to a soft cream then stir in the flaked mackerel, seasoning the mixture with salt, pepper, parsley and a pinch of ground mace. Melt the butter and stir it into the pâté. Serve on lettuce leaves.

FRITTO MISTO

This classic Italian dish is made of different kinds of fish, some coated in batter, some egged and breadcrumbed or tossed in seasoned flour, and all fried in deep fat. Choose as many varieties as possible; at least five to make an interesting and tasty dish. Traditionally often added to the fish given here are small octopus, small crabs and soft clams, as well as the more readily obtainable whiting, lobster and oysters. A *fritto misto* can be made with as few or as many ingredients as you like. The amount shown in the photograph on page 11 would be enough for about 8 people. Serve the fish all together on a large platter, each variety grouped separately. Lemon wedges, fried parsley and small mushrooms coated in batter are all excellent additions.

FOR THE BATTER
8 oz. plain flour	$\frac{1}{2}$ pint water
$\frac{1}{4}$ level teaspoon salt	1 level teaspoon
2 tablespoons salad oil	baking powder

FOR THE SEASONED FLOUR
1$\frac{1}{2}$ oz. plain flour	pepper
1 level teaspoon salt	

FOR THE EGG AND BREADCRUMBS
2 eggs, lightly beaten	dried white bread-crumbs

FOR THE FISH
8 small plaice fillets	1 lemon
1 lb. fresh filleted cod	enough oil to come
8 oz. whitebait	two-thirds up the
1 tin mussels in brine	side of a deep fat
($4\frac{1}{2}$ oz.)	frying pan (about
2 large scallops,	2$\frac{1}{2}$ pints)
cleaned	2 large handfuls of
4 oz. packet of frozen	washed and very dry
prawns, thawed	parsley sprigs

First make the batter: sift the flour and salt together into a basin. Make a hollow in the centre and pour in the oil then, stirring gently from the centre, work the oil into the flour, adding the water gradually at the same time. Mix the batter until it is smooth, then beat it very thoroughly and leave it, if possible, for an hour. Just before you are ready to use the batter, beat in the baking powder.

Mix together on a plate all the ingredients for the seasoned flour.

TO FRY THE FISH
Coat the small plaice fillets with egg and breadcrumbs and leave them on one side. Cut the cod fillet into finger widths and egg and breadcrumb these as well. Fry all the coated fish in deep fat, allowing the fat to reheat between the batches. Drain them on a wire tray and keep them hot in a warm oven.

Toss the whitebait in seasoned flour then fry them in deep fat, not too many at a time. They will become crisp in a few seconds.

Drain the tinned mussels and dip them in the batter. Transfer them to the deep fat from a fork and fry them until the batter is crisp. Lift them out and drain them. Cut the scallops in quarters, dip them in batter then fry them in deep fat. Dip and fry the prawns.

Cut the skin off the lemon including the white pith and cut it in wedges; dip these in the batter and fry them in the deep fat.

When all the fish and lemon fritters have been fried, arrange the fish in groups on the serving dish. Put half the parsley into the deep fat basket and lower it slowly into the hot fat; hold the handle of the basket with a cloth covering your hand as the parsley splutters when it touches the fat. Leave it for a second, just until the spluttering lessens, then lift it out and arrange it round the groups of fish. Fry the other half in the same way.

PRAWN AND MELON COCKTAIL

FOR 4 PEOPLE
4 oz. packet frozen prawns	a few drops of Tabasco sauce
$\frac{1}{2}$ ripe melon, with seeds removed	1 dessertspoon sherry
1 firm-hearted lettuce	salt and pepper if required
4 tablespoons mayonnaise (see page 85)	four slices of lemon
3 tablespoons tomato ketchup	brown bread and butter

Make sure the prawns are completely thawed. Cut out balls from the half melon with a vegetable ball cutter or a small teaspoon. Leave them on one side to allow some of the juice to run out.

Wash the lettuce and shred it in half-inch lengths so that it will be easy to eat. Divide the lettuce among four dishes. Mix the mayonnaise with the tomato ketchup, Tabasco sauce and sherry and season with salt and pepper if required. Add the prawns. Drain the melon balls (you can use all the scraps of melon and juice for the base of a fruit salad); add to prawns, mix well and heap on to the shredded lettuce. Garnish the dishes with a slice of lemon and serve the brown bread and butter separately.

NOTE: When fresh prawns are available buy $\frac{1}{2}$ pint. Keep four to put on the edge of each dish for garnish.

PÂTÉS

BACON AND VEAL PÂTÉ

1 lb. piece of very fat bacon (the small end of the forehock is good for this)	2 oz. butter
	pinch of cayenne pepper
12 oz. stewing veal, without bone	$\frac{1}{4}$ level teaspoon ground mace
	salt and pepper

Soak the bacon in cold water overnight. Then put it into a pan with cold water to cover it and bring slowly to the boil, skimming the surface when necessary. Put a lid on the pan and simmer the bacon for 45 minutes, then add the veal to the cooking bacon and simmer them together for a further 45 minutes. Lift the bacon and veal out of the liquid to cool. Remove the rind from the bacon.

Cut the bacon and the veal into a convenient size for your mincer and mince them twice, as finely as possible. Put the minced meat into a basin.

Melt the butter and add this to the meat mixture with the cayenne pepper and the ground mace. Work the mixture well with a wooden spoon and add seasoning if necessary. Press the mixture into a dish or small separate pots or jars, and smooth over the surface.

If you are going to keep the pâté for several days, melt an ounce of butter and run it over the surface of the pâté. It will keep longer in a refrigerator.

Prawn and melon cocktail (see page 15)

BEEF AND BACON TERRINE

FOR 4/5 PEOPLE

8 oz. thinly cut streaky
  bacon
1½ lb. thinly cut stewing
  steak
2 tablespoons stock or
  water
salt and pepper
¼ level tablespoon nutmeg

a bouquet garni (a
  sprig of thyme, a
  sprig of parsley and
  a bay leaf)
an ovenproof pie dish
  holding 1½ pints of
  liquid will be
  required

Cut the rind and any gristle off the bacon. Line the bottom
of the pie dish with some of the bacon and pour in 1 tablespoon of the stock. Put in a layer of steak, fitting it well into
the bottom of the dish. Sprinkle it well with salt, pepper and
some of the nutmeg. Lay more bacon lengthwise in the
dish, then add alternate layers of seasoned steak and bacon,
finishing with a steak layer. Pour in the other tablespoon of
stock, lay the bouquet garni across the top and cover the
dish with kitchen foil.
Bake the terrine on a baking tray in a moderate oven, at
Gas Mark 4 or 350 degrees F., for 30 minutes, then lower
the heat to *Gas Mark 2 or 300 degrees F.* for 1½ hours. As
soon as the terrine comes out of the oven, remove bouquet
garni, put a heavy weight on the top, and leave it overnight.
Turn out and slice thinly to serve.

TURKEY POTTED MEAT

8 oz. minced turkey
salt and pepper
½ level teaspoon ground
  mace

5 oz. butter
2 bay leaves
1 oz. lard

Mix the minced turkey, salt, pepper and ground mace
together. Melt the butter and stir it into the mixed ingredients. Taste the mixture to make sure it is seasoned
sufficiently. Pat the mixture into a shallow dish and level the
surface. Lay the bay leaves on top. Melt the lard, run it over
the surface and leave to set.

CHICKEN FILLET SALADS

FOR 5 PEOPLE

5 even sized lettuce
  leaves
1 head of chicory,
  finely shredded
1 carrot, grated
1 small beetroot,
  finely chopped
½ bunch radishes,
  finely chopped

about 4 tablespoons
  mayonnaise (see
  page 85)
5 small slices of cold
  chicken
cress
1 good sized firm
  tomato, sliced

Wash and dry the lettuce leaves carefully. Mix all the
vegetables together—except the tomato—and moisten
them with mayonnaise. Put a spoonful of the mixture into
each lettuce leaf. Lay a slice of chicken across each salad.
Spoon a little mayonnaise over it and flank it with cress.
Garnish each salad with a slice of tomato.
Alternatively, top the salads with smoked salmon or smoked
saithe instead of the chicken and garnish with lemon. Or
halve hard-boiled eggs and cover them with caviar-style
lumpfish roe.

Chicken fillet salads

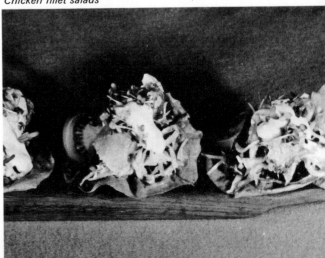

SOUPS

A thick, rich vegetable soup is a wonderful warmer-up on a cold day, and is really "a meal in itself". But there is a great variety of other kinds of soup too . . . a light, delicately flavoured consommé, for instance, makes a perfect prelude to a substantial three-course dinner and chilled soups are delicious and refreshing in hot weather.

In these days of convenience foods, when you can buy so many excellent soups in tins, I have concentrated in this chapter mainly on recipes for soups which don't come in tins—like creamy, green-tinted watercress soup, and delicious soups made from artichokes and sweetcorn. They are so easy to make—and really will give a wonderful start to a meal.

THE STOCKPOT

In the days of kitchen ranges when there was constant heat in the kitchen the stockpot was kept simmering continually in the winter. Nowadays that is rarely practicable, yet it is nice to make stock now and again and store it in a bowl in the refrigerator ready for instant use.

POINTS TO WATCH WHEN MAKING STOCK
Never mix cooked and uncooked bones in stock-making as the stock will not keep well.

Do not add carbohydrates, such as cooked potato or bread crusts, to bone stock as they will cause it to turn sour quickly, even when it is kept in a refrigerator.

LIGHT BONE STOCK

2 lb. beef bones, sawn or chopped	6 peppercorns
6 oz. coarsely sliced carrot	a bouquet garni (a bay leaf, a sprig of thyme and a few parsley stalks)
6 oz. coarsely sliced onion	salt
1 leek (white part only) small stalk of celery	4 pints cold water

Wash the bones carefully and put them, with the vegetables, herbs and seasoning, into a large pan. Add the water and bring the stock to the boil quite quickly, without a lid. Skim the surface carefully. Cover the stock with the lid and simmer the stock continuously for 3 or 4 hours (turning the heat on and off is apt to turn it sour). Strain the liquid off the bones and leave it overnight. Next day skim the fat from the surface, but keep it and clarify it (see below).

BROWN STOCK

Some soups and casseroles require a brown stock. For this use bones and vegetables as given in the recipe for light stock. Dry them carefully, which helps them to brown more quickly, and put them into a roasting tin in a hot oven. When the tops of the bones and vegetables are brown, turn them over and give the other sides a chance to colour.

Afterwards put them into the large pan and continue making the stock in the same way as the light stock.

VARIATIONS
Many different ingredients can be used for stock. Veal bones are good, so are chicken or turkey carcasses (add bacon rinds to these last two for extra flavour). Simply simmer the bones or carcasses with the vegetables and strain them afterwards. Bacon bones are also good, but should be used with caution as they tend to be rather salty.

VEGETABLE STOCKS
When no bones are available use the liquid in which vegetables have been cooked; it is an excellent substitute and even potato water is good. When using vegetable stock, the soup should be used the same day.

TO CLARIFY THE FAT AFTER STOCK-MAKING
Put the fat into a pan and cover it with cold water; bring it to the boil and pour it into a basin. Leave to get quite cold, overnight if possible.

Next day, lift off the cake of fat which has formed on top of the liquid, and scrape away any liquid which sticks to it. Put the fat into a strong pan and boil it until it stops bubbling, by which time the water will have evaporated and pure fat will remain. Strain it into a basin through a fine strainer or a piece of muslin. Store in the refrigerator or a cold larder until it is required.

CREAM OF WATERCRESS SOUP

FOR 6 PEOPLE

3 bunches watercress
¼ pint single cream

1½ pints chicken stock
    made from cubes
    and allowed to cool

Wash, dry and put aside a few sprigs of watercress for the garnish. Chop the rest very roughly and put it into a liquidiser with the stock. Switch on for just a few seconds until the watercress is chopped—alternatively chop with a sharp knife. Stir in the cream, chill and serve garnished with sprigs of watercress.

TO SERVE HOT

Blend 2 level dessertspoons cornflour with enough milk to make a thin cream. Put the soup into a pan, stir in the slaked cornflour and stir until the soup comes to the boil. Serve with Melba toast (see below). Can be prepared early in the day; avoid boiling the soup for more than a second after the addition of the thickening.

MELBA TOAST

medium thick slices from a large white sliced
    loaf

Toast both sides of the bread and cut off the crusts. Slip a knife through the centre of each slice and toast the remaining sides. Can be kept several days in an airtight tin.

CHILLED ASPARAGUS CREAM SOUP

FOR 8 PEOPLE

1 lb. 3 oz. tin of
    asparagus spears
1 lb. potatoes, peeled
1 small onion, peeled
the asparagus juice made
    up to 1½ pints with
    light stock

salt and pepper
1 pint milk
¼ pint single cream

Open the tin of asparagus spears. Cut off the tips of half the spears and keep them aside to add to the soup after it is cooked.

Slice the potatoes and onion thinly and put in a pan with the rest of the asparagus and the juice and stock. Add a little salt and pepper and simmer the soup until the potatoes are tender.

Sieve the soup, or put it through a vegetable mill, then stir in the milk, half the cream and the remaining asparagus tips. Season the soup very carefully, then chill it. Pour the soup into little bowls and float a dessertspoon of cream on top of each helping just before serving.

NOTE: This soup can also be served hot.

VICHYSSOISE SOUP

This is a cream soup which is usually served cold; the flavour is very delicate and the consistency velvet-smooth. It can also be served hot.

FOR 6 PEOPLE

1½ lb. leeks
3 oz. butter
6 oz. potatoes, peeled
1 medium sized onion
1½ pints chicken or veal
    stock (a stock cube
    could be used)

salt and white pepper
generous ¼ pint milk
¼ pint single cream
a few chopped chives

Take off the outside and top leaves of the leeks, slit them lengthwise and wash them under cold running water to remove every particle of grit. When prepared, three-quarters to one pound of leeks will remain. Chop them into half-inch lengths.

Melt the butter, add the leeks and cook them very slowly over a gentle heat for 10 to 15 minutes, stirring occasionally, until fairly tender.

Meanwhile, chop the potatoes, and peel and chop the onion. Add them to the leeks and cook them slowly for a few minutes before adding the stock and seasoning. Simmer the soup until all the vegetables are really soft; it will take about 30 minutes.

Sieve the soup. Rinse the pan and return the soup with the milk. Bring it to the boil and sieve it again; this gives it the velvety texture.

Chill the soup thoroughly before serving it. At the last minute stir in the cream and sprinkle with a few chopped chives.

GAZPACHO

FOR 6 PEOPLE

2 lb. tomatoes
½ cucumber
1 red pepper
1 green pepper
3 spring onions
1 tablespoon salad oil
1 tablespoon wine
    vinegar

about ½ pint cold
    water
a clove of garlic
salt and freshly
    ground black pepper
the yolk of a hard-
    boiled egg
ice cubes

Roughly chop and sieve the tomatoes (or, if you have a liquidiser, skin and liquidise them). Dice the cucumber very finely. Cut the red and green peppers in half and remove all the seeds; finely dice the red pepper, and cut the green one into fine shreds. Slice the spring onions in fine rings. Stir all these vegetables into the tomato purée together with the salad oil, the wine vinegar and the cold water, to make the consistency of thick soup. Peel the outer skin off the clove of garlic, slice it, sprinkle it with salt, and crush it to a smooth cream under the blade of a heavy knife. Stir it thoroughly into the mixture with salt and pepper.

Serve the cold soup in glass bowls. Sprinkle the centre of each with sieved yolk and add a few ice cubes before serving.

SCOTCH BROTH

FOR ABOUT 8 PEOPLE

1 lb. scrag end neck of lamb	2 large leeks, washed carefully and cut into $\frac{1}{2}$-inch lengths
1 turnip (8 oz.), peeled and diced	
$\frac{1}{2}$ large swede (8 oz.), peeled and diced	1 oz. barley
	4 pints water
1 lb. carrots, scraped, half diced and half kept for grating	salt and pepper

Put the meat into a large saucepan with the vegetables. Add the barley and the water and season the soup carefully with salt and pepper. Bring the soup to the boil and simmer steadily for two hours. Grate the remaining carrots, add to the broth and simmer for a further hour.

CONSOMMÉ

FOR 6 PEOPLE

1 lb. shin beef	a good pinch of salt
1 lb. veal bones, chopped	a few peppercorns
3 carrots, peeled and sliced	a bouquet garni (a bay leaf, a sprig of thyme and a few parsley stalks)
3 small onions, peeled and roughly sliced	
1 stalk celery, chopped	4 pints water

TO CLEAR THE CONSOMMÉ

2 egg whites and the shells	4 tablespoons medium sherry

Cut the meat into cubes. Brown the bones over a sharp heat, take them out and fry the meat in the fat from the bones. Add the vegetables, salt, peppercorns and bouquet garni. Pour over the water and bring the soup to the boil slowly. Skim the top carefully then simmer gently for about 3 hours, until the liquid is reduced by about a quarter. Season, strain and cool. The meat can be used for rissoles or shepherd's pie, but most of the value is in the soup.

TO CLEAR THE CONSOMMÉ

Fill the soup pan with cold water and bring it to the boil to sterilise it and clean it thoroughly. Put a clean tea towel and a large wire whisk into a fairly big basin, and when the water boils pour it into the basin on top of the tea towel and the whisk, then pour it off, leaving towel and whisk ready for straining the consommé.

Whisk the egg whites until they are slightly fluffy. Crush the shells and add these to the whites. Put the stock and sherry into the pan and add the egg whites and shells. Bring the consommé very slowly to the boil, whisking slowly all the time. As it starts to boil, stop whisking and allow it to boil up the top of the pan. The egg whites and shells make a crust on the surface and this acts as a filter in clearing the soup. Draw the pan off the heat, allow it to settle then boil it up once again, and again draw it off the heat. Be very careful not to break the crust. Line the basin with the tea towel with the corners over the sides. Pour the consommé and the crust into the tea towel then lift the tea towel gently out of the soup and let it drip for a few minutes. The consommé is now ready to serve.

GARNISH FOR CONSOMMÉ

It is usual to serve consommé with a garnish. This is very often small fancy pasta, boiled and rinsed in cold water; or neat strips of carrot, turnip or leek, boiled and rinsed then added to the soup. Be very careful not to add any garnish which will cloud the consommé.

TO SERVED CHILLED

Pour the consommé either into individual dishes or into one large dish and allow to cool and set. Serve chilled and sprinkle a little sieved egg yolk on to the top.

MINESTRONE SOUP

Minestrone soup varies so much from district to district in Italy that there is no traditional recipe. The main ingredients are a variety of vegetables in season, herbs and pasta. I have suggested a selection of vegetables in my recipe but many other interesting combinations can be used.

FOR 4 PEOPLE

1 red pepper	a sprig of parsley
1 tablespoon cooking oil	2 pints stock or water
	4 oz. shelled peas
1 carrot, diced	4 oz. shredded cabbage
1 medium sized onion, skinned and sliced	
1 medium sized potato, peeled and diced	3 oz. short macaroni
	salt and pepper
$\frac{1}{4}$ bay leaf	grated Parmesan cheese

Cut the red pepper in half and remove all the seeds from inside. Then slice it fairly finely. Heat the oil in a large pan and fry the carrot, onion, potato and red pepper very gently, turning them continuously, until light brown in colour. This will take about 10 minutes. Add the piece of bay leaf and parsley and the stock, then bring to the boil; reduce the heat and simmer for about 30 minutes. Add the peas, cabbage and macaroni, then test for seasoning. Bring the soup up to the boil again and simmer for about another 20 minutes. Serve with a bowl of grated Parmesan cheese.

LENTIL AND TOMATO SOUP

FOR 4/5 PEOPLE

4 oz. red lentils	1$\frac{1}{2}$ pints stock
8 oz. potatoes, peeled and diced	$\frac{1}{2}$ pint tomato juice
	salt and pepper
8 oz. carrots, peeled and sliced	

Put the lentils into a large saucepan with the potatoes and carrots. Add the stock and tomato juice. Season with salt and pepper, if using unseasoned stock. Bring the soup to the boil; put on the lid and simmer until the lentils are tender; this will take 1$\frac{1}{2}$-2 hours.
Whisk either with a hand whisk or an electric mixer until the soup is completely smooth.

NOTE: If you can soak the lentils in cold water overnight they will cook more quickly.

Brown onion soup

COCKIE LEEKIE SOUP

FOR 8 PEOPLE

1 boiling fowl	salt and extra pepper
8 peppercorns	if required
1 bay leaf	2 oz. Patna rice
1 lb. leeks, slit, cleaned,	4 oz. dried prunes,
and cut into inch	soaked for at least
lengths	1 hour

Put the bird, with the giblets, into a large saucepan and cover it with cold water. Add the bay leaf, peppercorns and leeks and a good pinch of salt. Bring to the boil and skim the surface, then put on the lid and simmer the fowl for 2 to 3 hours or until it is tender. Take it out of the pan. Add the rice and prunes, drained of liquid and simmer the soup for a further 20 minutes. Taste the soup and adjust the seasoning with salt and pepper.

NOTE: A nice way to serve the boiling fowl is to take the meat off the bone and coat it with egg sauce.
If the bird is eaten hot, the soup can be used that evening or the following day.

BROWN ONION SOUP

FOR 6 PEOPLE

1 lb. onions	salt and pepper, if
2 oz. dripping	required
pinch of sugar	a French loaf
1 oz. plain flour	French mustard
2 pints brown stock	3 oz. cheese, grated
(this can be made	
with a stock cube)	

Peel the onions and chop them finely. Heat the dripping in a large pan and cook the onions very slowly with the pinch of sugar to brown them. This should take about 20 minutes; if it is hurried the onions could burn and give the soup a bitter taste. Sprinkle over the flour and continue cooking until the flour is also golden brown. Pour over the stock and stir until the soup comes to the boil. Simmer for a few minutes and check seasoning.
Just before serving the soup slice the French loaf, spread the slices with French mustard and sprinkle them heavily with grated cheese. Grill for a few seconds, then float some on top of the soup and serve the rest separately.

Cockie leekie soup (see opposite)

Sweetcorn soup

SWEETCORN SOUP

FOR 6 PEOPLE

1 tin sweetcorn kernels (11½ oz.)	a bouquet garni (a sprig of parsley, a
3 medium sized potatoes, peeled	sprig of thyme and a small bay leaf)
1 onion, sliced	salt and pepper, if
1½ pints stock	required
	1 pint milk

Put the sweetcorn into a large pan with the potatoes, onion, stock and bouquet garni. Season with salt and pepper if the stock is unsalted. Simmer the soup, with the lid on the pan, for about 30 minutes or until the vegetables are tender. Lift out the bouquet garni, add the milk; whisk soup with hand whisk or electric mixer until smooth. Reheat and reseason if required.

ARTICHOKE SOUP

FOR 4/5 PEOPLE

1½ lb. artichokes	salt and pepper
2 medium sized potatoes	a little top of milk,
1 small onion	if liked
2 oz. margarine	a sprinkling of
1½ pints stock	paprika

First peel the artichokes: this should be done in cold water with a good pinch of salt added. As they are peeled, slice them and put them into a bowl of cold water to which a dessertspoon of vinegar has been added.

Peel potatoes and onion and slice them. Melt margarine in a large pan and stir in the sliced vegetables, tossing them gently over a moderate heat for a few minutes without allowing them to brown. Add stock, and salt and pepper, bring them to the boil over a gentle heat.

Simmer the soup for about 30 minutes until all the vegetables are tender. Sieve the soup, or put it through a vegetable mill, or into a liquidiser for a few seconds. Reheat the soup in the rinsed pan, adjust the seasoning and add a little top of milk, if you like a creamy soup.

Serve in hot soup cups with a little paprika pepper.

CREAM OF SPINACH SOUP

FOR 5/6 PEOPLE

1 oz. butter	1 packet of frozen,
1 oz. plain flour	chopped spinach
1¾ pints milk	(11 oz.)
	salt and pepper

Melt the butter, remove it from the heat and stir in the flour. Add the milk and stir over a gentle heat until the mixture is smooth. Bring to the boil, stirring all the time. Add the spinach, thawed or straight from the freezer, and cook gently until the soup is hot again. Season.

Cream of watercress soup (see page 18)

CARROT SOUP

FOR 6/7 PEOPLE

1½ lb. carrots, weighed after scraping	1½ pints light stock or vegetable stock
1 onion	1 bay leaf
1 oz. butter	salt and pepper
4 oz. red lentils	1 pint milk

Slice the carrots roughly, and peel and slice the onion. Melt the butter in a large pan and add the carrots, onion and washed lentils. Stir them over a gentle heat until the butter is absorbed. Add the stock, bay leaf, and salt and pepper, then bring the soup to the boil and simmer it for 1½ hours. Sieve the soup, then return it to the pan with the milk. Reheat and reseason the soup.

NOTE: If you have one or two egg yolks to spare they will improve the soup. Mix them well with two tablespoons of cream (single), then stir ¼ pint of hot—not boiling—soup gradually into the mixture. Add this to the soup, which will then thicken, stirred over a gentle heat. Never boil soup after adding egg yolk or it may curdle.

BORTSCH

FOR 5/6 PEOPLE

1 large cooked beetroot, weighing about 6 oz.	¼ pint double cream
beef bouillon cubes to make 2 pints of stock	

This soup is very quickly made. Rub the skin off the cooked beetroot and grate the beetroot finely. Stir this into the stock and bring the soup almost to boiling point. Leave it at this temperature for 30 minutes, but be very careful not to allow it to boil or the colour will spoil. It should be bright red—boiling the soup would turn it slightly brown. Strain the soup, pour it into soup dishes, and serve it with the cream in a bowl with a small sauce ladle or in a small jug.

NOTE: If you want to use fresh beetroot, cook it unpeeled, in boiling water to cover. When the skin will rub off easily, the beetroot is ready.

CURRIED LENTIL SOUP

FOR ABOUT 8 PEOPLE

1 oz. dripping—bacon dripping is best	1 onion, peeled and chopped
1½ level tablespoons curry powder	1 carrot, scraped and sliced
8 oz. red lentils	4 pints stock or water
the rinds of 6 or 7 rashers of bacon	salt and pepper
8 oz. turnip, peeled and roughly chopped	¼ pint milk
4 outside stalks celery, scrubbed and chopped	lemon wedges for serving with the soup

Melt the dripping in a large pan; add the curry powder and cook it gently for a few seconds. Stir in the lentils and the

bacon rinds and toss these over a moderate heat until all the dripping is absorbed. Stir in all the prepared vegetables and then the stock. Season the soup with salt and pepper and simmer it gently for 2-2½ hours, stirring occasionally. Sieve the soup, return it to the pan with the milk and reheat slowly. If necessary add more salt and pepper. Serve the lemon wedges separately.

QUICK MUSHROOM SOUP

FOR 6 PEOPLE

2 oz. butter	½ level teaspoon ground mace
2 oz. plain flour	salt and pepper
1 pint milk	4 oz. mushrooms
1 pint light stock (chicken, veal or made from a stock cube)	

Melt the butter in a large saucepan, take it off the heat and stir in the flour. Add the milk, stock and ground mace and stir the soup over a gentle heat until it is smooth. Increase the heat and bring the soup to the boil, stirring all the time. Simmer it for 2 minutes, then season it with salt and pepper. Wash the mushrooms and cut a few slices from one of the smallest ones to use for garnish. Chop all the rest or put them through a vegetable mill. (If you have a liquidiser, they can be liquidised with some of the soup, but they should not be too finely chopped so only give them a second). Put them into the soup, bring to the boil again and serve the soup with a thin slice of mushroom on top of each helping.

CREAM OF CUCUMBER SOUP

FOR 4/5 PEOPLE

1 large cucumber	1 level dessertspoon cornflour
1½ pints chicken stock (this can be made from stock cubes)	4 tablespoons single cream
1 level teaspoon chopped onion	salt and pepper
1 oz. butter	a few drops of green colouring
1 oz. plain flour	

Skin the cucumber with a potato peeler, and keep a little of the skin for garnish. Slice the cucumber, and add it to the stock with the chopped onion. Simmer gently for 20 minutes, or until the cucumber is tender.

Sieve the soup, either through a nylon sieve or the finest plate of a vegetable mill (if you have one, an electric blender is the quickest of all). Rinse the pan, put in the butter, and melt it over a gentle heat. When it has melted, remove the pan from the heat, and stir in the flour. Whisk in the sieved liquid, and when it is smooth return the soup to a moderate heat. Stir until it comes to the boil. After simmering the soup for a few minutes, take it off the heat. Blend the cornflour with the cream, and stir into the soup.

Bring to the boil again and season carefully with salt and pepper. Add a few drops of green colouring and finely shredded cucumber skin.

A sprinkling of chopped parsley also makes a good garnish.

RICE AND PASTA

In this chapter you'll find a selection of quick and easy recipes using rice and pasta. These dishes are all simple and economical to prepare and can be served as tasty supper meals, as first courses, or snack lunches.

Remember, too, that both these useful, versatile foods can take the place of potatoes for they happily combine with most meat and fish dishes, and are a marvellous store-cupboard standby for unexpected entertaining.

As a rule, 2 oz. of uncooked pasta or rice doubles its weight when cooked because of its high absorption rate of water. Finely grated Parmesan cheese is the traditional accompaniment to many rice and pasta dishes. This can be bought in packets, ready-grated, but the flavour is better if it is grated off a whole piece. For family cooking, however, especially for small children, it is probably a good idea to use one of the milder-flavoured cheeses.

Want a meal in a hurry? Then cook some spaghetti in plenty of boiling salted water, drain well and toss in melted butter. Top with grated cheese. What could be more delicious?

SMOKED COD IN A RING OF RICE

FOR 5 PEOPLE

12 oz. Patna rice	1 oz. plain flour
8 oz. packet mixed frozen vegetables	¾ pint milk
12 oz. smoked cod	2 oz. cheese, finely grated
a good knob of butter	salt and pepper
1 medium sized onion, finely chopped	a ring mould

Put the rice and vegetables into plenty of boiling, salted water and boil them briskly until they are tender, then drain thoroughly. Rub the inside of the ring mould with butter and put the rice and vegetables round it, pressing the surface down lightly. Leave the ring in a warm place.

Put the fish into an ovenproof dish with ¼ pint water, cover it and cook it in a warm oven, *Gas Mark 3 or 325 degrees F.*, for 20 minutes or until it will flake easily. Drain off the liquid and flake the fish, removing all traces of bone and skin.

Melt the butter and cook the chopped onion very slowly without browning until it is tender, then take it off the heat and stir in the flour. Add the milk and stir the sauce over a very gentle heat until it is smooth and comes to the boil. Do not season the sauce until you have added the cheese and fish. Take the sauce off the heat and beat in first the grated cheese, and then the flaked fish; season the mixture with pepper (it may not need salt).

Turn the rice ring on to a large plate and fill the centre with the fish mixture, serving any extra separately.

CHICKEN AND RICE PIE

FOR 8 PEOPLE

FOR THE PASTRY

12 oz. plain flour	1 egg yolk
a good pinch of salt	cold water to mix
8 oz. margarine	

FOR THE FILLING

3 lb. roasting chicken, uncooked	salt and pepper
4 oz. Patna rice	2 hard-boiled eggs
the finely grated rind and juice of 1 lemon	a little beaten egg to glaze the pastry
1 small onion, finely sliced	an 8 inch round spring-clip tin
1 level dessertspoon chopped parsley	

First make the pastry. Sift the flour and salt into a mixing bowl then rub in the margarine. Bind the pastry with the egg yolk and just enough water to make a pliable dough, and leave it in a cool place while making the filling.

Using a sharp knife take the skin off the chicken; carefully cut the meat from both sides of the breast bone and put this meat on one side. Cut the rest of the meat off the carcass (it is easiest to cut through the thigh joint first) and mince this meat through the coarse cutter of a mincer. The carcass can be used for making chicken soup. Meanwhile boil the rice in plenty of boiling salted water, drain it when it is tender and mix it with the minced chicken, the lemon rind and juice, the sliced onion and the parsley. Season the mixture carefully with salt and pepper.

Roll out three-quarters of the pastry into a circle and line tin; trim neatly round the top and add the trimmings to the rest of the pastry. Cover the base of the pie with some of the filling mixture, levelling the surface. Cut the chicken breasts in half and lay them over the surface. Shell the hard-boiled eggs, cut them in half lengthwise and arrange them round the pie. Top them with the remaining mixture. Roll out the rest of the pastry to fit the top of the pie. Moisten round the pastry lining and cover the pie with the top; press the join together firmly, trim it carefully and flute it with your fingers. Brush the surface with beaten egg and make a hole in the centre; use any trimmings to decorate the pie but do not block the hole. Glaze the decoration.

Bake the pie in a fairly hot oven, about *Gas Mark 6 or 400 degrees F.*, for 20 minutes, then reduce the heat to *Gas Mark 4 or 350 degrees F.* for a further $1\frac{1}{4}$ hours.

The pie is equally good hot or cold.

FLAMENCO RICE

FOR 4 PEOPLE

$1\frac{1}{2}$ oz. butter	2 tablespoons oil and
6 oz. Patna rice	2 oz. butter for
1 pint stock	frying
salt and pepper, if	4 eggs
required	tomato sauce as for
4 bananas	Cannelloni (see page 27)

Melt the butter in a fairly large saucepan, add the rice and stir it over a gentle heat until the butter is absorbed. Add the stock, bring the rice to the boil, put on the lid and simmer very gently for 10 to 15 minutes or until the rice is tender and the liquid has been absorbed. Season carefully with salt and pepper. The rice can be cooked in the centre of a moderate oven, *Gas Mark 4 or 350 degrees F.*, for 20 to 25 minutes. Prepare the tomato sauce.

Peel the bananas and slit them in half lengthways. Fry them gently on both sides in the mixture of oil and butter. Lift them out of the pan and keep them warm. Fry the eggs in the remaining fat.

Cover the base of a hot dish with the rice, arrange the bananas at either side and lay the eggs along the centre. Serve the tomato sauce separately.

TUNA FISH AND RICE CASSEROLE

FOR 2/3 PEOPLE

3 oz. Patna rice	1 pint chicken stock
1 tin tuna fish (7 oz.)	salt and pepper
1 small packet frozen	2 tomatoes
peas	3 oz. cheese, grated
1 small onion, chopped	

Put the rice into a casserole, flake the fish on top then sprinkle the peas and chopped onion over it and pour on the stock. Season with salt and pepper, unless a stock cube is being used in which case no extra seasoning should be needed. Cut the tomatoes in fairly thick slices and lay them round the dish then sprinkle the cheese over the top. Bake the casserole without the lid just above the centre of a fairly hot oven, *Gas Mark 6 or 400 degrees F.*, for 20 minutes; lower the heat to *Gas Mark 5 or 375 degrees F.*, for about 40 minutes or until the rice is cooked.

RISOTTO

FOR 4 PEOPLE

1 medium sized onion	1 clove of garlic
$1\frac{1}{2}$ oz. butter	salt and pepper
6 oz. Patna rice	1 pint stock
2 oz. mushrooms	grated Parmesan cheese

Slice the onion and cook it lightly in the butter; add the rice and stir it over a gentle heat for a few minutes. Wash the mushrooms (there is no need to peel cultivated ones), cut them in quarters and add them to the rice. Peel the outer skin off the clove of garlic, chop garlic, sprinkle it with a good pinch of salt then beat it to a smooth cream under the blade of a heavy knife. Add the creamed garlic to the rice with the stock. Cover the pan and cook the rice very gently until the liquid is absorbed; it will take about 25 minutes. If the rice is not tender when the liquid has been absorbed, add a little extra stock. Season carefully with salt and pepper; if using seasoned stock less will be required. Serve sprinkled with grated Parmesan cheese.

RICE SALAD

FOR 4 PEOPLE

6 oz. Patna rice	salt and freshly
1 level teaspoon salt	ground black pepper
a large packet of frozen	2 tablespoons salad oil
mixed vegetables,	2 tablespoons vinegar
cooked and cooled	4 stuffed olives, sliced

This can be served with many summer dishes. Wash the rice, plunge it into boiling salted water, and boil it rapidly until a grain will rub away between the fingers. Drain the rice and rinse it through with cold water to remove the excess starch and separate the grains. Put the rice into a bowl and toss in the cooked mixed vegetables, salt and pepper, salad oil, vinegar and sliced stuffed olives. Serve cold.

CHERRY AND ALMOND SALAD

FOR 6 PEOPLE

8 oz. Patna rice	8 oz. fresh ripe
2 tablespoons salad oil	cherries
2 tablespoons vinegar	2 oz. browned
salt, pepper and a	shredded almonds
pinch of sugar	sprigs of watercress

Cook the Patna rice in plenty of boiling, salted water until it is just tender. Strain it through a rounded strainer and pour cold water through it to separate the grains and remove the excess starch. Put the cooked rice into a bowl and mix it thoroughly with the salad oil, vinegar and seasoning of salt and pepper with a pinch of sugar. Stone the cherries and mix them in lightly together with the browned shredded almonds (see below). Serve cold, garnished with the sprigs of watercress.

BROWNED SHREDDED ALMONDS

First skin the almonds: put them into a bowl and pour boiling water over them; after a few seconds the skins will loosen. Slip them out of the skins, dry them and shred them into fairly fine slices lengthwise. Scatter these on a baking tray and brown them in a fairly hot oven, about *Gas Mark 6 or 400 degrees F.*, for a few minutes. Watch them carefully as they burn easily.

CHICKEN AND PINEAPPLE SALAD

FOR 4 PEOPLE

8 oz. Patna rice	a small tin of
2 tablespoons vinegar	pineapple rings
1 tablespoon salad	2 oz. peanuts or hazel
oil	nuts
salt and pepper	2 oz. button
a bunch of radishes	mushrooms
$\frac{1}{2}$ cold cooked chicken	

Cook the rice in boiling, salted water until it is just tender, drain it and pour through cold water to separate the grains and remove the excess starch (cold water is used as the rice is to be served cold). Stir the vinegar and salad oil into the rice and season it well with salt and pepper. Wash the radishes, chop half, mix with rice and lay down a dish.

Chicken and pineapple salad

Take all the bones and skin off the chicken and cut it into strips, laying these along the top of the rice. Drain the pineapple, cut the rings in half and arrange them along the top of the chicken with a radish between each.

Put the peanuts or hazel nuts at one end of the salad, wash the mushrooms (there is no need to peel cultivated ones), slice them and put them at the other end of the dish. Garnish the salad with a little watercress.

PASTA

CANNELLONI

FOR 2 PEOPLE

5 cannelloni pieces	a $\frac{3}{4}$ inch plain pipe and
1 oz. grated Parmesan	a large piping bag,
cheese	and 2 ovenproof
	dishes each holding
	$\frac{3}{4}$ pint liquid will be
	required

FOR THE STUFFING

1 oz. butter	1 egg
6 oz. minced ham	2 oz. white or brown
1 oz. parsley, chopped	bread
2 oz. Cheddar cheese,	4 tablespoons milk
grated	salt and pepper

FOR THE TOMATO SAUCE

1 oz. butter	$\frac{1}{2}$ teaspoon Worcester
1 small onion, chopped	sauce
1 level tablespoon	1 level teaspoon
plain flour	concentrated
15 oz. tin of tomatoes	tomato purée
1 small bay leaf	salt and pepper
a few stalks of parsley	1 clove of garlic
1 level teaspoon castor	
sugar	

First cook the cannelloni. Have ready a pan of boiling salted water and place the cannelloni in it. Boil gently for about 10 minutes until tender, then drain well; cut one in half. Meanwhile make up the stuffing. Melt the butter over a gentle heat then fry the ham in it for about 2 to 3 minutes. Stir in the parsley and Cheddar cheese; then beat the egg, soak the bread in the milk, and add them to the mixture. Mix the ingredients well and taste for seasoning. Fill a large piping bag with the stuffing and pipe it into the cannelloni. Arrange 2$\frac{1}{2}$ cannelloni in each dish.

TO MAKE THE TOMATO SAUCE

Melt the butter, add the chopped onion and fry it gently for 2 to 3 minutes without allowing it to colour. Stir in the flour, then the tin of tomatoes and stir it over a gentle heat until it comes to the boil. Add the bay leaf, stalks of parsley, castor sugar, Worcester sauce, tomato purée and salt and pepper. Peel the clove of garlic, chop it, then sprinkle it with salt, and crush it to a cream under the blade of a knife, and add it to the sauce. Cover the pan with a lid and simmer very gently for about 25 minutes. Sieve the sauce, return it to the heat and boil rapidly without a lid for a few minutes. Sprinkle the cannelloni with the Parmesan cheese then cover them with the tomato sauce. Place on the shelf above the centre of a moderate oven, *Gas Mark 4 or 350 degrees F.*, and cook for 15 to 20 minutes.

LAYERED LASAGNE

FOR 4/5 PEOPLE

tomato sauce as given
  for Cannelloni (see
  page 27)
1 oz. lard
8 oz. pork chipolata
  sausages
6 oz. lasagne verdi,
  or noodles
1 oz. grated Parmesan
  cheese

8 oz. packet cheese
  slices
1 oz. butter
an ovenproof dish
  holding 1½ pints
  of liquid will be
  required

First make the sauce. While it is cooking, melt the lard in a roasting tin, prick the chipolata sausages and place them in the hot fat (there is no need to divide the sausages). Return the tin to a fairly hot oven, *Gas Mark 6 or 400 degrees F.*, for 20 minutes until the sausages are golden brown.

Have ready a large pan half-filled with boiling salted water, and into it place the lasagne. Boil it gently for about 10 minutes until the pasta is tender, then drain it well.

Thoroughly grease the ovenproof dish and into it place alternate layers of lasagne, Parmesan cheese, tomato sauce and cheese slices, then all the sausages cut into pieces. Repeat these layers, ending with the cheese slices, then pour over the remaining sauce and sprinkle it generously with the remaining Parmesan cheese. Dot the top with butter.

Bake the lasagne in the centre of a moderate oven, *Gas Mark 4 or 350 degrees F.*, for 20 minutes.

MACARONI CHEESE

FOR 5/6 PEOPLE

1 lb. tomatoes

FOR THE SAUCE
3 oz. margarine
3 oz. plain flour
1½ pints milk
6 oz. Leicester cheese,
  grated

FOR THE TOP
2 oz. Leicester cheese,
  grated

4 oz. macaroni

2 level teaspoons
  powdered mustard
salt and pepper

an ovenproof dish
  holding 2¾ pints of
  liquid will be
  required

Slice the tomatoes. Keep 8 slices for the garnish. Place the remainder in the bottom of a buttered ovenproof dish.

Half-fill a large pan with salted water and bring it to the boil; add the macaroni and simmer until it is tender; this will take about 15 minutes. Drain it well.

Next make the sauce. Melt the margarine in a large saucepan over a gentle heat, take it off the heat and stir in the flour. Gradually add the milk, then stir the sauce over a gentle heat until it is smooth. Bring it to the boil and simmer for a few minutes. Take the sauce off the heat and beat in the grated cheese, the powdered mustard and enough salt and pepper to season it well. Stir in the macaroni and pour the mixture over the sliced tomatoes.

Macaroni cheese

Sprinkle the top thickly with the grated cheese and place the dish in a fairly hot oven, *Gas Mark 6 or 400 degrees F.*, for about 15 minutes until the macaroni cheese is crisp on top. Alternatively, it can be placed under a hot grill until golden brown in colour.

Place the slices of reserved tomato diagonally across the dish.

SPAGHETTI BOLOGNAISE

FOR 6/8 PEOPLE

2 oz. lard or dripping
2 oz. bacon rashers,
  chopped
8 oz. onion, chopped
12 oz. raw minced beef
4 oz. mushrooms,
  roughly chopped

2 carrots, sliced
1 large tin (2 lb. 3 oz.)
  of tomatoes
salt and pepper
12 oz. spaghetti
grated Parmesan
  cheese

Melt the lard or dripping in a fairly large saucepan and fry the bacon and onion for a few minutes; the onion should be soft but not coloured. Add the minced beef, mushrooms and carrots and fry again for about 2 minutes. Next add the tomatoes and a little salt and pepper, then bring the mixture slowly to the boil. Reduce the heat and simmer the sauce for about 1 to 1¼ hours. The sauce should by then have reduced considerably and become much richer. Season carefully with salt and pepper, if required.

Meanwhile, cook the spaghetti. Have ready a large pan half-filled with boiling, salted water and put into it one end of the spaghetti, then curl the rest into the water as it softens (never break it). Simmer the spaghetti for 15 to 20 minutes until it is tender, then drain it in a colander and pour through boiling water to separate the strands.

Finally, toss the spaghetti in a little grated Parmesan cheese, heap it on to a plate and pour the sauce over it. Sprinkle the top with a little cheese and serve more separately.

Spring pasta

SPRING PASTA

FOR 5 PEOPLE

4 oz. macaroni
2 oz. margarine
2 oz. flour
1 pint milk
salt and pepper
6 oz. Cheddar cheese,
    grated

8 oz. cooked chicken,
    cut into strips
1 tin of asparagus
    spears (14 oz.)
a lightly greased oven-
    proof dish holding $2\frac{1}{2}$
    pints of liquid will
    be required

Half-fill a pan with salted water and bring it to the boil. Add the macaroni and simmer until it is tender; this will take about 15 minutes. Drain it well.

Next make the sauce: melt the margarine in a large saucepan over a gentle heat, take it off the heat and stir in the flour. Add the milk, then return the pan to a gentle heat and stir it until smooth. Season with salt and pepper, and bring the sauce to the boil; simmer for a few minutes. Take the sauce off the heat and beat in three-quarters of the grated cheese, the chopped cooked chicken, and the cooked macaroni.

Check for seasoning, then pour half the mixture into the dish. Drain the tin of asparagus and lay all but 5 spears on top; cover with the rest of the mixture, and sprinkle the top with the remaining grated cheese.

Place the spring pasta under a pre-heated grill and brown it lightly: it will take about 5 to 7 minutes. Decorate it with the reserved asparagus.

FISH

There is nowadays an enormous variety of both fresh and frozen fish available, and it's fun to experiment with new and unusual recipes. In this chapter, I give ideas for hot and cold dishes, some simple, some special—there are traditional favourites too, like fried fish and chips and herrings in oatmeal, as well as some more unfamiliar recipes that I know you will enjoy.

An important point to remember is that although fish is an excellent source of nourishment, in order to obtain the best value from it, you should never overcook. Buy it as fresh as possible, and poach rather than boil to avoid breaking up the flakes. The fishmonger will usually clean the fish for you and remove heads, tails, fins and scales.

1

FRIED FISH AND CHIPS

For each person allow one or two fillets of fish, depending on their size. Skinned and filleted sole, plaice, cod or haddock are all good. Small whole haddock (if you can get them), skinned and filleted, have a delicious nutty flavour, and are just right for serving even-sized portions of the same thickness.

2

3

fish fillets	dry white
beaten egg (1 egg is	breadcrumbs
enough for about	fat for deep frying
7 fillets)	1 lemon
	potatoes

The secret of nicely fried fish is to drain it well after frying and to serve it hot, crisp and attractively arranged.
Wipe the fillets with a damp cloth and if they are too large cut them into pieces of a suitable size.

COATING THE FILLETS

Put the beaten egg on a plate and have a brush ready to coat the fillets with the egg. Put the dry white crumbs on to a square of paper.
Lay a fillet of fish in the egg and brush it all over. Lift the fillet up for a few seconds to allow any surplus egg to run

off, then transfer it to the crumbs. Lift one edge of the paper and flick the crumbs over the fish. When the fish is evenly coated, press the crumbs to it with a palette knife, then transfer it to a board or large plate ready for frying. Coat the remaining fillets in the same way.

FRYING THE FISH

Half-fill the deep fat pan with clean oil, lard or cooking fat; and heat it slowly. If the fat is too cool it will make food greasy, while if it is too hot it is not only dangerous but the fat will be spoiled too. The correct temperature for frying fish is about 375 degrees F. If you do not have a fat thermometer, the temperature can be tested by putting a cube of white bread into the hot fat. If the temperature is correct the bread should turn golden brown in about a minute.

Lower one fillet, or more if there is room, into the fat (there is no need to use a basket) and fry briskly until it is golden brown. Lift the fillet out of the fat, and lay it on a piece of absorbent kitchen paper. Fry all the fillets in the same way, remembering to reheat the fat after each frying.

Serve the fish heaped on a hot dish. Arrange slices of lemon, not too thinly cut, round it.

THE CHIPS

Peel and cut the potatoes into chips. To make nice even-sized chips cut a rectangle of potato as seen in photograph 1, and from it cut chips the size you like. The remaining scraps can be used for soup or mashed potato. Put the chips into a bowl of cold water as you cut them. Before frying however the chips must be dried very thoroughly in a clean towel (photograph 2). This is important because wet chips will not only make the fat splutter, but will also cool it more than necessary. Put the chips into the deep fat basket. Heat the fat to about 380 degrees F., just a little hotter than for fish, and lower the chips slowly into the fat. It will froth up at first then quieten as the chips begin to cook (photograph 3). Fry the chips over a moderate heat for about 5 minutes (less for really small chips). By this time, although they are still white, the chips are cooked through to the centre. Lift the basket out of the pan, put it on a plate to catch the drips of fat, and reheat the fat in the pan to the original temperature. Return the chips to the pan for just a minute until they are lightly golden and crisp. Lift them out of the pan, tip them on to absorbent kitchen paper, sprinkle with salt and then put them into a hot dish for serving; the hotter the chips are when served, the better. This method of twice frying chips is the best way to make them crisp. When you are frying both fish and chips it is best to pre-fry the chips before the fish, then fry the fish and finally fry the chips for just one minute. In this way both fish and chips will be hot, fresh and crisp at the same time.

LOOKING AFTER THE DEEP FAT

Always start with a clean dry pan; even a single drop of water will make the fat splutter as it is heating. Try never to overheat the fat as it will spoil, but also never fry with too cool fat as the food will be greasy and the flavour of the food can be drawn into the fat.

Fry with the handle of the pan turned to the back of the cooker; this is most important when there are children about.

Let the fat cool before moving it. Never strain very hot fat, but when it is cool lay a piece of muslin in a rounded

strainer and run the fat through the muslin to catch any particles of food or crumbs.

Keep the fat in a cool place.

TO SKIN AND FILLET A PLAICE

Using a sharp knife, slit the fish down the backbone from the head to the tail. Separate the fish from the bone, running the knife flat against the bone. Remove the rest of the fillets in the same way, turning the fish to lie in the other direction, with the tail away from you.

Place the fillet skin-side downwards on a board and sprinkle the tail with salt to give your fingers a good grip. Scrape the fillet off the skin, holding the knife at a more upright angle, as in the second picture.

1

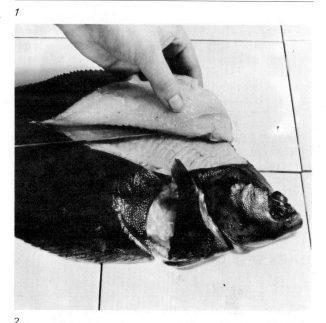

2

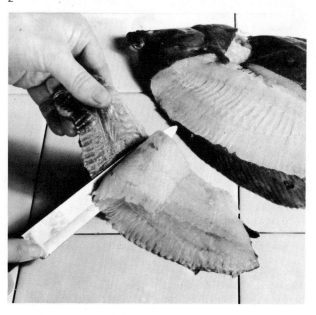

FISH SALAD PLATTER

FOR 8 PEOPLE

FOR THE BASE

6 oz. plain flour	2 oz. lard
a good pinch of salt	cold water to mix
2 oz. margarine	

FOR THE TOP

1 tin (15 oz.) vegetable salad	½ cucumber, thinly sliced
1 tin (3⅔ oz.) smoked oysters	2 tins sardines
	1 tin anchovy fillets
1 tin (7 oz.) tuna fish	1 small tin shrimps
1 tin (15 oz.) potato salad	a little watercress and 4 wedges of lemon

Sift the flour with the pinch of salt. Rub in the fats and mix the pastry to a stiff dough with a little cold water. Turn the pastry on to a lightly floured board and roll it into a circle, then trim it neatly to 9 inches in diameter. Slip the pastry circle on to a baking tray, prick it all over and bake it in a fairly hot oven, *Gas Mark 6 or 400 degrees F.*, for 25 to 30 minutes. Leave it on a wire tray to cool.

Put the pastry base on to the serving dish and spread the vegetable salad evenly over it. Edge the platter with a ring of smoked oysters then flake the tuna fish and spread it in the centre of the ring. Add a layer of potato salad, then cover the surface with thinly sliced cucumber.

Arrange in a star shape on top the sardines alternately with twists of anchovy fillets. Decorate the sardines with the shrimps.

Garnish the dish with watercress and lemon wedges.

DRESSED CRAB

FOR 4/5 PEOPLE

2 boiled crabs, weighing about 2 lb. each	salt and freshly ground black pepper
5 rounded dessert-spoons white breadcrumbs	finely grated nutmeg
	2 hard-boiled eggs
2 to 3 dessertspoons mayonnaise (see page 85)	1 rounded dessert-spoon chopped parsley

Pull the legs and claws from one of the crabs, close to the body. Turn the crab upside down and, holding it firmly with one hand, insert the thumb and first finger of the other hand into the sockets from which the large claws came and pull out the centre of the crab. To this centre the tail, stomach and gills are attached; the stomach is the little bag near the eyes. The feathery-looking gills are round the centre and some may still be attached to it. Both the stomach and gills should be removed and thrown away. The white hard centre shell will be left. Remove the crab meat from it, crack it open and pick out all the little pieces of meat with a skewer. With a spoon, remove the brown meat from all round the inside edges of the shell. Keep the white and the dark meat separate.

Next scrub the outside of the shell and wash the inside, drying it carefully. Break away the edge from the main shell leaving a large space: press firmly with your thumb and the shell will crack off quite easily round the natural line. Rub the outside of the shell with a little cooking oil to make it shiny.

Crack the large claws with a kitchen weight and remove the meat from inside them. Mix this meat with the rest of the white crab meat. Take great care not to allow any splinters of shell to fall into the meat. Detach the small claws at the ends of the legs, wash and dry them and keep them for a garnish. Crack the legs and remove the meat from each section.

Prepare the other crab in the same way.

Mix half the breadcrumbs into the dark crab meat and the rest with the white meat. Moisten each with some of the mayonnaise and season with salt, pepper and a little nutmeg. Refill the shells with crab meat, the white meat at one side and the dark meat at the other.

Sieve the yolks of the hard-boiled eggs and chop the whites roughly. Coat half of each crab with sieved yolk and the other half of each with chopped egg white. Sprinkle chopped parsley thickly down the centre. Decorate the crabs with the small claws sticking from the parsley.

FRIED SCAMPI AND MUSHROOMS

FOR 4 PEOPLE

4 oz. button mushrooms	dry white bread-crumbs
2 tablespoons French dressing (see page 86)	cooking oil for deep frying
1 egg	a slice of lemon
12 oz. frozen scampi	

Wipe the mushrooms (there is no need to peel them), toss them into the French dressing and leave them for 10 minutes. Beat the egg and coat the scampi, first in the egg then in the crumbs. Drain the mushrooms and coat them in the same way.

Heat the oil (if using a thermometer, to 360 degrees F.) and fry the scampi for 3 or 4 minutes. Drain them on absorbent kitchen paper. Fry the mushrooms for 2 minutes. Heap the scampi into the centre of a plate, surround them with the mushrooms, and garnish with lemon.

The scampi and mushrooms can be fried beforehand, kept in a warm (but not hot) oven, and garnished at the last minute.

FRESH SALMON

A piece of fresh salmon is always best cooked simply. No matter what size of piece, the cooking method is always the same.

FOR 6/8 PEOPLE

2 lb. fresh salmon or salmon trout	1 level teaspoon salt
	1 bay leaf
6 peppercorns	a sprig of parsley
2 tablespoons cider or wine vinegar	

THE THREE-MINUTE METHOD

Wipe the fish and place it on the tray of a fish kettle, or into a large saucepan. Cover the fish with cold water and add the peppercorns, cider or wine vinegar, the salt, bay leaf

and the sprig of parsley. Cover the pan tightly with a lid and bring the fish to the boil very slowly. Boil it briskly for exactly 3 minutes, then take it off the heat and remove the lid. Leave the fish to cool in the liquor. Take it out as soon as it has cooled. (If the fish is going to be served hot, leave it for 10 minutes before lifting it out of the pan.)
Serve with Hollandaise sauce (see page 86).

SALMON SOUFFLÉ

FOR 3/4 PEOPLE

1¼ oz. butter	1 level tablespoon
1¼ oz. plain flour	chopped parsley
¾ pint milk (this can	a few drops of
include liquid from	Tabasco sauce
the tinned salmon)	a pinch of ground
2 tins of salmon (7¾ oz.)	mace
2 eggs	salt and pepper
½ oz. gelatine	a soufflé dish which
3 tablespoons water	holds 1½ pints of
scant ¼ pint single cream	liquid will be required

FOR THE DECORATION

¼ pint aspic jelly, made	½ cucumber
up from aspic jelly	a few watercress
crystals	leaves

First prepare the soufflé dish as for Raspberry Soufflé on page 111.
Then make the sauce. Melt the butter in a saucepan, take it off the heat and stir in the flour. Add the milk and salmon juice and stir the sauce over a gentle heat until it is smooth, then bring it to the boil, stirring all the time. Separate the yolks from the whites of the eggs. Add a little of the sauce to the egg yolks and stir well, then stir them into the sauce. Stir the sauce over a gentle heat without allowing it to boil, just warming it sufficiently to thicken it with the egg yolks. Leave the sauce to cool.
Put the gelatine into a small pan, with the water, and dissolve it over a gentle heat, then stir it into the sauce. Remove any bones and skin from the salmon, flake the fish with a fork and stir it into the sauce with the cream, chopped parsley, Tabasco sauce, ground mace, and salt and pepper to flavour.
Whisk the egg whites stiffly and stir a tablespoon of egg white into the mixture. Lightly fold in the rest. Pour the mixture into the prepared dish; it should come an inch above the top of the dish and be held in position by the paper collar. Leave the soufflé for 30 minutes to set.

TO DECORATE THE SALMON SOUFFLÉ

Run 2 tablespoons of cold, but not set, jelly aspic over the surface of the soufflé; the paper collar will hold it in place. Leave it to set. Score the sides of the cucumber with the prongs of a fork, then cut it into thin slices. Arrange these, overlapping, round the top of the soufflé and place a few watercress leaves inside the cucumber ring. Gently run the rest of the aspic jelly over the surface and leave it to set. Untie the string and remove the paper collar carefully, holding a palette knife behind the paper and against the edge of the soufflé.
This is delicious served with a salad as a summer supper dish, or makes an unusual first course for a dinner party.

COD EN PAPILLOTE WITH EGG SAUCE

FOR 6 PEOPLE

2 oz. butter	6 oz. mushrooms
3 lb. cod, unboned and	a large sheet of
in one piece (middle	doubled greaseproof
cut is best)	paper will be
a good sprig of parsley	required
1 lemon	
salt and freshly ground	
black pepper	

Smear the centre of the doubled greaseproof paper with the butter and put it into a roasting tin. Lay the cod in the centre of the paper. Open the fish and put the sprig of parsley down the centre, then grate the rind of the lemon into the centre of the fish. Sprinkle well with salt and pepper and close the fish.
Wash and thickly slice the mushrooms and lay them round the fish. Slice the lemon and arrange the slices along the top of the fish.
Fold the greaseproof paper into a parcel around the fish, folding the ends of the paper upwards so that no juice can escape.
Put the fish into the centre of a moderately hot oven, about *Gas Mark 5 or 375 degrees F.*, for 1 hour.
To serve the fish, cut round three sides of a rectangle to make a "door" in the top of the parcel and fold back the paper to expose the fish. Serve the fish and mushrooms straight from the parcel, and the buttered egg sauce separately.

THE EGG SAUCE

3 hard-boiled eggs	salt if necessary
6 oz. butter	a pinch of cayenne
2 heaped tablespoons	pepper
chopped parsley	the juice of 1 lemon

Shell the hard-boiled eggs and chop them finely. Melt the butter gently, then stir in chopped hard-boiled eggs and the parsley. Season with salt, if required, and a pinch of cayenne pepper, and add the lemon juice. Serve the sauce from a small casserole or large sauceboat.

FISH IN A PUFF PASTRY PARCEL

FOR 4 PEOPLE

4 frozen cod or	salt and pepper
haddock steaks	a little lemon juice
1 small packet frozen	a little beaten egg to
puff pastry	glaze
2 oz. butter	
1 level tablespoon	
chopped parsley	

Leave the fish and pastry at room temperature just long enough to thaw the pastry sufficiently to make it pliable. Roll the pastry into a rectangle on a floured board and trim it neatly to 10 inches wide by 12 inches long. Keep the scraps for decoration. Lay the fish along the pastry, leaving

¼-inch space between each piece. Beat the butter to a soft spreadable consistency then beat in the chopped parsley, and heap this on top of the fish. Sprinkle the parsley butter with salt and pepper and squeeze a little lemon juice over the fish.

Moisten the edges of the pastry with water, fold up the two long sides on top of the fish and pinch them together all down the centre. They will split a little during cooking but the pastry should keep the parsley butter inside. Press the ends firmly together. Roll out the scraps into a strip, trim it to 1 inch wide and cut eight little diamonds for leaves. Stick them on the pastry with a dab of water.

Using a fish slice and a palette knife, transfer the parcel to a baking tray and brush it with a little beaten egg.

Bake the parcel in a hot oven, about *Gas Mark 7 or 425 degrees F.*, for 20 minutes then lower the heat to *Gas Mark 5 or 375 degrees F.* for 10 minutes.

FINNAN HADDOCK

These come in various sizes; the medium ones are best for serving whole. Make sure the fish are moist.

Cut off the fins and lay the fish in a pan large enough to hold it, then pour round a little milk and dot the fish with butter. Cover the haddock with a lid to keep it moist and heat it very gently without allowing the milk to boil. Simmer it gently until the fish will flake easily, but be careful not to over-cook. Serve it with more butter pats on top.

When cooking more than one, the fish can be heated in a roasting tin in the oven; again, remember to cover them with a baking tray or a piece of kitchen foil to keep them moist.

CREAMED HADDOCK SAVOURIES

FOR 4 PEOPLE

1 oz. butter	6 oz. cooked smoked
1 oz. plain flour	haddock, flaked
½ pint milk	salt and pepper, if
2 egg yolks	required
3 tablespoons double	pinch of ground mace
cream	paprika pepper

Melt the butter in a saucepan, take it off the heat and stir in the flour. Add the milk and stir the sauce over a gentle heat until it comes to the boil, then simmer the sauce for a few minutes. Beat the yolks and the cream together and add 2 tablespoons of the sauce to it; stir well and add to the sauce, return the saucepan to a gentle heat, then stir for a few minutes without allowing the mixture to boil. Stir the fish into the sauce, season it with salt, pepper and ground mace. Heat the fish and then turn the mixture into 4 small individual dishes. Sprinkle the tops with paprika and keep the savouries in a warm place until they are required.

FISH AND CHICKEN NEST

This unusual blend of flavours is delicious.

Arbroath smokies are whole, small haddock smoked over oak chips until they are cooked. To use them for breakfast or supper, heat them gently in milk with a dot of butter, keeping a lid on the pan so that they stay moist. Heat them only, because they are already cooked and further cooking would dry them. Smokies are not available everywhere but cooked finnan haddock can be substituted in the following recipe.

FOR 3/4 PEOPLE

1 Arbroath smokie	pinch of cayenne
(8 oz. cooked finnan	pepper
haddock can be used	salt if required
instead, if preferred)	a little lemon juice
2 helpings of cooked	1 lb. cooked potato,
chicken	creamed
2 hard-boiled eggs	a little beaten egg
1 oz. margarine	1 oz. cheese, finely
1 oz. plain flour	grated
¼ pint milk	a forcing bag with a
½ pint chicken stock	large star pipe
(this can be made	a plate 10 inches in
from a stock cube)	diameter

Skin and flake the smokie or finnan haddock. Remove any skin from the chicken and take out the bones then cut it into small pieces. Shell the hard-boiled eggs and cut each into about 8 pieces.

Melt the margarine in a saucepan, take it off the heat and stir in the flour. Add the milk and chicken stock and stir the sauce over a gentle heat until it is smooth, then bring it to the boil, stirring all the time. Season the sauce with a small pinch of cayenne pepper, salt if necessary, and a little lemon juice, then stir in the fish, chicken and egg.

Meanwhile fill a forcing bag with the creamed potato and pipe a border of potato round the edge of the plate, finishing it off with a row of stars. Brush the potato stars very lightly with beaten egg. Pour the prepared mixture into the centre

Fish and chicken nest

and scatter the surface with a little grated cheese. Thoroughly heat the potato and brown the surface in a fairly hot oven, about *Gas Mark 6 or 400 degrees F*. It will take about 20 minutes.

HASTY PLAICE

FOR 4/5 PEOPLE

a knob of butter	1 carton (2 oz.)
1 large packet (13 oz.)	potted shrimps
frozen individually	½ cucumber
packed plaice fillets	salt and pepper

Rub a flat ovenproof dish with butter then arrange the fillets of plaice on it, overlapping slightly. Put a few potted shrimps on each one. Bake the fish in a moderately hot oven, about *Gas Mark 5 or 375 degrees F.*, for about 10 minutes; if the fish is still frozen, it may take a little longer.
Dice the cucumber, put it into a pan with enough water almost to cover it, season it with salt and pepper and simmer it for 5 minutes. Drain the cucumber and arrange it at either end of the dish of fish.

SOLE DUGLÉRÉ

FOR 6 PEOPLE

1 onion	12 fillets of sole, with
6 peppercorns	the black skin
a blade of mace	removed (ask the
	fishmonger to let
	you have the bones)
	salt and pepper

FOR THE SAUCE

2 oz. butter	¼ pint single cream
1½ oz. plain flour	¾ lb. firm tomatoes
¼ pint dry white wine	1 level tablespoon
¾ pint fish stock (the	finely chopped
liquid in which the	parsley
fish is cooked)	salt and pepper, if
	needed

Peel and slice the onion. Put the onion, peppercorns, mace and the sole bones into a saucepan with a pint of cold water. Bring the water to the boil, skim the surface and simmer the stock without a lid for 20 minutes. Strain the stock and measure ¾ pint; if there is less, make it up with water. Meanwhile season the skin side of each fillet with salt and very lightly with pepper. Fold the fillets in three with the seasoning inside. Lay the fillets in an ovenproof dish and pour the stock over them. Cover the dish with a lid or greaseproof paper and cook the fish in a moderate oven, about *Gas Mark 4 or 350 degrees F.*, for about 20 minutes or until the fish is cooked; it will look opaque instead of transparent. Strain off the fish stock and again make it up to ¾ pint with water. Leave the fish covered and keep it hot while making the sauce.
To make the sauce, melt the butter in a saucepan, take it off the heat and stir in the flour. Add the wine and fish stock and stir the sauce over a gentle heat until it comes to the boil. Boil the sauce rapidly until it is reduced by about a quarter; it should be a thick, syrupy consistency which

will coat the back of the wooden spoon. Add the single cream, reboil the sauce, and season it carefully with salt and pepper if required.
Meanwhile peel the tomatoes. Quarter them and scoop out the pips and juice (this can be used for tomato sauce, soup or in stews). Cut the quarters of tomato into strips. Stir them into the sauce with all but a sprinkling of chopped parsley.
Drain off any liquid which has formed round the fish and coat the fish carefully with the sauce. Sprinkle the surface lightly with the rest of the chopped parsley.

ADVANCE PREPARATION

The fish is best cooked and the sauce made just before it is required; the tomatoes and chopped parsley can be prepared earlier in the day.

DEEP-FRIED SPRATS

FOR 2 PEOPLE

8 oz. sprats	paprika pepper
1 oz. plain flour	brown bread and
salt and pepper	butter
deep fat for frying	lemon wedges

Rinse the sprats and dry them well. Dust them with the flour, mixed with salt and pepper. Heat the fat in a deep frying pan until there is a slight haze from it. Fry the fish for a minute or two until they are golden brown, then drain them on kitchen paper. Sprinkle the fish with paprika and serve them with brown bread and butter and lemon wedges.

CHOOSING HERRINGS

To tell at a glance if the herrings you are buying are really fresh, make sure they are firm, shiny and have plenty of scales. The eyes should be bright and prominent, not shrunken, and the gills should be pink. The fishmonger will clean them for you and bone them too, if you wish. If you prefer to do this yourself follow our instructions carefully.

TO CLEAN A HERRING

1. Remove the scales by scraping from the tail to the head of the fish with the blunt edge of a knife.
2. Cut off the fins and head, just behind the gills, with a pair of scissors or a sharp knife.
3. Still using scissors or a knife, slit all the way down the front of the herring towards the tail and remove the inside. Have a piece of newspaper ready in which to wrap up the pieces and throw them away at once. Keep the roes if there are any as they can be cooked with the fish.
4. Rinse a cloth in cold water and wipe out the inside of the fish. Rub off all the black skin which lies next to the bone and inside the flaps.

BONING A HERRING

1. Take a cleaned herring and lay it, inside downwards, flat on a board and press firmly all the way along the backbone.
2. Turn the fish over and lift out the backbone.

GRILLED HERRINGS

FOR 4 PEOPLE

4 cleaned herrings
salt and pepper

2 oz. butter
4 slices of lemon

Open the herrings and sprinkle the insides with salt and pepper. Using a sharp knife make 3 incisions along each side of each herring. Brush one side of each herring with melted butter. Brush the grill pan grid also and lay the herrings on it, buttered side upwards. Grill the herrings under a moderate heat for 3 or 4 minutes, turn them over, brush their other sides with melted butter and grill them for the same time. The fish must be cooked to the centre but overcooking will dry the flesh and spoil the flavour.
Serve the herrings with slices of lemon. One of the nicest accompaniments is plain boiled potatoes plus more melted butter.

HERRING FILLETS IN OATMEAL

MAKES 6 FINGER SNACKS

3 boned herrings
2 level tablespoons
 medium Scotch
 oatmeal
1 level teaspoon salt
a good pinch of pepper
a little fat for frying
3 slices of fairly thickly
 cut brown or white
 bread and butter

2 level tablespoons
 chopped parsley
finely grated rind of 1
 lemon
slices of lemon for the
 garnish
a little paprika pepper

Cut each herring into 2 fillets. Mix the oatmeal, salt and pepper together and coat the fillets in this.
Heat enough fat to cover the base of the frying pan and fry the fish briskly for a few minutes on both sides, using a little more fat if required. Lift the fish on to a piece of absorbent kitchen paper to drain. Keep them hot.
Cut the crusts off the bread and cut each slice in half. Mix the chopped parsley and grated lemon rind together. Lay a fillet on each piece of bread and butter and sprinkle the lemon parsley mixture down the centre of each.
Arrange the snacks on a dish with a slice of lemon between every alternate one. For colour, spread half a slice of lemon with chopped parsley and half with paprika pepper. The flavour of lemon is delicious with most fish but is especially good with herrings as the acid counteracts their richness.

HERRINGS IN A PARCEL

FOR 4 PEOPLE

4 large or 6 small
 herrings, boned
1½ oz. butter
salt and pepper
3 oz. onion, finely
 chopped

4 oz. mushrooms,
 finely chopped
4 teaspoons chopped
 parsley

Cut a piece of greaseproof paper for each fish, large enough to parcel it up. Rub some of the butter on to each piece and sprinkle it with salt and pepper.
Melt the rest of the butter and cook the onion and mushrooms slowly for about 10 minutes without allowing the onion to colour. Add the parsley, and more salt and pepper. Spread the mixture down the centre of each open fish, close it, and wrap it in the greaseproof paper. Lay the fish parcels in an ovenproof dish. Cook at *Gas Mark 4 or 350 degrees F.* for 40 minutes. The herrings can be served in the parcels; this keeps all the goodness of the fish—and the smell—inside the parcels until just before they are eaten.

BUCKLING SALAD

Bucklings are smoked herrings; they can be grilled or fried quickly just to heat them, or they make a very good salad.

FOR 3 PEOPLE

2 bucklings
freshly ground black
 pepper
1 tablespoon salad oil
1 dessertspoon white
 vinegar
1 dessertspoon lemon
 juice

salt
1 lb. boiled potatoes
1 level teaspoon
 chopped parsley
a few large rings from
 a raw onion
curls of lemon

Skin the bucklings and remove the backbones. Arrange the pieces of fish on a dish and sprinkle them with a little black pepper. Mix the oil, vinegar and lemon juice and season the dressing well with salt and freshly ground black pepper. Dice the potatoes and toss them into the dressing, sprinkle over the parsley then arrange it beside the fish. Top the potatoes with onion rings and garnish the fish with lemon curls.

POACHED MACKEREL

FOR 4 PEOPLE

4 mackerel
water to cover
1 medium onion, sliced
2 tablespoons vinegar
1 level teaspoon salt

freshly ground pepper
1½ lb. boiled potatoes
1 level teaspoon
 chopped parsley
4 oz. melted butter

Wash the fish and cut off the heads and fins. Put the fish into a fish-kettle or large pan. Cover them with water, add the sliced onion, vinegar, salt and pepper. Bring *very* slowly to the boil—they will then be cooked.
Serve with boiled potatoes and chopped parsley, and hand the melted butter separately as a sauce.

MEAT

For a traditional—and satisfying—Sunday lunch, there is nothing quite to compare with a good succulent joint of beef, perfectly cooked and served with classic accompaniments. But meat comes in many other shapes and sizes, too, and at all prices. As most of us have to watch the pennies, you will probably be interested in the cheaper cuts and ways to prepare them.

In most cases, it is the meat from the forequarters of an animal—beef, lamb or pork—which gives the cheaper cuts. Remember cheaper cuts often come from top-quality animals. They do need slow and careful cooking, but the flavour can be better than expensive joints.

Beef varies in quality more than any other meat. When first cut, the lean should be dark, almost dull, and should turn bright red on exposure to the air. The fat should be creamy in colour. Lamb nowadays is available throughout the year, although it is especially good in April. The lean can vary from clear pink to a darker red, depending on age and variety.

Pork may be fresh, salted or smoked like bacon. When fresh, it should have firm lean of a good pinkish colour, with clear creamy white fat. Pork must always be well cooked.

In this chapter I give ideas for using many different cuts of meat—the cheaper ones and the more expensive. There are also recipes for veal, bacon and offal, and some ideas for that ever-popular standby—mince.

ROASTING TIMES

LARGE JOINT OF BEEF

20 minutes per lb. plus 20 minutes added to total for rare joint. Add extra 20 minutes for medium-done, plus another 20 minutes for well-done. Start in fairly hot oven (*Gas Mark 6 or 400 degrees F.*) for 20 minutes, reduce to *Gas Mark 5 or 375 degrees F.* for remainder.

LAMB

20 minutes per lb. plus 20 minutes added to total. Start in fairly hot oven (*Gas Mark 6 or 400 degrees F.*) for 20 minutes, reduce to *Gas Mark 4 or 350 degrees F.* for remainder.

PORK

25 minutes per lb. plus 20 minutes added to total. Rub scored joint with salt. Roast in fairly hot oven, *Gas Mark 6 or 400 degrees F.* Pork must be thoroughly cooked.

VEAL

25 minutes per lb. plus 25 minutes added to total. Start in fairly hot oven (*Gas Mark 6 or 400 degrees F.*) for 20 minutes, reduce to *Gas Mark 4 or 350 degrees F.* for remainder. Veal should be thoroughly cooked.

GAMMON

Soaked overnight then usually baked or boiled. For both, allow 25 minutes per lb. plus 25 minutes added to total. Boil, calculate cooking time from boiling point. Bake, wrapped in kitchen foil, starting in fairly hot oven (*Gas Mark 6 or 400 degrees F.*) for 40 minutes, reduce to *Gas Mark 3 or 325 degrees F.* for remainder.

BEEF

TRADITIONAL ROAST BEEF

FOR A JOINT WEIGHING BETWEEN 5 AND 7 LB.

Good cuts to buy for roasting are sirloin or rib. Both can be boned and rolled by the butcher if you wish.

Calculate the roasting time by the weight of the joint. Allow 20 minutes to every pound and add 20 minutes to the total time for a rare joint; add another 20 minutes for medium cooking and a further 20 minutes for a well-done joint.

Prick the fat surface of the joint with a fork, then rub it with cooking salt; this crisps the fat and, incidentally, makes it delicious for cutting cold. Put the meat into a roasting tin with some dripping and put it in a moderately hot oven, about *Gas Mark 6 or 400 degrees F.*, for the first 20 minutes, then reduce the heat to *Gas Mark 5 or 375 degrees F.* for the remaining time. Baste the joint once or twice during the cooking.

Beef should be carved in thin slices across the grain. The exception to this is the undercut of sirloin when it is roasted on the bone, and which should be carved in thick slices running in the same direction as the grain of the meat.

NOTE: Before carving a large joint, let it rest in a warm place for 15 minutes. This improves the texture and makes it easier to slice.

TO MAKE THE GRAVY

Spoon off the fat into a basin, leaving only the brown sediment in the tin. Dust in a level dessertspoon of flour and stir into the sediment. Add half a pint of stock or vegetable water, and stir the gravy over a low heat until it comes to the boil. Add pepper to flavour and strain the gravy into a sauceboat. Gravy to serve with beef should be thin, but rich brown from the meat sediment.

ACCOMPANIMENTS

Horseradish sauce and English mustard are the traditional accompaniments to roast beef, and roast, boiled or creamed potatoes are essential. One of the nicest accompanying vegetables is a mixture of boiled carrots and white turnips in equal quantities, drained, chopped (not mashed), and tossed in butter, salt and pepper.

YORKSHIRE PUDDINGS

4 oz. plain flour	$\frac{1}{4}$ pint water
$\frac{1}{2}$ level teaspoon salt	little dripping
1 egg	12 little individual bun
$\frac{1}{4}$ pint milk	tins or a bun tray

These are often baked in a bun tray. Baked in this way they are easier to serve and cook more quickly.

Sift the flour and salt into a mixing bowl. Break the egg into the centre of the sifted ingredients and add the milk. Start mixing from the centre and gradually incorporate all the flour. Beat the batter well until it is smooth, and add a little water. When bubbles start to rise to the surface of the batter, stir in the rest of the water.

Heat a speck of dripping in each little bun tin. Beat the batter again then fill the tins almost to the top with batter. Put the tins into a hot oven, about *Gas Mark 7 or 425 degrees F.*, for 20 to 25 minutes.

STAPHADO

FOR 4 PEOPLE

2 lb. shin beef	$\frac{1}{4}$ pint red wine
4 tablespoons cooking oil	5 oz. tin concentrated tomato purée
3 lb. small onions	$\frac{1}{2}$ pint stock (this can
1 clove of garlic	be made with a
salt and pepper	stock cube)

Cut the beef into fairly large pieces. Fry it briskly in a tablespoon of the cooking oil, then transfer it to a casserole. Peel the onions and fry them briskly, adding the rest of the oil, and add them to the meat. Crush the clove of garlic

with a pinch of salt, mix it with the wine and tomato purée, then stir it into the meat with the stock. Season carefully. Cook the staphado in the centre of a moderate oven, about *Gas Mark 4 or 350 degrees F.*, for 1 hour then reduce the heat to *Gas Mark 2 or 300 degrees F.* for a further 2 hours or until the meat is tender.

STEAK AND KIDNEY PUDDING

FOR 6 PEOPLE

FOR THE PASTRY

12 oz. self-raising flour	scant $\frac{1}{2}$ pint milk and
1 level teaspoon salt	water in equal
3 oz. shredded suet	proportions

FOR THE FILLING

1$\frac{1}{2}$ lb. stewing steak, cut thinly	1 medium sized onion, sliced
4 oz. ox kidney	3 tablespoons cold water
2 level tablespoons flour	little stock for gravy
$\frac{1}{2}$ level teaspoon salt and a good pinch of pepper	a pudding basin holding 3 pints will be required

Cut stewing steak into strips 2$\frac{1}{2}$ inches long and 1 inch wide. Cut the kidney into $\frac{1}{2}$-inch dice and wrap steak round each little piece of kidney. Sift the flour and seasoning together on to a plate and coat the meat rolls with it.

Grease the pudding basin thoroughly.

Make the pastry: Sift the self-raising flour, and salt together, then mix in shredded suet and stir to a soft dough with milk and water. Turn on to a well-floured board and cut off a quarter of the pastry. Roll the remainder into a round the size of a dinner plate, being careful to keep it of even thickness—it should be at least $\frac{1}{2}$ inch thick. Dust the pastry with flour, fold it lightly in four and lift into the greased basin. Unfold the pastry quickly and press it up the sides of the basin until it just overlaps the top. Fill the pastry with sliced onion and prepared meat to the top of the basin. Add 3 tablespoons water. Moisten the edge of the suet pastry. Roll out the lid from the remaining quarter of pastry and place it in position. Press the edges firmly together.

Cut a double thickness of greaseproof paper, large enough to cover the basin and come well down the sides. Make a pleat, about 1$\frac{1}{2}$ inches wide, in the centre of the paper— this fold allows for the pudding to rise—then grease the paper where it will touch the pudding. Tie the paper over the pudding, keeping the fold in position. Surplus paper below the string can be cut away.

Steam the pudding for about 6 hours (if the steak is particularly tender it may require only 4 to 5 hours). Use a double steamer or a large saucepan, but be sure it has a well-fitting lid and is considerably deeper than the pudding basin. A steamer should be replenished with extra boiling water as it evaporates; water in a saucepan should be maintained at a level halfway up the sides of the basin, by adding *boiling* water as required.

When the pudding is ready, lift it out of the pan and remove the greaseproof paper. Cut a round in the crust and lift it off. Stir a little boiling stock into the pudding to increase the gravy.

Top: cannelloni (see page 27); bottom: spaghetti bolognaise (see page 28)

BEEF OLIVES

MAKES ABOUT 6 OR 7

1¼ lb. chuck steak, in one piece
2 level tablespoons plain flour
salt and pepper
1 oz. dripping
¾ pint stock (this can be made from a stock cube)
wooden cocktail sticks

FOR THE STUFFING

2 oz. white breadcrumbs (about 10 level tablespoons)
2 level teaspoons chopped parsley
2 level tablespoons shredded suet
small pinch of dried mixed herbs
1 small onion, very finely chopped
1 level teaspoon grated lemon rind
1 large egg
salt and pepper

FOR SERVING THE OLIVES

2 lb. potatoes, weighed before peeling, boiled and beaten to a smooth cream with milk and butter, salt and pepper
1 large packet frozen peas, cooked as directed on the packet
little chopped parsley
little paprika

First make the stuffing: mix the breadcrumbs, parsley, suet, dried herbs, chopped onion and grated lemon rind together. Beat the egg and add it to the mixture with enough salt and pepper to season it.

Slice the meat as thinly as you can, cutting each slice across the grain as seen in the colour photograph on page 79; the meat should make six or seven slices. Roll up each piece of meat with a spoonful of stuffing inside and secure it with a cocktail stick. Season the flour with salt and pepper and dust the beef olives with the flour. Melt the dripping in a frying pan and fry the olives, turning them occasionally to brown them evenly. Transfer them to a casserole. Pour the stock into the frying pan and stir until it comes to the boil, then pour it over the beef olives.

Cook the beef olives in a very moderate oven, about *Gas Mark 2 or 300 degrees F.*, for 1½ hours.

Using a piping bag with a star pipe, pipe potato stars down the centre of a hot serving dish. Arrange the beef olives on top and take out the cocktail sticks. Pipe potato down either side of the olives. Sprinkle the olives with chopped parsley and colour a few of the potato stars with a little paprika. Arrange the peas at each side of the dish.

BOILED BEEF AND CARROTS

FOR 6/8 PEOPLE

3½ lb. salt silverside or salt brisket beef, boned and rolled
1 level dessertspoon demerara sugar
6 peppercorns
1 large parsnip
1 lb. carrots
1 lb. onions
8 oz. turnips

FOR THE DUMPLINGS

8 oz. plain flour
1 level teaspoon salt
3 level teaspoons baking powder
4 oz. shredded suet
almost ¼ pint water

Put the meat into a pan, cover it with cold water and leave it to soak for several hours or overnight. Next day, weigh the meat and calculate the cooking time: allow 30 minutes to each pound of weight, plus an extra 30 minutes. Thus a joint weighing 3½ lb. will need to boil for 2¼ hours.

Rub the lean surface of the meat with demerara sugar and leave it for 10 minutes, then put it into a pan and cover it with cold water. Add the peppercorns and bring the meat slowly to the boil, skimming the surface as necessary. The moment the water comes to the boil, start the calculated cooking time, covering the pan and leaving the meat to simmer. It should *not* boil rapidly.

While the meat is simmering, peel the vegetables and cut them into fairly large pieces. If the carrots and onions are small, leave them whole.

Add the vegetables to the pan when the meat has been simmering for about an hour. You may have to remove a little of the water to make room for them all. Bring the vegetables quickly to the boil, then reduce the heat and continue simmering.

Next prepare the dumplings. Sift together the flour, salt and baking powder, then mix in the shredded suet. Make a hollow in the centre of these ingredients, pour in almost all the water and mix to a soft but not sticky dough. Add a little extra water if necessary.

Form the dough into 10 little balls between the hands. Flour them, then 15 minutes before the cooking time is up, drop the dumplings into the simmering liquid. Replace the lid and bring the liquid swiftly back to simmering point for the final 15 minutes.

Lift out the meat and cut off the string. Serve on a hot dish surrounded with vegetables and dumplings.

NOTE: For a cold meal, cook the brisket as described, without dumplings and with fewer vegetables and leave it in the liquid until it is cold to keep it moist.

TO COOK RUMP STEAK

This is usually fried or grilled, and extra delicious when it is cut ¾ to 1 inch thick. If possible, allow 8 oz. per person.

1 lb. rump steak, cut ¾ to 1 inch thick
freshly ground black pepper
2 oz. butter
1 tablespoon cooking oil
watercress to garnish

FRIED RUMP STEAK

Score the steak on both sides with a sharp knife and sprinkle it thickly on both sides with freshly ground black pepper. Melt the butter and oil in the frying pan. When it is hot, fry the steak for 3 minutes on each side. If it is preferred well done, allow a little longer. For extra flavour, add a few drops of Worcester sauce to the butter.

GRILLED RUMP STEAK

Score the steak on both sides with a sharp knife. Melt the butter and oil and brush this over one side of the steak, then sprinkle this thickly with freshly ground black pepper. Grill this side of the steak under a fairly hot grill for about 3 minutes, turn it and brush the other side with melted butter and oil and sprinkle it with black pepper. Grill this side for 3 minutes in the same way. If it is preferred well done, allow a few minutes longer at a slightly reduced heat. For extra flavour, rub the steak with a cut clove of garlic after scoring it.

Grilled herrings and herring fillets in oatmeal (see page 36)

CORNISH PASTIES

Chuck steak should be used, for this is a tender stewing cut, but minced steak is also good and is usually cheaper. Because it is minced, it will cook as quickly as chuck steak.

MAKES 4 LARGE PASTIES

FOR THE PASTRY

12 oz. plain flour	3 oz. lard or cooking
good pinch of salt	fat
3 oz. ~~margarine~~ butter	cold water to mix

1½ c

FOR THE FILLING

3 medium sized potatoes	salt and pepper
2 medium sized onions	4 small dots of
12 oz. chuck steak	~~margarine~~ butter

FOR THE GLAZE

½ an egg beaten	good pinch of salt
with 1 tablespoon	a plate 7 inches in
of cold water	diameter

First make the pastry. Sift the flour with the salt, rub in the fats and mix the pastry to a stiff dough with a little cold water. Cut the pastry into four and roll out one piece into a round, the size of the plate. Put it on the plate and trim round to neaten the edge.

Peel the potatoes and onions and slice them very thinly indeed; a potato peeler is good for slicing the potato really thinly. Dice the meat finely; this is very easy with a sharp knife on a wooden board.

Put a small line of sliced potato across the centre of the pastry circle and cover it with sliced onion, then put a layer of meat on top, nestling it into the vegetables so that the filling is firmly packed. Sprinkle with salt and pepper and put a small dab of ~~margarine~~ butter in the centre.

Crown of lamb—joining the ends with string and trussing needle

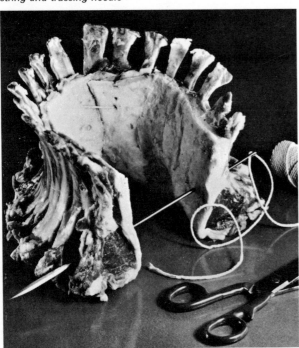

Damp round the edges of the pastry and draw opposite sides of the circle on top of the filling, enclosing it completely. Crimp the edge with the forefinger and thumb and as you do this, draw the edge up and fold it over making a neat pleat as seen in the photograph on page 79.

Make the other three pasties in the same way. Brush the pasties with the glaze and bake them in a fairly hot oven, just above the centre, at *Gas Mark 6 or 400 degrees F.*, for 1 hour.

LAMB

CROWN OF LAMB

FOR 6 PEOPLE

2 pieces of 6 bones	salt and pepper
each of best end neck	2 oz. lard
of lamb	12 small onions

TO ACCOMPANY THE CROWN WHEN SERVED HOT

2 lb. creamed potatoes	sprig of mint
lightly whipped	knob of butter
and well-seasoned	pinch of castor sugar
1 lb. new carrots,	a forcing bag and a
cooked	large star pipe

TO GARNISH THE CROWN WHEN SERVED COLD

¼ pint apple mint jelly	½ a lemon
(see page 201)	2 tomatoes
2 tablespoons water	a punnet of cress
1 level dessertspoon	6 cutlet frills
powdered gelatine	6 maraschino
rice salad (see page 26)	cherries
½ an orange	

The cutlets will be in two pieces, taken from either side of the backbone. Ask the butcher to chop between the joints at the thick end of each cutlet so that the joints will curve as seen in the photograph, left.

Trim all the meat off the tips of the bones, leaving about an inch of bone showing on each cutlet. Using string and a trussing needle, push the string through one end of each joint and tie firmly. Similarly, join the other ends as in the photograph, left. This forms the crown of lamb.

Weigh the crown and allow 20 minutes cooking time for each pound and add 20 minutes to the total time. Sprinkle the inside of the crown (this is the fat surface) with salt and pepper and smear the outside with the lard. Put the crown in a roasting tin. Peel the onions and put them into the tin. Roast the crown in a moderately hot oven, about *Gas Mark 5 or 375 degrees F.*, for the calculated time, basting it and turning the onions once or twice.

TO SERVE HOT

Fill a forcing bag, with a large star pipe attached, with the creamed potato. Make a bed of potato in the centre of a hot serving dish then put the crown in the middle. Pipe a little potato inside the crown and rosettes of potato round the base. Toss the cooked carrots with a sprig of crushed mint, a knob of butter and a pinch of castor sugar. Heap them into the crown and spear a little onion on to each bone.

TO SERVE COLD

Cook the crown as described above, but omit the onions. Put the mint jelly, water and gelatine into a small pan and dissolve them together over a gentle heat. Let the mixture become cold, but not set, and when it is thickening put the cold crown of lamb on a wire tray and brush it thoroughly with this glaze. Give it several coats if necessary.

Put the crown of lamb on a serving dish and heap rice salad round the base. Garnish it with alternate wedges of orange and lemon. Fill the centre of the crown with rice salad, halve and slice the tomatoes and surround the rice salad with slices of tomato so that they can be seen through the bones, as in the photograph on page 62. Mound the centre with cress. Put a cutlet frill or a maraschino cherry on alternate cutlet bones.

MEDITERRANEAN LAMB

FOR 6 PEOPLE

1 medium sized leg of lamb weighing about 4 lb.	1 level teaspoon salt
3 tablespoons oil	1 level teaspoon paprika
2 medium sized onions	sprig of rosemary
4 oz. mushrooms	8 olives
$\frac{1}{4}$ pint red wine	4 level tablespoons concentrated tomato purée
$\frac{1}{2}$ pint stock	
clove of garlic	a covered roasting tin will be required

Wipe the leg of lamb with a damp cloth. Leave the knuckle attached to the leg as it helps to prevent the meat shrinking up the bone. Heat the oil in the base of the covered roasting tin and brown the leg of lamb in it as evenly as possible over a fairly strong heat. Take out the meat.

Peel and slice the onions finely, add them to the oil and fry for a few minutes. Wipe and slice the mushrooms (there is no need to peel them), add to the onions and cook for a few minutes. By this time all the oil should be absorbed. Add the red wine and the stock. Peel the papery skin off the clove of garlic, chop the garlic and sprinkle the salt over it. Crush the garlic to a cream under the blade of a heavy knife and add it to the pan. Stir in the paprika, rosemary, olives and tomato purée. Stir the mixture over a gentle heat until it comes to the boil. Put the meat back into the tin, baste it with the ingredients, cover the tin with the lid and cook the joint in a slow oven, *Gas Mark 2 or 300 degrees F.*, for $2\frac{1}{2}$ hours.

Cut the knuckle off the joint before serving and pour the gravy from round the joint into a sauceboat.

LANCASHIRE HOTPOT

FOR 4/5 PEOPLE   *23 = 4½ lbs.?*

lamb shanks	
2$\frac{1}{2}$ lb. best end neck of lamb, chined by the butcher *2-3 split lengthwise*	1 level teaspoon curry powder
4 lamb kidneys	$\frac{1}{2}$ pint stock or water
4 medium sized onions, peeled	a little melted butter
1$\frac{3}{4}$ lb. peeled potatoes	an ovenproof dish with a fairly wide top
salt and pepper	

Trim a little of the fat off the meat and divide the lamb into cutlets between the bones. Arrange a layer of cutlets in the base of the dish. Peel the transparent skin off the kidneys and slice them, removing the central core; cover the meat with half the kidneys. Season with salt and pepper and a sprinkling of curry powder. Halve five potatoes and slice the rest fairly finely; slice the onions and cover the meat

Mediterranean lamb

with a layer of sliced potatoes and onions, and season this layer with salt and pepper and curry powder.

Continue with a layer of meat, seasoning, then potatoes and onions. Now pour the stock round. Top the hotpot with the halved potatoes and brush them with melted butter, to give them a golden gloss as they cook.

Do not cover the dish, but put it into the centre of a moderate oven, about *Gas Mark 4 or 350 degrees F.*, for $2\frac{1}{4}$ to $2\frac{1}{2}$ hours. It will do no harm to cook the hotpot for 3 to $3\frac{1}{2}$ hours if the heat is turned down to *Gas Mark 2 or 300 degrees F.* after the first 30 minutes.

LEMON LAMB

FOR 6/7 PEOPLE

2 breasts of lamb, boned (about $2\frac{1}{2}$ lb.)	2 oz. plain flour
$1\frac{1}{2}$ pints stock (this can be made from stock cubes)	1 dessertspoon water juice of 2 lemons
2 medium onions, sliced	4 egg yolks
8 oz. young carrots, washed and scraped	salt and pepper if required
$\frac{1}{2}$ level teaspoon dried marjoram	8 oz. Patna rice
1 oz. dripping	1 lemon for garnish

Cut the meat into $1\frac{1}{2}$-inch squares. Put it into a fairly large pan with the sliced onion, carrot, marjoram and stock. Bring the meat to the boil without a lid, skim the surface, then put on the lid and simmer gently for an hour or until it is tender. Strain off the liquid for the sauce and keep the meat and carrots hot.

Melt the dripping, take the pan off the heat and stir in the flour. Whisk in the strained liquid from the meat, and when the sauce is smooth, stir it over a gentle heat until it comes to the boil. Simmer for 5 minutes. Beat the egg yolks, a dessertspoonful of water and the lemon juice together, add two tablespoons of the sauce to this mixture and stir well, then whisk the mixture slowly into the sauce. Season with salt and pepper, if required, and keep the sauce warm without allowing it to come to the boil.

Meanwhile put the rice into boiling salted water and boil it until it is tender. A grain should just rub away between the finger and thumb. Drain off the liquid and pour boiling water through the rice to separate the grains.

Turn the rice on to a hot dish, lay the meat and carrots down the centre of the rice and coat the meat and rice with the sauce. The sauce should sink through into the rice, moistening and flavouring it. Garnish with lemon.

MIXED GRILL

Cutlets are the "back-bone" of this grill. Chops, which are cut a little lower down the side of lamb than cutlets, are excellent but more expensive. You can also use steak, pork chops, liver or beefburgers.

Buy the number of cutlets you require in one piece—this joint is called best end of neck. Not only is it cheaper to buy the cutlets this way but the trimmings can be used too. Ask the butcher to chine the joint for you: this means saw across the bones. The bones can be used to flavour soup. Also ask him to saw through the ends of the bones making 3 to 4-inch-long cutlets.

Using a sharp knife cut off the back bones and cut off the meat behind the bone tips; this piece is grilled with the cutlets to make a cushion to arrange them on, as well as providing a little extra meat. Cut off the cutlets making them as even in thickness as possible.

FOR 4 PEOPLE

a 4-bone piece of best end neck of lamb	4 oz. mushrooms
salt and pepper	2 large tomatoes
4 chipolata sausages	1 bunch watercress
2 lamb kidneys	a pinch of sugar
	cooking oil

Divide the meat into cutlets as described. Pepper the meat if you wish but never salt meat before grilling as it tends to draw out the juice. There is no need to prick the sausages. Peel the encasing suet off the kidneys, this is often done for you by the butcher, but you can render down this fat and use it for frying. Nick the outside transparent skin with a sharp knife and peel it off. Cut the kidneys in half then cut out the central core with a sharp knife. Wash or wipe the mushrooms, there is no need to peel the cultivated ones. Cut the tomatoes in half.

GRILLING THE FOOD

Turn on the grill and leave for a few minutes on a fairly strong heat with the grill pan beneath. Brush the grill pan grid with oil and lay the cutlets and the bone end on it and brush the tops with oil; take out the grill pan and arrange the sausages, tomatoes, half kidneys and mushrooms in it. Brush them all with oil and sprinkle the mushrooms and tomatoes with salt and pepper, and add a pinch of sugar to each tomato. Replace the grid in the grill pan and cook the grill under a sharp heat for a few minutes until the meat surface is seared, then turn the cutlets and brush them with oil on the other side. Reduce the heat and cook a little more slowly but they must cook through to the centre. Brush the meat with oil again if it seems at all dry.

The sausages, tomatoes, kidneys and mushrooms in the grill pan cook a little more slowly and of course catch any drips from the meat. Turn the sausages during the cooking —it is most important that they are cooked right through. When completely cooked they can be browned on top of the grid. The exact cooking time depends on the thickness and the heat from the grill. When cooked, dust the meat with a little salt.

Lay the end piece of grilled cutlet on a hot serving dish and arrange the cutlets with their bones tipped against it. Place the kidneys alongside the cutlets and the sausages at one end and the mushrooms at the other. Put two tomatoes right at each end. Garnish the dish with a few sprigs of watercress and serve the rest separately.

Hand potato crisps or chips and Maître d'Hôtel butter (see below) separately.

MAÎTRE D'HÔTEL BUTTER

2 oz. butter	a little lemon juice
2 level dessertspoons finely chopped parsley	a pinch of cayenne pepper

Mixed grill

Beat the butter to a soft cream and add the chopped parsley, lemon juice and cayenne pepper. Spread the butter about ½ inch thick on a plate and leave in a cool place. Cut into neat pieces before serving.

LAMB BREDIE

FOR 4/5 PEOPLE

1 level tablespoon dripping	1 level teaspoon ground cinnamon
2 lb. middle neck of lamb, cut in pieces	1 oz. demerara sugar
3 oz. onions, skinned and sliced	1 large tin tomatoes (2 lb. 3 oz.)
2 level tablespoons plain flour	salt and pepper
	1 bay leaf

Melt the dripping in a frying pan and fry the meat to brown the surface. Transfer the meat to an ovenproof casserole. Using the remaining dripping, fry the onions rather more slowly, turning them frequently until they are golden brown. They will take from 5 to 7 minutes. Add the flour, cinnamon and sugar and stir in the contents of the tin of tomatoes. Bring the mixture to the boil, season it with salt and pepper and add the bay leaf. Pour it over the meat. Cover the casserole with a tight-fitting lid and cook the meat just above the centre of a slow oven, about *Gas Mark 2 or 300 degrees F.*, for 1½ hours or until the meat is tender. Re-season before serving if required.

PORK

ROAST PORK

FOR 4/5 PEOPLE

5 lb. loin of pork	3 rounded table-
salt	spoons dripping

SAGE AND ONION STUFFING

3 medium sized onions	3 level teaspoons sage
6 oz. fresh white breadcrumbs	salt and pepper
	dusting of flour

ROAST POTATOES

12 even-sized potatoes	salt

GRAVY

dusting of flour	½ pint stock or
salt and pepper	vegetable liquid

APPLE SAUCE

1 large cooking apple	knob of butter
castor sugar to sweeten	

When you have chosen your joint of pork ask the butcher to score it for you. The skin is actually cut through the surface in lines a quarter of an inch apart across the joint. It is a good idea to have the joint scored lengthwise too, as this makes it easier to carve through the crackling. Ask the butcher to chine the joint (to saw through the backbone) lengthwise so that after roasting the bone can be quickly removed, making it easy to carve between the chop joints. Calculate the time the joint will require, allowing 25 minutes to the pound and adding 20 minutes to the total time. Thus a 5 lb. piece of pork will need 2 hours 25 minutes. Rub the outside of the joint with salt. Heat the dripping in a roasting tin in a fairly hot oven, *Gas Mark 6 or 400 degrees F.* When the dripping is hot, put in the pork and baste it well with the fat. Roast the joint just above the centre of the oven for the required cooking time. Baste it occasionally.

SAGE AND ONION STUFFING

Peel the onions and chop them fairly finely. Put them in a pan and cover with cold water, bring to the boil and simmer until tender, then drain off the water. Mix the onions with the breadcrumbs and sage, and add salt and pepper to season the stuffing well. Add enough cold water to bind the mixture, then roll it into balls between the hands and dust the balls with flour. Roast them round the joint; they will take about 30 minutes.

ROAST POTATOES

Wash and peel the potatoes, put them into a pan and cover with cold water, then bring to the boil and simmer for exactly 5 minutes. Drain off the liquid. Holding each potato in turn in a clean tea-towel, scrape the surface with the prongs of a fork; this will help to make them crisp. Place the potatoes round the joint and baste them with the hot dripping. Roast them for 1¼ hours, basting occasionally.

NOTE: The potatoes will crisp more easily if they are roasted in a tin by themselves near the top of the oven, where the heat is greatest; in this case, you can move the joint down to the middle shelf when you put the potatoes in.

GRAVY

Spoon the dripping out of the roasting tin, leaving the brown sediment. Stir a little flour into the sediment to absorb any remaining fat. Add the stock and stir the gravy over a moderate heat until it comes to the boil and thickens. Season with salt and pepper and strain it into a sauceboat.

APPLE SAUCE

Wash the apple and cut it into small pieces without removing the skin or core. Cook it in just enough water to prevent it from sticking to the pan until it is pulped, then sieve it and sweeten it with castor sugar to taste. Stir in a knob of butter and serve it in a small sauceboat.

LOIN OF PORK WITH MACEDOINE OF TOMATOES

FOR 5/6 PEOPLE

3 lb. loin of pork, chined
(this means it is sawn
through the back bone
to make carving easier.
Ask the butcher to
score the fat surface)
1 oz. lard
8 oz. salt belly of pork
1 lb. tomatoes

2 medium sized
onions
½ cucumber
1 level teaspoon
cinnamon
1 oz. demerara sugar
1 bay leaf
salt and pepper

Using a large frying pan, fry the loin of pork briskly on all sides in the lard; this is to brown the surface. Lift it out and put it in a roasting tin (a covered one is ideal if you have one). Cut the salt belly of pork in strips and fry them in the lard until they are nicely browned. Peel the tomatoes, cut them in eighths and peel and slice the onions. Dice the cucumber and add it to the strips of pork with the tomatoes and onions. Sprinkle over the cinnamon and demerara sugar,

and stir them into the vegetables with a little salt and pepper to season. Add the bay leaf. Surround the joint with the vegetables. Put on the lid and cook the pork in a moderate oven, about *Gas Mark 3 or 325 degrees F.*, for 2 hours. Serve it surrounded by vegetables.

ESTOFADO

FOR 6 PEOPLE

6 tablespoons oil
1 lb. 6 oz. fillet of pork,
cut into chunks
1 oz. plain flour
salt and pepper
¼ level teaspoon
paprika pepper
pinch of cinnamon
1 onion, sliced
2 aubergines, sliced

1 level tablespoon
tomato purée
¼ pint red wine and
¼ pint stock (or all
stock could be used)
8 oz. tomatoes,
skinned and cut in
halves
8 olives

Heat the oil and fry the chunks of pork lightly. Add the flour, salt and pepper, paprika, cinnamon, sliced onion and aubergine. Stir in the tomato purée with wine and stock. Put the Estofado into a casserole and cook it in the centre of a warm oven, about *Gas Mark 3 or 325 degrees F.*, for an hour; reduce the heat to *Gas Mark 2 or 300 degrees F.* for a further 1½ hours. Add the tomatoes and olives and return the Estofado to the oven for a final 30 minutes to heat them thoroughly.

NOTE: Serve with plain boiled potatoes, boiled rice or pasta and a green salad.

PORK CHOPS IN TOMATO AND RICE

This is a course all in one dish, and is both easy to cook and serve. A green salad need be the only accompaniment.

FOR 6 PEOPLE

6 pork chops
2 oz. lard or dripping
2 medium sized onions
1 small green pepper
6 oz. Patna rice
salt and pepper
1 level teaspoon ground
cinnamon

1 large tin of tomato
juice, made up
with stock to
1½ pints
sprig of thyme
1 lb. small tomatoes

Fry the chops briskly in the lard or dripping to brown them. Meanwhile peel and slice the onions, slice the green pepper and wash out all the seeds. Transfer three chops to a large ovenproof casserole, sprinkle over them half the rice, green pepper and onion, and sprinkle with salt, pepper and cinnamon. Add the rest of the chops and cover with the remaining rice, onion and green pepper. Pour over the liquid then add the sprig of thyme. Put on the lid and cook the chops in a slow oven, about *Gas Mark 2 or 300 degrees F.*, for about 1½ hours. After the chops have been cooking for an hour, peel and add the whole tomatoes. Remove the thyme when the chops are cooked.

Loin of pork with macedoine of tomatoes

GLAZED PORK CHOPS

FOR 2 PEOPLE

1 level tablespoon soft brown sugar	2 pork chops, about an inch thick
2 level teaspoons dry mustard	1 dessertspoon lemon juice
salt and pepper	

Mix the brown sugar, dry mustard and a good pinch of salt and pepper together. Dust this mixture thickly all over the chops and lay them in an ovenproof dish. Sprinkle over the lemon juice.

Bake the chops in a moderately hot oven, about *Gas Mark 5 or 375 degrees F.*, for 40 minutes.

VEAL

WIENER SCHNITZEL

FOR 4 PEOPLE

4 very thinly cut escalopes of veal	cooking oil
2 oz. flour seasoned with salt and pepper	1 lemon
1 beaten egg	8 fillets of anchovy
dry white breadcrumbs	4 olives
	watercress for garnish

Put each slice of veal between two pieces of damp, grease-proof paper and flatten to $\frac{1}{4}$ inch thick with a rolling pin. Dust the meat with seasoned flour. Dip each piece of meat in egg then coat it in breadcrumbs.

Heat 3 tablespoons of cooking oil in a frying pan and fry each escalope, not too quickly, on both sides. Allow about 5 minutes on each side, using more oil as required. Drain the meat on absorbent kitchen paper. It can be kept in a warm (but not hot) oven until required. Arrange the Wiener Schnitzel on a long dish with a slice of lemon on top of each. Cross this with fillets of anchovy and put an olive in the centre of each one. Garnish with watercress.

ESCALOPE DE VEAU VALENTINO

FOR 4 PEOPLE

1 lb. veal bones, chopped	salt and pepper
4 escalopes of veal	2 oz. mushrooms
$2\frac{1}{2}$ oz. butter	a little lemon juice
$\frac{1}{2}$ level tablespoon plain flour	1 small tin asparagus tips
$\frac{1}{4}$ pint single cream	creamed potatoes
	sprinkling of paprika

First make the veal stock with the bones. Put the bones into a saucepan with a good pinch of salt, cover them with cold water and bring them to the boil, then simmer them steadily for $1\frac{1}{2}$ to 2 hours.

Put the slices of veal on a chopping-board and stretch them out with a palette knife. Flatten them still further by batting them with the back of a large wooden spoon or a rolling pin. Melt $1\frac{1}{2}$ ounces of the butter in a frying-pan, then gently fry the pieces of veal for a few minutes on each side. When the escalopes are cooked, put them between two hot plates and keep them in a warm place.

Dust the flour into the fat in the pan and stir it in, then add $\frac{1}{4}$ pint of veal stock and the single cream. Stir the sauce until it comes to the boil, season it well with salt and pepper, and leave it aside ready for coating the veal.

Wash and slice the mushrooms. Melt half the remaining butter in a small pan, add the sliced mushrooms and fry them briskly until they are just cooked and the moisture has evaporated. Add a squeeze of lemon juice and a little salt and pepper. Keep the mushrooms hot.

Open the tin of asparagus at the base instead of the top to prevent damaging the tips when you turn them out. Stand the opened tin, still upside down, in a saucepan of hot water to heat the asparagus.

Prepare the creamed purée potatoes and heap them down the centre of a hot serving dish.

Arrange the veal, the slices overlapping, down the centre of the potatoes. Add the rest of the butter to the prepared sauce and boil it briskly. If the sauce seems too thin, boil it rapidly for a few seconds to reduce and thicken it, then coat the pieces of veal. Garnish the dish with the mushrooms and the drained asparagus. If you prefer it, a few of the asparagus tips can be cut into smaller pieces and added to the sauce.

Sprinkle a little paprika down the centre of the dish.

NOTE: When it comes into season, fresh asparagus is excellent for this dish. Quite often it can be bought fairly inexpensively by weight. Eight ounces would be quite sufficient for this dish.

TYROLEAN VEAL

FOR 4 PEOPLE

4 veal chops	2 rashers of streaky bacon, chopped
$\frac{1}{2}$ oz. plain flour	15 oz. tin tomatoes
2 tablespoons oil	4 thin slices of Cheddar cheese, each slice about 1 oz.
1 clove of garlic	
salt and pepper	

Coat the chops with the flour and fry them in the oil until they are golden brown. Transfer them to a casserole. Crush the clove of garlic with a little salt and put it into the frying pan with the chopped bacon and cook them for a few minutes. Add the tomatoes and season the mixture with salt and pepper; when it comes to the boil pour it over the meat. Put a lid on the casserole and cook it in a slow oven, about *Gas Mark 2 or 300 degrees F.*, for $1\frac{1}{2}$ hours. Take off the lid and put a slice of cheese over each chop, and return the casserole to the oven for a further 20 to 30 minutes.

If wished, put the Tyrolean Veal under the grill for a few minutes to brown the cheese. Serve piping hot with peas or runner beans and plain boiled potatoes. This is a good satisfying dish for a cold winter day.

JELLIED VEAL

FOR 4 PEOPLE

1 lb. stewing veal	drop of cooking oil
½ bay leaf	2 tomatoes, skinned
strip of thinly peeled lemon rind about 1 inch long	a plain mould or soufflé dish holding 1½ pints of liquid will be required
salt and pepper	
¼ oz. gelatine	

Put the veal into a saucepan with a pint of water, the half bay leaf, the lemon rind and a little salt and pepper. Simmer the veal gently for about 1½ hours or until it is tender. Strain off the liquid and measure ¾ pint, making it up with water if necessary. Remove the bay leaf and the lemon rind and chop the veal roughly. Melt the gelatine in a little of the measured liquid in a small pan over a gentle heat, stir it into the rest of the liquid, then into the veal. Season the mixture carefully with salt and pepper, remembering that the meat should be fairly highly seasoned when it is cold.

Rub the mould with a drop of salad oil and when the mixture is cold—but not set—pour it into the mould. Leave it to set, then turn it out on to a plate and place slices of tomato round it.

BACON

BAKED GAMMON AND MADEIRA SAUCE

FOR 6/8 PEOPLE

corner of gammon; this can weigh between 3 and 5 lb.	1 bay leaf
	brown breadcrumbs
1 oz. demerara sugar	kitchen foil

FOR THE DUCHESSE POTATOES

2 lb. potatoes, weighed when peeled	little beaten egg for the glaze
2 oz. butter	a large forcing bag and a large rose pipe
1 egg	
salt and pepper	

FOR THE MADEIRA SAUCE

1 oz. dripping	1 pint brown stock (this can be made from stock cubes)
2 medium sized onions, finely chopped	
2 rashers of bacon, chopped	salt and pepper
	3 tablespoons Madeira
1 level tablespoon flour	4 oz. green grapes
2 level teaspoons tomato purée	

Weigh the corner of gammon and calculate the cooking time. Allow 25 minutes for every pound and add 25 minutes. Soak the gammon in cold water overnight. Take it out of the water and dry it and scrape the surface with a knife to remove any "bloom". Put the gammon on a large sheet of kitchen foil and rub the lean surface with demerara sugar.

Put the bay leaf on it, wrap the gammon into a foil parcel and fold up the ends. Lift it into a roasting tin.
Bake the gammon in a moderately hot oven, *Gas Mark 5 or 375 degrees F.*, for the calculated time.
Unwrap the gammon, peel off the outside skin and dust the surface with browned crumbs.

THE DUCHESSE POTATOES

Boil the potatoes until they are tender, then sieve or beat them in an electric mixer with the butter, egg and salt and pepper to season. Fill a large piping bag, with a large rose pipe attached, with potato and pipe rosettes on to a greased baking tray. Allow them to cool then brush the tops with beaten egg. Heat and lightly brown them in a moderately hot oven, *Gas Mark 5 or 375 degrees F.*, for 20 minutes.

THE MADEIRA SAUCE

Melt the dripping in a saucepan, add the onions and bacon and fry them to a good golden brown. With a metal spoon, stir in the flour and allow it to brown; do this quite slowly, the ingredients must not burn or the sauce will be bitter. Add the tomato purée, stock and salt and pepper and bring the sauce to the boil. Simmer it for 15 to 20 minutes then strain it. Add the Madeira, bring it to the boil and simmer it for another 10 minutes, or until reduced and thickened. Remove the pips from the grapes; the easiest way to do this is with the doubled end of a sterilised hair grip. Add the grapes to the sauce and bring it to the boil.

CALIFORNIAN STUFFED FOREHOCK

ENOUGH FOR 4/5 PEOPLE—A HOT MEAL ONE DAY, A COLD MEAL THE NEXT

1 forehock of bacon, (7 or 8 lb.) boned and rolled, and soaked	¼ pint water

FOR THE STUFFING

3 level tablespoons peanut butter	3 oz. fresh white breadcrumbs
grated rind and juice of half an orange	4 oz. dates or prunes, stoned and chopped

FOR THE GLAZE

1 level teaspoon ground ginger	2 level tablespoons thick honey
1 tablespoon orange juice	

First prepare the stuffing. Mix together the peanut butter, grated rind and juice of the orange. Lightly work in the breadcrumbs and dates or prunes.

Remove the string from the bacon, then open the cavity from where the bone was cut and fill it with the stuffing. Use the handle of a wooden spoon to push the stuffing into the joint. Retie the joint securely by stringing it at 1 to 2-inch intervals. Put the joint, fat side up, in a roasting tin and pour round the water. Cover the joint with kitchen foil and bake the forehock on the shelf above the centre of a warm oven, *Gas Mark 3 or 325 degrees F.*, for 2 hours.
Then add the glaze: remove the string and skin from the joint and score the fat surface in diamond shapes. Mix the ground ginger, orange juice and honey together, then spread it over the surface. Return the joint to a moderately hot oven, *Gas Mark 5 or 375 degrees F.*, for 15 to 30 minutes until the joint is golden brown.

Fish salad platter (see page 32)

Above: fried fish and chips (see page 30); right: salmon soufflé (see page 33)

Scotch mince (page 55), moussaka (page 56), flat and pastry-wrapped rissoles (page 55), veal and ham balls (page 57), fresh pork patties with sliced apple (page 57)

BACON AND MUSHROOM DUMPLING

FOR 6 PEOPLE

FOR THE SUET PASTRY
12 oz. self-raising flour	5 oz. shredded suet
good pinch of salt	cold water to mix

FOR THE FILLING
8 oz. cooked forehock	4 level tablespoons
8 oz. mushrooms	water
10½ oz. tin of	a pudding basin
condensed mushroom	holding 3 pints of
soup	liquid

Sift the flour and salt; stir in the suet, then mix the pastry with just enough cold water to make a soft but not sticky dough. The consistency should be a little softer than for short crust pastry.

Grease the pudding basin. Cut off three quarters of the pastry and roll this into a circle. Flour the top, fold it lightly in four and lift it into the basin; then unfold it and press it to the sides of the basin, working the pastry just over the rim.

Next make the filling. Cut the forehock into cubes of about 1 inch and layer them alternately with whole mushrooms until the pudding basin is full. Mix the mushroom soup with the water and pour it round the filling.

Roll out the rest of the pastry into a circle to fit the top of the basin. Moisten the edge of the pastry lining the basin, lift the lid into position and press the pastry edges firmly together. Trim round the edge neatly with scissors.

Cover the pudding with a double sheet of greased grease-proof paper large enough to fold a good pleat across the top. Tie it firmly round the basin with a piece of string. Put the pudding into a large pan with enough boiling water to come at least halfway up the sides of the basin. Put a lid on the pan and cook the pudding in the boiling water for 1½ to 1¾ hours. During this time keep an eye on the water and replace it with more boiling water as required.

TO SERVE THE PUDDING
Take the pudding out of the pan; remove the paper and cut a slice from the suet crust. Fold a large napkin or teacloth to the depth of the basin and wrap the cloth around it. This not only looks attractive but it also helps to keep the pudding warm.

CIDER BAKED GAMMON STEAK

FOR 2 PEOPLE
1 gammon steak,	½ pint cider
about 14 oz. in weight	2 level teaspoons
and cut ¾ inch thick	arrowroot
4 oz. prunes	1 large packet frozen
1 inch cinnamon	spinach, cooked as
stick	as directed on the
½ pint water	packet

Soak the gammon and the prunes, in the same basin if you like, in cold water overnight.

Cut the skin off the gammon steak. Lay the gammon surrounded by the prunes, in an ovenproof dish. Add the cinnamon stick and pour the water and cider round the steak; cover the dish and bake the gammon in a moderately hot oven, *Gas Mark 5 or 375 degrees F.*, for 30 minutes, then reduce the heat to *Gas Mark 2 or 300 degrees F.*, for a further 45 minutes. Strain off half a pint of the liquid, and remove the cinnamon stick. Blend the arrowroot with a few drops of cold water to a thin cream, then stir it into the liquid. Stir this in a saucepan, over a gentle heat, until it comes to the boil and thickens. Pour over the gammon steak and round the prunes.

Arrange the cooked spinach round one side of the dish.

OFFAL

BRAINS IN BATTER

FOR 4 PEOPLE
2 sets of sheep's brains	1 tablespoon white
a bouquet garni (a sprig	vinegar
of parsley, thyme	salt and pepper
and a medium sized	few sprigs of parsley
bay leaf)	tomato sauce (see
	page 27)

FOR THE BATTER
6 oz. plain flour	½ pint milk
1 level teaspoon dried	1 oz. butter
yeast	fat for deep
1 level teaspoon sugar	frying

Soak the brains in plenty of cold salt water for at least 4 hours, changing the water frequently.

Sieve the flour into a bowl and place it in a warm place. Meanwhile, put the yeast and sugar into a small bowl, heat the milk to just blood heat and then stir half of it into the yeast mixture. Leave the mixture in a warm place for the yeast to dissolve and prove. Put the butter to melt in the other half of the milk. When the yeast is ready (it should take about 10 to 15 minutes, and will have a good froth on top) pour it into a well in the centre of the flour, with the rest of the milk and the melted butter. Stir in all the flour to make a thick batter, then beat it well for a few minutes. Cover the bowl with a damp tea cloth and leave it in a warm place to prove for about an hour, until it is about double its size and has a bubbly appearance.

Meanwhile, prepare the brains: remove the very thin skin and any white fatty tissues and split each brain in half. Place the brains in a saucepan with the bouquet garni, the vinegar and salt and pepper, cover them with cold water then bring them slowly to the boil. Reduce the heat and simmer them over a very gentle heat for 20 minutes. When they are cooked, drain the brains well and divide each into three.

Half fill a deep fat pan with fat and heat it until the fat is fairly hot. To test, drop a teaspoon of the batter into it and if it becomes golden brown in about a minute the fat is ready to use. Dip each piece of brain in the batter then place it in the hot fat, a few pieces at a time. Fry them gently until the batter is golden brown then remove the brains and drain them well on paper. Dip a few sprigs of parsley into the batter and fry them quickly.

Serve the brains and parsley together with tomato sauce.

Oxtail casserole

OXTAIL CASSEROLE made in a pressure cooker

FOR 6 PEOPLE

3 oz. butter beans
1 oxtail (about 2 lb.)
   cut at the joints
4 oz. streaky bacon
2 oz. dripping
2 oz. flour
12 oz. onions, peeled
   and sliced
1 lb. carrots

1 small turnip
1 parsnip
salt and pepper
a bouquet garni (a
   sprig of parsley,
   thyme and a
   medium sized bay
   leaf)
2 pints stock

Cover the beans with cold water and soak overnight.
Wash and dry the oxtail, cutting the meat into joints if necessary, and trim off the surplus fat. Remove the rind from the bacon and cut up the rashers. Melt the dripping in a pressure cooker and fry the meat and bacon together until the oxtail is brown all over; sprinkle in the flour and fry for a few more minutes. Lift out the meat and put in the pressure cooker rack. Return meat to pan with onion.
Peel the carrots, turnip and parsnip; cut the carrots into four lengthways and the other vegetables into fairly large cubes. Add all these to the pan with the drained butter beans. Sprinkle over the salt and pepper; add the bouquet garni and the stock.
Put on the lid and stand the pressure cooker over a sharp heat until the steam comes out in a long jet, then put the pressure valve on and cook the oxtail at 15 pounds pressure for 45 minutes. Cool the pressure cooker under cold water.

TO COOK IT IN THE OVEN

Prepare the stew in the same way as for the pressure cooker but cook it in the centre of a moderate oven, *Gas Mark 4 or 350 degrees F.*, for 30 minutes then reduce the heat to *Gas Mark 2 or 300 degrees F.* for a further 3½ hours.

SWEETBREAD FRICASSEE WITH TOAST TRIANGLES

FOR 4 PEOPLE

12 oz. sweetbreads
1 medium bay leaf
1 small blade of mace
6 black peppercorns
1½ oz. butter
1 medium sized
   onion, finely
   chopped

1½ oz. flour
½ pint stock
¼ pint milk
salt
4 oz. packet frozen
   peas
3 slices of white
   bread

Wash the sweetbreads well, then place them in a saucepan with plenty of cold water, the bay leaf, mace and peppercorns and bring them to the boil. Drain them, then remove the membranes, using a very sharp knife.
Melt the butter in a saucepan, add the chopped onion and fry gently over a fairly low heat until it is cooked but not coloured. Stir in the flour, then remove the pan from the heat and gradually blend in the stock and milk. Return the saucepan to the heat and, stirring the sauce all the time, gradually bring it to the boil. Season with salt. Add the sweetbreads and the peas and simmer the mixture over a gentle heat for about 15 minutes, until the peas are tender and the sweetbreads heated through. Meanwhile toast the slices of bread on both sides, remove the crusts and cut each slice of toast into 4 triangles.
Serve the Sweetbread Fricassee in a dish with 4 of the toast triangles as decoration. Serve the remaining triangles separately.

STUFFED LAMBS' HEARTS

FOR 4 PEOPLE

4 lambs' hearts

FOR THE STUFFING

4 oz. freshly made
   white breadcrumbs
1 onion, finely chopped
1 level teaspoon dried
   sage
1 level tablespoon finely
   chopped parsley

grated rind of 1
   small orange
salt and pepper
1 small egg
1 tablespoon
   orange juice

FOR THE GRAVY

2 oz. dripping
2 oz. flour
1 pint stock

1½ lb. potatoes,
   creamed with
   seasoning, a knob of
   butter and a little
   hot milk

Soak the hearts in plenty of salted water for about 1 hour to remove the blood, then remove any tubes or gristle with a sharp knife or a pair of scissors and wash the hearts again. Mix the white breadcrumbs, onion, finely chopped herbs, and finely grated orange rind together. Season the mixture with salt and pepper. Beat the egg and add it to the mixture with the orange juice to bind the ingredients together.
Divide the stuffing into 4 and put each quarter into a heart, packing it well in. Melt the dripping in a saucepan then fry the hearts until they are slightly brown. Remove them

from the pan, stir in the flour and leave it to brown. Then take the pan off the heat and blend in the stock gradually. Return the gravy to the heat and, stirring continuously, bring to the boil. Add the stuffed hearts to the gravy and simmer them gently for about 2 hours until tender.

Meanwhile prepare the potatoes, and when the hearts are cooked, pipe the mashed potato in a dish and arrange the hearts on top. Serve the gravy separately.

OX HEART STEW

FOR 6 PEOPLE

1 ox heart (2 lb. sliced heart)	8 oz. carrots, peeled and quartered
1 oz. plain flour seasoned with salt and pepper	2 medium sized parsnips, peeled and quartered
2 tablespoons oil	$\frac{3}{4}$ pint stock
2 lb. onions, peeled and quartered	salt and pepper

Soak the ox heart in plenty of cold salted water for at least 2 hours, changing the water once. Dry the heart and cut it into rings about $\frac{1}{2}$ inch thick. Toss the rings in the seasoned flour, then heat the oil in a frying pan and fry the ox heart on both sides of each slice to brown them. Transfer the meat to an ovenproof casserole. Lightly fry the vegetables and add them to the meat. Pour the stock into the frying pan and stir it until it comes to the boil, then pour the stock over the meat. Cook the casserole in a slow oven, just above the centre, at *Gas Mark 2 or 300 degrees F.*, for $3\frac{1}{2}$ to 4 hours. Check the seasoning before serving and accompany the ox heart with redcurrant jelly.

NOTE: Ox heart stew is excellent cooked in a pressure cooker. If you do this, reduce the stock by $\frac{1}{4}$ pint; it will take 35 minutes at 15 lb. pressure.

MINCE

SCOTCH MINCE

FOR 4 PEOPLE

$\frac{1}{2}$ oz. dripping	$\frac{1}{2}$ pint stock
1 lb. raw minced beef	salt and pepper
2 small onions	triangles of toast
1 level tablespoon flour	

Melt the dripping in a stewpan; when it is hot add the mince and fry over a brisk heat. Break up the meat so there are no lumps (a potato masher is excellent for this); and stir the meat frequently until it is evenly browned. Meanwhile chop the onions and add them to the mince. Stir in the flour and cook it for a few minutes then stir in the stock and bring the mince slowly to the boil, stirring all the time. Season the mince with salt and pepper, put on the lid and simmer for about 45 minutes, stirring occasionally.

Alternatively turn the mince into a casserole and cook it in the oven at *Gas Mark 2 or 300 degrees F.* for about an hour. Top the dish with triangles of toast.

NOTE: Chopped carrot and white turnip can be added to the mince with the onion.

TWO KINDS OF RISSOLE

FOR FLAT RISSOLES
MAKES ABOUT 9

8 oz. cold roast meat	2 level tablespoons flour, seasoned with salt and pepper
12 oz. cold mashed potato or small packet of instant potato made as described on the packet	1 beaten egg
	dried white breadcrumbs
2 tablespoons tomato ketchup	fat for shallow frying
salt and pepper	a round cutter $2\frac{1}{2}$ inches in diameter

Mince the cold roast meat and mix it with the potatoes and tomato ketchup, seasoning the mixture well with salt and pepper.

Turn the mixture on to a floured board and, using a rolling pin, roll it to just over $\frac{1}{2}$ inch thick. Cut out rounds $2\frac{1}{2}$ inches in diameter with the cutter then roll up the scraps and make a few extra. Dust the rissoles with seasoned flour. Put the beaten egg on to a plate and have the dry white crumbs ready on a square of kitchen paper. Put one of the rissoles into the egg and brush it all over with egg, then lift it on a palette knife and transfer it to the crumbs. Hold the corners of the paper and flick the crumbs on to the rissole to coat it completely, then transfer it to a board and press the crumbs firmly to the surface. Coat the other rissoles in the same way.

Heat enough fat or oil in a frying pan to cover the base well, put in the rissoles and fry them, not too quickly, on both sides to heat them through thoroughly. Drain them on a piece of absorbent kitchen paper before serving.

FOR PASTRY-WRAPPED RISSOLES
MAKES ABOUT 9

4 oz. cold roast meat	dry white breadcrumbs
6 oz. mashed potato	fat for deep frying
1 tablespoon tomato ketchup	a round cutter $3\frac{3}{4}$ inches in diameter (a small saucer will do)
salt and pepper	
1 beaten egg	

FOR THE PASTRY	
6 oz. plain flour	$1\frac{1}{2}$ oz. lard
$1\frac{1}{2}$ oz. margarine	cold water to mix

Mince the cold meat and mix it with the mashed potato, tomato ketchup and salt and pepper to season.

Sift the flour for the pastry, rub in the margarine and lard, then mix the pastry to a stiff dough with a little cold water. Roll it out thinly and cut rounds with the cutter. Put a teaspoon of the meat mixture on to one of the rounds of pastry; moisten round the edges and draw the pastry up to the centre on four opposite sides to form a square; pinch the edges firmly together. Make all the others in the same way. Coat the rissoles in beaten egg then in breadcrumbs. Heat enough fat in the deep pan to cover the rissoles. When a cube of white bread, placed in the fat, browns slowly put 2 or 3 rissoles into the deep fat basket and lower them into the fat. Fry them for 2 or 3 minutes until they are golden

Moussaka

brown, then drain them on a piece of absorbent kitchen paper. Fry the rest in the same way, reheating the fat between each batch.

MOUSSAKA

FOR 4/5 PEOPLE

3 aubergines
salt
2½ oz. butter
2 onions, finely chopped
1 lb. raw minced beef
¼ pint red wine or stock
2 level tablespoons concentrated tomato purée
pepper

about 6 tablespoons cooking oil
1 oz. browned breadcrumbs
1½ oz. flour
¾ pint milk
2 egg yolks
2 oz. cheese, finely grated

Wash the aubergines and remove the stalks, then cut them into slices about ¼ inch thick. Lay these slices on a board, sprinkle them liberally with salt and leave them for 15 minutes; this helps to remove some of the extra moisture. Meanwhile melt 1 oz. of the butter, add the chopped onion and mince and fry them gently in the butter until it is a light golden brown, breaking the mince up as it cooks. Stir in the wine or stock and concentrated tomato purée and season with salt and pepper. Cover the pan and simmer very gently for 30 minutes.

Rinse the aubergine slices under cold water and dry them between pieces of absorbent kitchen paper. Heat the oil in a large frying pan and when it is hot fry the slices of aubergine until lightly browned on both sides.

Brush the inside of a shallow ovenproof dish with oil and dust the crumbs round the inside. Cover the base with a third of the aubergine slices and cover them with half the meat, then aubergine and top with the rest of the meat. Finish with a layer of aubergine.

Melt the remaining 1½ oz. butter in a saucepan, take it off the heat and stir in the flour. Add the milk and stir the sauce over a gentle heat until it is smooth, then bring it to the boil and simmer it for a few minutes. Take the sauce off the heat. Beat the egg yolks in a small basin and gradually stir in a tablespoon of hot sauce. Beat this into the sauce to thicken it, gradually stirring in three-quarters of the cheese, making the sauce smooth and glossy. Pour it over the top of the aubergine and sprinkle over the rest of the cheese.

Heat the Moussaka in a fairly hot oven, about *Gas Mark 6 or 400 degrees F.,* just until it is thoroughly hot. If necessary, brown the top under the grill.

VEAL AND HAM BALLS

MAKES 14

1 lb. minced raw bacon (collar is a good cut to choose; it must be soaked overnight)

8 oz. stewing veal (this can be minced by the butcher)

1 medium sized onion, minced or chopped

1 large egg

½ level teaspoon mixed herbs

salt and pepper

1 tin condensed mushroom soup (10½ oz.)

¼ soup tin of water

FOR THE JULIENNE STRIPS
2 carrots   2 stalks of celery

Soak the collar of bacon in cold water overnight. Next day remove the outside skin and chop bacon roughly. Mince the bacon with the veal (if you are doing it yourself) and the onion.

Break the egg into a mixing bowl and beat it with the mixed herbs, salt and pepper, add the minced meat and mix all the ingredients together really well.

Empty the soup into an ovenproof dish and stir in a quarter of a tin of water.

Roll the meat mixture into balls between the palms of your hands and drop them into the soup. Cover the dish with a lid or a piece of foil and cook the meat balls in a moderate oven, about *Gas Mark 3 or 325 degrees F.*, for 1½ hours.

Meanwhile make the julienne strips. Scrape the carrots and cut them into neat strips about 1½ inches long. Wash the celery and cut it into strips of the same length. Put the carrot and celery strips into a pan, add enough water to cover them, salt them and bring them to the boil, then simmer until they are just tender.

When the meat balls are ready, drain the julienne strips and scatter them over the surface.

MINCE ROAST

FOR 4 PEOPLE

3 oz. freshly made brown breadcrumbs

4 tablespoons milk

1 onion

½ oz. butter

8 oz. minced pork (raw)

8 oz. minced beef (raw)

salt and pepper

1 level teaspoon chopped parsley

1½ oz. dripping

4 oz. bacon ends, sliced

halved orange slices for garnish

FOR THE ORANGE BEETROOT
1 lb. cooked beetroot   juice of ½ orange
2 oz. butter   salt and pepper

Mix the breadcrumbs and milk together and leave them on one side to soak.

Dice the onion finely, fry it gently in the butter, and add it to the breadcrumb mixture with the minced pork and beef. Season the mixture and add the chopped parsley.

Turn the mixture, which will be quite soft, on to a well-floured board and shape it into a roll. Melt the dripping in the roasting tin in a moderate oven, about *Gas Mark 4 or 350 degrees F.*, and put the roll into the tin. Cover it with

fat bacon ends and put the roast into the oven just above the centre. Roast for 1¼ hours, basting occasionally.

Lift the roast on to a hot dish and cut it into thick slices. Heap the prepared beetroot along one side and garnish it with halved slices of orange.

THE ORANGE BEETROOT
Skin the beetroot and grate it on a coarse grater. Melt the butter in a pan and add the orange juice, then the beetroot. Heat it thoroughly, stirring constantly, and season with salt and pepper.

FRESH PORK PATTIES WITH SLICED APPLE

MAKES ABOUT 15

1 oz. butter

1 tablespoon cooking oil

1 medium sized onion

4 oz. freshly made breadcrumbs

12 oz. fresh minced pork (this can be pie pork)

1 level teaspoon dried sage

salt and pepper

1 egg

¼ pint plus 4 tablespoons milk

1 green-skinned dessert apple

Melt the butter and oil in a large frying pan and fry the onion very slowly until it is tender. Add it to the bread-crumbs with the pork, sage and seasoning, leaving the fat in the pan ready to fry the patties. Beat the egg and the milk thoroughly and add to the mixture.

Heat the fat and drop tablespoons of the mixture into it. Fry the patties fairly quickly to start with, then reduce the heat slightly. Allow about 7 minutes on the first side then turn the patties over and fry for about the same time on the other side. Drain them on a piece of absorbent kitchen paper and keep hot. Fry the rest in the same way.

Quarter and remove the core from the apple, slice it without taking off the skin, and arrange the patties on a hot dish with slices of apple between them.

POULTRY AND GAME

Once a luxury reserved for Christmas and celebrations, chicken nowadays, with prices at rock-bottom, has become a valuable and tasty addition to our everyday family menus. And it is still exciting enough, with a sauce or interesting accompaniments, to make good party fare.

Most butchers sell individual chicken joints, which are marvellous for meals for two or three people, but if you are catering for larger numbers, why not try jointing a chicken yourself? It is not so difficult as you might think and in this chapter I show you exactly how to do it. And—if you want to be even more ambitious—you might like to try boning a bird. You'll find step-by-step instructions for this opposite. It's very economical, too.

As game is becoming more popular, I have included some recipes for different varieties—including pigeon, rabbit and hare.

These make a pleasant change from poultry, and need be no more difficult or expensive to prepare.

POULTRY

STUFFED BONED CHICKEN

Boning a chicken (see opposite) is not a quick job, so allow yourself plenty of time. You will find your second attempt will take about half as long. Do not despair if the chicken looks wrecked without the bones; stuffings will take their place and the chicken can be reshaped almost perfectly. Absolutely essential for boning is a small sharp-pointed knife; there's no use trying unless you have one of these. The chicken's skin is pushed back and left intact while the flesh is worked off the bone, leaving the chicken almost inside out by the time you've finished. Then you turn the skin back again. If you're using a frozen chicken, it will have to be thoroughly thawed before you start boning it.

FOR 6 PEOPLE

6 oz. streaky bacon
1 roasting chicken (about 3½ lb. trussed)

2 oz. butter

FOR THE SAUSAGE STUFFING

the chicken liver
4 oz. lamb's liver
1 shallot or small onion
2 oz. mushrooms, wiped but unpeeled
2 oz. liver sausage

8 oz. pork sausage-meat
1½ oz. freshly made white breadcrumbs
1 beaten egg
salt and pepper

FOR THE LEMON AND PARSLEY STUFFING

6 oz. freshly made white breadcrumbs
6 level tablespoons chopped parsley
3 oz. shredded suet

grated rind and juice of 1 lemon
1 beaten egg
salt and pepper

TO MAKE THE STUFFINGS

For the sausage stuffing mince the chicken liver with the lamb's liver, the shallot or onion and the mushrooms. Take the skin off the liver sausage and mix it with the pork sausagemeat; add the minced mixture, then the breadcrumbs, and bind the mixture with the beaten egg. Season it with salt and pepper.

For the lemon and parsley stuffing mix together all the ingredients and season them with salt and pepper

TO STUFF THE BONED CHICKEN

Lay the boned bird on its breast and put in the lemon and parsley stuffing against the breast meat. Press a little stuffing into the wings and legs to reshape them. Put the sausage stuffing inside on top of the first, then, with the bird still on its breast, secure the loose neck skin and the wings by threading a skewer through one wing, taking in the loose skin of the neck and continuing on to the other wing.

Turn the bird over, press it into shape, and skewer the legs closely to the bird. Wrap a folded strip of greaseproof

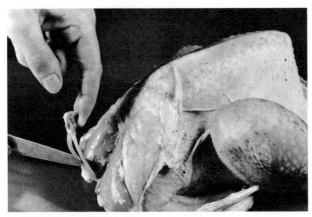

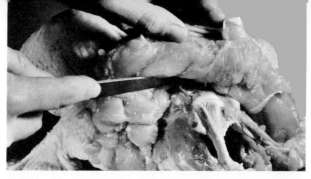

BONING A CHICKEN

1 Remove any trussing string. Loosen the skin over the breast by working your hand between the breast and the flesh, being very careful not to tear the skin. Turn back the skin and, using a sharp knife, cut away the flesh on either side of the wishbone and gradually remove the bone.

Then sever both shoulder joints at the base of the wings.

4 Now work down the carcass under the breast meat and as close to the breast bone as you can.

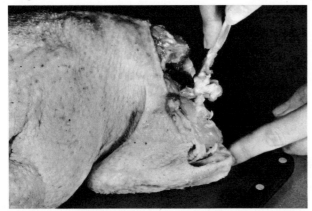

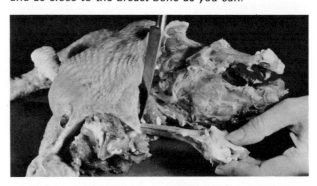

2 Turn the bird breast downwards and cut out the two sharp little bones from beneath the skin.

3 Work the flesh from the wing bone. Gradually remove the bone and sever it at the wing tip; the tip is left on to keep the shape of the wing. Remove the other wing bone in the same way.

5 Continue working down the leg, removing the thigh bone, then remove the drumstick, but leave the end of the leg up to the joint as this helps the bird to look more shapely when it is cooked and can easily be removed before carving. Remove the other leg in the same way. Continue working round the carcass and when the "parson's nose" is reached, cut the bone inside it. This should loosen the whole bone structure, which should then be removed.

6 All the bones are now removed and the chicken is ready to be stuffed. Keep it in a cool place while making the stuffing.

7 The bird back to its original shape after being stuffed. A skewer secures the loose neck skin and the wings and the legs are skewered close to the bird. Wrap a folded strip of greaseproof paper round the bird to keep it in good shape while it is roasting.

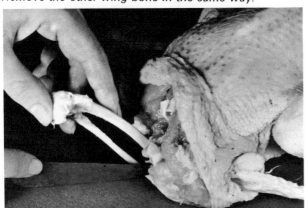

paper round the bird (photograph 7) to keep it a good shape while it is roasting. Fix it firmly with a paper clip.

TO ROAST THE BONED CHICKEN

Melt the butter in a roasting tin, put in the chicken and baste it well with butter. Cut the rind off the bacon and lay rashers over the breast. Roast the chicken in a fairly hot oven, about *Gas Mark 6 or 400 degrees F.*, for 20 minutes. Reduce the heat to *Gas Mark 4 or 350 degrees F.* for a further 1 hour 20 minutes. Twenty minutes before the end of the roasting time remove the paper collar.

TO SERVE HOT

Accompany the chicken with roast potatoes or boiled new potatoes and vegetables. Carving presents no problem; carve in fairly thick slices straight across the bird.

TO SERVE COLD

Surround the bird with Summer Salad (see below). It is best carved after it has been cooled overnight. If the weather is hot, put the chicken into the refrigerator for an hour before serving. Carve it crossways into thick slices.

SUMMER SALAD

1 bunch of watercress	2 heads of chicory
1 red dessert apple	2 oz. cottage cheese
the juice of 1 lemon	2 oz. halved walnuts
1 banana	1 oz. seedless raisins
	1 orange

Wash and dry the watercress. Slice and core the apple and turn the slices in the lemon juice. Slice the banana and turn these in the lemon juice. Separate the leaves of the chicory and arrange them round one side of the dish, heap the wide inner curve of each piece of chicory with cottage cheese and put a walnut on each. Stand slices of apple in the cottage cheese. Heap the banana slices and the raisins at one end of the serving dish. Cut two slices from the orange. Press the leg-ends of the chicken through the larger slice as a garnish on top of the bird. Cut the other slice in four and slip the slices under the first slice of chicken. Cut the skin off the rest of the orange with a very sharp knife, slice orange in wedges and heap on top of the quartered slices. Heap the watercress in the centre and garnish the orange slice on top of the bird with a few small leaves.

CHICKEN CURRY

FOR 4 PEOPLE

8 oz. cooked chicken	1 level teaspoon
2 oz. margarine	turmeric
1 level tablespoon	1 pint chicken stock
curry powder	1 tablespoon
1 onion, finely sliced	mango chutney
$\frac{1}{2}$ cooking apple,	1 oz. sultanas
finely chopped	salt and pepper
2 oz. plain flour	

FOR THE RICE AND ACCOMPANIMENTS

8 oz. Patna rice	little lemon juice
4 slices of lemon	1 oz. sultanas or
1 banana	seedless raisins

Chop the chicken roughly. Melt the margarine in a fairly large pan and add the curry powder and sliced onion. Cook them slowly together until the onion is almost tender. Add the chopped apple and cook this too for about 5 minutes. Stir in the flour and turmeric then add the chicken stock and stir it over a gentle heat until it comes to the boil and thickens. Simmer the sauce for a few minutes then add the chutney and sultanas and season the curry with salt and pepper. Stir in the chicken and heat it thoroughly without actually boiling it.

Put the rice into boiling salted water and boil it steadily for 12 to 15 minutes until the grains are tender. Strain the rice and pour a little boiling water through it to separate the grains and remove the excess starch. Heap it round the edge of a serving dish and pour the curry into the centre, garnishing the ring with slices of lemon. Slice the banana and mix it with a little lemon juice and the sultanas or raisins and arrange at either end of the dish.

SUNDAY CHICKEN

FOR 5/6 PEOPLE

a roasting chicken	2 oz. butter
(about 4 lb. trussed)	$\frac{1}{4}$ pint stock
salt and pepper	6 bananas
1 level teaspoon curry	
powder	

FOR THE FRITTERS

$\frac{1}{2}$ tin sweetcorn kernels	2 tablespoons milk
(11$\frac{1}{2}$ oz. tin)	salt and pepper
1 egg	a little fat for
3 oz. self-raising flour	frying

FOR THE GARNISH

3 good sized tomatoes	a knob of
salt and pepper	butter
$\frac{1}{2}$ tin sweetcorn kernels	
(the other half of the	
11$\frac{1}{2}$ oz. tin)	

Put the chicken in the roasting tin and sprinkle it with salt, pepper and the curry powder. Dot the top with butter and pour round the stock.

Roast the chicken in a fairly hot oven, about *Gas Mark 6 or 400 degrees F.*, for 1$\frac{1}{4}$ to 1$\frac{1}{2}$ hours. Baste the bird once after the first 15 minutes.

Meanwhile make the fritters. Mix the half tin of sweetcorn, the egg, self-raising flour and milk to a batter, and season with salt and pepper. Heat a little fat in a frying pan, put in spoonfuls of the batter and fry the under-sides until they are golden brown, then turn the fritters and fry them on the other side. Lift them out of the pan and drain them on absorbent kitchen paper for a few minutes before arranging them in a dish. Keep warm.

Fifteen minutes before the chicken is ready, skin the bananas, and put them round the chicken.

Cut the tomatoes in half, scoop out the centres, sprinkle the insides with salt and pepper, and fill them with sweetcorn kernels. Dot the tops with butter and put the tomatoes in the oven with the chicken for 10 minutes.

Put the chicken on a hot dish and arrange the bananas and some of the stuffed tomatoes round it. Serve the rest with the fritters. Serve the gravy from the tin in a sauceboat.

Lemon lamb (see page 44)

CHICKEN À LA KIEV

FOR 6/8 PEOPLE

2 roasting chickens,
  about 3½ lb. each,
  trussed (the legs,
  wings and carcass
  can be added to any
  chicken casserole
  dish)
6 oz. butter, well chilled
salt

freshly ground black
  pepper
4 level tablespoons
  flour, seasoned with
  salt and pepper
2 eggs
dry white
  breadcrumbs
deep fat for frying

THE ACCOMPANIMENT

smoothly creamed, well
  seasoned potatoes
  (1½ lb. when peeled)
1 small tin asparagus
  spears
3 large tomatoes

salt and pepper
1 large packet frozen
  peas, cooked as
  directed and tossed
  with a knob of
  butter
8 large flat cultivated
  mushrooms
little melted butter

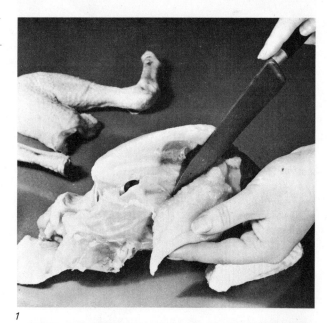

1

This dish is rather unusual as each little parcel of chicken breast is filled with butter. When it is cut, the melted butter deliciously spurts out and soaks into the creamed potatoes. First remove the legs of the chickens by cutting through the thigh joints. Now remove one of the breasts; to do this, keeping the knife against the breast bone and starting at the tip, fillet off the breast to the wing joint (photograph 1). Cut through the joint. Cut the breast off the wing; only the breast is used. Cut the other pieces of breast off both chickens in the same way.

Lay one piece of breast on a board and slit it in half, holding the knife horizontal to the table. Halve the other pieces in the same way, making 8 slim pieces. Place each piece of breast between two pieces of damp, greaseproof paper and flatten it with a rolling pin (photograph 2), but be careful not to break the flesh.

Next make the parcels. Cut the butter into 8 fingers. Place one of them in the centre of a piece of breast. Sprinkle it with salt and freshly ground black pepper. Roll the chicken over the butter once, fold in the edges like a parcel, then finish off the roll. It will stick without a skewer. Make all the other rolls in the same way.

Put the seasoned flour on a fairly deep plate. Beat the eggs and put them in a shallow bowl. Have the crumbs on a sheet of paper. Lightly toss one roll in flour, then stand it in the egg and brush it with beaten egg. Transfer it to the crumbs and coat it by lifting the edges of the paper and flicking the crumbs over the surface. Press the crumbs to the surface with a palette knife. Coat the rest of the rolls in the same way. Coat them all a second time. The rolls can be left in the refrigerator for several hours at this stage.

Heat the deep fat to *360 degrees F.* or until it is hot enough to brown a cube of white bread fairly quickly. Put 2 to 3 chicken rolls into the basket and lower them into the fat and fry them for about 7 minutes. Give them the full time to ensure the flesh is cooked to the centre. Drain them on a piece of absorbent kitchen paper. Fry the rest of the rolls in the same way, remembering to reheat the fat between batches. The fried rolls keep hot well, so you can assemble

2

the dish before the meal if you wish.

ASSEMBLING THE DISH

Pipe or spoon the creamed potato down the centre of a serving dish. Stack the rolls along it, putting asparagus tips between the 4 lower ones. The rest of the asparagus can be served separately. Keep the dish hot.

Skin and halve the tomatoes and remove the centres. Season, and heat them in a moderate oven. Fill them with the cooked peas; the rest of the peas can be served separately. Arrange the stuffed tomatoes at either side of the rolls. Wipe the mushrooms; there is no need to peel them or cut off the stalks. Brush them with melted butter and grill them for a few seconds, then arrange them down both sides of the dish.

Crown of lamb (see page 42)

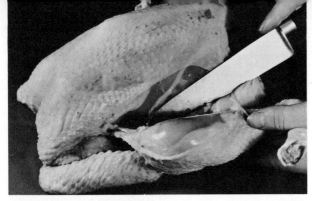

JOINTING A CHICKEN

1 Using a sharp knife, cut the flesh round the leg joint. Pull the leg from the carcass and sever through the joint. Cut the joint in half at the drumstick. Remove the other leg in the same way. Cut off the wings, taking a small piece of breast with each; again sever through the joint.

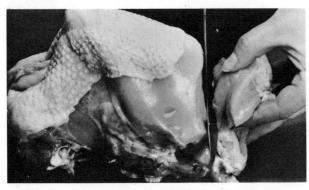

2 Cut off the wishbone, taking a little of the breast with it.

3 Using kitchen scissors, cut through the rib cage on each side of breast bone to separate back from front.

4 Plunge the knife into the centre of the breast bone from inside bird and cut breast in half along the bone.

CHICKEN JULIENNE

FOR 4/5 PEOPLE

1 roasting chicken (about 2¾ lb. trussed)
2 medium sized leeks
8 oz. celery
8 oz. carrots
1 oz. butter
pinch of sugar
¾ pint water
¼ pint white wine
salt and white pepper

FOR THE VELOUTÉ SAUCE

1 oz. butter
1 oz. plain flour
1 pint stock, strained after cooking the chicken
1 teaspoon lemon juice
salt and white pepper

Joint the chicken (see left). The remaining carcass and giblets can be used for making soup.

Wash the vegetables very thoroughly, and cut strips of leek 1½ inches long and about ¼ inch wide from the medium green part of the leek. Cut about half a cupful of these neat strips which are known as *juliennes;* they are for the garnish. Cut up the rest of the leek roughly to cook with the chicken. Cut thin julienne strips of celery and carrot in the same way and place the strips in water for the time being, as they are cooked separately. Cut the rest of the carrot and celery roughly to cook with the chicken.

Melt the butter in a large saucepan and add all the roughly cut vegetables and toss them over a moderate heat until the butter is absorbed. Put in the chicken joints. The remaining chicken carcass can be put on top and will add flavour, though it should be taken out before serving. Add the pinch of sugar, the water and the wine, and a sprinkling of salt and pepper. Bring to the boil, cover the pan with a tight-fitting lid and simmer the chicken very gently for about an hour or until it is tender. Alternatively it can be transferred to a slow oven, about *Gas Mark 2 or 300 degrees F.*

Meanwhile, boil the julienne strips of vegetable separately; they will take about 7 minutes to cook. Drain them and keep them hot. Lift the chicken joints on to a hot plate and strain off the stock, measure it and make up to a pint with water, if necessary. Melt the butter for the sauce, take it off the heat and stir in the flour. Cook the roux over a very gentle heat until it is straw coloured, then take it off the heat and add the stock. Whisk the sauce until it is smooth, then stir it over a moderate heat until it thickens. Boil it rapidly to reduce it to a syrupy consistency, then add the lemon juice and salt and pepper if required. Skim the sauce when necessary. Heap the cooked vegetables round the chicken, and pour the sauce over the joints.

HARLEQUIN CASSEROLE

FOR 6 PEOPLE

1 roasting chicken (about 3 lb. trussed)
3 oz. flour seasoned with salt and pepper
8 oz. fresh belly of pork
little made mustard
2½ oz. lard

1 pint stock
4 oz. mushrooms
3 medium onions
3 cloves
pinch of fresh chopped or dried thyme

Cut the chicken into joints (see left) and toss them in the seasoned flour. Remove all the skin and bones from the pork, then cut it into fairly large cubes, about 1 inch square, and spread each cube with a little made mustard. Melt the lard in a frying pan and fry the chicken joints lightly until they are golden brown all over, then transfer them to a casserole. Stir the remainder of the seasoned flour into the lard left in the frying pan. Remove it from the heat and gradually add the stock then return the pan to the heat and bring to the boil, stirring all the time. Pour into the casserole. Add pork.

Slice the mushrooms and the onions and add them to the casserole with the cloves and the thyme. Put the lid on and cook the casserole in the centre of a moderate oven, *Gas Mark 4 or 350 degrees F.*, for 1½ to 1¾ hours.

CHICKEN AURORE

FOR 5/6 PEOPLE

1 roasted chicken (about 3½ lb. before cooked)	salt and pepper
	½ pint mayonnaise (see page 85)
1 lb. tomatoes	few drops of Tabasco
12 oz. Patna rice	1 dessertspoon sherry
a slice of lemon	½ level teaspoon finely grated orange rind
2 tablespoons cooking oil	
2 tablespoons distilled white vinegar	

FOR THE GARNISH

1 lb. tomatoes	1 orange (it can be the orange from which the rind was grated)
1 oz. shredded browned almonds	

Cut the roasted chicken into pieces. Remove the legs and make 2 portions from each by severing at the joint. Cut off each wing with a piece of the breast, then cut off the remaining breast from either side of the bone. Remove all the skin. Cut the tomatoes in quarters, put them into a pan and cook them briskly without a lid until they are a very thick consistency. Sieve the pulp and allow the purée to get cold. Cook the rice in plenty of boiling, salted water, adding a slice of lemon to keep it white. When the rice is tender, drain it and pour cold water through it to remove the excess starch and separate grains. Put it into a bowl and mix in the cooking oil, vinegar, salt and pepper. Heap the rice on to a large dish and arrange the pieces of chicken round it.

Mix the tomato purée into the mayonnaise, add the Tabasco, sherry and finely grated orange rind, season the sauce with salt and pepper and coat the joints of chicken. For the garnish, peel the tomatoes, quarter them and scoop out the seeds (use these in soups, sauces or stews). Scatter these tongues of tomato over the dish and sprinkle browned almonds over the top.

Cut 3 inches of the rind off the orange with a potato peeler and cut it in very thin shreds. Put these into a small pan, cover them well with water and simmer them for 5 minutes, then drain them. Cut off the skin of the orange, including the inner white skin, using a very sharp knife and cutting spirally round the orange. Cut the orange in half lengthways, then cut slices from each half. Nestle these slices round the dish beside the tomatoes and scatter the top with shredded orange rind.

Serve the dish with a green salad.

ROAST TURKEY

ROASTING TIMES AND TEMPERATURES
Weigh the bird, trussed but not stuffed. Allow 20 minutes for every pound and add 20 minutes to the total time. Roast the turkey at *Gas Mark 6 or 400 degrees F.* for the first hour then reduce the heat to *Gas Mark 4 or 350 degrees F.* for the rest of the time. For very large birds above 18 lb. reduce the heat to *Gas Mark 2 or 300 degrees F.* after the first hour. Make sure the turkey is ready 30 minutes before the meal; it will give you time to make the gravy and the turkey will carve better, too.

A FROZEN TURKEY
Do remember that a frozen turkey must have time to thaw slowly. It will take anything up to 36 hours in the refrigerator or 24 hours in the larder. The giblets are usually packed inside the carcass so remember to remove them.

THE GIBLET STOCK
This is used for the gravy; the meat from the cooked giblets can be chopped and added to the stuffing.

Wash the neck, gizzard and heart in cold salted water and dry them. Keep the liver, chop this and add it raw to the stuffing. Heat a teaspoon of cooking oil in a strong pan and when it is hot, brown the giblets and a small, sliced onion quickly on all sides, to make a brown stock. Add 2 pints of water, bring it to the boil, skim it, put on the lid and simmer the giblets for about 1½ hours or until the meat will come easily off the bone. Strain the stock. Skim the fat from the surface before using it.

STUFFING THE TURKEY
Choose two stuffings from the stuffing section on page 89. Work your hands under the skin of the bird as far along the breast as you can. Put one stuffing carefully into the neck end of the turkey, pressing it well into the bird under the breast skin so that during roasting the stuffing will help to keep the breast moist. Make sure the stuffing makes the breast look well-rounded. Tuck the loose skin, which covered the neck, under the wings; this keeps the stuffing in place. Spoon the other stuffing into the carcass.

PREPARING THE TURKEY FOR THE OVEN
Put the turkey into the roasting tin and rub the breast with a cut lemon to whiten it. Cover the breast and the top of the legs with slices of very fat bacon and *loosely* top this with a piece of kitchen foil.

ROASTING
Roast the turkey for the calculated time. There is no need to baste the bird to start with but take off the foil and bacon for the last 30 minutes of cooking, and baste the bird.

THE GRAVY
Lift the turkey on to a hot dish and leave it in a warm place while making the gravy. Spoon off the fat, leaving only the sediment below. Stir a level dessertspoon of flour into the tin and stir it over a gentle heat to brown the flour lightly. Pour on a pint of giblet stock and stir the gravy over a low heat until the sediment has melted into the gravy. As the gravy heats it becomes smooth; bring it to the boil, simmer it for a few minutes and season it with salt and pepper.

THE OTHER ACCOMPANIMENTS
Most people like sausages; bread sauce is a *must*, cranberry sauce if you like (recipes on pages 86 and 87).

ROAST GOOSE

1 roasting goose, trussed	1 lemon
salt and pepper	1 tablespoon dripping

Weigh the trussed goose before stuffing it. Choose sage and onion stuffing (see page 89). Allow 15 minutes cooking time for every pound in weight.

Wipe out the inside of the goose with a damp cloth before stuffing it. Season the inside with a little salt and pepper then put the whole lemon into the carcass, towards the neck end. This gives the goose a delicious flavour.

THE STUFFING

Put the stuffing into the tail end of the carcass, not too far inside so that it is easy to get out with a spoon. Make a small incision in the skin above the "parson's nose" and button the "parson's nose" through the loop to keep the stuffing nicely secure.

ROASTING THE GOOSE

Heat the dripping in a roasting tin in a moderately hot oven, about *Gas Mark 5 or 375 degrees F.*, put the goose into the tin and baste it with the dripping, then put it into the centre of the oven. Baste the goose occasionally during cooking and if the surface should brown too quickly cover it with a piece of dampened, clean brown paper. When the goose is ready, put it on a hot dish and keep it warm while making the gravy.

THE GRAVY

This is made from giblet stock in exactly the same way as described for turkey (see page 65) using half the quantity of liquid as the giblets are smaller.

GLAZED APPLE RING GARNISH

This is a pleasant change from apple sauce, which is often served with roast goose. Alternatively, orange salad (see below right) can be served.

Cut two peeled and cored cooking apples into rings about ¼ inch thick. Brush them with a little melted butter and sprinkle them with castor sugar. Cook them under a moderate grill to soften them and lightly glaze the sugar. Arrange them round the goose.

NOTE: It is always correct and rather nice to serve a green salad—tossed with French dressing, if you like—with the goose.

FESTIVE ROAST DUCK

FOR 4 PEOPLE

1 roasting duck, trussed	juice and rind of
salt and pepper	1 orange
2 tablespoons clear honey	1 tablespoon brandy

TO ACCOMPANY THE DUCK

duchesse potatoes (see page 75) made from 1 lb. potatoes	green peas orange salad

Roast goose with glazed apple ring garnish

Pepper and salt the inside of the duck. Wash the giblets in cold salt water then put them back into the carcass. Put the duck into a roasting tin. Mix the honey with the orange juice and rind and spoon it over the duck.

Roast the duck in a moderately hot oven, about *Gas Mark 5 or 375 degrees F.*, for 30 minutes, reduce the heat to *Gas Mark 4 or 350 degrees F.* for a further hour or until the duck is tender, basting it occasionally with the honey and orange juice which should put a glaze on the surface.

Put the duck on to a hot plate, with the duchesse potatoes. Warm the brandy in a pan, set it alight in the pan then pour it over the bird. This can be done at the table in exactly the same way as you would flame a Christmas pudding. As well as adding flavour, it gives the skin a delicious crispness. Serve duchesse potatoes and green peas with the duck, also an orange salad (see below).

NOTE: Duck cooked in this way is very good served cold for a buffet party.

ORANGE SALAD

Peel the outer skin very thinly off one small orange (a potato peeler is best for this). Shred it into very thin strips across the peel. Put them into a pan, cover well with water and simmer them for 5 minutes. Drain them. Cut the skins off four more small oranges, using a sharper knife and cutting both the outer and inner white skin spirally off the orange. Slice the oranges and arrange them on a dish. Sprinkle over them the cooked orange rind. The salad can be sprinkled with French dressing or serve the dressing separately if you prefer.

Lift out the duck and the giblets, mace and thyme, then sieve the sauce or put it through the finest plate of a vegetable mill. Put it back into a pan, bring it to the boil, skim off any fat and add the orange juice and maraschino syrup. Boil the sauce rapidly without a lid to evaporate some of the liquid and concentrate the flavour. When there is three-quarters of a pint left add the maraschino cherries, and season the sauce with salt and pepper. Put the duck back into the sauce and heat it gently for about 30 minutes. Serve the duck on a hot plate, pour round the sauce and garnish the duck with a thinly sliced orange. Surround it with sprigs of watercress, sections of orange and a few extra maraschino cherries.

GAME

ROASTING GAME

Roast only young birds. The older ones are ideal for stewing, or making into casserole dishes or pies, but it is a mistake to roast them as they would be dry and tough. Young birds should have soft, pliable feet and the tip of the breast bone and back should be soft and pliable.

PHEASANTS
Time—Between 45 minutes and $1\frac{1}{4}$ hours: it depends how large the bird is and how long it has been hung.
Temperature—*Gas Mark 5 or 375 degrees F.* for all the cooking time.
Tip—Cover the breast with fat bacon to prevent it from drying.

PARTRIDGE AND GROUSE
Time—Allow 25 to 35 minutes, depending on the size and how long the birds have hung.
Temperature—*Gas Mark 5 or 375 degrees F.* for all the cooking time.
Tip—Baste well during roasting and serve each bird on a square of toast or fried bread.

PIGEON AND BEEF CASSEROLE

FOR 6 PEOPLE

3 stewing pigeons	2 small onions
2 oz. dripping	salt and pepper
$1\frac{1}{2}$ lb. shin of beef	1 tin cherries (15 oz.)
2 oz. plain flour	6 tablespoons
$\frac{1}{4}$ pint red wine	yoghourt
2 pints stock	

Split the pigeons in half and take the skin off the breasts. Brown them well in the dripping, then transfer them to the casserole. Cut the beef into cubes, brown these, and scatter them over the pigeons. Add the flour to the remainder of the dripping then pour over the wine and stock. Add the onions, quartered. Bring the sauce to the boil, season it with salt and pepper, then pour it over the pigeons. Put on a lid and cook the casserole in a slow oven, about *Gas Mark 2 or 300 degrees F.*, for 2 hours or until the pigeons are tender.
Strain the juice off the cherries and stone them. When the pigeons are tender, strain off the gravy and mix it with the yoghourt and stoned cherries, season it again if required then pour it over the pigeons.

BRAISED DUCK WITH ORANGE AND CHERRY SAUCE

FOR 4 PEOPLE

1 medium sized duck, trussed and with the giblets (about $3\frac{1}{2}$ to 4 lb.)	1 clove of garlic
	sprig of thyme
thinly peeled rind of $\frac{1}{2}$ small orange	1 blade of mace
	1 pint water
$1\frac{1}{2}$ oz. dripping	$\frac{1}{4}$ pint white wine
1 medium onion, sliced	salt and pepper
2 rashers of bacon, with the rinds	juice of the peeled orange
2 carrots, scraped and cut lengthwise	1 tablespoon maraschino syrup from the cherries
2 oz. mushroom stalks	12 maraschino cherries

FOR THE GARNISH

2 small oranges watercress	few extra cherries

Wash the inside of the duck, then put the orange rind inside. Melt the dripping and fry the duck quickly to brown it. Put it into an ovenproof pan or casserole. Fry the onion until it is lightly browned, then add the bacon and fry it to a golden brown with the onions. Add the carrots and washed mushroom stalks, and the garlic, crushed under the blade of a knife with a pinch of salt. Add the thyme and mace, then the water and wine. Season the braise lightly with salt and pepper, bring it to the boil and pour it round the duck. Add giblets to casserole. Put on the lid and cook the duck in a cool oven, about *Gas Mark 2 or 300 degrees F.*, for $2\frac{1}{2}$ hours or until the duck is tender. It can be left overnight at this stage.

TERRINE OF PIGEON

FOR 6 PEOPLE

2 pigeons
8 oz. belly of pork
8 oz. lamb's or pig's liver
1 small onion
8 oz. sausagemeat
8 oz. minced beef
2 level tablespoons
  chopped parsley
3 oz. freshly made brown
  breadcrumbs

4 tablespoons milk
2 dessertspoons
  sherry or brandy
salt and pepper
12 oz. streaky bacon,
  cut in thin
  rashers
1 bay leaf

Remove the skin from and slice the meat off the pigeon breasts and as much meat as possible from the carcass. Finely chop the belly of pork, the liver and the onion; these can be minced through a coarse cutter. Add the sausagemeat, minced beef, chopped parsley, breadcrumbs and mix well adding the milk and sherry or brandy. Season the mixture carefully with salt and pepper.

Cut the rinds off the bacon rashers, and stretch them under a heavy knife. Line an ovenproof dish with the bacon leaving four rashers for the top. Put half the meat mixture into the dish and cover it with the slices of pigeon, then add the rest of the mixture. Cover the top with the rest of the bacon and put the bay leaf on top. Put on a tight-fitting lid. Stand the terrine in a roasting tin and surround it with hot water. Cook it in a moderate oven, *Gas Mark 4 or 350 degrees F.*, for 2 hours.

Take off the lid, press the terrine surface with a small plate and some kitchen weights and leave in a cool place overnight. Cut large slices of terrine for each person and serve with a green salad, and hot garlic or mustard bread (see below).

GARLIC OR MUSTARD BREAD

Slice a French loaf thickly to within $\frac{1}{4}$ inch of the base. Beat French mustard or a creamed clove of garlic into 2 oz. softened butter and spread this between the slices. Crisp in a hot oven for 10 minutes.

RABBIT AND PORK CASSEROLE

FOR 4 PEOPLE

1 large onion
2 small cooking apples
1 lb. belly of pork
4 rabbit joints
salt and pepper

2 level tablespoons
  tomato purée
$\frac{3}{4}$ pint stock
$\frac{1}{4}$ pint apple juice

Peel and slice the onion and lay the slices over the base of a casserole. Peel and core the apples; slice them in rings and lay them over the onion. Cut the pork into fairly large cubes and put it, with the rabbit, on top of the apples. Season the meat with salt and pepper. Mix the tomato purée with the stock and apple juice and pour the mixture over the meat. Cover the casserole with a lid and cook it in a warm oven, about *Gas Mark 3 or 325 degrees F.*, for 1 hour, then reduce the heat to *Gas Mark 2 or 300 degrees F.* for a further hour, or until the rabbit is tender.

JUGGED HARE

FOR 6/7 PEOPLE

1 hare, paunched and
  jointed (ask for the
  blood, too)
2 oz. dripping
4 oz. streaky bacon
  cut into strips
2 medium sized onions,
  peeled and each stuck
  with a clove
6 peppercorns
salt

a bouquet garni (bay
  leaf, a sprig of thyme
  and a sprig of parsley)
1 level teaspoon
  allspice berries
1 stalk of celery,
  washed and
  chopped
3 medium sized
  carrots, quartered
juice of 1 lemon
2 pints of stock

FOR THE STUFFING BALLS

2 oz. streaky bacon,
  with rinds removed,
  chopped
$\frac{1}{2}$ oz. dripping
1 medium sized onion,
  peeled and chopped
  finely
2 level tablespoons
  shredded suet

4 oz. freshly made
  white breadcrumbs
4 level teaspoons
  chopped parsley
salt and pepper
1 beaten egg
little butter for
  frying

TO THICKEN AND FINISH

2 level dessertspoons
  cornflour
the hare's blood
2 level dessertspoons
  redcurrant jelly

salt and pepper,
  if required
1 small tin red
  cherries
4 tablespoons port

Soak the joints of hare in salted water for 2 or 3 hours. Drain and dry them thoroughly, cut leg joints in half.

Melt the dripping and fry the strips of bacon until they are crisp, then lift them out of the fat. Brown the joints of hare on both sides then pack them into a large casserole with the bacon. Add the onions, peppercorns, bouquet garni, allspice berries, celery and carrots. Sprinkle with salt and pour over the lemon juice and stock. Put on the lid. Cook the hare in a moderate oven, about *Gas Mark 4 or 350 degrees F.*, for 1 hour, then reduce the heat to *Gas Mark 2 or 300 degrees F.* for a further 2 hours or until the hare is tender. While it is cooking make the stuffing balls.

THE STUFFING BALLS

Fry the bacon in the dripping until it is cooked, remove it and fry the chopped onion gently until it is tender. Mix the remaining fat with the onion, bacon, shredded suet, breadcrumbs and chopped parsley. Season the mixture with salt and pepper and bind it with the beaten egg.

Heat a little butter in a frying pan and fry the stuffing balls gently over a moderate heat, rolling them round the pan.

THE GRAVY

Pour the gravy off the hare into a pan. Blend the cornflour with the hare's blood, and stir in a little of the gravy. Sieve the redcurrant jelly into this, and then add the rest of the gravy, return it to the pan and stir it over a gentle heat until it thickens and becomes dark brown and shiny, which it will do quite suddenly. Re-season with salt and pepper. Add the cherries, drained of their juice, and the port. Pour over the hare. Serve with the stuffing balls.

SUPPERS AND SNACKS

Light lunches . . . children's tea . . . snack suppers by the fire. These are often the most difficult meals to think of, and to vary day by day. In this chapter, I suggest many new and interesting ideas for these "in-between" meals, using mainly simple ingredients that you could well have in your store cupboard. Eggs and cheese are among the most useful foods for snack dishes, so I have included some recipes using these. However, if you want a snack meal in a hurry, and there isn't a thing in your store cupboard, remember you cannot go far wrong with a good chunk of cheese, fresh bread and plenty of butter, washed down with mugs of strong, hot coffee, or glasses of milk, followed by fresh fruit.

KIDNEY, MUSHROOMS AND TOAST

FOR ABOUT 4 PEOPLE

1 oz. dripping	1 oz. plain flour
2 rashers streaky bacon	1 tin tomatoes
1 small onion	(14 oz.)
6 lamb's kidneys,	salt and pepper
skinned and	7 large mushrooms
quartered, with	little melted butter
cores removed	7 triangles of toast

Melt the dripping gently; chop the bacon and fry it gently in the dripping. Skin and slice the onion finely and add to the bacon. Add the kidneys and fry them with the other ingredients for a few minutes just to brown them lightly. Add the flour then stir in the contents of the tin of tomatoes. Stir over a gentle heat until the mixture comes to the boil, season it with salt and pepper and simmer it gently for 20 to 30 minutes.
Wipe the mushrooms with a damp cloth (there is no need to peel them). Brush them with a little melted butter and grill them for a few seconds.
Turn the kidney mixture into a hot dish and arrange the mushrooms down one side of the dish and the triangles of toast down the other.

SALMON FISHCAKES

MAKES 6 LARGE CAKES

1 small packet of instant	1 beaten egg
mashed potato	dry white
1 small tin of salmon or	breadcrumbs
tuna fish (about 4 oz.)	fat for deep or
salt and pepper	shallow frying

Make up the potato as directed on the packet. Open the tin of salmon or tuna fish, drain off the liquid and remove any bones. Flake the fish, mix it well with the potatoes and season carefully with salt and pepper. Turn the mixture on to a floured board and roll it to just over $\frac{1}{2}$ inch thick. Cut out rounds with a cutter $2\frac{3}{4}$ inches in diameter. Press the scraps together and shape these as well. Brush the fishcakes with beaten egg, cover with breadcrumbs, reshape with a palette knife and fry them in deep or shallow fat.

PARSLEY AND CHEESE CAKES

MAKES 5 CAKES

1 small packet of instant	1 beaten egg
mashed potato	white breadcrumbs
1 tablespoon chopped	fat for deep or
parsley	shallow frying
5 triangular sections of	
processed cheese	

Make up the potato according to the directions on the packet, roll half of this made-up potato on a floured board to just under $\frac{1}{2}$ inch thick and cut out rounds with a cutter $2\frac{3}{4}$ inches in diameter. Mix the parsley with the other half, roll it out and cut it into rounds in the same way. Press rounds of parsley and plain potato together with a wedge of cheese between, and reshape with a palette knife. Egg and breadcrumb the potato cakes twice before frying them in deep or shallow fat.

KEBABS

FOR 3 PEOPLE

1 large packet instant
  mashed potato
2 oz. lamb liver cut into
  6 small pieces
1 lamb kidney, skinned
  and halved
3 tomatoes, halved
6 chipolata sausages,
  each twisted and
  cut into two

3 bay leaves
3 slices of orange
3 small mushrooms,
  washed but not
  peeled
1 tablespoon
  cooking oil
1 tablespoon tomato
  ketchup

Thread the liver, kidney, tomatoes, sausages, bay leaves, orange and mushrooms on to 3 long skewers, with a good selection on each, and lay them on the grill grid. Mix the oil and tomato ketchup and brush it over the meat. Grill the kebabs under a moderate heat until they are lightly browned, then turn them and brush them before grilling the other sides.

Make up potato according to directions on packet; divide among three serving plates; lay kebabs on top of potato.

BACON AND BANANA CORKSCREWS

FOR 4 PEOPLE

4 long rashers of
  streaky bacon
4 small bananas

$\frac{1}{2}$ pint cheese sauce
  (see page 86)
6 oz. Patna rice

Cut the rinds off the bacon. Peel the bananas and wrap each banana in a rasher of bacon. Grill the bananas gently under a slow heat to brown and crisp the bacon. Turn the bananas and cook the other side. Meanwhile make the sauce with the milk and cook the rice as directed on the packet. Drain the rice and turn it on to a hot plate, pour over the cheese sauce and serve the bananas on top.

POTATO RING

FOR 3/4 PEOPLE

1 large packet instant
  mashed potato
little beaten egg
4 oz. button mushrooms
  washed and sliced
1$\frac{1}{2}$ oz. butter

1 level tablespoon
  plain flour
$\frac{1}{4}$ pint stock
2 oz. ham, chopped
salt and pepper if
  needed

Make up the potato as directed on the packet. Put the potato into a forcing bag with a large star pipe attached. Pipe a 6$\frac{1}{2}$ inch wide circle on a heatproof plate, and another circle on top of it. Pipe a circle of potato stars round the top and another round outside of ring on the plate. Brush the case with egg then bake in a moderate oven, about *Gas Mark 4 or 350 degrees F.*, for about 20 minutes.
While the case browns, make the filling. Cook the sliced mushrooms for 3 minutes in the butter. Lift out the same number of slices as there are stars round the top of the case, add the flour to the rest, then the stock and stir the sauce

until it comes to the boil. Add the chopped ham and simmer the sauce for a few minutes. Season it with salt and pepper, if necessary. Pour the sauce into the centre of the potato case and slip the slices of mushroom between the stars on the top.

SANDWICHES AND SPREADS

TOMATO AND CREAM CHEESE FILLING

ENOUGH FOR 6 WHOLE ROUNDS

4 oz. cream cheese
8 oz. tomatoes

salt and pepper

Spread 6 rounds with cream cheese. Slice the tomatoes fairly thinly (they can be peeled beforehand if you like), cover the cream cheese with the sliced tomatoes and add salt and pepper.

AN ALTERNATIVE FILLING WITH TOMATOES

Instead of cream cheese, beat a little mayonnaise into 8 oz. chutney.

BANANA AND RASPBERRY

ENOUGH FOR 6 WHOLE ROUNDS

3 bananas
1 level tablespoon castor
  sugar

squeeze of lemon
  juice
little raspberry jam

Mash the bananas with a fork. Beat in the sugar and lemon juice. Spread the rounds of bread with raspberry jam, then cover the jam with mashed banana.

APPLE AND RAISIN

ENOUGH FOR 6 WHOLE ROUNDS

2 sharp-flavoured
  dessert apples

2 oz. stoned raisins

Grate the apple (there is no need to remove the skin) using a coarse grater. Chop the raisins and mix them with the apple.

CREAM CHEESE AND WALNUT

ENOUGH FOR 6 WHOLE ROUNDS

1 oz. walnuts, chopped
  or minced

salt and pepper
6 oz. cream cheese

Beat the walnuts and seasoning into the cream cheese.

CURRIED CHICKEN

ENOUGH FOR 4 WHOLE ROUNDS

1 cooked chicken joint	½ level teaspoon
1 stick celery	curry powder
2 oz. butter	salt and pepper

Mince the chicken and celery or chop very finely. Melt the butter, add the curry powder and cook for a few seconds. Stir in the chicken and celery and season the mixture with salt and pepper.

LIPTAUR

6 oz. butter, softened	3 level teaspoons
8 oz. cottage cheese	French mustard
½ small tin anchovies	good pinch of
3 gherkins	paprika
1 level dessertspoon	salt and pepper
chopped chives	

This makes a delicious spread on French bread. It is also excellent stuffed into potatoes baked in their jackets.
Beat the butter and cottage cheese thoroughly together. Chop the anchovies and gherkins and add them to the mixture with the chopped chives, French mustard, paprika and salt and pepper. Serve while it is soft and easy to spread. Although liptaur keeps well in the refrigerator allow time for it to soften before serving it.

DANISH BLUE AND CHIVES SPREAD

4 oz. Danish blue cheese	salt and pepper
4 oz. butter	
1 level teaspoon	
chopped chives	

Sieve the Danish blue cheese. Soften the butter, and beat the butter and cheese together until they are well blended. Add the chives and seasoning.

NOTE: This spread can be made in seconds in a liquidiser. Melt the butter, put it into a blender with the cheese, and switch on for a few seconds until the mixture is a smooth blend. Season with salt and pepper and chives.

LIVER SAUSAGE AND CREAM CHEESE SPREAD

4 oz. liver sausage	1 teaspoon
4 oz. demi-sel cream	Worcester sauce
cheese	1 tablespoon sherry
2 oz. butter, melted	1 tablespoon double
good pinch of curry	cream or
powder	evaporated milk

Remove the skin from the liver sausage, then put the liver sausage into a basin with the demi-sel cheese and beat both of them together until they are thoroughly mixed. Stir in the melted butter, curry powder, Worcester sauce, sherry and cream or evaporated milk.

EGGS AND CHEESE

PANCAKES

MAKES ABOUT 10 PANCAKES

4 oz. plain flour	1 dessertspoon salad
pinch of salt	oil
1 egg	little oil for frying
¼ pint milk	the pancakes
¼ pint water	

Sift the flour with a pinch of salt into a mixing bowl. Break the egg and drop it into the centre of the flour, then add the milk. Mixing from the centre, gradually incorporate the flour from round the sides and when it is all mixed in beat the batter well with the back of a wooden spoon; this helps to add air. When it is ready the batter should be smooth and shiny, and small bubbles should rise to the surface. Stir in the water and salad oil. Pour the batter into a jug; this is the easiest way to pour and judge the right amount for each pancake.

Have a clean strong frying pan 8 inches in diameter ready for making the pancakes. Heat a little oil in the pan and when it is hot pour off all that will run, leaving only the oil that clings to the surface of the pan. Heat this again until it is really hot then lift the pan off the heat and pour in about two tablespoons of batter from the jug and swirl it quickly round the base of the pan to coat it evenly, and thinly. Put the pan back on to a sharp heat for a few seconds. Loosen the pancake round the edges with a palette knife, then turn over the pancake and fry it for a few seconds on the other side. Both sides should be lightly browned. Turn the pancake on to a piece of absorbent kitchen paper. Fry the rest of the pancakes in the same way stacking them on top of each other as they are fried.

STUFFED PANCAKES

The pancakes and the finish for the topping are the same in all three recipes. The topping keeps the pancakes moist while they are reheating.

FOR 4 PEOPLE

8 pancakes (see above)

FOR THE TOPPING

1 oz. butter, melted	¼ pint stock
2 oz. Cheddar cheese,	
grated	

SMOKED HADDOCK FILLING

¼ pint milk	3 oz. Cheddar cheese
¼ pint water	10 oz. cooked and
2 oz. butter	flaked smoked
2 oz. plain flour	haddock (about 1 lb
freshly ground black	fish will be
pepper	required)

Put the milk, water, butter, flour and freshly ground black pepper into a saucepan and stir the mixture over a very gentle heat until the sauce is smooth; increase the heat and continue stirring until the mixture boils. Take it off the heat and beat in the cheese, then stir in the flaked fish. Put a good spoonful of the mixture on to each pancake and fold the pancake in three.

Arrange the pancakes in a well-greased heatproof dish and brush with melted butter. Scatter with grated cheese and pour the stock round them. Heat the pancakes in a fairly hot oven, about *Gas Mark 6 or 400 degrees F.*, for 15 minutes when they should be thoroughly hot and the topping lightly browned.

KIDNEY FILLING

12 oz. ox kidney	1 level tablespoon
1½ oz. butter	plain flour
4 medium sized	¼ pint plus 4
onions, sliced	tablespoons stock
	salt and pepper

Slice the kidney, cover it with cold salted water and leave it for 30 minutes. Dry it and cut out the central core from each slice with a sharp knife, then chop the kidney, not too finely.

Melt the butter and fry the onion very slowly until it is tender, add the kidney and toss over the heat for 5 or 6 minutes. Stir in the flour then add the stock; stir the mixture until it comes to the boil then season carefully. Simmer the filling gently for 15 to 20 minutes. Fill and cook pancakes as for smoked haddock filling.

CHICKEN LIVER AND SPINACH FILLING

8 oz. chicken liver	2 eggs
1 large packet frozen	salt and pepper
spinach	

Chop the chicken liver, not too finely. Cook the spinach as directed, drain it, then return it to the pan with the chopped chicken liver and cook them over a very gentle heat for 6 or 7 minutes until the liver is tender. Beat the eggs; gradually stir in the liver and spinach mixture. Season carefully with salt and pepper. Fill and cook pancakes as for smoked haddock filling.

SPANISH OMELET

FOR 4 PEOPLE

1 lb. potatoes	2 tablespoons oil
bunch of spring onions	6 eggs
(2 sliced onions could	1 tablespoon water
be used instead, if	salt and pepper
wished)	

Peel and dice the potatoes. Take the outside skin off the spring onions and cut them in half if they are large ones. Heat the oil and fry the diced potato very slowly until almost tender. Add the onions and cook with the potatoes until they are both tender and lightly golden.

Break the eggs into a bowl, add the water and season with salt and pepper. Beat the eggs just to break them. Pour the eggs on to the vegetables and cook the omelet over a fairly brisk heat until the egg is set. To cook the other side lightly, slip the omelet on to a baking tray, turn the pan over on top of it and turn the whole thing over. When cooked, serve at once.

72

Spanish omelet

HAM SOUFFLES

FOR 4 PEOPLE

8 oz. lean ham	4 or 5 drops of
¾ oz. butter	Tabasco sauce
¾ oz. plain flour	1 level teaspoon
½ pint milk	condensed tomato
2 eggs	purée
½ oz. gelatine	salt and pepper
2 tablespoons water	4 individual
½ gill single cream	soufflé dishes, each
1 level dessertspoon	holding ¼ pint liquid,
sieved chutney	will be required

FOR THE DECORATION

little horseradish sauce	1 tinned pimento
finely chopped	2 slices of hard-boiled
parsley	egg

Round each soufflé dish tie a collar of doubled greaseproof paper about 1 inch deeper than the dish, making the collar tight and overlapping the ends to prevent any of the mixture running between the paper and the dish.

Mince the ham finely, or put it through the fine cutter of a vegetable mill. Melt the butter in a saucepan, take it off the heat and stir in the flour. Add all the milk and stir the mixture over a gentle heat until it is smooth, then increase the heat and bring to the boil. Simmer it for a few minutes. Separate the yolks from the whites of the eggs. Stir two tablespoons of the sauce into the egg yolks, mix together, then add this to the sauce and stir over a gentle heat for a few minutes without allowing it to boil. Stir in the minced ham, and leave the mixture to cool.

Put the gelatine into a small pan, with the water, and dissolve it over a gentle heat. Add this to the mixture with the cream, sieved chutney, Tabasco sauce, tomato purée and salt and pepper. Whip the egg whites stiffly and stir a dessertspoon of egg white into the mixture. Lightly fold in the rest. Divide the mixture among the little dishes; it should come about half an inch above the top rims. Leave the soufflés for an hour or so to set.

Remove the paper collars carefully, then spread the edge of each soufflé with horseradish sauce and roll it in the finely chopped parsley. Cut thin strips of pimento and lay them across the top of each soufflé. Put half a slice of hard-boiled egg in the centre of each.

CHEESE SOUFFLÉ

FOR 3 PEOPLE

¾ oz. margarine
¾ oz. plain flour
¼ pint milk
2 oz. cheese, finely
  grated
salt and a pinch of
  cayenne pepper

2 large eggs or
  3 small ones
a straight-sided
  soufflé dish 6
  inches in diameter
  will be required

Tie a double strip of greaseproof paper round the outside of the dish, to come at least an inch above the rim. It is best not to grease the dish—the soufflé will rise better without it. Melt the margarine in a fairly large saucepan, take it off the heat and stir in first the flour, then the milk. Put the pan over a gentle heat and using a small whisk beat the mixture until it is quite smooth. Continue beating as it comes to the boil to keep it smooth. Simmer the mixture (it is called a *panada* at this stage) for a few seconds, then take it off the heat and beat in the grated cheese. Season the mixture well with salt and cayenne pepper.

Separate the yolks from the whites of the eggs and beat the yolks into the cheese mixture. Whisk the whites stiffly and fold them into the mixture. Turn the mixture into the soufflé dish, put it on a baking tray and put the tray straight into a moderately hot oven, about *Gas Mark 5 or 375 degrees F.*, for 30 to 35 minutes. The soufflé should rise above the surface of the dish and be lightly browned on top. A hot soufflé should still be moist in the centre.

NOTE: Be ready to serve the soufflé immediately; this is one dish which must be eaten straight from the oven and very hot.

TELEVISION EGGS

FOR 4 PEOPLE

2 large tomatoes,
  skinned
salt and pepper
1 small tin asparagus
  (this can be cut
  pieces)

4 eggs
knob of butter
4 ovenproof cups each
  holding a quarter of
  a pint of liquid will
  be required

Grease the cups. Cut the tomatoes in small pieces and divide them among the cups. Season with salt and pepper. Drain the asparagus, cut it into small pieces and divide among the cups. Break an egg into each. Sprinkle with salt and pepper and dot the tops with butter.
Bake the eggs in a moderate oven, *Gas Mark 4 or 350 degrees F.*, for 10 minutes or until the eggs are set. Stand each cup on a saucer and serve with toast and butter.

Cheese and raisin grill

CHEESE AND RAISIN GRILL

FOR 4 PEOPLE

2 eggs
8 oz. Cheddar cheese,
  grated
4 oz. stoned raisins
salt and pepper

4 slices bread
2 oz. butter
little made mustard
4 large tomatoes,
  sliced

Lightly beat the eggs, then add the cheese and raisins, and season.
Toast the bread on one side only, turn over and butter the other side. Lightly spread with the mustard, then arrange the sliced tomatoes on top. Finally pile the cheese mixture over the tomatoes and place under a hot grill to brown the surface and heat the cheese mixture. The tomatoes should remain firm.

SURPRISE RAREBIT

FOR 4 PEOPLE

6 oz. cheese, grated
3 tablespoons
  mayonnaise or salad
  cream (see pages 85
  and 86)

4 large slices of brown
  or white bread
1 jar beef spread with
  butter (1¼ oz.)

Mix the grated cheese with the mayonnaise or salad cream. Toast the bread on both sides and spread it with the beef spread, then top with the cheese mixture. Grill till lightly browned. Serve with sliced tomatoes.

CHEESE PUDDING

FOR 4 PEOPLE

4 oz. thinly cut bread spread with butter	salt and pepper
2 eggs	2 oz. Lancashire cheese, crumbled
¼ pint milk	watercress to serve with the puddings
1 dessertspoon double cream	

Butter four individual ovenproof dishes. Cut the bread and butter in squares. Break the eggs into a bowl and beat them well, then stir in the milk and cream and pour this mixture on to the bread squares. Season the mixture with salt and pepper, then mix in the crumbled cheese. Divide the mixture among the dishes and bake them in a moderately hot oven, about *Gas Mark 5 or 375 degrees F.*, for 20 to 25 minutes. They should rise well and brown on the surface. Serve the cheese puddings immediately, as the consistency is that of a soufflé. Serve the watercress separately.

SCOTCH EGGS

MAKES 5

1 lb. sausagemeat	browned breadcrumbs
5 hard-boiled eggs	fat for deep frying
1 egg, beaten	

Shell the eggs. Divide the sausagemeat into five even pieces. Flatten each piece with your hand on a floured board, into a round big enough to cover an egg. Work the sausagemeat round each egg in the palm of your hands until it is completely smooth. Brush each Scotch Egg with beaten egg, then toss it in the breadcrumbs to coat evenly. Heat the fat, which should be deep enough to cover the eggs, to a medium heat, for if it is too hot the outside of the sausagemeat will be too brown before the inside is cooked. Put the Scotch Eggs into the deep fat basket and lower them into·the fat. Fry them for about 5 minutes then lift them out of the fat and drain them for a few seconds before serving.

FIRESIDE EGGS

FOR 4 PEOPLE

½ head of celery	1 small tin sweetcorn kernels (7 oz.)
3 tablespoons salad oil	2 oz. cheese, grated
4 tomatoes	4 small eggs
1 large onion	a flameproof or ovenproof dish holding 2 pints of liquid
1 green pepper	
1 red pepper	
1 clove of garlic	
salt and pepper	

Scrub the stalks of celery and cut them into ½ inch lengths. Cook them gently in the oil while preparing the other vegetables. Peel and quarter the tomatoes. Peel and slice the onion. Cut the peppers into rings, removing all the seeds. Keep aside the two nicest green and the two nicest red pepper rings for the top. Peel the papery skin off the clove of garlic, slice it and sprinkle it with salt. Beat the garlic to a soft cream under the blade of a heavy knife. Transfer the celery to an ovenproof dish, unless it is already in a flameproof one, and add all the other vegetables including the garlic. Season with salt and pepper. Add contents of tin of sweetcorn. Put the best pepper rings on top. Put on the lid.

Cook the vegetables in a moderate oven, about *Gas Mark 4 or 350 degrees F.*, for about 1 hour or until the vegetables are tender.

Lift off the four top pepper rings and sprinkle the top with grated cheese. Lay the pepper rings on top of the cheese and make a slight dent in the centre of each ring. Break an egg into each ring.

Return the dish to the oven and cook it for a further 10 minutes or until the eggs are set, but not hard.

CHEESE AND BACON SNACKS

FOR 6 PEOPLE

6 thick slices white or brown bread	3 tomatoes
about 2 dessertspoons sweet chutney	12 small rashers of streaky bacon, with the rinds cut off
6 slices of cheese	
1 large cooking apple, peeled and cored	

Toast the bread on both sides. Spread each slice thinly with chutney and cover with a slice of cheese. Slice the apple fairly thinly and put a slice on top of the cheese. Grill for a few seconds just to start the apple cooking; then halve the tomatoes and put a half tomato, cut side downwards, in the centre of the apple. Cook under a slow grill to soften the tomato slightly. Transfer the snacks to a dish and quickly grill the rashers of bacon until they are almost crisp. Serve two on top of each snack.

SCRAMBLED EGGS AND MUSHROOMS

FOR 5 PEOPLE

5 large cup-shaped mushrooms	salt and pepper
little cooking oil	knob of butter
8 eggs	5 half-slices of hot buttered toast
8 tablespoons milk	

Wash the mushrooms (there is no need to peel cultivated ones) and brush them lightly with cooking oil. Put the mushrooms, cupped side upwards, on to the grill and grill them lightly and slowly.

Beat the eggs and milk, and season with salt and pepper. Melt the butter in a pan and add the egg mixture, stirring slowly over a very gentle heat until the eggs are scrambled. Put the mushrooms on to the toast and fill each one with scrambled egg.

VEGETABLES AND SALADS

Fresh vegetables can be obtained all the year round, and there is an excellent variety of canned and frozen vegetables available, so that there is no longer any excuse for serving the same one too often.

It is very important, I think, to take extra time and trouble over cooking and presenting vegetables. So often endless care may be taken to prepare a complicated meat dish, but the vegetables to go with it are dull and unimaginative. Potatoes especially lend themselves to being presented in interesting and appetising ways—try croquettes, for instance, or oven potatoes. When you do decide to have plain boiled, add colour with simple garnishes.

Try some of the more unusual vegetables, too—braised celery is delicious, so is sweetcorn, and swedes mashed well with plenty of seasoning and butter will just melt in your mouth!

POTATO CROQUETTES

MAKES ABOUT 24

3 lb. peeled potatoes	dusting of flour
1 oz. butter	2 eggs, beaten
1 egg	dry white breadcrumbs
salt and pepper	fat for deep frying

Boil the potatoes, drain them and then toss over a gentle heat for a few minutes to dry. Sieve the potatoes or put through a vegetable mill. If you have a mixer, beat them to a smooth cream with the flat beaters. Thoroughly beat in the butter and the egg, and season the potatoes well with salt and pepper.
The quickest way to shape the croquettes is to weigh 2-oz. portions of potato and roll them into balls, using a light dusting of flour. They can also be made into little cork shapes. Beat the eggs for the coating and pour them into a fairly deep plate. Have the crumbs ready on a sheet of kitchen paper.

Stand one croquette in the beaten egg and brush it with egg. Lift it on to a plate, then brush five more croquettes. Working in rotation, coat this batch, one at a time, in dry breadcrumbs, using the edge of the paper to flick the crumbs over the surface. Coat the rest in the same way. The croquettes will remain a better shape if coated again.
Heat the fat; when it is hot enough to brown a cube of white bread almost immediately (about *375 degrees F.*), it is ready for frying. Lower each croquette into the fat on a draining spoon. The pan will hold three or four croquettes. Fry them to a golden brown, turning when necessary. Lift out on to a piece of absorbent paper to drain. Fry the next batch, remembering to reheat the fat between batches.

SAUTÉ POTATOES

FOR 4/5 PEOPLE

1½ lb. potatoes, unpeeled	1 dessertspoon frying oil
2-3 oz. butter	salt

Scrub the potatoes but do not peel them. Cover them with cold salted water, bring them to the boil and boil them steadily until they are almost tender. Drain off the water, peel the potatoes (hold each one in a cloth whilst peeling it) and cut them into cubes.
Melt 2 oz. of the butter in a frying pan, add the oil and, when it is hot, stir in the cubed potato. Sauté the potatoes for 10 to 15 minutes, or until they are cooked, and lightly touched with brown. Use the extra butter if it is required. Sprinkle the potatoes lightly with salt before serving.

DUCHESSE POTATOES

FOR 6/8 PEOPLE

2 lb. potatoes, weighed when peeled	little beaten egg for the glaze
2 oz. butter	large piping bag and a large rose pipe
1 egg	
salt and pepper	

Boil the potatoes until they are tender, then sieve or beat them in an electric mixer with the butter, egg and salt and pepper to season. Fill a large piping bag, with a large rose pipe attached, with potato and pipe rosettes on to a greased baking tray. Allow them to cool then brush the tops with beaten egg. Heat and lightly brown them in a moderately hot oven, about *Gas Mark 5 or 375 degrees F.*, for about 20 minutes.

OVEN POTATOES

FOR 6 PEOPLE

12 medium sized potatoes	**¼ pint stock**
1 oz. butter	**salt and pepper**
	1 small bay leaf

Peel the potatoes and slice each one to within ½ inch of one side so that it is still held together. Put the potatoes into a heatproof dish and dot them with butter. Pour round the stock, sprinkle them with salt and pepper and add the bay leaf. Cover the dish with a lid and put it in a warm oven at *Gas Mark 3 or 325 degrees F.* Cook for 2 hours.

AUBERGINES

Aubergines are an unusual vegetable, and very easy to cook. Stuffed, they make a good first course or light supper dish.

TO COOK AUBERGINE

Cut the aubergine in rounds ¼ inch thick. Lay them on a plate, sprinkle with salt and leave for 30 minutes. This draws out some of the moisture and flavours the aubergine. Rinse and dry the rounds. Heat 1 oz. butter and 1 tablespoon of oil in a frying pan and fry the slices of aubergine on one side for a few seconds. Add a little more oil, turn them over and fry on the other side for 2 or 3 minutes. Sprinkle a little freshly ground pepper and a few drops of lemon juice over the aubergine.

Aubergines are especially nice with fish, chicken, lamb, veal or any mild-flavoured dish.

STUFFED AUBERGINE

FOR 2 PEOPLE

1 fairly small aubergine	**2 hard-boiled eggs**
½ small onion	**salt and pepper**
¾ oz. butter	**½ oz. cheese, finely grated**
2 tomatoes	
1 tablespoon thick soup or 1 dessertspoon stock	

Cut the aubergine in half lengthways, sprinkle the cut sides with salt, and leave them for 30 minutes.

Meanwhile peel and chop the onion. Melt the butter in a frying pan and fry the onion gently until it is almost tender. Skin the tomatoes by first pouring boiling water over them; count 20, then pour off the water and the tomatoes will skin easily. Slice them, add to the onions, and cook for a few minutes. Scoop out the centres of the aubergine and dice them. Cook the aubergine with the other ingredients in the frying pan for 5 or 6 minutes until the aubergine is cooked. Add the soup. Chop the hard-boiled eggs and add to the mixture. Season it well with salt, if necessary, and pepper, and heap the mixture back into the empty aubergine cases. Sprinkle the surface with grated cheese and put them into a fairly hot oven, about *Gas Mark 6 or 400 degrees F.*, for 7 to 10 minutes to heat and brown.

SWEETCORN

Sweetcorn makes a most delicious first course in itself, or is a good main course for a light supper. It is speared with little corn skewers or eaten with the fingers.

It is best to buy sweetcorn when it is still wrapped in its green sheath leaves. Pull the sheath down a little way before buying to make sure that the cob is filled to the top. The cob should not be too big or the corn may be tough.

When you are cooking sweetcorn for the family it is a good idea to cook one or two extra cobs, as there are many good ways of using it to make your menus more interesting. A sweetcorn sauce is particularly nice with fish or fishcakes, sweetcorn fritters (see page 60) go well with sausages or fried chicken, and sweetcorn also makes a very good base for savoury flans and supper dishes.

TO COOK SWEETCORN

Pull off the green outside sheath leaves and remove the green silky strands from inside. Plunge the cobs into boiling water and boil until the corn is tender; the time depends on the size of the cob—young ones from the garden will take 5 or 10 minutes, but some cobs can take up to 20 minutes. Add a teaspoon of salt to the water just before they are ready.

Brush the cobs with melted butter, and serve them with more melted butter.

SWEETCORN SAUCE

½ oz. butter	**1 head cooked sweetcorn**
1 level tablespoon plain flour	**salt and pepper**
½ pint milk	

Melt the butter in a saucepan, then take it off the heat and stir in the flour. Add all the milk and stir the sauce over a very gentle heat until it is smooth, then increase the heat and bring it to the boil, stirring all the time. Take the corn off the cob; the easiest way is to scrape it off with the back of a knife. Add it to the sauce with salt and pepper and simmer it for 5 or 6 minutes.

NOISETTES OF LAMB WITH AUBERGINE AND SWEETCORN

FOR 6/8 PEOPLE

2 best end necks of lamb, each five bones and weighing about 1¾ lb.; ask the butcher to bone them	**3 tablespoons frying oil**
	1 tinned red pepper
	5 stuffed olive halves
salt and pepper	**2 heads of cooked sweetcorn, stripped from the cob, or an 11½ oz. tin of sweetcorn kernels**
1 large aubergine	
2 tablespoons plain flour	
1 level teaspoon turmeric	**1 oz. butter**

Shave some of the fat from the outside of the pieces of neck of lamb. Season the inside of each well with salt and pepper. Roll one up tightly, lengthways, and tie it tightly with string at 1½ inch intervals. Then cut between the string so that each piece of meat remains tied. Roll, tie and slice the other piece in the same way; each piece should make about five noisettes.

Next, prepare the aubergine. Slice it in $\frac{1}{4}$ inch slices, lay them on a plate and sprinkle with salt; leave for 30 minutes, then rinse and dry them. Mix the plain flour, turmeric, salt and pepper together and dust the slices with the mixture.

Heat the oil in a large frying pan and fry the noisettes on both sides over a moderate heat until they are cooked. Lift them out of the pan and fry the aubergine slices on both sides. Arrange as many aubergine slices as there are noisettes round the edge of a large dish and put a noisette of lamb on top of each.

Garnish every other one with a criss-cross of red pepper strips and half a stuffed olive. Melt the butter in a pan and toss the sweetcorn over a gentle heat to heat it thoroughly. Heap it in the centre with any extra slices of aubergine on top.

MARROW WITH WHITE SAUCE

1 young marrow (about 1 lb.)	$\frac{1}{2}$ pint milk
large pinch of salt	salt and pepper
1 oz. margarine	3 or 4 slices of toast
1 oz. plain flour	paprika pepper

Wipe the rind of the marrow with a damp cloth. Bring a pan of salted water to the boil, and put in the marrow. Bring it to the boil again, and boil gently for about 40 minutes, or until the marrow is tender. Drain off the water, and cut the rind off the marrow with a sharp knife. Keep the marrow warm while you make the sauce.

Melt the margarine in a pan, take it off the heat and stir in the flour. Stir in the milk gradually over a gentle heat, until it comes to the boil. Let it boil for a minute, then season with salt and pepper.

Use three or four slices of toast according to the size of the marrow. Lay the toast on a serving dish and put the marrow on top. Cover it with the sauce and shake on a little paprika pepper. Garnish with a slice of toast with the crust cut off, cut into four triangular pieces.

CRAB-STUFFED MARROW

FOR 4 PEOPLE

1 marrow (about 1½ lb.)	2 level tablespoons chopped parsley
tin of crabmeat (7 oz.)	1 beaten egg
2 oz. fresh white breadcrumbs	1 level teaspoon salt
2 celery stalks, finely chopped	pepper
	1 oz. dripping

Preheat the oven at *Gas Mark 7 or 425 degrees F.*
Peel the marrow, cut it in half lengthways and scoop out the seeds.

Open the tin of crabmeat, turn it on to a plate and flake it. Add the breadcrumbs, chopped celery, parsley, egg, salt and pepper. Mix well and fill one half of the marrow with the mixture. Place the other marrow half on top of the stuffed half and secure the two halves together with four lengths of string.

Melt the dripping in a roasting tin. Put in the marrow, baste it well, and bake it in the hot oven for 40 minutes. Turn the oven down to *Gas Mark 6 or 400 degrees F.* for a further 15 minutes.

Baste the marrow well every 15 minutes throughout the baking time. Take off the string before serving.

PIQUANT CABBAGE

FOR 4 PEOPLE

3 rashers of streaky bacon, chopped	3 oz. cooking apple, chopped
1 small onion, finely sliced	salt and pepper
1 tablespoon frying oil	good pinch of brown sugar
1¼ lb. firm-hearted cabbage, shredded	1 lb. tomatoes
$\frac{1}{2}$ pint boiling water	2 frankfurter sausages

Fry the bacon and the sliced onion in the oil in a large saucepan. When they are cooked add the shredded cabbage and pour over the water. Cover the cabbage with a lid and simmer it until the cabbage is tender; this will take 20 to 25 minutes.

Stir in the chopped apple and season the mixture with salt and pepper and brown sugar.

Peel and quarter the tomatoes and slice the frankfurters crossways and put them all in the pan on top of the cabbage. Cook them without a lid for a further 10 minutes to reduce the liquid and heat the tomatoes and frankfurters thoroughly. Tip the cabbage mixture on to a hot dish to mix in the tomatoes without spoiling their shape.

OVEN-COOKED CARROTS

Scrape the carrots and slice them into rounds about $\frac{1}{4}$ inch thick. Put them in a fireproof dish with seasoning, a pinch of sugar, a knob of butter and just enough stock to cover the bottom of the dish. Cook them at *Gas Mark 5 or 375 degrees F.* for 50 minutes.

OVEN-COOKED TOMATOES AND CUCUMBER

Peel both vegetables, cut them into fairly large chunks and put them in a fireproof dish. Sprinkle them with chopped fresh herbs—mint, parsley or chives—and add a little seasoning and a knob of butter. Cover with a lid or a piece of buttered paper and cook at *Gas Mark 5 or 375 degrees F.* for 50 minutes.

RATATOUILLE

FOR 4/6 PEOPLE

2 small aubergines or 1 large one	1 sweet red pepper
1 lb. tomatoes	1 clove of garlic
2 large onions	4 tablespoons salad oil
1 sweet green pepper	salt and pepper

Cut the aubergines into 1 inch cubes, but do not skin them. Peel and quarter the tomatoes, then peel and slice the onions. Cut the peppers in half and remove all the seeds as these are very bitter, then cut into slices. Peel the papery skin off the clove of garlic and slice it, sprinkle with salt and crush it to a cream under the blade of a heavy knife.

Heat the oil in a large frying pan, add all the vegetables and cook together for about 8 minutes. Transfer to a casserole and season with salt and pepper. Put on a lid and cook the Ratatouille in a warm oven, about *Gas Mark 3 or 325 degrees F.*, for 2 hours.

TOMATO CRUSTADE

FOR 6 PEOPLE

6 oz. butter	8 oz. broad beans, cooked
1 large white loaf 2 or 3 days old, thinly sliced	1 small tin sweetcorn kernels, drained
6 oz. cold meat, tongue and ham mixed, luncheon meat or cold roast beef	1 lb. new potatoes, cooked
1 lb. tomatoes	mayonnaise, see page 85
8 cooked baby beetroot (larger beetroot, sliced could be used)	chopped chives rectangular tin 12 inches by 8 inches

Butter the inside of the tin. Spread about three-quarters of the loaf with the rest of the butter (if you like garlic, see note below); this is most easily done with a palette knife when the butter has been softened. Cut off all the crusts. Line the base of the tin with squares of bread and butter. Cut the rest of the slices in half and arrange them round the edge of the tin, slightly overlapping and with a corner of each slice showing above the tin. You may need a little more bread, depending on how much you overlap.

Put another tin or pie dish inside, with a weight in it to hold down the bread in the centre. Put the crustade into a moderate oven, about *Gas Mark 4 or 350 degrees F.*, for 30 minutes. Remove the weighted tin and leave the crustade for a further 15 minutes until the bread is crisp and golden round the edges. If a little more colour is required, increase the oven heat for a few minutes.

When the crustade is cold, cut the cold meat into strips and line the base with the meat. Peel the tomatoes. Cut them in slices and arrange them diagonally from corner to corner of the crustade, dividing it into four.

Fill one of the sections with baby beetroot, one with drained sweetcorn kernels, one with cooked broad beans, popped out of their "jackets", and the fourth section with new potatoes. Coat the potatoes with mayonnaise and sprinkle them with chopped chives.

Note: Add a clove of garlic to the butter if you like the flavour; to do this, peel the papery skin off the clove of garlic, slice the garlic and sprinkle with salt, then crush to a soft cream under the blade of a knife. Beat it into the butter before spreading it on the bread.

NOTE: The crustade can be made in the morning and filled just before it is needed.

SPANISH STUFFED PEPPERS

FOR 5 PEOPLE

5 sweet peppers, red or green	2 tablespoons salad oil
4 oz. uncooked pork	2 oz. fresh white breadcrumbs
4 oz. uncooked pie veal	1 egg yolk
4 oz. uncooked bacon	salt and pepper
1 onion, finely diced	
1 carrot, finely diced	

FOR THE SPANISH RICE

1 diced onion	$1\frac{1}{2}$ pints hot stock
2 tablespoons oil	salt and pepper
8 oz. Patna rice	

Tomato crustade

FOR THE ACCOMPANYING VEGETABLES

1 lb. courgettes	1 oz. butter
salt and pepper	2 aubergines
little lemon juice	little oil for frying

Cut off the tops of the peppers and cut out the central cores, being careful not to pierce the skins. Wash out all the seeds as they taste bitter. Plunge the peppers into boiling water, one at a time, for a minute.

Mince all the meats together. Fry the onion and carrot gently in the oil until they are tender, then add the meats and cook them, stirring most of the time. When the meat is cooked add the breadcrumbs, egg yolk and season with salt and pepper. Stuff the peppers with the mixture and put on the tops.

THE RICE

Cook the onion gently in the oil, then add the rice and stir it over a gentle heat until all the oil has been absorbed. Put the rice in a roasting tin, stir in the hot stock and season it with salt and pepper. Stand the peppers in the rice, cover them with kitchen foil and put them into a moderately hot oven, about *Gas Mark 5 or 375 degrees F.*, for about 40 minutes or until the rice is tender and all the liquid is absorbed. The peppers will also be cooked in this time.

Meanwhile cook the courgettes and aubergines. Slice the courgettes in half and put them in an ovenproof dish, sprinkle them with salt and pepper and lemon juice, dot them with butter and cover with a lid. Cook in the same oven as the peppers; they will take about the same time.

Slice the aubergines, spread the slices on a plate and sprinkle with salt. Leave them for about 10 minutes; this draws out some of the liquid. Wash and dry the slices and fry them briskly in the oil.

Serve the peppers on the bed of rice, and arrange the sliced aubergines and the courgettes between them.

OVEN-COOKED ONIONS

Peel and blanch the onions. To blanch them, put into cold water and bring slowly to the boil. Put the blanched onions in a fireproof dish with a knob of butter and cook them at *Gas Mark 5 or 375 degrees F.* for an hour.

Top: Wiener schnitzel (see page 47); bottom: Cornish pasties (see page 42) and beef olives (see page 41)

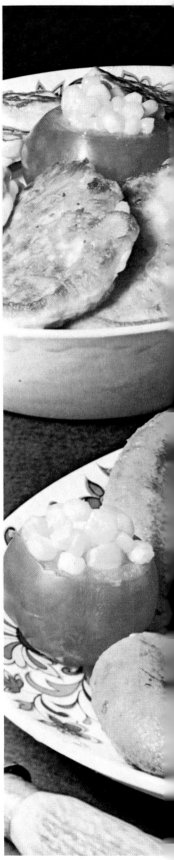

Lancashire hotpot (see page 43)

Sunday chicken (see page 60)

BRAISED CHICORY

FOR 4 PEOPLE

4 large heads of chicory	salt and pepper
1 oz. butter	squeeze of lemon juice

Cut off the base of each chicory head and remove any discoloured leaves. The heads can be slit in half lengthways if liked. Plunge the heads into a pan of boiling salted water and boil them for 1 minute. Drain the chicory and arrange it in a buttered fireproof dish. Sprinkle it with salt and pepper and squeeze over it a few drops of lemon juice. Dot it with the remaining butter. Cover the dish with a tight-fitting lid and cook it in a moderately hot oven, about *Gas Mark 5 or 375 degrees F.*, for about 30 minutes or until the chicory is tender.
NOTE: Celery is good cooked in the same way, but it will take a little longer to cook than chicory.

TOMATO AND COURGETTE RICE

FOR 6 PEOPLE

2 oz. Patna rice	1 oz. butter
1 lb. courgettes	¼ pint stock
6 large tomatoes	salt and pepper

Sprinkle the rice into a shallow ovenproof dish. Wipe the courgettes with a damp cloth and put them whole and unpeeled over the rice. Peel the tomatoes and arrange them among the courgettes. Dot the butter over the surface. Pour on the stock and sprinkle with salt and pepper.
Cover the dish with a lid or a piece of kitchen foil and bake in a moderate oven, about *Gas Mark 4 or 350 degrees F.*, for 1¼ to 1½ hours. The courgettes should be tender and the rice cooked but moist.

FRESH ASPARAGUS

Fresh asparagus is in the shops during the latter half of May and all through June.
Served with melted butter is the favourite, traditional way to eat asparagus as a first or extra course. To make a supper meal add a hot, hard-boiled egg for each person. Sprinkle the eggs with freshly ground black pepper. Serve them in thick Chinese spoons, if you have them, surrounded with hot, melted butter. Serve brown bread and butter separately.

TO COOK ASPARAGUS

Cut off the stalks just beyond the purply green colouring. Wash the asparagus well and scrape the ends of the stalks, if necessary, to clean them. Lay the asparagus in a shallow, wide pan with the tips all facing in the same direction. Cover them with boiling water, salt it well and put on the lid. (A covered roasting tin makes an ideal container for cooking asparagus). Simmer the asparagus until the coloured parts of the stalks are tender; the tips will be ready first. Lift the stalks out of the water with a fish slice, lay the slice on a piece of absorbent kitchen paper for a few seconds to drain the asparagus then slip it on to a hot plate. Coat the tips with hot melted butter.

SALADS

WINTER CHICKEN SALAD

FOR 6 PEOPLE

1 head of chicory	sliced cooked chicken or other poultry
1 head of celery	
1 green dessert apple	
1 red dessert apple	6 cooked prunes
	little lemon juice

FOR THE DRESSING

½ pint soured cream	dash of Worcester sauce
4 oz. cottage cheese	
1 tablespoon lemon juice	salt and pepper

Remove the outside leaves of the chicory and the coarser stalks of the celery. Wash the chicory and celery well and chop both fairly finely. Cut the apples into quarters without peeling them and remove the cores. Chop two quarters of each apple and add to the chopped chicory and celery. Heap the chopped fruit and vegetables in the centre of a dish.
Mix the soured cream gradually into the cottage cheese, add the lemon juice and the Worcester sauce and enough salt and pepper to season the mixture. Pour the dressing over the chopped fruit and vegetables.
Arrange the sliced poultry at opposite ends of the dish. Slice the remaining apple quarters, toss in lemon juice and arrange between the poultry slices. Garnish with the prunes.

CABBAGE COLESLAW

FOR THE DRESSING

1 level teaspoon castor sugar	¼ pint vinegar
	1 small egg
½ level teaspoon plain flour	½ oz. butter
1 level teaspoon salt	little cream or evaporated milk, if liked, to mellow the flavour
½ level teaspoon dry mustard	

FOR THE SALAD

1 small firm-hearted cabbage, finely shredded	1 sliced green dessert apple
2 carrots, scraped and grated on a coarse grater	1 sliced red dessert apple
	1 oz. walnuts, chopped

Mix the castor sugar, flour, salt and dry mustard together, then stir in the vinegar. Put these ingredients into a pan and stir them over a gentle heat until they come to the boil. Simmer the dressing for about 15 minutes. Beat the egg, add a tablespoon of dressing to it and mix well, then stir it into the dressing and beat in the butter. Since the dressing is a sharp one, a little cream or evaporated milk can be added to soften the flavour. Cool the dressing and store it in a screw-topped jar in a cold place. It will keep for several weeks.
When required, stir the dressing into the shredded cabbage, then mix in the grated carrot, sliced apples and chopped walnuts.

Stuffed boned chicken (see page 58)

SALAD PLATTER SELECTION

This selection has traditional ingredients, but also includes some new ideas for people who feel a little more adventurous. The apricot mayonnaise goes well with chicken, while the tomato mayonnaise is nice with ham and tongue.

FOR 4 PEOPLE

1 cucumber	6 tinned apricot halves
1 tin kipper fillets	4 firm tomatoes
9 small slices of roast beef	2 tablespoons tomato ketchup

Slice the cucumber and spread the slices over a large round plate. Arrange the kipper fillets round one side of the plate; curl the slices of beef into cones and arrange them in trios round the other side of the plate. Place the apricots, cut side down, between the kipper fillets. Pour boiling water over the tomatoes, count 20, then pour off the water and slip off the skins. Cut the tomatoes in quarters, remove the seeds and arrange these tongues of tomato in groups between the meat cones.

THE TOMATO AND APRICOT MAYONNAISE

½ pint mayonnaise or salad cream (see page 85 and 86)	2 level tablespoons apricot jam, sieved
1 teaspoon horseradish sauce	

Mix half the mayonnaise with the tomato ketchup and horseradish, and the other half with the sieved apricot jam. Serve them in separate small dishes.

CUCUMBER AND MINT SALAD

½ cucumber	1 teaspoon chopped mint
salt	
French dressing (see page 86)	

Slice the cucumber thinly and lay the slices on a plate. Sprinkle them with salt and leave them for 30 minutes. Drain off any liquid which has formed and sprinkle over enough French dressing to moisten the cucumber. Arrange it in a dish and sprinkle the chopped mint over the surface.

NEW POTATO SALAD

1½ lb. new potatoes	1 tablespoon chopped chives
pinch of salt	3 cooked carrots
sprig of mint	3 tablespoons cooked green peas
2 tablespoons French dressing (see page 86)	

Boil the potatoes with a pinch of salt and sprig of mint. Drain them, and while they are still hot slice fairly thickly and toss them in two tablespoons of French dressing; the potatoes should absorb all the dressing. Heap the potatoes in a dish and sprinkle well with chopped chives. Surround them with cooked sliced carrot, and sprinkle the peas between the carrot rings and the potatoes.
NOTE: There are many variations of this salad.
To make Potato Mayonnaise pour a little mayonnaise (see page 85) over the potato salad, or mix it in lightly, if you prefer.

BACON AND APPLE SALAD

FOR 4 PEOPLE

½ firm-centred cabbage	little lemon juice
2 rosy dessert apples	3 rashers streaky bacon

FOR THE DRESSING

1 tablespoon vinegar	1 tablespoon salad oil
salt and pepper	
pinch of castor sugar	

Remove any discoloured leaves from the cabbage, wash it well, dry it and shred it. Wash apples and polish the skins; cut the apples into quarters; core and slice the quarters fairly finely. Toss in lemon juice. Mix half the slices of apple with cabbage.
Mix the vinegar with a good pinch of salt, pepper, and sugar, then gradually beat in the salad oil. Toss the cabbage and apple in this dressing, then heap it into a shallow bowl. Cut the rind off the bacon and remove any little pieces of bone. Cut the bacon into thin strips, and fry them briskly, stirring all the time, till they are crisp and brown. Heap them on top of the salad. Surround the bacon with the remaining slices of apple.

WALDORF SALAD

6 oz. celery, chopped	salt and pepper
8 oz. cooked potato, diced	1 green dessert apple
1 oz. walnuts, chopped	1 red dessert apple
2 tablespoons mayonnaise (see page 85)	little lemon juice
	walnut halves for garnish

Mix the celery, potato and chopped walnuts. Add the mayonnaise, or salad dressing, and salt and pepper to season. Quarter and core the apples and slice them thinly. Toss in lemon juice. Arrange the salads on individual plates: form a circle of alternate colours of apple round the edge of each plate and heap the salad in the centre. Garnish with the walnut halves.
This is a nice salad to serve alone or with any cold meat; it is especially pleasant with cold lamb or cold pork.

PINEAPPLE WHEELS

1 large pineapple	1 oz. salted peanuts
4 oz. ripe cherries	4 oz. cream cheese

This is a suitable dish for a buffet table centrepiece, and a splendid accompaniment to cold ham or any smoked or salted meat.
Cut the pineapple in half across and with a very sharp knife cut out the central core from each half. Stone and quarter the cherries and roughly chop the nuts. Mix these with the cream cheese and fill both pineapple halves with the mixture. Cut the pineapple in thick slices across and arrange these on a dish, using the green spiky top for decoration. A half of a slice is enough for each helping.
Alternatively, the wheels can be cut into small wedges and spiked with cocktail sticks for unusual cocktail party snacks.

SAUCES AND STUFFINGS

It is the sauce, they say, that makes the dish. And certainly it is worth taking a few extra minutes to create an appetising, velvety smooth sauce to transform what might otherwise be a fairly ordinary meal. It's fun, too, to experiment and try different sauces with different accompaniments: don't, for instance, always serve cheese sauce with cauliflower—try a spicy sauce au diable (see page 87) instead; or combine sauce poulette (see page 88) with ham; or sauce duxelles (see page 88) with fish.

To serve the sauce, you can either pour it over the food or serve it separately in a gravy boat, so those who prefer food "neat" can leave off the sauce. Most savoury sauces belong to one of three "families"—béchamel, velouté and brune. I give a selection of recipes for each here, plus some ideas for more unusual stuffings.

SAUCES

MAYONNAISE

3 egg yolks (2 whole eggs if using the liquidiser method)
¾ pint salad oil
3 level teaspoons French mustard
good pinch of castor sugar

salt and freshly ground black pepper
about 2 tablespoons distilled white or wine vinegar

Mayonnaise is one of the most popular dressings for salads. The following recipe makes just over ¾ pint of mayonnaise. The eggs and oil should be at room temperature. Mix the yolks with the mustard, sugar, pepper and a good pinch of salt. Measure the oil into a jug, then add a drop at a time to the yolks, beating all the time with a wooden spoon. When the mayonnaise starts to thicken, but not before, the oil can be added a little more quickly. When it is really thick, add

a little vinegar to thin it and to keep it the right consistency, then reseason. Mayonnaise keeps well in a screw-topped jar in the refrigerator.

LIQUIDISER METHOD
If your blender is a small one it is better to make the mayonnaise in two batches. Use 2 whole eggs instead of 3 yolks. Put the eggs into the liquidiser with the mustard, sugar, salt, pepper and vinegar and blend them together for a second; then add the oil in a steady thin stream. It should suddenly start to thicken and when it does, add the oil more quickly.

LEMON MAYONNAISE
Make as above, substituting lemon juice for vinegar.

HOME-MADE SALAD CREAM

¾ oz. margarine	salt and pepper
1½ level tablespoons plain flour	1 level teaspoon castor sugar
½ pint milk	½ level teaspoon French mustard
1 egg yolk	good dash of Worcester sauce
3 dessertspoons malt vinegar	

Melt the margarine in a saucepan, then take it off the heat and stir in the flour. Add all the milk and stir the sauce over a very gentle heat until it is smooth then continue stirring until it comes to the boil. Beat the egg yolk, then add two tablespoons of the sauce and beat it well. Gradually stir this mixture back into the sauce in the saucepan. Add the vinegar gradually then the salt and pepper, castor sugar, French mustard and Worcester sauce. Extra vinegar or seasoning can be added if liked. Store the dressing in a screw-topped jar and keep it in a cool place.
NOTE: This dressing is fairly thick and can be diluted with a little top milk or cream as it is required.

FRENCH DRESSING

¼ pint salad oil	1 level teaspoon salt
3 tablespoons distilled white vinegar, cider vinegar or wine vinegar	good sprinkling of freshly ground black pepper
1 level teaspoon castor sugar	1 level teaspoon French mustard

Pour oil and vinegar into a bottle. Put the seasonings on to a small piece of paper, curve the paper and shoot them into the bottle. Add the French mustard and cork the bottle. Shake vigorously until all ingredients are well mixed. This dressing keeps well.

HOLLANDAISE SAUCE

6 tablespoons wine or distilled white vinegar	2 blades of mace
12 peppercorns	8 oz. butter
1 bay leaf	4 egg yolks
	salt and pepper if necessary

This sauce has a texture similar to home-made mayonnaise. Put the vinegar into a pan with the peppercorns, bay leaf and mace and boil them together until the vinegar is reduced by half. Leave on one side for the flavours to infuse into the vinegar.
Beat the butter to a soft consistency. Put the egg yolks into a basin with a small nut of the butter and beat well. Strain the vinegar over the egg mixture. Stand the basin in a roasting tin half filled with hot water, heat to simmer gently but not boil. Stir the sauce briskly until it is thick, then add the rest of the butter a little at a time, stirring

continuously. The sauce should just hold its shape. If necessary, season with salt and pepper.
If not required immediately, store the sauce in a screw-topped jar in the refrigerator (I have kept it successfully up to a week). To reheat it, turn it into a basin and put the basin into a pan of warm water. Stir the sauce until it is slightly warm then beat it with a wooden spoon to smooth it completely.

TARTARE SAUCE

4 tablespoons mayonnaise (see page 85)	1 level tablespoon chopped gherkins
2 level tablespoons chopped capers	1 level teaspoon chopped parsley

Make the mayonnaise (see page 85) and stir in the chopped capers, gherkins, and parsley.

CHEESE SAUCE

1 oz. butter	3 oz. grated cheese
1 oz. plain flour	salt and
¾ pint milk	pepper

Put the butter in a saucepan (to be accurate mark an 8 oz. block of butter into eight 1 oz. pieces, and use one for the sauce). Melt the butter over a gentle heat without allowing it to fizzle. Take it off the heat and add the flour. Stir in the flour, then pour in all the measured milk.
Using a small wire whisk beat the sauce over a very gentle heat until it is absolutely smooth, then increase the heat slightly and whisk or stir it briskly until it comes to the boil. Whisk the cheese into the sauce—it will melt quite quickly. Season the sauce with salt and pepper. Heat it again before serving it; the smooth coating consistency will remain even if the cheese sauce is boiled.
This is a coating sauce to serve as an accompaniment, or to pour over vegetables, or to add to many savoury dishes.
For extra flavour add a quarter of a level teaspoon of dry mustard with the flour.

BREAD SAUCE

1 onion	salt
8 cloves	cayenne pepper
just over ½ pint milk	½ oz. butter
1½ oz. freshly made white breadcrumbs	

Peel the onion and push the cloves into it. Put the milk in a saucepan with the onion and leave it over a very gentle heat so that the flavour from the onion and cloves infuses into the milk. This will take a little over 30 minutes. The milk can be allowed to get quite hot but it should not boil. Strain the milk, measure it and make it up to half a pint with extra milk, if necessary, then return it to the saucepan. Mix the breadcrumbs very thoroughly with a good pinch of salt and of cayenne pepper. Add them to the hot milk with the butter. Reheat the sauce thoroughly and reseason it. Pour it into a sauceboat.

MINT SAUCE

Wash a handful of mint, chop it and mix it with 2 level teaspoons of sugar. Stir in 1 tablespoon of boiling water, and then add 2 tablespoons of vinegar.

BLENDER METHOD
Put all the ingredients into the blender goblet and switch on for 30 seconds.

CRANBERRY SAUCE

4 oz. cranberries	3-4 oz. castor
$\frac{1}{4}$ pint water	sugar

Simmer the cranberries in the water until they are tender. Then sweeten them with castor sugar. The berries are rather bitter so the sauce should be fairly sweet.

SAUCE BRUNE

Stock is an essential part of this sauce. Make it as for the white stock for Velouté Sauce on page 88. It can be darkened by frying the bones in a very little dripping to brown them before adding the water.

$\frac{1}{2}$ oz. dripping	1 level teaspoon
1 small shallot or onion, finely diced	finely chopped mushroom
1 rasher of bacon diced	peelings or stalks
$\frac{1}{2}$ oz. plain flour	1 level tablespoon concentrated
$\frac{3}{4}$ pint stock, slightly warm	tomato purée
	salt and pepper

Melt the dripping and add the shallot or onion and bacon and fry gently until they are golden brown. Add the flour, and stir it over a gentle heat until it is golden (be careful not to make the roux too dark or the sauce will be bitter). This is called a *roux brune*. Add the stock and whisk until it is smooth then stir over a gentle heat until it comes to the boil. Add the tomato purée and mushroom stalks or peelings. Simmer the sauce for about 15 minutes, skimming it when necessary. It should be syrupy or of a slightly thickened gravy-like consistency. Strain it, and season with salt and pepper.
NOTE: Serve this sauce in a hot sauceboat with any meat fries or grills. It will keep well in a refrigerator for several days.

SAUCE AU DIABLE

$\frac{1}{4}$ oz. butter	1 level teaspoon
1 level tablespoon finely chopped shallot or onion	chopped parsley cayenne pepper (the amount scooped up
3 tablespoons brandy (a miniature bottle)	on a knife-point)
1 level dessertspoon concentrated tomato purée	$\frac{1}{2}$ teaspoon Worcester sauce salt and pepper
$\frac{1}{2}$ pint Sauce Brune (or the amount in the Sauce Brune recipe)	if required

Melt the butter in a small saucepan, add the shallot or onion and fry it very gently until it is golden brown. Pour in the brandy and simmer until it is reduced by half. Add tomato purée and the sauce and simmer for 3 minutes. Add the chopped parsley, cayenne pepper and Worcester sauce. Season if necessary.
NOTE: Serve with grilled meats, chicken and turkey.

SAUCE CHASSEUR

$\frac{1}{2}$ oz. butter	$\frac{1}{2}$ pint Sauce Brune
1 level tablespoon chopped shallot or onion	(or the amount in the Sauce Brune recipe)
3 oz. mushrooms, washed, dried and finely sliced, but not peeled	1 level teaspoon chopped parsley salt and pepper if required
$\frac{1}{4}$ pint white wine	a small piece of
1 level dessertspoon tomato purée	butter

Melt the butter and fry the shallot or onion gently until lightly golden. Add the mushrooms and fry them for a minute or two. Add the white wine and simmer it over a gentle heat until it is reduced by half. Add the tomato purée and Sauce Brune, and simmer for about 2 minutes. Stir in the chopped parsley, then take the pan off the heat and beat in the butter, a tiny piece at a time, stirring until it is melted. Season if necessary.
NOTE: A good sauce with chicken and rabbit; it is sometimes served separately and sometimes used to cook with the meat.

BÈCHAMEL SAUCE

$\frac{1}{2}$ pint milk	1 blade of mace
slice of onion	$\frac{1}{2}$ oz. butter
3 slices of carrot	$\frac{1}{2}$ oz. plain flour
5 peppercorns	(scant measure)
1 bay leaf	salt and white pepper

Put the milk into a pan with the onion, carrot, peppercorns, bay leaf and blade of mace. Stand the pan over a *very* gentle heat to extract the flavours from the vegetables and herbs, and infuse them in the milk. Remove from the heat before the milk boils, and strain it.
Melt the butter in a saucepan which is large and wide enough to allow a quick stirring movement. When the butter has melted take the pan off the heat and stir in the flour; this thickening is called a *white roux*. Add all the milk and, using a small sauce whisk or a wooden spatula, stir the sauce until it is smooth. If the milk is still warm from the infusion this will not take long, but if the milk is cold, stir the sauce over a very gentle heat until it is smooth. Stir the smooth sauce over a gentle heat until it comes to the boil, simmer it for a few minutes and add seasoning. Use white pepper to retain the light appearance of the sauce. This is a sauce of a semi-coating consistency. Should a thicker sauce be required, boil it quickly for a few minutes without a lid. This will reduce and thicken the sauce. Seasoning should be added after reduction.
NOTE: This sauce can be used to coat vegetables, fish, chicken or eggs.

SAUCE SOUBISE

6 oz. onions, finely chopped	1 tablespoon double cream
½ pint Béchamel sauce (see page 87)	salt and white pepper if required

Cover the onions with cold water, add a pinch of salt and boil them until they are soft. Strain and sieve them and add the purée to the sauce. Heat the sauce and add the cream. Boil the sauce for 2 minutes, or until the desired consistency is reached. Season if necessary.

NOTE: Serve with roast mutton, egg dishes, or with roast vegetables such as potatoes or artichokes.

SAUCE AURORE

½ pint Béchamel sauce (see page 87)	1 tablespoon double cream
2 level tablespoons concentrated tomato purée	salt and white pepper if required

Heat the sauce and add the tomato purée. Stir in the cream and bring the sauce to the boil. Season it if necessary.

NOTE: Serve with eggs, fish or vegetables.

VELOUTÉ SAUCE

This is a sauce made from stock. It can be chicken, white meat or fish stock. The sauce is always well reduced to concentrate the flavour, so be careful not to season it too much before reducing it. As its name implies, it is a sauce with a velvet texture.

STOCK FOR VELOUTÉ SAUCE

2 lb. veal bones, roughly chopped (a calf's or pig's head can be used)	a bouquet garni (sprig of thyme, a sprig of parsley and a bay leaf)
1 onion, peeled and halved	6 white peppercorns
1 carrot, peeled and sliced	salt

Wash the bones, put them into a large pan and cover them with water. Add the onion, carrot, bouquet garni and peppercorns and bring the stock slowly to the boil, skimming the surface when necessary. Add salt, put on a lid and simmer the stock steadily for 2½ to 3 hours. Strain off the liquid and leave it to get cold; it should be quite a stiff jelly. Skim all the fat from the surface.

This jellied stock keeps well for a few days in a refrigerator and apart from making the following sauces it is most useful to add to everyday soups, sauces and gravies.

VELOUTÉ SAUCE

good ½ oz. butter	1 teaspoon lemon juice
½ oz. plain flour	
¾ pint stock given above (easier to blend with the roux if it is warm)	salt and white pepper if required

Melt the butter in a saucepan over a gentle heat, then take it off the heat and stir in the flour. Cook the roux very gently, stirring it all the time, until it is a light straw colour; it is now called a *roux blond*. This must be done slowly and carefully and should take about 10 minutes. Too quick cooking will make the sauce bitter.

Take the pan off the heat and allow it to cool. Stir in the warm stock and stir rapidly, or use a small wire sauce whisk, to work the roux smoothly into the stock. When the sauce is smooth bring it to the boil over a gentle heat, stirring all the time.

Continue cooking the sauce until it is of a slightly syrupy consistency, skimming the surface when necessary. To do this most easily, keep the pan tilted on a skewer and skim from the side of the pan inwards. When the consistency is correct, add the lemon juice. Add salt and white pepper, if required.

This sauce is now ready to use as a base for any of the following sauces. It keeps well in a refrigerator.

NOTE: A Velouté sauce can be made from the liquid left after cooking fish, veal or chicken, as in the recipe for Chicken Julienne on page 64.

SAUCE DUXELLES

2 oz. mushrooms	½ pint Velouté sauce (see left)
½ oz. butter	
1 level dessertspoon finely chopped onion	salt and pepper if required
4 tablespoons white wine	

Wash the mushrooms, dry them and chop them as finely as possible. Melt the butter in a saucepan, add the chopped onion and cook very slowly in the butter until tender, but not coloured. Add the mushrooms and cook them briskly until the moisture is absorbed. Pour over the white wine and reduce by fast boiling to one tablespoon. Heat the Velouté sauce then add the onion and mushrooms to it. Season with salt and pepper, if required.

NOTE: This is a good sauce with rabbit or veal, root vegetables, cauliflower or celery. It is often served with white fish and is excellent with mixed vegetables.

SAUCE POULETTE

½ pint Velouté sauce (see left)	1 egg yolk
1 teaspoon lemon juice	1 tablespoon double cream
pinch of chopped savory	salt and pepper if required
1 level teaspoon finely chopped parsley	

Heat the Velouté sauce gently with the lemon juice, savory and parsley. Mix the egg yolk and the cream very thoroughly together, and then mix in a little of the hot sauce. Add this to the rest of the sauce in the pan and stir over a gentle heat until the sauce thickens; do not boil it. Season if necessary.

NOTE: This sauce can be served with calf's head, boiled tongue, new potatoes, carrots, broccoli or broad beans.

STUFFINGS

CHRISTMAS TURKEY STUFFINGS

BASIC MIXTURE

14 oz. freshly made breadcrumbs (almost all of a large white loaf after the crusts are removed)	2 level teaspoons salt
	freshly ground black pepper
6 oz. shredded suet	3 eggs
finely grated rind of 1 lemon	3 or 4 tablespoons milk

Mix the crumbs, suet, lemon rind, salt and pepper together. Beat the eggs and add them to the mixture with enough milk to moisten the stuffing and make it bind together. Do not overwork it at this stage as it is easier to add the other ingredients if the mixture is open in texture.

GREEN HERB AND LEMON STUFFING

the basic mixture	juice of 1 lemon
3 level tablespoons chopped parsley	

Mix the parsley and lemon juice into the basic stuffing mixture. Add a dusting of dried herbs if you like.

DARK MUSHROOM STUFFING

the basic mixture	2 oz. butter
4 oz. mushrooms	$\frac{1}{2}$ level teaspoon paprika

Wipe the mushrooms with a damp cloth (there is no need to peel them). Chop them finely. Melt the butter in a frying pan, add the mushrooms, and stir them over a gentle heat until they are cooked. Add the paprika, then stir this mixture into the basic stuffing mixture.

PINK HAM AND PIMENTO STUFFING

the basic mixture	1 tinned pimento
4 oz. cooked ham	1 tablespoon tomato ketchup

Chop the ham finely. Cut the pimento into thin slivers and stir ham and pimento into the basic stuffing mixture with the tomato ketchup.

CHESTNUT STUFFING

ENOUGH FOR A 12 LB. TURKEY

1 lb. chestnuts	chopped cooked giblets
$\frac{1}{2}$ pint giblet stock or water	1 egg
6 oz. freshly made white breadcrumbs	a little of the liquid in which the chestnuts were cooked
1 small onion, finely chopped	
2 oz. celery, finely diced	salt and pepper to season

Take the shells and inner skins off the chestnuts. The easiest way to do this is to cut a fairly large cross in the centre of each chestnut; put them in an ovenproof dish in a very hot oven, about *Gas Mark 7 or 8 or 450 degrees F.*, for 10 to 15 minutes. Then the outer and inner skins should come off quite easily.

Put the skinned chestnuts into a saucepan with the stock or water, put on the lid and cook the chestnuts gently for about 20 minutes, until they are tender. Drain off the stock. Sieve the chestnuts or chop them finely. Add the breadcrumbs, onions, celery and chopped, cooked giblets to the chestnuts. Beat the egg and add it to the stuffing with just enough liquid to bind it. Finally, season the stuffing.

SAGE AND ONION STUFFING

ENOUGH FOR A MEDIUM SIZED GOOSE

4 large onions, peeled	1 level teaspoon dried sage
6 oz. freshly made white breadcrumbs	salt and pepper

Peel and halve the onions and put them into a pan. Cover them with cold water and bring to the boil. Simmer for 10 minutes, then drain off and reserve the water. Chop the onions quite finely, mix the onions, breadcrumbs and sage together and add plenty of salt and pepper. Bind the stuffing with just a little of the onion liquid.

SAUSAGE STUFFING

ENOUGH FOR A 3 LB. CHICKEN

the chicken's liver	8 oz. pork sausage-meat
4 oz. lamb's liver	
1 shallot or small onion	1$\frac{1}{2}$ oz. freshly made white breadcrumbs
2 oz. mushrooms, wiped but unpeeled	1 beaten egg
2 oz. liver sausage	salt and pepper

Mince the chicken's liver with the lamb's liver, the shallot or onion and the mushrooms. Take the skin off the liver sausage and mix the liver sausage with the pork sausage-meat; add the minced mixture, then the breadcrumbs, and bind the mixture with the beaten egg. Season it with salt and pepper.

APRICOT STUFFING

3 oz. dried apricots	grated rind and juice of 1 lemon
9 oz. freshly made white breadcrumbs	1 egg
4 oz. shredded suet	salt and pepper
3 level tablespoons chopped parsley	

Put the apricots into a pan, cover them with cold water. Bring them slowly to the boil then pour off the water and chop the apricots. Mix the chopped apricots with the white breadcrumbs, suet, parsley, lemon rind and juice.

Beat the egg and stir it into the mixture with the salt and pepper.

This stuffing is ideal for a shoulder of lamb.

PASTRY DISHES

Steak and kidney pie . . . fruit tarts . . . lemon meringue pie . . . so many of the traditional family favourite dishes require a pastry base. And nowadays there is no need to despair if your hand is not quite light enough to produce really flaky puff pastry, for excellent results can be achieved with the convenient, inexpensive packets of ready-prepared frozen pastry. In this chapter I give a selection of recipes for sweet and savoury flans and pies, most of which can be made with short crust pastry or frozen puff pastry. But whichever pastry you use, the rolling and lining of flan tins is exactly the same, so I have included a few useful hints to help you do this. Also, of course, there are some pastries which are a little more unusual—like choux and pâté sucrée. You'll find instructions for making choux pastry on page 107, and pâté sucrée on page 156, in the Party Fare chapter.

SAVOURY RECIPES

QUICK FLAKY PASTRY

THIS AMOUNT IS NEEDED FOR EACH OF THE FOLLOWING FOUR SAVOURY PIES

9 oz. plain flour
1 level teaspoon salt
8 oz. margarine in a hard block, preferably straight from the refrigerator

1 dessertspoon lemon juice
cold water to mix

Sift the flour and salt into a mixing bowl. Coarsely grate the margarine straight into the flour, dusting it occasionally with flour to keep the grated pieces separate. Mix the grated margarine evenly into the flour with a knife. Add the lemon juice and water gradually, mixing with your hand so you can feel the consistency. The dough should be smooth but not too stiff, pliable but not sticky.

Wrap the pastry in greaseproof paper and leave it in a cool place for 15 minutes, when it will be ready for rolling out. The pastry keeps well for several days in a polythene bag in the refrigerator.

SAVOURY MINCE PIE

FOR 4/5 PEOPLE

1 lb. minced steak
1 level tablespoon tomato ketchup
2 teaspoons Worcester sauce
2 oz. rolled oats

salt and pepper
¾ pint stock
the quick flaky pastry as in the recipe
little beaten egg
10 inch pie plate

Put the mince in a large frying pan and fry it gently without extra fat, breaking it down in the pan with a wooden spoon. When it is brown, stir in the tomato ketchup, Worcester sauce, rolled oats and salt and pepper. Stir in the stock and bring to the boil. Leave the mince filling to cool before putting it in the pie.

Cut the pastry in two pieces, one a little larger than the other, and roll the smaller piece into a round to fit the pie plate. Line the plate and trim the edges. Fill the pie with the cold mince mixture.

Roll out the rest of the pastry, with any scraps, into a round a little larger than the plate to allow for the domed top. Moisten the edge of the pastry base and put the top on the pie. Trim the edges, knock them up and flute them as described for the steak and kidney pie on page 00. Use any pastry scraps to make leaves to decorate the top.

Brush the top of the pie with beaten egg. Make a hole in the centre, arrange the leaves round it and brush them with beaten egg also.

Leave the pie in a cold place for at least an hour for the pastry to rest; it will then keep its shape better.

Bake the pie in a hot oven, about *Gas Mark 7 or 425 degrees F.,* for 20 minutes, then reduce the heat to *Gas Mark 5 or 375 degrees F.* for a further 25 to 30 minutes.

This pie is good hot or cold.

Jugged hare (see page 68)

Above: potato ring (see page 70); right: kebabs (see page 70)

Top: salmon fishcakes and parsley and cheese cakes (see page 69); bottom: noisettes of lamb with sweetcorn and aubergines (see page 76)

STEAK AND KIDNEY PIE

FOR 6 PEOPLE

2 lb. stewing steak,
  thinly sliced
6 oz. kidney
2 level tablespoons
  plain flour
salt and pepper
1 small onion, sliced into
  rings
just over $\frac{1}{4}$ pint stock or
  water

the quick flaky pastry
  as in the recipe on
  page 90
little beaten egg
little extra stock
  to add to the pie
  when serving
2 pint pie dish and
  a pie funnel will
  be required

Cut the steak into 1 inch strips. Remove the central core of the kidney and cut the kidney into small pieces. Roll each piece of kidney in a strip of steak.

Season the flour with salt and pepper, turn the meat and kidney rolls in the seasoned flour and arrange them in the pie dish round the pie funnel. Scatter the onion rings over the top and pour the stock round the meat.

Roll the pastry into an oval about $1\frac{1}{2}$ inches larger all round than the top of the pie dish, and cut off an inch-wide strip from all round the edge. Moisten the rim of the pie dish with cold water and lay the strip of pastry round the rim of the dish. Join the ends by overlapping them slightly. Lift the pastry lid on the rolling pin carefully over the pie to make sure it is large enough. If it seems too small do not stretch it, or it will sink during the baking and fall into the pie; instead, roll it a little larger. Moisten the pastry strip with water and cover the pie with the pastry lid, pressing the edges very firmly together.

Trim the edges of the pastry by holding the pie on one hand and cutting smartly round the edge with a sharp knife, keeping the handle well under the pie dish so that the blade slopes upwards and outwards. Trimmed in this way, the pastry will overlap the dish very slightly and if it shrinks a little in cooking it will still remain on the rim of the dish.

Knock up the edge of the pastry with a sharp knife, holding the pastry firmly on the rim of the pie dish with one finger of the other hand so that the pastry remains just over the rim.

Using the back of the knife, make $\frac{1}{2}$ inch flutes round the edge of the pie. Brush the top of the pie with beaten egg, and make a hole in the centre just over the funnel.

Stack the scraps of pastry in a heap without kneading them and roll them out into a rectangle. Trim the rectangle into strips an inch wide and cut them into diamond shapes for leaves. Mark veins on the leaves with the back of a knife and arrange them round the pie, pointing inwards. Brush the leaves also with beaten egg.

Rest the pie in a refrigerator or a cold place for at least 30 minutes before baking (it is often helpful to leave it overnight). This allows the pastry to settle, and prevents it shrinking from the edges.

Bake the pie in a hot oven, about *Gas Mark 7 or 425 degrees F.*, for 20 minutes, then reduce the heat to *Gas Mark 2 or 300 degrees F.* for a further 1 hour 40 minutes. After the first hour, cover the pie with a double layer of greaseproof paper as the pastry is apt to brown too quickly. When serving the pie, pour a little extra boiling stock or water into the dish after cutting the first slice.

CHICKEN, TOMATO AND BACON PIE

FOR ABOUT 5 PEOPLE

1 small roasting
  chicken
4 oz. streaky bacon
$1\frac{1}{2}$ oz. plain flour
salt and pepper
$\frac{1}{2}$ level teaspoon ground
  mace
1 large tin whole peeled
  tomatoes (2 lb. 3 oz.)

little beaten egg
the quick flaky pastry
  as in the recipe on
  page 90
round deep pie plate
  about $8\frac{1}{2}$ inches in
  diameter, holding
  $1\frac{1}{4}$ pints of liquid,
  will be required

Using a sharp knife, cut the chicken into joints (see page oo). Remove as much skin as you can.

Remove the rind from the bacon, cut the bacon into strips and fry slowly until crisp. Season the flour with the salt, pepper and mace and dust the chicken joints with this mixture. Arrange the joints in the pie plate. Scatter the bacon over the top and pour round the tomatoes.

Roll out the pastry into a round about $1\frac{1}{2}$ inches larger all round than the top of the pie dish, and cut off an inch-wide strip from all round the edge. Moisten the rim of the pie plate with cold water and lay the strip of pastry round the rim of the plate. Join the ends by overlapping them slightly. Lift the pastry lid, on the rolling pin, carefully over the pie to make sure it is large enough. If it seems too small do not stretch it, or it will sink during the baking and fall into the pie; instead, roll it a little larger. Moisten the pastry strip with water and cover the pie with the pastry lid, pressing the edges very firmly together.

Trim the edges of the pastry by holding the pie on one hand and cutting smartly round the edge with a sharp knife, keeping the handle well under the pie plate so that the blade slopes upwards and outwards. Trimmed in this way, the pastry will overlap the plate very slightly and if it shrinks a little in cooking it will still remain on the rim of the plate.

Knock up the edge of the pastry with a sharp knife, holding the pastry firmly on the rim of the pie plate with one finger of the other hand so that the pastry remains just over the rim.

Using the back of the knife, make $\frac{1}{2}$ inch flutes round the edge of the pie. Brush the top of the pie with beaten egg, and make a hole in the centre.

Stack the scraps of pastry in a heap without kneading them and roll them out into a rectangle. Trim the rectangle into strips an inch wide and cut them into diamond shapes for leaves.

Mark veins on the leaves with the back of a knife and arrange them round the pie, pointing inwards. Brush the leaves also with beaten egg.

Rest the pie in a refrigerator or a cold place for at least 30 minutes before baking (it is often helpful to leave it overnight). This allows the pastry to settle, and prevents it shrinking from the edges.

Bake the pie in a hot oven, about *Gas Mark 7 or 425 degrees F.*, for 20 minutes, then reduce the heat to *Gas Mark 2 or 300 degrees F.* for a further hour, or until the chicken is tender when tested through the hole in the pie top with the tip of a sharp pointed knife.

This pie is good hot or cold. If serving hot, a green vegetable is the best accompaniment. Serve cold with a green salad—the pie is excellent for a picnic.

PORK FILLET ROLL

FOR 4/5 PEOPLE

the quick flaky pastry as
in the recipe on
page 90
1 pork fillet, about 8 oz.
in weight
salt and pepper

1 level tablespoon
sage and onion
stuffing crumbs
from a packet
little beaten egg
for the glaze

Roll the pastry into a rectangle wide enough to encase completely the pork fillet, plus 2 inches. Centre the fillet on the pastry and sprinkle it with salt and pepper and the sage and onion stuffing crumbs. Moisten the pastry edges with water and wrap the fillet in the pastry, overlapping the sides and folding the ends up to keep in all the juices. Turn the roll over, so that the joins in the pastry are underneath, and transfer it to a baking tray.

Brush the roll with a little beaten egg, then score the top with a sharp knife in a diamond pattern. Make a small slit at each end of the roll, to allow the steam to escape. Leave the roll in a cool place for 30 minutes before baking it.

Put the roll into a very hot oven, about *Gas Mark 8 or 450 degrees F.,* for 10 minutes; this quick heat makes the pastry rise and sets it. Reduce the heat to *Gas Mark 5 or 375 degrees F.* for a further 25 to 30 minutes. If the roll should brown too much, cover with damp greaseproof paper.

GAME PIE

I have chosen pigeons to accompany the other meats in the pie because they are almost always available, but any other game, such as a duck, a stewing pheasant or 2 stewing grouse, would also be nice; stewing birds are always cheaper than young ones. Joints of hare are good, too. Larger birds should be cut into joints (see instructions for jointing a chicken on page 64). Pigeons should be cut in half down the centre.

FOR 6 PEOPLE

3 pigeons
1 lb. chuck steak
1 lb. pieces of boned
rabbit
2 oz. plain flour
seasoned with salt and
pepper

4 oz. streaky bacon,
cut fairly
thinly
$\frac{1}{2}$ pint stock

FOR FORCEMEAT
(this is packed between the pieces of meat)

2 oz. shredded suet
4 oz. freshly made
white breadcrumbs
2 oz. streaky bacon,
chopped
2 teaspoons chopped
parsley

$\frac{1}{4}$ level teaspoon
mixed herbs
grated rind of $\frac{1}{2}$ lemon
salt and pepper
1 egg

FOR TOP OF THE PIE

2 large packets frozen
puff pastry (about 1 lb.
6 oz. pastry)

a beaten egg
salt

a pie dish holding 3 pints of liquid will
be required

Halve the pigeons. Cut the steak into fairly large cubes. Separate the pieces of rabbit. Dust these and the pigeons with the seasoned flour. Cut the rinds off the bacon.

Next make the forcemeat balls. Mix the suet, breadcrumbs, chopped bacon, parsley, herbs and lemon rind. Season the mixture with salt and pepper. Add the egg to bind the mixture; form it into small balls—the mixture makes about 8.

Pack half the meat—not the bacon—into the pie-dish, filling any gaps with half the forcemeat balls. Cover the meat with a layer of bacon, then fill the pie with the rest of the meat and forcemeat and pour round the stock.

Roll out each packet of pastry to 11 inches long by $7\frac{1}{2}$ inches wide. Cut each piece of pastry into five strips each $1\frac{1}{2}$ inches wide by 11 inches long. Put five pastry strips side by side and weave the other five strips through them. Fold back the ends of the strips and brush the pastry beneath with water; gently press the top strips back in place. Roll the woven pastry rectangle gently from corner to corner until it will fit the top of the pie when the ends are trimmed. Moisten round the top of the pie dish and lift the pastry top into position. Trim round the edge with a pair of scissors.

Roll out the scraps of pastry and cut them into strips each $\frac{1}{2}$ inch wide. Take two strips, plait them and place them round the edge of the pie, moistening beneath with water. Beat the egg well with a good pinch of salt to make the glaze shiny, and brush over the surface of the pie.

Bake the pie just above the centre of a hot oven, about *Gas Mark 7 or 425 degrees F.,* for 20 minutes. Slip a piece of damp greaseproof paper on top of the pie, and lower the heat to *Gas Mark 3 or 325 degrees F.* for a further 2 to $2\frac{1}{2}$ hours.

CHICKEN AND HAM PIE

FOR 6/8 PEOPLE

FOR THE FILLING

$1\frac{1}{2}$ lb. uncooked lean
bacon (a slipper is
about the right size)
1 roasting chicken,
about $3\frac{1}{2}$ lb.
salt and freshly ground
black pepper

2 hard-boiled
eggs
about $\frac{1}{4}$ pint
jellied stock or
dissolved aspic

FOR THE PASTRY

$1\frac{1}{2}$ lb. plain flour
2 level teaspoons salt
$7\frac{1}{2}$ oz. lard

just over $\frac{1}{4}$ pint water
a little beaten egg
for the glaze

An open raised pie mould measuring 8 inches by 5 inches will be required. (This is an oval-shaped metal collar fastening with a clip at each end. A cake tin 6 inches in diameter, with a loose base, could be used instead.)

First prepare the filling. Put the piece of bacon into a bowl, cover it with cold water and leave it overnight. Mince it through a coarse mincer plate or chop it, not too finely.

Cut off all the flesh from the chicken, working round the bones with a very sharp knife. Remove the skin and keep

Chicken and ham pie

heat to *Gas Mark 4 or 350 degrees F.* for another 30 minutes. Finally, reduce the heat to *Gas Mark 3 or 325 degrees F.* for another hour, making 2 hours in all. As soon as the top of the pie starts to brown, cover it with damp greaseproof paper. When the pie is cooked, take it out of the oven but leave it inside the mould on the tray until next day.

Remove the mould very carefully; the best way is to warm the pie in the oven for a few seconds as this loosens the mould. Unclip it and remove as seen in photograph above. Melt the jellied stock or aspic and cool it without allowing it to set. You can use ¼ pint of the stock from the chicken carcass—dissolve 1 teaspoon gelatine in the stock over a gentle heat, then cool before pouring into the pie. Put the tip of a funnel into one of the holes in the pie and slowly pour the liquid in to fill the pie completely; it will set in the spaces round the meat.

Leave the pie in a cool place for the liquid to set to a firm jelly.

the pieces of dark and light meat in separate heaps. Put the carcass into a pan, cover it with cold water and simmer it steadily to get a well-reduced, good-flavoured stock. Strain the stock, season it and leave it overnight.

Next make the pastry. Sift the flour and salt into a mixing bowl. Put the lard and water into a saucepan and melt the lard over a low heat, then bring the mixture to the boil and pour it immediately into the flour, using a knife to mix it, then knead the dough with your hand until it is smooth. Cut off a quarter of the pastry for the lid and put it in a warm place to keep it pliable. Clip the raised pie mould together and stand it on an upturned baking tray. Put the large piece of pastry into the mould and, with your fingers, work the pastry up the sides of the mould. It must come ¼ inch above the top.

Put the chopped or minced bacon into pie; sprinkle with freshly ground black pepper. Shell the hard-boiled eggs and lay them end to end on top of the bacon. Add a layer of the dark chicken meat, season it with salt and pepper, then add the white meat. It is best to pack the pie loosely with the meats; if it is too firmly packed the juices cannot circulate through the meat. Season the chicken before putting on the lid; no extra liquid is added at this stage.

Form the remaining piece of pastry into an oval to fit the top of the pie. Damp the edges of the pastry above the pie mould and place the lid in position, pressing it well on to the pastry beneath. Trim the edges and keep the trimmings in a warm place as they will be needed for the decoration. Make a crimped edge round the top of the pie and brush the surface with beaten egg. Make two holes in the lid to allow the steam to escape. Roll out the scraps of pastry and cut four diamond shapes for leaves. Cut a strip an inch wide and "fringe" one long edge with cuts ¼ inch apart. Roll up this strip to form a tassel. Put the tassel in the centre of the pie with the leaves curved round beneath it. Brush the decoration with beaten egg.

Bake the pie in the centre of a fairly hot oven, about *Gas Mark 6 or 400 degrees F.*, for 30 minutes then reduce the

CUTLET PIE

FOR 6 PEOPLE

1½ lb. best end neck of lamb (about 6 cutlets)
3 lamb kidneys
2 oz. mushrooms

1 level tablespoon flour seasoned with salt and pepper
about 4 tablespoons stock

FOR THE PASTRY

6 oz. plain flour
good pinch of salt
1½ oz. margarine
1½ oz. lard
cold water to mix
little beaten egg for the glaze

6 cutlet frills
a pie dish holding 1½ pints of liquid will be required

Cut the meat into cutlets and scrape the meat off the ends of the bones; put these scraps into the pie dish.

Skin the kidneys, cut them in half and cut out the cores with a sharp knife. Wipe the mushrooms with a damp cloth, and slice them thickly—there is no need to peel them.

Toss the meat and kidneys in seasoned flour then arrange them in the pie dish with the cutlet bones sticking upwards. Put the mushrooms round the meat, then add the stock.

Sift the flour and salt, then rub in the fats. Mix with just enough cold water to make a stiff paste. Roll the pastry larger than the top of the pie, cut a strip from the edge and lay it round the rim, having first moistened the rim with water. Roll the pastry to fit the pie. Moisten the pastry band and lift the lid on to cover the pie, making holes for the bones to stick through. Trim the edges, press the pastry firmly round the join, then knock it up and flute the edge. Roll any scraps of pastry into a long strip and cut diamond shapes for leaves and arrange them on top of the pie. Brush the surface of the pastry with beaten egg.

Bake the pie in a fairly hot oven, about *Gas Mark 6 or 400 degrees F.*, for 15 minutes then reduce the heat to *Gas Mark 4 or 350 degrees F.* for a further hour. Slip on the cutlet frills before serving the pie.

SWEETCORN FLAN

MAKES 6 LARGE SLICES

FOR THE PASTRY

6 oz. plain flour	1½ oz. vegetable
salt	shortening
1½ oz. margarine	little cold water to mix

FOR THE FILLING

2 cooked heads of	½ pint milk
sweetcorn (or an	1 small egg
11½ oz. tin sweetcorn	cayenne pepper and
kernels)	salt
6 rashers of bacon	a flan ring 8 inches in
1 oz. butter	diameter will be
1 small onion	required
1 level tablespoon plain	
flour	

Sift the flour with a pinch of salt, rub in the fats and mix the pastry with just enough cold water to make a stiff dough.

Put the flan ring on an upturned baking tray. Roll out the pastry and use to line the flan ring neatly (see below). Keep any scraps to make a trellis on top of the flan.

Remove the sweetcorn from the cobs (or drain the tin of sweetcorn). Cut the rinds off the rashers of bacon, chop bacon finely and fry it in the butter. Dice the onion and fry it slowly with the bacon. Take the pan off the heat and stir in the flour; add the milk and bring the mixture gradually to the boil, stirring all the time. Take it off the heat and add the prepared sweetcorn. Beat the egg thoroughly, add a little of the mixture to the egg then pour this back into the sweetcorn mixture. Season with a tiny pinch of cayenne pepper and salt. Allow the mixture to get cold.

When cold, turn the mixture into the lined flan. Make a trellis over the surface with some strips of pastry. Bake the flan in a fairly hot oven, about *Gas Mark 6 or 400 degrees F.*, for 10 minutes, then reduce the heat to *Gas Mark 4 or 350 degrees F.* for 30 minutes. Slip the flan off the ring for the last 5 minutes of baking.

Serve hot or cold with watercress.

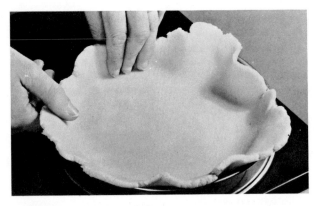

LINING A FLAN RING

1. Place the flan ring on an upturned baking tray (the tart is then easily slipped on to a serving plate after baking). Roll the pastry into a circle an inch larger than the ring. Slip the rolling pin underneath the pastry and lift the pastry into the ring.

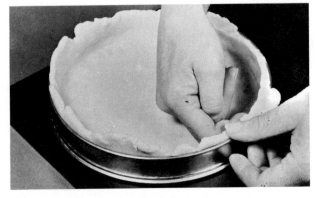

2. Line the ring very carefully, keeping the pastry fairly thick where the baking tray and the ring meet, and pressing it down firmly. Place the first finger of your right hand inside and just under the rim and press the pastry over this finger with your left thumb.

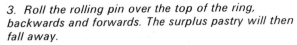

3. Roll the rolling pin over the top of the ring, backwards and forwards. The surplus pastry will then fall away.

4. Flute the edge of the flan: press the top of the pastry edge with the first finger of your right hand and pinch the pastry with your left hand.

SWEET RECIPES

SHORT CRUST PASTRY

THIS AMOUNT IS NEEDED FOR EACH OF THE FOLLOWING FIVE SWEET PIES

8 oz. plain flour	2 oz. lard
good pinch of salt	cold water to mix
2 oz. margarine	

Sift the flour and salt into a basin. Add the margarine and lard and work into the flour by rubbing it across the tips of the fingers until the pastry is of an even consistency rather like freshly made white breadcrumbs. Keep your hands well above the basin, in order to incorporate as much air as possible with the flour as you work it through your fingers. Mix the pastry with just enough cold water to bind it. It is best to use your hand for mixing as you can feel the consistency much better—too much water makes tough pastry. The pastry is now ready to use.

JAM TART

MAKES 8 SLICES

the short crust pastry given in the recipe above	12 oz. strawberry jam 9 inch plate will be required as a cutting guide
1 teaspoon lemon juice	

Roll the pastry into a large round about 10 inches in diameter. Put the plate, upturned, in the centre and cut round it. Form the remainder of the pastry into an inch-wide band. Lay the round on a baking tray, moisten round the edge of the top and lay the band round it, joining the ends with a dab of water. Knock up the pastry edges and mark the top in a criss-cross pattern with the back of a knife. Prick the centre with a fork.

Mix the lemon juice and the jam. Put just over half the jam in the centre of the pastry and spread it evenly. Bake the jam tart in a moderately hot oven, about *Gas Mark 5 or 375 degrees F.*, for 30 to 40 minutes. Take it out of the oven, spread over the rest of the jam, and return to the oven for about another 5 minutes.

RASPBERRY MERINGUE TARTLETS

MAKES 12 TARTLETS

the short crust pastry given in the recipe above	12 paper cases a piping bag and a $\frac{1}{4}$ inch round meringue pipe, and 12 shallow tartlet tins will be required
1 tin raspberry pie filling (18 oz.)	
2 egg whites	
4 oz. castor sugar	
little redcurrant jelly	

Roll the pastry to about $\frac{1}{8}$ inch thick and cut out rounds with a fluted cutter just larger than the top of the tartlet tins. Line the tartlet tins with the pastry.

Put a good spoonful of the raspberry filling in each tartlet and bake the tartlets in a moderately hot oven, about *Gas*

Mark 5 or 375 degrees F., for about 30 minutes. Slip the tartlets out of the tins, but leave them on a baking tray to cool.

When the tartlets are cold, whisk the egg whites stiffly and when they are stiff enough to stand in sharp points beat in a level dessertspoon of the measured sugar. Whisk again until the same stiff consistency is reached, then fold in the rest of the sugar lightly. Fill the piping bag, with the pipe attached, with the meringue mixture.

Pipe a zigzag of meringue over the top of each tartlet and smooth it over with a palette knife. Then pipe three circles of meringue in a clover leaf pattern on top of each tartlet and top with a fourth circle (see colour photograph on page 104). Put the tartlets into a cool oven, about *Gas Mark 2 or 300 degrees F.*, for about 20 minutes to set the meringue and to brown the tops lightly.

Sieve the redcurrant jelly and drop a little into each meringue circle. Put the tartlets into paper cases for serving.

APPLE AND APRICOT PIE

FOR 4/5 PEOPLE

1 red-skinned dessert apple	the short crust pastry given in the recipe above left
2 large cooking apples	little sifted icing sugar
1 small tin apricots ($7\frac{1}{2}$ oz.)	a pie dish holding $1\frac{1}{2}$ pints of liquid will be required
2 oz. soft brown sugar	
2 cloves	
little beaten egg	

Quarter and core the dessert apple and slice it without skinning it. Peel, core and slice the cooking apples. Arrange the apples in layers in the pie dish with the tinned apricots, drained. Sprinkle the layers with soft brown sugar, and put a clove at each end of the dish.

Roll the pastry into an oval about $1\frac{1}{2}$ inches larger all round than the top of the pie dish, and cut off an inch-wide strip from all round the edge. Moisten the rim of the pie dish with cold water and lay the strip of pastry round the rim of the dish. Join the ends by overlapping them slightly. Lift the pastry lid, on the rolling pin, carefully over the pie to make sure it is large enough. If it seems too small do not stretch it, or it will sink during the baking and fall into the pie; instead, roll it in a little larger. Moisten the pastry strip with water and cover the pie with the pastry lid, pressing the edges very firmly together.

Trim the edges of the pastry by holding the pie in one hand and cutting smartly round the edge with a sharp knife, keeping the handle well under the pie dish so that the blade slopes upwards and outwards. Trimmed in this way, the pastry will overlap the dish very slightly and if it shrinks a little in cooking it will still remain on the rim of the dish. Knock up the edge of the pastry with a sharp knife, holding the pastry firmly on the rim of the pie dish with one finger of the other hand so that the pastry remains over the rim.

Using the back of the knife, make $\frac{1}{2}$ inch flutes round the edge of the pie. Brush the top of the pie with beaten egg, and make a slit in the centre.

Bake the pie in a fairly hot oven, about *Gas Mark 6 or 400 degrees F.*, for 20 minutes, then reduce the heat to *Gas*

Mark 4 or 350 degrees F. for a further 20 to 25 minutes, or until the apples are tender when tested with a skewer. The pie can also be cooked at *Gas Mark 3 or 325 degrees F.* for 2½ hours.

Sift a little icing sugar through a rounded strainer over the surface of the pie before serving it, and accompany the pie with cream or thin custard.

RHUBARB AND BANANA PIE

FOR 4 PEOPLE

the short crust pastry given in the recipe on page 99	2 tablespoons plum jam
1 lb. rhubarb	sprinkling of castor sugar
2 bananas	7 inch pie plate will be required
2 oz. soft brown sugar	

Cut the pastry in two pieces, one slightly smaller than the other, and roll out and line the pie plate with the smaller piece.

Wipe the rhubarb and cut off any pieces of leaf or root, then cut into 1 inch pieces. Peel the bananas, cut them in slices and mix with the rhubarb. Add the brown sugar, mix well and heap into the pie. Dot the plum jam over the top.

Roll the rest of the pastry into a round a little larger than the plate to allow for the domed top. Moisten round the edge of the pastry base with water and cover the fruit with the pastry top, pressing the joins firmly together. Knock up the edges. Using a large, round cutter, cut almost through the pastry in semi-circles, working from the centre round the pie (see colour picture on page 104). Open up the pastry top where the lines meet, thus making a hole in the top.

Brush the pie with cold water and dust it with castor sugar. Bake the pie in a fairly hot oven, about *Gas Mark 6 or 400 degrees F.*, for 20 minutes, then reduce the heat to *Gas Mark 3 or 325 degrees F.* for a further 20 to 25 minutes.

TRADITIONAL APPLE PIE

FOR ABOUT 6 PEOPLE

the short crust pastry given in the recipe on page 99	little lightly beaten egg white
2 lb. cooking apples	castor sugar
6 oz. granulated sugar	a pie dish holding 1½ pints of liquid will be required
3 cloves	
4 tablespoons water	

First make the pastry and leave it in a cool place while filling the pie dish.

Peel the apples, cut them in quarters and cut out the cores, then slice the apple quarters and heap them into the pie dish, adding layers of sugar between. Make sure the pie dish is well mounded.

Put the cloves between the apple slices, spreading them round the dish. Add the water to start forming the juice. Roll out the pastry and use to cover the pie as shown in photographs 1 to 4. Bake the pie in a fairly hot oven, about *Gas Mark 6 or 400 degrees F.*, for 20 minutes then reduce

the heat to *Gas Mark 4 or 350 degrees F.* for a further 30 minutes or until the apples are tender; some apples take a little longer to cook but most cooking apples will be ready in this time—there is no need to cook them beforehand.

NOTE: You can vary the pie filling by using: apple and bramble (blackberry), apple and thinly sliced quince, apple and grated lemon rind, apple with a little mincemeat, apple and tinned apricot, apple and sliced orange. All delicious!

1. Roll the pastry into a rectangle 1½ inches larger than the pie dish top—hold the pie dish above the pastry to check the size.

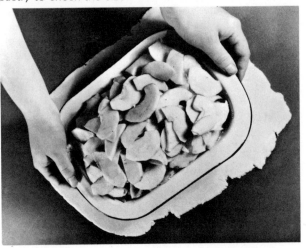

2. Cut a 1 inch strip from round the rectangle, and lay it on the rim of the dish. Lift the rectangle of pastry on the rolling pin and check its size. It should fit without stretching and overlap the rim by ¼ inch. If the pastry is stretched it will fall back into the pie during baking. Roll it to the right size if necessary. Moisten the rim with water and put the pastry top back on the pie, pressing the edges together. Trim the edges by lifting the pie dish on your left hand and holding the knife at an acute angle, so that the pastry slightly overhangs.

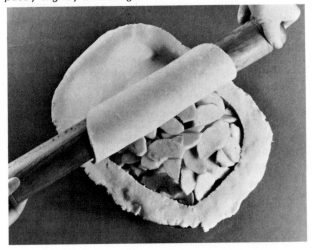

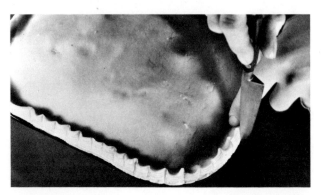

3. Knock up the edges of the pie by pressing your finger along the rim and making small cuts into the edge with the back of a knife.

4. Flute the edge at $\frac{1}{4}$ inch intervals, keeping the knife upright and the pastry well forward to the edge of the dish. Criss-cross the pie top with the back of a knife, taking care not to spear the pastry. Brush the top (not the edge) with beaten egg white and sprinkle with castor sugar. Make a slit in the centre of the pie.

5. The pie baked and ready to serve.

MINCE PIES

MAKES 24

8 oz. plain flour
good pinch of salt
2 oz. margarine
2 oz. lard
cold water to mix
1 lb. mincemeat (see page 196)

little lightly beaten egg white
dusting of castor sugar
tartlet tins

Sift the flour with the salt, then rub the fats into the flour. Add just enough cold water to make a stiff dough. Roll out the pastry to about $\frac{1}{8}$ inch in thickness and cut out rounds just larger than the tartlet tins. Line the tins with the pastry. Put a good spoonful of mincemeat into each. For traditional mince pies, cut rounds to cover the tops of the pies, and using a little water to moisten the meeting edges, press each cover and base firmly together.

Brush the tops of the pies with lightly beaten egg white and sprinkle with castor sugar. Make one or two little snips in the pastry with a pair of kitchen scirrors.

Bake the mince pies in a moderately hot oven, about *Gas Mark 5 or 375 degrees F.*, for about 20 minutes. Slip them out of the tins, and reheat them when required.

LEMON MERINGUE PIE

MAKES 6 SLICES

FOR THE PASTRY
6 oz. plain flour
$1\frac{1}{2}$ oz. margarine

$1\frac{1}{2}$ oz. vegetable shortening
cold water to mix

FOR THE FILLING
finely grated rind of 2 lemons
the juice of 2 lemons made up to $\frac{1}{2}$ pint with water
2 level tablespoons cornflour

4 level tablespoons castor sugar, or to taste
1 oz. butter
2 egg yolks

FOR THE MERINGUE
2 egg whites

4 oz. castor sugar

a flan ring 8 inches in diameter will be required

First make the pastry. Sift the flour into a mixing bowl then rub in the fats and mix the pastry to a stiff dough with cold water.

Place the flan ring on an upturned baking tray. Roll out the pastry to about an inch larger in diameter than the ring, then lift it into the ring and press it well down into the base where the ring and the tray meet. With the rolling pin, roll off the surplus pastry from the top of the ring (see photographs on page 98). Line the pastry case with a little crumpled kitchen paper and fill it with some beans or dried crusts to prevent the pastry from rising while it is baking. Bake the case in a hot oven, about *Gas Mark 7 or 425 degrees F.*, for 20 minutes then remove the beans and paper, lower the heat to *Gas Mark 5 or 375 degrees F.*, and continue baking for a further 15 minutes. Just before the flan is ready, slip off the ring and finish the baking without it.

THE FILLING
Mix the lemon rind, juice and water together and blend the cornflour to a smooth cream with a little of the mixture. Put the remaining liquid into a saucepan, add the blended cornflour and stir the mixture until it comes to the boil. Take it off the heat, stir in the sugar, then beat in the butter and the egg yolks. Turn the mixture into the baked pastry case.

THE MERINGUE TOP
Whisk the egg whites until they will stand in straight peaks (see photograph on page 139), then beat in a dessertspoon

of the measured sugar. Whisk again then lightly fold in the remaining sugar. Spread meringue over the top of the flan filling level with the top of the pastry. Fill a piping bag with the remaining meringue and pipe a trellis pattern over the surface. Put the lemon meringue pie into a slow oven, about *Gas Mark 2 or 300 degrees F.*, for 30 minutes to dry the meringue and colour it lightly. If it does not have this drying time it may soften when it is cold.

The pie can be browned more quickly if it is to be served hot. Set oven at *Gas Mark 6 or 400 degrees F.*

RASPBERRY AND REDCURRANT CRISP FLAN

MAKES 5 SLICES

FOR THE FLAN CASE
a little tasteless salad oil
2 oz. butter
3 oz. icing sugar, sifted
2 level tablespoons golden syrup
4 oz. Rice Krispies

FOR THE FILLING
8 oz. fresh raspberries
few large redcurrants
$\frac{1}{8}$ pint double cream

a flan ring 7 inches in diameter will be required

Brush the inside of the flan ring with salad oil and place it on the plate from which you will serve the flan.

Melt the butter in a fairly large pan, over a gentle heat. Remove the pan from the heat and stir in the icing sugar and golden syrup. When they are thoroughly mixed stir in the Rice Krispies. Turn the mixture into the flan ring and smooth it over the base and up the sides of the ring with the back of a wooden spoon. Do this while the mixture is hot. Leave it to cool and set, then carefully slip off the flan ring. Fill the flan case with the raspberries. Keep nine well-shaped redcurrants to one side and scatter the rest over the raspberries. Whip the cream lightly until it will just hold its shape and pipe it in nine stars round the flan. Put a redcurrant on top of each cream star.

CURRANT ALMOND FLAN

MAKES 6 LARGE SLICES

FOR THE PASTRY CASE
6 oz. plain flour
pinch of salt
1½ oz. margarine
1½ oz. lard
1 oz. castor sugar
1 egg yolk
1 dessertspoon water

FOR THE FILLING
2 tablespoons redcurrant jelly
1 egg white
4 oz. castor sugar
3 oz. ground almonds
½ teaspoon almond essence
4 oz. red or white currants or a mixture of the two
a flan ring measuring 8 inches in diameter will be required

Sift the flour and salt into a mixing bowl. Rub in the fats, then stir in the sugar. Mix the egg yolk and water together and add them to the pastry. Work it to a stiff dough, adding just a little more water if necessary.

Put the flan ring on an upturned baking tray. Roll the pastry into a round 2 inches larger all round than the flan ring. Lift the pastry into the ring and line the ring carefully, taking special care to press the pastry well into the base where the ring and the tray meet. Roll over the top of the flan—the surplus pastry will fall away (see photographs 1-3 on page 98). Gently pull the top edge of the pastry out a little above the ring and indent it every ½ inch with a skewer to give a scalloped effect. Spread the base of the flan case with redcurrant jelly. Whisk the egg white stiffly, lightly fold in the castor sugar and ground almonds and finally the almond essence. Turn the mixture into the flan case and bake in a moderate oven, about *Gas Mark 4 or 350 degrees F.*, for about 20 minutes, then sprinkle the currants on top of the flan, and return the flan to the oven for a further 10 to 15 minutes. Slip the flan ring carefully off the flan about 5 minutes before it is ready to be served.

LITTLE MARRON TARTLETS

MAKES 10 TARTLETS

FOR THE PASTRY
2½ oz. plain flour
1 oz. castor sugar
1½ oz. softened butter
1 egg yolk

FOR THE FILLING
1 tin chestnut purée (8 oz.)
1½ oz. castor sugar
drop of vanilla essence
1 teaspoon lemon juice
¼ pint single cream
¼ pint double cream
1 oz. plain chocolate, grated

a cutter 3 inches in diameter and 10 small, deep tartlet tins, each with a capacity of 2 tablespoons of liquid, will be required

First make the pastry. Sift the flour on to the kitchen working surface and form it into a small circle. Into the centre put the castor sugar, softened butter and egg yolk. Using the tips of the fingers of your right hand only, squeeze the ingredients in the centre of the ring together until they are well mixed, then, using a palette knife in the other hand, gradually flick in the flour from round the sides. Knead the ingredients into a soft though not sticky dough. Wrap it up and put it in a cold place for 30 minutes. Roll out the pastry fairly thinly and cut out 3 inch rounds with the cutter, re-rolling and using up the scraps. Line the tartlet tins with the pastry. Then cover the pastry with squares of crumpled kitchen paper filled with dry beans to weight the pastry while it is cooking.

Bake the tartlets in a moderately hot oven, about *Gas Mark 5 or 375 degrees F.*, for 10 minutes; lift out the beans and paper and return the tartlets to the oven for a further 5 minutes. After they have cooled, the tartlets can be kept in an airtight tin for several days; they can always be warmed through in a moderate oven to crisp them before filling them.

To make the filling, put the chestnut purée into a mixing bowl and beat in the castor sugar, vanilla essence and the lemon juice. Fill a forcing bag with a small round pipe attached, and pipe squiggles of the mixture into each tartlet, overlapping the edges slightly.

Whip the cream together until it will hold its shape and then put a good dessertspoon of it on top of each tartlet. Dust with grated chocolate.

Opposite: salad platter selection (see page 84). Overleaf: rhubarb and banana pie (see page 100), apple and apricot pie (see page 99), raspberry meringue tartlets (see page 99), jam tart (see page 99)

Pavlova gâteau (see page 141)

CHOUX PASTRY

Choux pastry is exciting and very easy to make, once you have mastered a few important points.

First, accuracy in weighing and measuring the ingredients must be observed.

Second, the eggs must be beaten into the mixture *very thoroughly* because choux paste should be very light and airy when it is baked. The lightness depends entirely on the air beaten in with the eggs as there is no other raising agent.

Third, choux paste is baked most successfully in a hot oven so that it will rise quickly and keep its shape.

Fourth, choux pastry should be well baked and it often looks ready before it actually is. If it is taken out of the oven too soon it will shrink and soften.

Finally, choux paste should always be used the day it is made—in fact, the sooner it is eaten the better.

2½ oz. plain flour	¼ pint water
pinch of salt	2 eggs
2 oz. margarine	

Sift the flour with the salt on to a piece of kitchen paper. Put the margarine and water into a fairly large pan and heat gently until the margarine melts. Bring the mixture to a rapid boil, take the pan off the heat and immediately shoot in the flour from the paper then, using a wooden spoon, beat the mixture vigorously until it is smooth and leaves the sides of the pan. It is essential to beat the mixture as soon as the flour has been added.

Cool the mixture slightly. Break one egg into a cup and beat it into the mixture using a wooden spoon, bowl side upwards, to incorporate as much air as possible. When the mixture is smooth and glossy, add the other egg.

ÉCLAIRS

MAKES ABOUT 15

the choux pastry given in the recipe above

FOR THE FILLING
just under ½ pint double cream	a forcing bag with a round pipe ½ inch in diameter will be required
1 level teaspoon castor sugar	

FOR THE CHOCOLATE ICING
3 oz. icing sugar, sifted	water to mix
1 oz. cocoa powder	

FOR THE COFFEE ICING
3 oz. icing sugar, sifted	a few drops of water
coffee essence	about 15 paper sweet cases

Put the choux pastry mixture in a forcing bag, with a plain round pipe ½ inch in diameter attached. Lightly grease two baking trays and pipe straight lines of the mixture on to them. Each éclair should be about 3 inches long.

Put the éclairs into a hot oven just above the centre, at *Gas Mark 7 or 425 degrees F.*, for 10-15 minutes. Take out

of the oven and slit open the side of each to allow the steam to escape, then return to the oven for 2 minutes.

THE FILLING
Whip the cream with the castor sugar until it will hold its shape. Fill the éclairs using a teaspoon, or a piping bag and a round or star pipe.

THE ICING
Sift the icing sugar for the chocolate icing and the cocoa together, and add enough water to make a thick coating consistency. Coat half the éclairs with this icing.

Sift the icing sugar for the coffee icing and add coffee essence and a little water to make a good coffee flavoured icing. Coat the rest of the éclairs with this.

Put each éclair into a paper sweet case when icing has set.

PROFITEROLES

FOR 8/10 PEOPLE

double the choux pastry given in the recipe above left

FOR THE CHOCOLATE SAUCE
6 oz. plain dessert chocolate	3 tablespoons water
	3 level teaspoons
1½ oz. castor sugar	flavourless salad oil

TO FILL THE PROFITEROLES AND DECORATE THE SWEET
½ pint double plus ¼ pint single cream	a few fresh and sugared violets
1 level dessertspoon icing sugar	

a forcing bag with a plain ½ inch round pipe for the choux pastry and a large star pipe for decorating the sweet will be required

Put the choux pastry mixture into a forcing bag with the plain round pipe attached. Lightly grease a baking tray and pipe the mixture into small balls, each about the size of a walnut, cutting the choux pastry off from the pipe with a small knife. The mixture will make about 75 choux balls. Bake the balls in a hot oven, *Gas Mark 7 or 425 degrees F.*, for 10 to 15 minutes. The balls should be well browned, light and crisp. Leave them on a wire tray to cool.

TO MAKE THE CHOCOLATE SAUCE
Chop up the chocolate roughly and put it into a pan with the castor sugar, the water and the oil. Stir over a very gentle heat until the chocolate has melted and the mixture is smooth. Leave it to cool, stirring it occasionally.

TO ASSEMBLE THE SWEET
Whip the double and single creams with the sugar until it holds its shape. Use tip of knife to make small hole in each choux ball and fill with the whipped cream (it is easiest to pipe it in). Fill a forcing bag, with a large star pipe attached, with the whipped cream that is left, and heap up the choux balls, piping the cream between (see the colour photograph on page 198). Trickle the chocolate sauce over the top and down the sides and dot the sugared and fresh violets over the surface. Serve any remaining chocolate sauce separately.

PUDDINGS

What shall we have for pudding? Is this a constant cry in your house—do you find it difficult constantly to think up something new and appetising to round off a lunch or dinner? Here I have selected recipes for a variety of different sweets and puddings—mouthwatering hot puddings for chilly days, delicious tempting fruity sweets for hot weather, and melt-in-the-mouth ice creams. All should prove popular with the whole family!

Remember, too, that sweets to serve at parties need not always be light frothy concoctions . . . on a bleak winter evening, Granny's lemon pudding (see page 110) is hard to beat!

SUET PUDDINGS

RHUBARB OR BLACKBERRY AND APPLE DUMPLING

FOR 6 PEOPLE

FOR THE SUET CRUST
8 oz. self-raising flour	3 oz. shredded suet
pinch of salt	cold water to mix

FOR A RHUBARB DUMPLING
1½ lb. rhubarb	good pinch of ground
4 oz. castor sugar	ginger

FOR A BLACKBERRY AND APPLE DUMPLING
2 lb. cooking apples	4 oz. blackberries
4 oz. castor sugar	2 tablespoons
finely grated rind of	water
1 lemon	

pudding basin holding 2 pints of liquid will be required

Brush the pudding basin with melted fat. Sift the flour and salt and mix in the suet. Mix these ingredients with water to a soft but not sticky dough. Turn the dough on to a well-floured board and cut off a quarter and reserve. Roll the rest into a round, of the same thickness all over, large enough to line the basin. Lightly dust the pastry with flour then fold it lightly and lift it into the basin; unfold it and press it to the base and sides of the basin, allowing a little to come above the top.

FOR THE RHUBARB DUMPLING
Cut off and discard any rhubarb leaves; wipe the stalks with a damp cloth. Cut the rhubarb into ½ inch lengths. Pack the lined basin with rhubarb then cover it with sugar and a good pinch of ginger.

FOR THE BLACKBERRY AND APPLE DUMPLING
Peel the apples and slice them finely. Fill the basin to the top with layers of sliced apples, sprinkled with sugar and a little lemon rind, and dotted with blackberries. Add the water.

FOR BOTH DUMPLINGS
Fold the lining pastry above the top of the basin over the fruit. Moisten the edge. Roll out the remaining piece of pastry for the lid. Place it in position and press the joined edges firmly together.

Cut a double thickness of greaseproof paper large enough to cover the top of the basin and come well down the sides. Make a pleat in the centre, about 1½ inches wide, to allow the pudding to rise. Grease the paper where it will touch the pudding. Cover the pudding with the paper and tie it round the basin with string.

Steam the pudding for 2 hours. Use a double steamer or a large saucepan, considerably deeper than the pudding basin, with a well-fitting lid. If you are using a saucepan, the water should be kept at a level about halfway up the sides of the pudding basin. The water should be replenished with boiling water as it evaporates.

When the pudding is ready, lift it carefully out of the pan. Remove the string and paper and loosen round the edges with a knife. Have a hot plate ready for the pudding, turn it upside down over the pudding and turn the whole thing over. This will leave the pudding the correct way up in the centre of the dish, ready for serving.

SUET PUDDING WITH LEMON AND SYRUP

FOR 6 PEOPLE

the suet pastry as in
   rhubarb or blackberry
   and apple dumpling
   (see page 108)
1 lemon
a little soft brown sugar

golden syrup
pudding basin which
   holds 2 pints of
   liquid will be
   required

Prepare the suet pastry, but do not roll it out. Brush the inside of the pudding basin with melted fat and fill it with half the pastry.

Cut both ends off the lemon and dip it in water then in soft brown sugar. Put on top of the pastry in basin and cover it with the remaining pastry.

Cover the basin with greased greaseproof paper as for the dumpling.

Steam the pudding for 2 hours, then turn it out and cover it thickly with golden syrup. Serve more syrup separately.

JAM ROLY-POLY

FOR 6 PEOPLE

the suet pastry as in
   rhubarb or blackberry
   and apple dumpling
   (see page 108)

8 oz. strongly
   flavoured jam such
   as plum, gooseberry
   or raspberry

Prepare the pastry and roll it into a rectangle on a floured board. Spread it with jam to within $\frac{1}{2}$ inch of the edges. Roll it up and press the ends down firmly. Place the roly-poly in the centre of a large sheet of kitchen foil and wrap it up with the joins of the foil on top of the roll: be sure there is no split in the foil and leave space inside for the roll to rise. Steam the roly-poly for 2 hours in a steamer or in about 1 inch of boiling water, being very careful that the joins in the foil are above the water. The water will need replenishing during the cooking. Use a fish kettle with a grid on the base if you have one as the water can then be a little deeper. Serve with extra jam.

SPOTTED DICK

FOR 6/8 PEOPLE

6 oz. currants, cleaned
12 oz. self-raising flour
good pinch of salt

5 oz. shredded suet
cold water to mix
golden syrup

pudding basin holding 2 pints of liquid will
be required

Grease the basin with melted fat and sprinkle a ring of currants on the base. Sift the flour and salt, then mix in the suet and the rest of the currants. Mix with enough cold water to make a dropping consistency and turn the mixture into the basin. Cover the basin with a double layer of greased greaseproof paper, first making a pleat in the centre to allow the pudding to rise; tie securely with string. Steam the pudding for 2 hours. Serve with hot golden syrup.

SPONGE PUDDINGS

CANARY PUDDING

FOR 5/6 PEOPLE

4 oz. margarine
4 oz. castor sugar
2 eggs
finely grated rind of
   1 lemon
6 oz. self-raising
   flour
pinch of salt

2 tablespoons milk
1 tablespoon lemon
   juice
aluminium or oven-
   proof jelly mould
   holding 2 pints of
   liquid will be
   required

TO DECORATE THE MOULD
3 glacé cherries

Brush the inside of the mould with melted fat and arrange the cherries, cut in half, round the base.

Beat the margarine to a soft cream in a warmed mixing bowl, add the castor sugar and beat again until the mixture is light in colour and texture. Beat the eggs well together then add to the mixture, a little at a time, beating well after each addition. Add the grated lemon rind. Sift the flour and pinch of salt into the mixture and fold them lightly in with the milk and lemon juice.

Turn the mixture into the prepared mould and cover it with a double layer of greased greaseproof paper, first making a pleat in the centre to allow the pudding to rise; tie securely with string. Steam the pudding for $1\frac{1}{2}$ hours. Serve with syrup, jam, cream or custard.

SYRUP SPONGE

Instead of cherries put 3 rounded tablespoons golden syrup into the basin.

JAM OR MARMALADE SPONGE

Put 3 tablespoons of jam or marmalade into the greased mould before adding the pudding mixture.

SULTANA SPONGE

Add 3 oz. sultanas to the Canary Pudding mixture with the milk and lemon juice.

GOOSEBERRY EVE'S PUDDING

two 1 lb. 2 oz. tins or
   two 1 lb. jars of
   gooseberries
4 oz. castor sugar

canary pudding
   mixture
little sifted icing
   sugar

Turn the drained gooseberries into a rectangular ovenproof dish, add $\frac{1}{4}$ pint of the juice, and sprinkle them with the sugar. Spoon the pudding mixture over the gooseberries and bake the pudding in a fairly hot oven, about *Gas Mark 6 or 400 degrees F.*, for about 30 minutes, then reduce the heat to *Gas Mark 4 or 350 degrees F.* for a further 20 minutes or until the sponge mixture is cooked. Dust the top with icing sugar rubbed through a coffee strainer.

CHOCOLATE PUDDING

FOR 5 PEOPLE

3 oz. self-raising flour
4 level tablespoons
 cocoa powder
1½ oz. softened
 margarine

3 oz. castor sugar
5 tablespoons milk
few drops of vanilla
 essence
sprinkling of castor
 sugar

FOR THE SAUCE
(during baking this sauce sinks to the bottom
of the pudding)

2 oz. soft brown sugar
2 level tablespoons
 cocoa powder
½ pint boiling water

ovenproof dish which
 holds 1½ pints of
 liquid will be
 required

Sift the flour with the cocoa. Cut the margarine into small
pieces and mix into the sifted ingredients with the castor
sugar. Stir in the milk and vanilla essence. Grease the
ovenproof dish, turn the mixture into it and spread evenly
over the surface.

Mix the soft brown sugar and the cocoa together and
sprinkle over the pudding mixture. Pour over the boiling
water.

Bake the pudding in a moderate oven, about *Gas Mark 4 or
350 degrees F.*, for 35 minutes. Sprinkle the top with castor
sugar before serving.

PINEAPPLE UPSIDE-DOWN PUDDING

This is also good made with peaches or pears

FOR 4 PEOPLE

3 oz. butter
3 oz. soft brown sugar
4½ rings of tinned
 pineapple
4 glacé cherries, halved
2 oz. margarine
2 oz. castor sugar
1 egg

3 oz. self-raising
 flour
pinch of salt
1 tablespoon milk
thick frying pan
 7 or 8 inches in
 diameter will be
 required

Melt the butter and soft brown sugar in the frying pan
over a very low heat, without allowing the mixture to boil.
Drain the pineapple and place one whole ring in the centre
of the pan and the others in halves around it, straight edges
to the sides of the pan. Place half a cherry in the centre core
of each.

Beat the margarine and castor sugar to a very soft cream.
Break the egg into a small bowl and beat it well. Beat it
gradually into the creamed mixture. Sift the flour and salt
and fold them lightly into the mixture with the milk.

Spread the mixture over the pineapple and cover the pan
closely with kitchen foil. Place the pan over the lowest
possible heat for 25 to 30 minutes. Remove the foil and
turn the pudding out, so that the pineapple is on top.

*NOTE: This is a useful pudding for "one ring"
cookery though it can equally well be baked in an
8 inch sandwich tin in a moderately hot oven,
Gas Mark 5 or 375 degrees F., for about 20 minutes.*

GRANNY'S LEMON PUDDING

FOR 4/5 PEOPLE

4 oz. butter
4 oz. castor sugar
2 eggs
4 oz. self-raising flour
good pinch of salt
the finely grated rind and
 the juice of 1 large
 lemon, or 2 small ones

½ pint milk
straight sided
 soufflé dish which
 holds 2 pints of
 liquid will be
 required

Lightly grease the soufflé dish.

Beat the butter and the castor sugar to a very soft cream.
Separate the yolks from the whites of the eggs and beat
the yolks into the creamed mixture very thoroughly. Sift
together the flour and the pinch of salt. Beat the egg
whites to a stiff froth.

Fold the flour lightly into the yolk mixture with the lemon
juice, rind and half the milk. Lightly fold in the egg whites,
then add the remaining milk. Pour the mixture into the
soufflé dish and put it straight into a moderately hot oven
at *Gas Mark 5 or 375 degrees F.* for 30 to 35 minutes. The
pudding should rise well and beneath the spongy top there
should be a creamy lemon custard.

*NOTE: If you have no soufflé dish, a pie-dish is just
as good for baking the pudding; if the dish is
shallow, the pudding will cook a little more quickly.*

Granny's lemon pudding

1   2   3   4

5   6   7

SOUFFLÉS

All soufflés are made from a thick basic mixture into which egg whites are folded to give volume and lightness. For a sweet soufflé the basic mixture can be a fruit purée, an egg-thickened custard or whipped egg yolks and sugar. It is important that the flavour is fairly concentrated.

In hot soufflés the egg whites actively raise the basic mixture. In cold soufflés their addition achieves the final volume, so the mixture is set with gelatine.

When melted gelatine is added to a mixture the mixture should be slightly warm. This will avoid any "threadiness" caused by the gelatine setting before it is properly blended.

RASPBERRY SOUFFLÉ

FOR 6 PEOPLE

two 15 oz. tins raspberries	2 large eggs, separated
juice of 1 lemon	$\frac{1}{2}$ oz. gelatine
3 oz. castor sugar	3 tablespoons water
	$\frac{1}{4}$ pint single cream

FOR THE DECORATION

2 oz. hazelnuts	scant $\frac{1}{4}$ pint double cream

a straight-sided soufflé dish holding $1\frac{1}{2}$ pints of liquid will be required

Surround the dish with a collar of doubled greaseproof paper standing 2 inches above the dish, with the folded edge at the bottom. Tie it in place—photograph 1 shows how to do this: double the string, encircle the dish, put one end of string through the loop, pull tightly and knot with other end of string.

Drain the juice from the raspberries and put aside six nice ones for the decoration. Sieve the rest and measure the purée, making it up to $\frac{3}{4}$ pint with raspberry juice. Tip the raspberry purée into a mixing bowl with the lemon juice, sugar and egg yolks—the whites are added later. Suspend the bowl over a pan of simmering water and whisk the mixture with a hand, electric or rotary beater (photograph 2).

When the mixture falling from the whisk leaves a trail over the surface—it will take about 10 minutes to arrive at this point—remove the bowl from the heat. Transfer the mixture to a pan. Dissolve the gelatine in the water in a small pan over a gentle heat, then stir it into the raspberry mixture which should still be warm so that the gelatine will blend in evenly (photograph 3). Stir in the cream. Stand the pan on a tin of ice cubes, if you have them, and stir the mixture, taking particular care to stir well over the base of the pan, as it cools and sets most quickly when directly over the ice. A metal pan is a quick conductor and the mixture will cool amazingly quickly.

When the mixture is cold and starts to thicken, take pan off the ice, beat the egg whites fairly stiffly and, using a metal spoon, stir the first spoonful of egg white briskly into the mixture—this first introduction of egg white makes it

111

much easier to incorporate the rest. Fold in the egg white very lightly with almost a flicking movement, lifting up the heavier mixture on the spoon and dropping it over the egg whites and, as the spoon is returned to the mixture, cut through the egg white (photograph 4). At this stage the mixture has thickened enough to hold the air from the egg whites evenly.

Immediately pour the mixture into the prepared dish. The paper will hold the top inch of the mixture in place while it sets. Leave the soufflé in a cold place for at least 2 hours. It will set in minutes, but not firmly enough for the paper to be removed.

DECORATING THE SOUFFLÉ

Put the hazelnuts on a baking tray in a moderately hot oven, *Gas Mark 5 or 375 degrees F.,* for a few minutes to loosen the brown skins. Turn the nuts on to a tea towel and rub off the skins. Chop the nuts fairly coarsely, spread them on the baking tray again and return them to the oven for a few minutes, turning the nuts occasionally so that they brown lightly and evenly.

Remove the paper collar from the soufflé. The easiest way to do this is to dip a palette knife into a jug of boiling water and, while the knife is still hot, slip it between the grease-proof paper and stroke round the edge of the soufflé to loosen it (photograph 5). Reheat the palette knife by dipping it into the hot water as you work round the edge. Whip the double cream lightly so that it will just hold its shape—if it should thicken too fast, whip in a few drops of milk. Spread nearly all the cream round the outside edge of the soufflé. Form the chopped nuts in a circle on a sheet of greaseproof paper and stand the soufflé in the centre. Lift the nuts on to the palette knife and stick them to the cream (photograph 6).

Fill a forcing bag, with a star pipe attached, with the rest of the cream and pipe six stars on the soufflé and top each with a raspberry.

NOTE: This soufflé can be made with any fresh, frozen or stewed fruit; $\frac{3}{4}$ pint of purée is needed— usually 1 lb. of fresh fruit.

APRICOT SOUFFLÉ

Dried apricots also make a nice soufflé. Soak 8 oz. dried apricots overnight. Next day put them into a pan with the water in which they were soaked and simmer until tender. Sieve the apricots, measure the purée and make it up to $\frac{3}{4}$ pint with juice. Then proceed as for raspberry soufflé.

ORANGE SOUFFLÉ

FOR 6 PEOPLE

4 standard eggs	$\frac{1}{4}$ pint double cream
8 oz. castor sugar	
2 oranges	1 oz. grated chocolate
1 lemon	
$\frac{3}{4}$ oz. gelatine	2 thin slices of orange
6 oz. tin creamed rice pudding	7 diamonds of angelica
2 tablespoons single cream, or top of milk	2 glacé cherries

soufflé dish holding 2 pints of liquid will be required

First prepare the soufflé dish (see raspberry soufflé on page 111).

Separate the yolks of the eggs from the whites and put the yolks into a mixing bowl with the castor sugar. Finely grate the rind of the oranges and add to the mixture. Squeeze the juice from the oranges and lemon; measure it, and if necessary make up to $\frac{1}{4}$ pint with cold water. Add half the juice to the mixture and whisk this with a rotary beater, or an electric mixer if you have one, until it is light and creamy.

Put the gelatine into a small pan with the remainder of the fruit juice and dissolve over a gentle heat without allowing it to boil. Stir this into the mixture. Sieve or blend the creamed rice, and then mix in the single cream, or top of the milk. Stir this into the mixture, which will set rapidly at this stage, so quickly beat the egg whites until stiff and fold them in. Pour into the soufflé dish; the mixture should come well above the top of the dish. Leave the soufflé in a cold place to set. It will take about an hour.

Peel off the paper collar carefully, holding a palette knife dipped in hot water behind the paper and against the edge of the soufflé (see photograph 5 of raspberry soufflé on page 111). Whisk the double cream lightly until it will just hold its shape and spread a little round the edge of the soufflé. Stand the dish on a sheet of greaseproof paper and surround it with the grated chocolate. Lift the chocolate on a palette knife on to the sides of the soufflé (in the same way as the nuts are put on the raspberry soufflé—see photograph 6 on page 111). Fill a forcing bag (with a star pipe attached) with the rest of the cream, and pipe a trellis on top, with stars to finish the edge.

Decorate with orange slices, angelica and cherries.

SOUFFLÉ GRAND MARNIER

FOR 5 PEOPLE

2 oz. butter	2 oz. castor sugar
2 oz. flour	3 eggs
$\frac{1}{4}$ pint milk	3 tablespoons (or a miniature bottle) Grand Marnier
the grated rind and flesh of one orange	

A deep, straight-sided dish which holds 2 pints of liquid will be required. The soufflé will rise better if you don't grease the dish.

Melt the butter over a gentle heat then take the pan off the heat and stir in the flour and the milk. Stir the mixture over a gentle heat until it is smooth, then keep it smooth by beating well while it is thickening. When it has thickened, take it off the heat and add the grated rind of the orange with the castor sugar. Separate the egg yolks from the whites and beat the yolks into the mixture one at a time.

Peel the orange with a very sharp knife to remove both the remaining rind and the white pith beneath, then remove the flesh from between the segments. Add this to the mixture with the Grand Marnier.

Beat the egg whites until they are light and fluffy but not too dry; they should still have a slightly moist appearance. Stir a tablespoon of the beaten egg white into the Grand Marnier mixture, then fold in the rest of the white very lightly with a metal spoon. Turn the mixture into the dish and put the soufflé into a moderately hot oven, *Gas Mark 5 or 375 degrees F.,* for 40 minutes. Serve at once.

MISCELLANEOUS HOT PUDDINGS

OLD FASHIONED MILK PUDDINGS

THE FOLLOWING PROPORTIONS WILL SERVE 4 PEOPLE

CHOOSE FROM

Carolina pudding rice	barley
flaked rice	sago
tapioca	macaroni

For a creamy consistency use 2 oz. of any of above per pint of milk, plus 1 level tablespoon of castor sugar and a knob of butter.

Rub the knob of butter round the top edge of a pie dish; this makes the pie dish much easier to wash and helps to prevent the milk boiling over should the oven get too hot. The butter also improves the flavour and food value.

Scatter your choice in the pie dish and sprinkle over the sugar. Add the milk. If liked, add a sprinkling of nutmeg. Put the pudding in a cool oven, about *Gas Mark 2 or 3 or 300 to 325 degrees F.;* long slow baking is always best, and is essential to make the pudding creamy. If you prefer the pudding more lightly set, use a little less grain or pasta.

Rice takes the longest to bake (about 2 hours), while the others will be ready in about 1½ hours.

NOTE: Tinned evaporated milk, diluted as directed on the tin, also makes good milk puddings.

BANANA JAMAICA

FOR 4 PEOPLE

8 small bananas	good pinch of ground
juice of 2 oranges	cinnamon
5 level tablespoons soft brown sugar	2 teaspoons rum
½ level teaspoon grated nutmeg	single cream to accompany the pudding

Peel the bananas and arrange them in an ovenproof dish. Mix the orange juice with the sugar, grated nutmeg, cinnamon and the rum. Pour over the bananas. Bake the pudding in a very hot oven, about *Gas Mark 8 or 450 degrees F.*, for 15 to 20 minutes. Serve single cream separately. This pudding is also good served cold.

FROU-FROU PUDDING

CARAMEL FOR LINING THE BASIN

4 oz. castor sugar	¾ pint water

PUDDING

4 egg whites (the yolks are used for the accompanying Sauce Ambrose)	5 oz. castor sugar

pudding basin holding 3 pints liquid

Heat the pudding basin so that the caramel will coat it easily.

Put the sugar and water for the caramel into a pan over a very gentle heat and dissolve the sugar slowly, without allowing the syrup to boil. When all the sugar has completely dissolved, bring the syrup to a rapid boil. Do not stir again after it has come to the boil. Watch it, and when it is a deep golden brown pour it into the warm pudding basin. Hold the basin with an oven-cloth and twist it round so that the caramel coats the basin evenly.

The basin can be lined with caramel well beforehand, even overnight if it is more convenient, but keep it in a dry place.

TO MAKE THE PUDDING

Put the egg whites into a large, clean bowl. Beat them until they will stand up in stiff peaks when the whisk is lifted from the mixture. Fold in 2 level tablespoons of the castor sugar and whisk again until the consistency is as stiff as before. Fold in the rest of the sugar and turn the mixture into the caramel-lined basin.

Cover the pudding with a double thickness of greased greaseproof paper, large enough to come well down the sides of the basin. Make a pleat, about 1½ inches deep, in the centre of the paper; this leaves room for the pudding to rise. For extra protection cover with a single layer of kitchen foil, pleating it in the same way, and pressing it to the sides of the basin without tying it.

Stand a rack—one from a roasting tin or pressure cooker would be ideal—in the base of a saucepan large enough to allow the steam to circulate and tall enough to give the pudding headroom to rise below the lid. A fish kettle could be used. Steam the pudding for 1 hour, keeping the container half-full of boiling water all the time. This pudding must be cooked at an even heat.

Turn out the pudding just before required. Although it will keep its shape well for a few minutes after it is turned out, it is really best served at once. Serve with Sauce Ambrose (see below).

NOTE: Both the pudding and the sauce are very quick and easy to make using an electric mixer.

SAUCE AMBROSE

4 egg yolks	1 or 2 tablespoons
3 oz. castor sugar	curaçao
¼ pint water	

Beat the egg yolks with a fork to mix them. Dissolve the sugar in the water over a gentle heat in exactly the same way as for the caramel for the pudding. When the sugar has dissolved boil the syrup rapidly until it is thick enough to make a thread when tested between the finger and thumb; lightly touch the surface of the cooled syrup with your second finger, press it to your thumb and pull apart quickly—a thread should form between them. This test should take place just before the syrup changes colour.

Pour the syrup gradually on to the egg yolks, beating all the time until the mixture thickens, which will take about 10 to 15 minutes. Mix in the curaçao.

This sauce will stay fluffy for several hours if you wish to make it beforehand.

APPLE AND CINNAMON PANCAKES

2 cooking apples	2 oz. castor sugar
a little oil for frying	1 level teaspoon
pancake mixture (see	cinnamon
page 71)	

Peel, core and slice the apples very thinly. Heat a little oil in the pan, pour it off and pour in enough batter to coat the base of the pan. Arrange a few slices of apple over the batter and cook the pancake over a brisk heat until the batter between the apple is set. Turn it over and cook the other side, then turn it out on to a piece of kitchen paper. Mix the sugar and cinnamon thoroughly and sprinkle the pancake with cinnamon sugar. Make the rest of the pancakes in the same way, sprinkling the cinnamon sugar between them. To reheat them, put the stack of pancakes on to a hot plate then brush them with melted butter and sprinkle with more cinnamon sugar. Heat them in a fairly hot oven, *Gas Mark 6 or 400 degrees F.*, for about 15 minutes. Serve either separately or in a stack.

NOTE: Cider used instead of water is rather nice for mixing the batter.

APRICOT MERINGUE SURPRISE

FOR 4/5 PEOPLE

3 oz. cut macaroni	16 oz. tin halved
	apricots

SAUCE

1 oz. butter	1 oz. castor sugar
1 oz. plain flour	2 egg yolks
½ pint milk	

MERINGUE

2 egg whites	4 oz. castor sugar

lightly greased ovenproof dish holding 1¾ pints of liquid will be required

Cook the cut macaroni as directed on the packet, then drain it well. Drain the apricots, reserve the juice.

Meanwhile make the sauce. Melt the butter in a saucepan over a gentle heat, take it off the heat and stir in the flour. Gradually add the milk, then stir the sauce over a gentle heat until it comes to the boil. Boil it for a few minutes. Remove the sauce from the heat and stir in the juice from the tin of apricots, the castor sugar and the egg yolks, one at a time. Reserve 8 apricot halves for the decoration, then add the rest to the sauce with the macaroni. Pour the mixture into an ovenproof dish.

Next make the meringue. Place the egg whites in a bowl and whip them stiffly until they stand in peaks. Add 2 tablespoons of the sugar and beat again until the mixture is of the same stiff consistency. Lightly fold in the rest of the sugar. Spread the meringue over the pudding, pulling it into peaks with a palette knife and then place the eight remaining apricot halves on top.

Place the pudding in the centre of a moderate oven, *Gas Mark 4 or 350 degrees F.*, for about 10 minutes until the meringue is light golden.

114

1

COLD PUDDINGS

PEACH PARADISE PUDDING

This is a quickly made pudding that requires no cooking. It can be eaten 2 hours after it is made or it will keep quite safely for a couple of days. Fresh fruit can be used instead of the tinned peaches—fresh peaches, of course, are excellent. A fruit pie filling makes a very good, quick topping if you are in a hurry.

FOR 6/8 PEOPLE

PUDDING

26 sponge finger biscuits	⅜ pint evaporated
(just under 2 packets,	milk (chilled
or you can make your	beforehand, if
own—see page 137)	possible)
raspberry jam	½ pint double cream
6 sponge cakes or a	¼ pint soured cream
6½ inch sandwich	4 oz. castor sugar
sponge (see page 137)	15½ oz. tin peach
finely grated rind and	halves
juice of 1 lemon	

MELBA SAUCE

8 oz. fresh raspberries	cake tin, with a loose
4 level tablespoons	base, 7¾ inches in
sifted icing sugar	diameter will be
	required

Line the sides of the cake tin with sponge fingers (photograph 1). Spread a little jam down the edge of each so that they stick together. You may have to trim the last one to make it fit neatly. Line the base of the tin with sponge

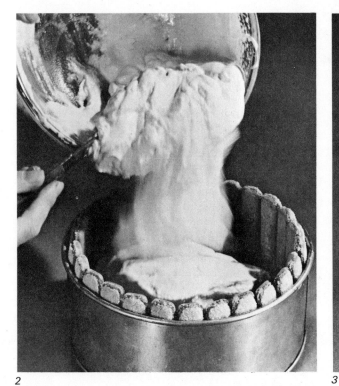

2

3

cakes, or the sandwich sponge, cutting them where necessary.

Add the lemon rind to the chilled evaporated milk and whip until it is thick and creamy (the milk whisks up more quickly if it is chilled first). Whisk the cream to the same light fluffy consistency as the evaporated milk. Stir the lemon juice, soured cream and sugar into the evaporated milk and lemon rind. Fold in the whipped cream. Pour the mixture into the lined tin (photograph 2).

Put the pudding in the refrigerator for at least 2 hours.

MELBA SAUCE

Sieve the raspberries, and then sweeten the purée with icing sugar.

TO SERVE THE PUDDING

Drain the juice off the peaches and put it into a jug to serve with the pudding. Arrange the peaches round the top of the pudding and pour the Melba sauce into the centre. To remove the cake from the tin, rest the tin on a bowl, the rim of which is smaller than the base of the cake tin. Carefully push the sides of the cake tin downwards (photograph 3) leaving the pudding standing free on the loose base of the cake tin on top of the bowl. Then put it on a pretty plate.

CARAMELLED ORANGES

FOR 4 PEOPLE

8 small oranges	few drops of cooking
8 oz. granulated sugar	oil
$\frac{1}{2}$ pint water	extra $\frac{1}{4}$ pint water for
	the sauce

TO PREPARE THE ORANGES

Peel the oranges with a very sharp knife to remove both the skin and white pith beneath. This is most easily done working spirally round the orange, using a sawing action. Slice the oranges, reassemble them, then arrange in a dish and put aside until the caramel sauce is made.

THE CARAMEL FOR THE TOP AND THE SAUCE

Put the sugar and $\frac{1}{2}$ pint of water into a fairly large pan over a very gentle heat. Stir from time to time to help the sugar to dissolve, but on no account allow the syrup to boil before every grain *has* dissolved. If there are any grains left in the sugar you will hear them crunch if you press the wooden spoon on the bottom of the pan. When all the sugar has dissolved, take the spoon out and do not put it back; the syrup must not be stirred after it has boiled or it will become opaque instead of clear. Boil the syrup as briskly as possible, without a lid, until it is a deep golden colour. Take it off the heat when it is a shade lighter than you need —remember the heat from the pan will continue to darken the caramel for a few more seconds. Meanwhile, rub an enamel tray or a baking tray with a few drops of cooking oil and, when the caramel is ready, pour half of it on to the oiled surface and leave it to cool and set. Add the extra $\frac{1}{4}$ pint of water to the rest of the caramel in the pan; stand away from it until the bubbles subside, then put it over a gentle heat for the caramel to melt with the water. Pour the caramel over the oranges; if the oranges are in a glass dish, cool the caramel first.

When the caramel in the tray has set, crush it with a kitchen weight or a rolling pin and put it into an airtight jar. Scatter it over the oranges just before serving.

PEAR AND LEMON SPONGE

FOR 5/6 PEOPLE

SPONGE FLAN BASE

4 oz. margarine	2 eggs
4 oz. castor sugar	4 oz. self-raising flour

sponge flan tin 9 inches in diameter will be required

FILLING

4 dessert pears, just under-ripe	$\frac{3}{4}$ pint water the juice of
8 oz. castor sugar	1 lemon

FLUFFY LEMON SAUCE

1 egg and 1 egg yolk	8 half slices of lemon for decoration

First make the sponge flan. Brush the inside of the flan tin very thoroughly with melted fat then dust it out with a thin layer of flour.

Have a moderately hot oven, about *Gas Mark 5 or 375 degrees F.*, ready for baking the flan.

Beat the margarine to a soft cream, add the castor sugar and beat again until it is a soft, light consistency. Add one of the eggs and beat it in very thoroughly; add the other in the same way, beating well. Lightly fold in the flour and turn the mixture into the tin. Smooth it round the sides and over the centre so that the surface is level. Bake the flan just above the centre of the oven for 25 to 30 minutes. Slip a sharp knife round the edge and turn the flan on to a wire tray to cool.

The flan case can be made beforehand; it will keep well for a day or two in an airtight tin.

Peel the pears (the easiest way is to use a potato peeler). Cut them in half and scoop out the cores with a teaspoon. Melt the sugar in the water, add the lemon juice and bring the syrup to the boil. Add the pears to the syrup and simmer them gently for about 10 minutes until they are tender. Leave until they are cold.

Put the flan on to a plate or dish and arrange the pears in the centre. Make the lemon sauce: break the egg into a bowl, add the extra yolk and $\frac{1}{4}$ pint syrup in which the pears were simmered and whisk them together over a saucepan of hot water or in a double saucepan until the sauce is light and frothy. Pour half over the pears and the rest into a sauceboat for serving.

Leave the pudding at least 2 hours; some of the froth will melt into the flan, moistening and flavouring it.

Decorate the sides of the flan with half slices of lemon, cut up to the skin and curled over the edge of the dish.

CRÈME RENVERSÉE AU CARAMEL

FOR 6 PEOPLE

4 oz. granulated sugar	1 egg yolk
4 tablespoons water	$1\frac{1}{2}$ pints milk
5 eggs	2 oz. castor sugar

straight-sided soufflé dish holding 2 pints of liquid will be required

Brush the base of the soufflé dish with cooking oil.
Dissolve the granulated sugar very slowly in the water in a pan without boiling. When *every grain* has dissolved, bring to a rapid boil and, without stirring, watch until the syrup is a rich golden brown. Then hold the pan with a thick cloth, wrapped round your hand, lift off the heat and plunge the base of the pan into cold water for a second to check the heat and prevent the caramel from darkening further. Turn it into the dish; hold the dish with a cloth and tip it from side to side so that the caramel covers the base of the dish evenly.

Break the eggs into a bowl, add the extra yolk and beat with a fork. Put the milk and castor sugar into a pan and, when almost boiling, pour the mixture on to the eggs, stirring briskly. Strain the custard into the caramel-lined dish. Leave for a few minutes for the bubbles to rise, then stand the dish in a roasting tin, pour cold water into the tin to come halfway up the dish, and cover the custard with greased, greaseproof paper. Bake in a moderate oven, about *Gas Mark 4 or 350 degrees F.*, for $1\frac{1}{4}$ to $1\frac{1}{2}$ hours. It should be just set in the centre. Lift out of the tin and leave overnight.

Next day run a knife round the top of the custard, turn a fairly deep serving dish over it and reverse the whole thing. The custard should turn out surrounded by liquid caramel. *NOTE: If you wish to serve hot, add an extra egg.*

TIPSY TRIFLE

FOR 6 PEOPLE

12 oz. sponge cake	1 pint milk
3 level tablespoons raspberry jam	1 oz. castor sugar
15 oz. tin peaches	1 egg white
2 tablespoons sherry	$\frac{1}{2}$ pint double cream
2 level tablespoons custard powder	36 ratafia biscuits
	12 glacé cherries

Cut the sponge cake into cubes, put into a glass dish and dot with raspberry jam. Open the tin of fruit and measure $\frac{1}{4}$ pint of the juice. Mix the juice with the sherry and pour it over the sponge cake. Cut the peaches neatly into cubes and scatter them over the sponge.

Blend the custard powder with a little of the measured milk to make a thin cream. Heat the rest of the milk, stir in the blended custard powder and stir over a moderate heat until it thickens and comes to the boil. Add the sugar, cool custard slightly, then pour it over the sponge and fruit. Put a plate on top of the bowl to prevent a skin forming and leave until the trifle is completely cold.

Whip the egg white stiffly. Whip the cream until it will just hold its shape, not too stiffly, then fold in the egg white. Spread this mixture over the surface and decorate the edge with biscuits and an inner circle of halved glacé cherries.

APRICOT ORANGES

FOR 6 PEOPLE

6 large oranges	$\frac{1}{2}$ pint milk
15 oz. tin apricots or fresh apricot purée	$\frac{1}{4}$ pint single cream
	$\frac{1}{4}$ oz. gelatine
3 level dessertspoons custard powder	sugar to sweeten
	$\frac{1}{4}$ pint double cream
	top of milk

Cut off the tops of the oranges and reserve; scoop out the orange flesh with a teaspoon. Put the flesh and juice aside to add later. Shave a very little off the base of each orange to make it stand firmly.

Open the tin of apricots, strain off the juice and sieve or liquidise them, making about $\frac{1}{2}$ pint purée.

Make the custard; blend the custard powder with a little of the measured milk, heat the rest of the milk then stir in the blended custard powder. Stir until the custard thickens and comes to the boil. Take it off the heat, stir in the purée and the single cream.

Take three dessertspoons of orange juice from the oranges and dissolve the gelatine in this juice in a small pan over a gentle heat. Stir this into the mixture with the flesh and remaining juice of the oranges. Sweeten to taste then pour into the orange cases. Leave in a cool place to set.

Whisk the double cream with a little top of milk to make it light and fluffy; put a spoonful on the top of each orange. Replace the lids at an angle to show some of the cream.

CHOCOLATE DREAM

FOR 6 PEOPLE

4 oz. fresh brown breadcrumbs	$\frac{1}{4}$ pint single cream
$4\frac{1}{2}$ oz. demerara sugar	$\frac{1}{2}$ pint double cream
8 level tablespoons drinking chocolate	2 oz. plain chocolate, coarsely grated
2 level tablespoons instant coffee powder	

glass dish holding $1\frac{1}{2}$ pints of liquid (a shallow one is best) will be required

Mix the brown breadcrumbs with the demerara sugar, drinking chocolate and coffee powder.

Lightly whip the creams together, then spread the base of the dish with a layer of cream. Sprinkle half the dry mixture over this and pack it down fairly firmly into the cream. Spread over a little more cream, just reserving enough for one good layer on top. Spread over the remaining crumbs, then the rest of the cream. Keep a palette knife on the surface of the pudding while spreading the cream; if you lift it the crumbs are apt to rise into the cream. Sprinkle the grated chocolate over the pudding and leave it at least 3 hours to allow the layers to combine well. The pudding can be made the day before and kept in a refrigerator.

COFFEE CREAM

FOR 4/5 PEOPLE

$\frac{1}{2}$ pint water	2 eggs
2 level dessertspoons instant coffee powder	2 oz. castor sugar
light $\frac{1}{2}$ oz. gelatine	$\frac{1}{4}$ pint double cream (half is for the decoration)
$\frac{1}{2}$ pint milk	walnut halves

Put the water, coffee powder and gelatine into a small pan over a gentle heat. When the coffee and gelatine have dissolved stir the mixture slowly into the milk.

Separate the eggs, and beat the yolks with the sugar in a bowl over a pan of hot water; the mixture should become thick and creamy. Stir in the cooled coffee mixture with

half the cream. Whip the egg whites really stiffly, then stir a tablespoon of egg white rather vigorously into the coffee mixture to accustom the mixture to it. Lightly fold in the rest. Pour into a glass dish and leave to set.

Whisk the rest of the cream until it will hold its shape. Take a piping bag, with a star pipe attached, and fill with the cream; decorate the top of the coffee pudding with lines of cream. Top with a few halved walnuts.

ICES

NOTES FOR FIRST-TIMERS

1. Freeze ice cream in ice-cube trays in their usual position in the refrigerator. Ices should be frozen as quickly as possible, as it helps to keep the ice cream texture smooth. For this reason, turn the refrigerator down to maximum coldness well before you require it for the ice mixture (remembering to turn it back to normal when the ice cream is frozen). If you do have a deep freeze or a freezing compartment in your refrigerator, it is ideal for ice cream making.

2. It helps to keep the texture smooth if the mixture is beaten twice during freezing. When it starts to freeze round the edges—after about 45 minutes—beat it well with a fork or rotary beater and put it back in the freezing compartment. Repeat the beating when the mixture freezes round the edges again.

3. Remember that ice cream mixtures should be well sweetened, as freezing reduces the effect of sweetening agents.

4. A real vanilla pod is best for flavouring a cream ice. If you have one, use it as described below, then wash and dry it and store in a jar of castor sugar—it will flavour the sugar mildly and pleasantly.

5. Water ices, or sorbets, as they are often called, should only be taken out of the refrigerator just before they are to be eaten; once out of the refrigerator they melt quite quickly.

VANILLA ICE CREAM

1 pint milk	$1\frac{1}{2}$ oz. castor sugar
vanilla pod	1 egg
1 level tablespoon custard powder	$\frac{1}{2}$ pint double cream

Heat the milk and the vanilla pod gently and allow them to infuse without boiling for about 15 minutes. Remove the pod.

Make the custard with the custard powder, milk and sugar, following the directions on the tin. Separate the egg, and beat the yolk well. Cool the custard slightly and add a tablespoon of custard to the egg yolk, then stir this into the custard.

Whip the cream fairly well, and when the custard is cool, stir it in. Beat the egg white until it will stand up in stiff peaks and fold it gently into the mixture. Put the mixture into an ice-cube tray and freeze as described in the notes above.

NOTE: If you have no vanilla pod, add a few drops of vanilla essence to the milk when making the custard.

Pineapple water ice

COFFEE ICE CREAM

2 oz. coffee beans
1 pint milk
4 oz. loaf sugar
¼ pint water

3 egg yolks
½ pint double cream,
lightly whipped

Put the coffee beans and the milk into a saucepan over a very gentle heat, and allow them to infuse without boiling for 45 minutes. Strain and cool the milk.

Dissolve the sugar and water together over a low heat, making sure every grain of sugar has dissolved before the water boils. Then boil the syrup rapidly for about 4 minutes or until it "forms a short thread." To test for this, touch the surface of the slightly cooled syrup very lightly with the third finger, press fingertip and thumb together, then separate them quickly and the syrup should form a short thread before breaking.

Beat the egg yolks, and pour the syrup very slowly on to them, beating all the time. The mixture should become rather fluffy in texture. Add the cold coffee-flavoured milk, and when this mixture is again quite cold, add the lightly whipped cream. Pour the mixture into the ice-cube tray and freeze as described in the notes on page 117.

Try adding 1½ oz. chopped glacé pineapple and 1½ oz. chopped glacé cherries when it is beaten for the second time.

PINEAPPLE WATER ICE

1 fresh ripe
pineapple, weighing
2½ lb.
¾ pint water
6 oz. castor sugar

very finely peeled
rind and juice of
1 lemon
1 egg white
strawberries for
decoration

Cut the pineapple lengthways through the leaves, cut out the hard white core and discard it. Scoop out all the fruit and chop it finely with a stainless steel knife. Keep the 2 shell halves.

Put the water and sugar into a pan with the thinly peeled lemon rind and dissolve the sugar very slowly over a gentle heat, stirring occasionally. When the sugar has dissolved, bring the syrup to a rapid boil and boil it without stirring for 5 minutes. The syrup will thicken slightly but the colour will remain clear. Strain and cool the syrup.

Add the lemon juice and chopped pineapple and pour the mixture into an ice cube tray. Leave the tray in the freezing compartment of the refrigerator until the mixture is of a slushy texture. Whip the egg white stiffly, fold it into the semi-set ice and return the ice to the refrigerator to freeze completely.

Cool the pineapple shell halves in the refrigerator, then fill them with spoonfuls of pineapple ice. Decorate with halved and whole strawberries.

LEMON OR ORANGE SORBET

¾ pint water
6 oz. castor sugar
juice and very finely
peeled rind of 3 lemons
or of 3 large oranges

½ egg white, stiffly
beaten
tuiles (see page 119)

Put the water and sugar into a pan with the lemon or orange rind, and dissolve the sugar very slowly over a gentle heat, stirring occasionally. When the sugar has dissolved, bring the syrup to the boil and boil it rapidly without stirring for 5 minutes. The syrup will thicken slightly, but the colour will remain clear. Strain and cool the syrup. Add the lemon or orange juice, pour into an ice cube tray, and place it in the freezing compartment of the refrigerator. When the sorbet is of a slushy texture, turn it into a bowl and fold in the beaten egg white. Return to the ice-cube tray to continue freezing. Serve with tuiles.

CRANBERRY FRUIT ICE

SYRUP
12 oz. loaf sugar
1½ pints water

rind and juice of
½ lemon

PURÉE
1 lb. cranberries
2 tablespoons water

3 oz. castor sugar
juice of ½ lemon

To make the syrup, put the sugar, water and lemon rind and juice into a pan over a low heat. Stir the sugar, taking care that every bit has dissolved before the water boils. Then boil the syrup rapidly for 10 minutes, strain through muslin or a fine sieve, and cool.

Stew the cranberries gently in the water for about 10 minutes or until the berries are soft. Sieve them, or put them through a vegetable mill. Stir in the sugar, lemon juice and syrup.

Pour the mixture into the ice-cube tray and freeze as described in the notes on page 117.

NOTE: This ice can be made with redcurrants, loganberries or raspberries.

INSTANT ICE PUDDING

The meringues (see page 139) can be made well in advance and stored in an airtight tin. The chocolate sauce will keep well for several days if placed in a covered dish and put in the refrigerator.

18 small meringues
  (see page 139)
2 family blocks vanilla
  ice cream

½ pint chocolate
  sauce (see below)

Line the base of a big glass bowl with half the meringues. Spoon 1 ice cream block over them and cover with a second layer of meringues. Spoon over the second ice cream block, heaping it well. Cover with the chocolate sauce.

CHOCOLATE SAUCE

This is intentionally strong in flavour, is not too sweet and blends ideally with the meringue and ice cream.

6 level tablespoons
  cocoa powder
½ pint water

6 level tablespoons
  castor sugar
2 level teaspoons
  arrowroot

Put the cocoa, water and sugar together into a pan and stir the mixture over a very gentle heat until the cocoa and sugar have dissolved. Blend the arrowroot with just enough cold water to make a thin cream and stir it into the mixture. Stir the sauce until it comes to the boil, then simmer for 2 or 3 minutes. Pour into a bowl, cover it and, when it is cold, store it in the refrigerator.

SAUCES AND TOPPINGS FOR ICE CREAM

Each recipe makes enough sauce to serve with a family block of ice cream

BUTTERSCOTCH SAUCE

2 oz. soft brown sugar
1 tablespoon golden
  syrup

1 oz. butter
4 tablespoons
  water

Dissolve the sugar, syrup and butter over a very gentle heat, and then boil them together for 3 minutes. Add the water; slowly bring the sauce to the boil and cook gently until it has blended evenly. The sauce can be served hot or cold. **Variation:** Substitute ginger syrup for golden syrup and add a tablespoon of lemon juice. When the sauce has cooled slightly add two pieces of stem ginger (chopped) and ½ oz. seedless raisins (chopped) with 2 teaspoons of rum.

MELBA SAUCE

1 lb. fresh or frozen
  raspberries

4 oz. sieved icing sugar

Sieve the raspberries through a nylon sieve and stir in the sieved icing sugar gradually.

CRÈME DE MENTHE SAUCE

¼ pint single cream
1 tablespoon crème de
  menthe liqueur

green colouring
  (optional)

Pour the cream into a jug and stir in the crème de menthe and a drop of green colouring if you are using it.

MALT CRUMB TOPPING

2 slices of fruit malt bread

Dry the slices of fruit malt loaf in the oven until they are crisp. Crush them with a rolling pin and sprinkle the crumbs over the top of the ice cream.

NUTTY CRUNCH TOPPING

4 level tablespoons
  powdered malt drink
2 level dessertspoons
  drinking chocolate

1 level dessertspoon
  instant coffee
8 walnuts

Mix the powders well. Chop the walnuts and add them to the mixture. Sprinkle over the ice cream.

TUILES

1 egg white
1 oz. butter

2 oz. castor sugar
1 oz. plain flour

Whip the egg white until it is frothy. Warm the butter slowly until it melts. Fold the castor sugar into the egg white, then add the flour alternately with the melted butter. Have at least two greased baking trays ready to bake the tuiles in batches. Put a small teaspoon of the mixture on a baking tray and work it round with the back of a spoon until it forms a round about 2 inches in diameter; there should be only a thin film of mixture. Put 6, or at the most 8, rounds on one tray because the tuiles have to be curled while they are hot, and if you bake more at a time some will become too cool to curl. Have ready a lightly oiled rolling pin on which to shape them.
Bake one tray of tuiles in a moderately hot oven, about *Gas Mark 5 or 375 degrees F.*, for between 5 and 7 minutes; they must be watched carefully as they burn easily. When the tuiles are ready, they should be golden brown.
Lift the tray out of the oven and slip a sharp knife under each wafer to loosen it. Lay the tuiles in a row over the lightly oiled rolling pin until they cool, when they will hold the shape of the rolling pin. Slip them off on to a wire tray.
Bake the rest in the same way. The mixture makes about 26.

NOTE: The tuiles are a nice accompaniment to any ice cream sweet and they keep well in an airtight tin, though they soften quickly when exposed to the air.

BREAD AND SCONES

There is something very exciting about making one's own bread . . . perhaps it is because it appeals to so many senses—there is the pleasure of watching the yeast grow almost before our eyes, there is the wonderful feel of the dough, pliable and elastic under our hands as we knead it, and then there is the glorious pungent smell which fills the whole house as the bread bakes. Finally, of course, there is the taste . . . what can possibly equal a slice of bread, hot from the oven, with a crisp golden crust, heaped with fresh butter and jam?

If you have never tried bread-making before, then I urge you now to try—it is not at all difficult, as you might imagine. Certainly it is a fairly lengthy process, though the actual handling time is fairly short, for time must be allowed for the dough to stand in a warm place so that the yeast can grow and multiply. A draught-free airing cupboard or the warming drawer of a cooker are excellent places.

I have included in this chapter a selection of different breads, and Danish pastry recipes which also require yeast dough as a base, plus some excellent tea breads and scones—everything, in fact, you will need for a delicious afternoon tea!

A BATCH OF WHOLEWHEAT BREAD

1 oz. dried yeast	1½ level tablespoons salt
2 level tablespoons soft brown sugar	3 lb. plain wholewheat flour
1½ pints water, and a little extra warm water if necessary	1 oz. butter

FOR THE GLAZE

1 egg	good pinch of salt

TO MAKE THE DOUGH

1 Put the dried yeast into a small bowl with 1 level teaspoon of the measured soft brown sugar.
2 Heat the water in a saucepan to a comfortable hand temperature *(100 degrees F.)*. This is important; if the water is cool the dough will take longer than it need to rise, if too hot it will kill the yeast.
3 Whisk half a pint of the warm water into the yeast and sugar with a fork and leave it in a warm place for the yeast to dissolve; this takes 10 to 15 minutes.
4 Add the salt and the remaining sugar to the water left in the pan; there is no need to reheat it.
5 Empty the flour from the bag on to the kitchen working surface and rub the butter lightly into the flour as seen in photograph 1 on the opposite page.
6 Form the flour into a large circular wall, making sure it is an even height all round with no breaks.
7 Pour the liquid from the pan, which should still be warm, into the centre of the ring, then pour in the dissolved yeast; by this time it should have worked a good froth on top, as seen in photograph 2.
8 Holding a palette knife in one hand, flick flour from the outside of the ring into the liquid in the centre, mixing it with the tips of your fingers with the other hand (photograph 3). Be careful not to break the wall.
9 When the liquid has absorbed enough flour to form a sticky dough, work in the rest of the flour (photograph 4). Should the dough seem dry at this stage, add a little more warm water.
10 Knead the dough for at least 5 minutes. It will change from a rough texture to an even and smooth one. The best movement is to work the outside of the dough continually to the centre.
11 Lightly grease a large bowl and drop the dough into it, cover with a greased piece of polythene or a damp tea towel and put the dough in a warm place to rise; in a warming drawer, by a solid fuel cooker, or in a warm airing cupboard is ideal. It should double in bulk in about 45 minutes. It is better to leave a dough to rise for a longer time than to increase the temperature.
12 Turn the dough on to a lightly floured working surface. Knead it lightly (photograph 5) to distribute the air evenly and give the bread an even texture, adding as little extra flour as possible to prevent altering the texture of the dough. The dough is now ready to shape.

The dough will make four 1 lb. tin loaves or one tin loaf, a plait, six rolls and three flower pot loaves, using a quarter of the dough for each.
NOTE: Steps 5 to 9 inclusive can be done in a large polythene or china bowl.

ONE POUND TIN LOAF

Grease the tin thoroughly with melted fat. Cut off a quarter of the dough, knead it to a smooth ball, and punch it out into a rectangle; the width should fit the base of the tin. Fold the dough in three (photograph 6) and drop it into the tin, fold downwards. Beat the salt into the egg and lightly brush the top of the loaf with the glaze.
Put the loaf back in a warm place to prove and regain its former bulk; this should take about twenty minutes. The loaf is ready when the dough reaches about ½ inch above the tin.
Bake the loaf just above the centre of a hot oven, about *Gas Mark 8 or 450 degrees F.*, for 20 minutes. Reduce the heat to *Gas Mark 6 or 400 degrees F.* for a further 20 minutes. Slip the loaf out of the tin, tap the base with the knuckles and if it sounds hollow the bread is ready.

WHOLEWHEAT PLAIT

Take the second quarter of dough and cut it into three equal pieces. Roll each one into a sausage shape about 14 inches long with a bulge in the middle. Put the pieces side by side and join the tops with a dab of water. Plait the three strands of dough; the plait will, of course, be thicker in the centre. Stick the ends together with water. Tuck both ends of the plait neatly beneath it. Put the plait on a greased baking tray and brush it with egg glaze. Prove the dough in a warm place until it regains its bulk; this should take about 15 minutes.
Bake the plait just above the centre of a hot oven, about *Gas Mark 8 or 450 degrees F.*, for 20 minutes, then lower the temperature to *Gas Mark 6 or 400 degrees F.* for a further 10 minutes. The bread should sound hollow when tapped on the base.

WHOLEWHEAT ROLLS

Take another quarter of the dough and cut it into six even-sized pieces. Knead each one into a ball and put it on a greased baking tray. Brush the top with egg glaze.
Prove in a warm place for 10 to 15 minutes until they regain their bulk, then bake them in a hot oven, about *Gas Mark 8 or 450 degrees F.*, for 15 to 20 minutes. Remove the loaf from the tin; the bread should sound hollow when tapped on the base.

FLOWER POT LOAVES

You will need three clean earthenware flower pots, each measuring 4 inches across the top. Brush the insides of the flower pots very thoroughly with melted fat.
Cut the last quarter of dough into three equal pieces, roll each into a ball and drop one into each flower pot. Brush the tops with egg glaze. Prove the little loaves in a warm place for 15 to 20 minutes and when they are almost at the top of the flower pots, put them into a hot oven, about *Gas Mark 8 or 450 degrees F.*, for 20 minutes. Then reduce the heat to *Gas Mark 6 or 400 degrees F.* for a further 10 to 15

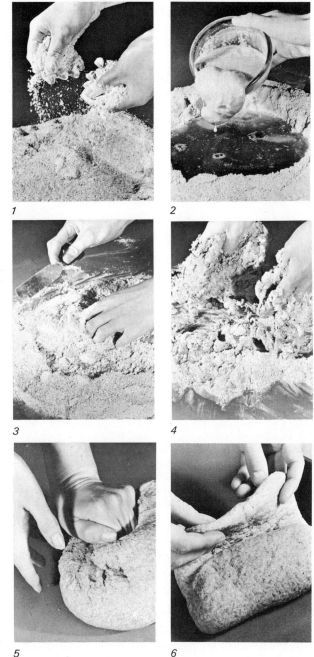

1   2
3   4
5   6

minutes. The loaves should come easily out of the pots and sound hollow when tapped on the bottom.

FARMHOUSE BREAD

Make the dough in exactly the same way as the wholewheat bread dough (page 120) but use plain white flour in place of the wholewheat flour.
The glaze is the same also.
From the dough I make one 2 lb. loaf (using half the dough), a roll cluster and a cottage loaf, using a quarter of the dough for each of these.

TWO POUND LOAF

You will need a 2 lb. loaf tin. Use half the total dough and shape, prove and bake it as described for the One Pound Wholewheat Tin Loaf on page 121, proving it for about 30 minutes and baking the loaf in a hot oven, *Gas Mark 8 or 450 degrees F.*, for 20 to 30 minutes; then reduce to *Gas Mark 6 or 400 degrees F.* for a further 25 to 30 minutes.
NOTE: Two 1 lb. tin loaves can be made with the same amount of dough. Prove and bake them in the same way as the One Pound Wholewheat Tin Loaf (page 121).

COTTAGE LOAF

Take a quarter of the total dough and from this cut off about a quarter. Knead the remainder into a smooth round and place it on a greased baking tray. Knead the small piece of dough, damp the base, and place it in the centre of the large loaf. Flour the handle of a wooden spoon and plunge it down quite deeply through the small loaf into the larger one. With a sharp knife make four slits round the top of the loaf and sprinkle it with a little flour. Prove the loaf in a warm place for 10 to 15 minutes. Bake in a hot oven, *Gas Mark 8 or 450 degrees F.*, for 20 minutes then reduce the heat to *Gas Mark 6 or 400 degrees F.* for a further 10 to 15 minutes.

ROLL CLUSTER

You will need a cake tin about $7\frac{1}{2}$ inches in diameter. Brush the inside of the cake tin with melted fat. Cut the remaining quarter of the dough into six even-sized pieces. Knead these into balls and place them in the tin, five round the edge and one in the centre. Brush the tops with egg glaze. Prove the roll cluster in a warm place for 15 to 20 minutes to regain the bulk then bake in a hot oven about *Gas Mark 8 or 450 degrees F.* for 20 minutes; lower the heat to *Gas Mark 6 or 400 degrees F.* for a further 15 to 20 minutes.

EMERGENCY BREAD

1 lb. self-raising wholewheat or plain white flour or a mixture of both	1 level teaspoon salt 1 oz. butter about $\frac{1}{2}$ pint milk

Mix the flour and salt then rub in the butter. Mix the dry ingredients to a soft dough with milk; turn this on to a greased baking tray in a round, and cross it in four with a knife.
Bake the bread in a fairly hot oven, about *Gas Mark 7 or 425 degrees F.* for 25 to 30 minutes.
NOTE: For a quick fruit bread, add 2 oz. cleaned currants and 1 oz. soft brown sugar to the dry ingredients.

DEEP-FREEZING LOAVES

If you have a deep freeze, this is ideal for storing a batch of bread until it is required. Put each loaf after it is cold into a polythene bag, exclude all the air and fasten it with a twist of paper-covered wire. Allow at least half a day to thaw the bread before use.

BRIOCHES

MAKES 10

8 oz. plain flour salt $\frac{1}{4}$ oz. dried yeast 1 level tablespoon castor sugar 3 tablespoons tepid water	2 eggs 4 oz. butter little beaten egg for the glaze 10 little brioche or queen cake tins will be required

Make the dough the day before and leave it overnight before baking.
Sift the flour and a good pinch of salt into a mixing bowl. Mix the yeast, sugar and tepid water and leave in a warm place, stirring occasionally until the yeast has dissolved.
Beat the eggs and pour them into the flour with the dissolved yeast. Melt the butter and add this as well. Beat the dough well then transfer it to a clean greased basin, cover it with a piece of polythene and leave it in a warm place until it has doubled in size; this will take about an hour. Take off the polythene and, with the back of your hand, knock back the dough into the base of the basin. Cover it again and leave it in a cool room overnight.
Next day divide the dough into ten even-sized pieces. Grease the tins well. Cut about a quarter off one of the pieces of dough and drop the larger piece into the base of a tin. Roll the small piece into a ball, cut a cross on top of the dough in the tin, and crown it with the small ball. Shape the rest in the same way.
Leave the brioches in a warm place to prove for about 20 minutes; they should rise to the tops of the tins. Brush the tops quickly with beaten egg. Bake the brioches in a hot oven, about *Gas Mark 7 or 425 degrees F.* for 15 to 20 minutes. Serve warm with butter and black cherry jam.

CHIVE AND CHEESE SCONES

$\frac{1}{2}$ lb. plain flour 1 level teaspoon bicarbonate of soda 2 level teaspoons cream of tartar pinch of salt $1\frac{1}{2}$ oz. margarine 1 rounded teaspoon finely chopped chives	$1\frac{1}{2}$ oz. cheese, finely grated just over $\frac{1}{4}$ pint milk little extra milk for the glaze cream cheese for the filling

Sift the flour, bicarbonate of soda, the cream of tartar and pinch of salt together. Rub in the margarine, then mix in the chopped chives and the grated cheese. Bind the mixture with the milk and turn it on to a well-floured board. The dough should be rather soft and only just firm enough to handle.
Roll the dough to about $\frac{1}{2}$ inch thick and cut out scones with a floured fluted cutter 2 inches in diameter. Put the scones on to a floured baking tray. Roll out the scraps and make more scones. Brush the tops of the scones with a little extra milk.
Bake the scones in a hot oven, about *Gas Mark 7 or 425 degrees F.*, for about 7 minutes until they are well risen and brown. Cool them on a wire tray and when they are cold fill them with cream cheese.

Frou-frou pudding (see page 113)

Soufflé Grand Marnier (see page 112)

A BATCH OF SCONES

The following quantities make 8 cheese scones, 8 plain scones, and 8 sultana scones

1¼ lb. plain flour	2 oz. grated cheese
1 level teaspoon salt	a pinch of cayenne
2½ level teaspoons	pepper
bicarbonate of soda	¾ pint milk
3½ level teaspoons	1½ oz. castor sugar
cream of tartar	2 oz. cleaned
4 oz. butter	sultanas

Sift the flour, salt, bicarbonate of soda and cream of tartar into a mixing bowl and rub in the butter. Put a third of this mixture into another bowl, mix in the grated cheese and the pinch of cayenne pepper, then stir in a quarter pint of the milk and form the mixture into a soft dough with as little handling as possible. Turn the dough on to a floured surface and pat it into a large round about ¾ inch thick. Cut out scones with a round cutter 2½ inches in diameter. Put the scones on a floured baking tray, gather up the scraps and use them to make another scone. Bake the scones in a hot oven, *Gas Mark 7 or 425 degrees F.*, for 10 minutes. Cool them on a wire tray.

Meanwhile add the sugar to the rest of the dry ingredients, put half of them into the other bowl, and mix them to a soft dough with another quarter of a pint of the milk. Shape the dough into two rounds and score a cross on the surface of each with the back of a floured knife, so that they are ready to break apart when they are baked. Put them on a floured baking tray.

Add the sultanas to the remaining mixture, and mix it to a soft dough with the rest of the milk. Form this dough into scones, using a floured fluted cutter 2½ inches in diameter.

Bake the sultana and the plain scones in the same way, at *Gas Mark 7 or 425 degrees F.* for 10 minutes. Cool them on a wire tray and serve them with plenty of butter.

DROP SCONES

MAKES 36 SCONES

1 lb. plain flour	3 level tablespoons
2 level teaspoons	castor sugar
bicarbonate of soda	2 eggs
3 level teaspoons	¾ pint milk
cream of tartar	

Sift the flour, bicarbonate of soda and cream of tartar into a mixing bowl and stir in the castor sugar. Break the eggs into the centre of the flour, and pour the milk into the centre. Using a wooden spoon and mixing from the centre, gradually incorporate the dry ingredients. Beat the mixture only until it is smooth—too much beating will reduce the action of the raising agent.

Meanwhile heat a griddle, moving it round over the heat so that it is evenly heated and fairly hot. Rub the surface with a little lard, then put a tablespoon of the mixture on to the griddle to test it for correct heat. After about a minute the mixture should be rising well and the bubbles bursting on the surface. Turn it over—the underside should be nicely browned—and brown the other side in the same way. Put the drop scone between a folded tea-towel to keep it moist while it cools. Once the heat of the griddle is right for one drop scone, cook as many as the griddle will hold, and cool them all in a tea-towel.

WHOLEMEAL SCONE RING

12 oz. wholemeal or	1 level teaspoon
wholewheat flour	salt
4 oz. plain flour	2 oz. margarine
2 level teaspoons	just over ½ pint
bicarbonate of soda	milk
4 level teaspoons	
cream of tartar	

Set the oven so that it will be ready for baking the scone ring. A hot oven will be required, about *Gas Mark 7 or 425 degrees F.*

Have a floured baking tray ready. Put the wholemeal flour into a mixing bowl, sift in the plain flour, the bicarbonate of soda, the cream of tartar and the salt. Rub the margarine into the mixture. Mix to a soft dough with the milk and turn it out on to the floured tray. Pat it into shape and mark the scone into eight pieces with a floured knife.

Put the scone into the oven in a fairly high position and bake it for 15 minutes, then reduce the heat to *Gas Mark 5 or 375 degrees F.* for a further 5 to 10 minutes. Break the scone and divide it into eight.

CRUMPETS

MAKES 8 OR 9 CRUMPETS

8 oz. plain flour	¼ pint plus 4
1 level teaspoon salt	tablespoons water
½ oz. dried yeast	4 egg poaching rings
½ level teaspoon	or biscuit cutters
castor sugar	(made of metal)
¼ pint milk	

An iron griddle should be used if you have one, but a large, thick frying pan or the solid plate of an electric cooker will do nicely instead.

Sift the flour and salt into a mixing bowl, then put the dried yeast and castor sugar in another bowl. Heat the milk and water together until they are comfortably warm to the touch, then pour the liquid on to the yeast and stir well.

Leave this mixture in a warm place for 10-15 minutes until the yeast has dissolved completely. Pour this into the flour and make a smooth batter. Leave the mixture in a warm place for half an hour; it should be light and frothy.

Grease the griddle and rings, then heat the griddle evenly, moving it over the heat occasionally if necessary. The griddle should be at a fairly sharp heat. Stand the rings on the griddle and pour about half an inch of batter into each one. Cook the crumpets briskly until bubbles rise to the surface and they are almost set. Remove the rings and turn the crumpets on to the other side to brown; this will only take a minute or two; most of the cooking is done on the first side.

Cool the crumpets, wrapped in a tea-towel to keep them moist and flexible until they are needed.

Toast them lightly on both sides and spread the "holey" side thickly with butter. Stack them up and keep them hot.

DANISH PASTRIES

Danish pastry is a puff pastry made with a yeast dough. If you visited the kitchens of a Danish pastry shop in Denmark, you would see a machine for rolling out the pastry. There it is rolled as many as 24 times, but in our own kitchens we content ourselves with five.

All these varieties of pastries are made with the same dough. The Danish ring uses the whole quantity but the others each need a quarter of the dough so you can make quite a nice selection with one batch, and if you are making the selection the trimmings can be used up to make some Short Plaits.

BASIC DOUGH

$\frac{1}{2}$ oz. dried yeast
1 oz. castor sugar
$\frac{1}{2}$ pint milk
1 lb. plain flour

good pinch of salt
1 egg
9 oz. butter

Put the dried yeast into a bowl with a teaspoon of the castor sugar. Heat the milk until it is comfortably warm to the touch; this is just a little above blood heat. Pour half the milk over the yeast and mix it thoroughly with a fork. Leave it on one side for about 10 minutes until a good froth has formed on the surface.

Meanwhile, sift the flour with the pinch of salt into a mixing bowl and add the rest of the sugar. Make a hollow in the centre of the flour and pour in the rest of the milk. Beat the egg and add this as well, then pour in the frothy yeast and milk mixture. Using your hand, stir well from the centre so that you gradually mix in the flour. The dough should be elastic but not sticky; if necessary add an extra dusting of flour. Turn the dough on to a floured surface and knead it for 2 or 3 minutes. Return it to the floured bowl, cover it with a damp cloth and leave it to rise for about 20 minutes until it has doubled in bulk.

Lightly flour the working surface, turn the dough on to it and knead it lightly, then roll it into a rectangle about 12 inches long and 10 inches wide; this will be about "finger thickness".

The butter should be the same consistency as the dough. The best way to ensure this is to take the butter out of the refrigerator, unwrap it, add the ounce to the half pound, put it between two butter papers, and beat it with a rolling pin to about a $\frac{1}{4}$ inch in thickness. This softens the butter without making it oily.

Lay the dough with one of the short sides towards you and put the butter squarely on the two-thirds of the dough farthest from you. Leave a border of pastry round the butter so that you can later seal the butter inside the dough. Fold the unbuttered third of dough to the middle as seen in photograph 1, and brush off any flour. Bring the top third of the dough down, complete with its butter, brush off any flour, and seal the edges by pressing them firmly with the rolling pin (photograph 2). Press the rolling pin three times one way and twice the other way across the dough; this distributes the air inside evenly.

Turn the dough so that the fat-folded side is to your right, and roll it out to an even thickness. Fold the dough in three, seal it, turn it, and roll it out again as before.

If the butter begins to soften and come through the dough, rest the dough for 30 minutes in a polythene bag in the refrigerator. Sometimes the dough becomes "tired" and will not roll out properly. Then, too, it improves with a rest in the refrigerator.

Fold and roll the dough five times in all. This distributes the butter and air in layers. These layers can be seen clearly in photograph 3, where we show the dough cut in half. At this stage the dough can be used, though it improves by being wrapped in polythene and rested in the refrigerator for half an hour.

As the pastries are best used the day they are baked, it may be more convenient to keep the dough, wrapped in polythene, overnight in the refrigerator; it will gain in bulk. If you are lucky enough to have a deep freeze the dough or the fresh baked pastries freeze beautifully. Allow the dough half a day to thaw slowly at room temperature or overnight in the refrigerator. The baked pastries only take about 2 hours to thaw; open the bag and separate them because of their stickiness.

NOTE: If you can get it and prefer to use fresh yeast, use 1 oz. for this quantity.

APPLE TURNOVERS

quarter of the basic dough (see left)
4 level teaspoons apple purée
egg glaze (as for Danish Ring, page 129)

1 oz. castor sugar
1 level teaspoon ground cinnamon

Roll the dough into a square about $\frac{1}{4}$ inch thick. Trim all edges cleanly. Cut the dough into four 4 inch squares.

1

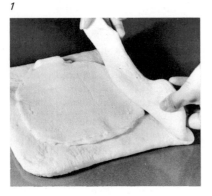

2

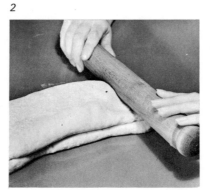

3

Leave the trimmings on one side for the Short Plaits in the last recipe (see page 129).

Spread the centre of one diagonal half of each square with one level teaspoon of the apple purée and brush all the edges with the egg glaze (see photograph). Fold the uncovered halves of the pastry over the filling to form a triangle and seal the edges well.

Mix the castor sugar with the cinnamon and dust each turnover liberally with the cinnamon and sugar. Then put them on a lightly floured baking tray and leave in a warm place to prove for 10-15 minutes. Bake them on the shelf above the centre of fairly hot oven, *Gas Mark 6 or 400 degrees F.*, for about 15 minutes.

WINDMILLS

quarter of the basic dough (see page 126)	half the glacé icing used for the Danish Ring
egg glaze (as for Danish Ring, page 129)	little redcurrant jelly
sugar glaze (as for Almond Apricots, below)	

Roll out the dough, trim all the edges cleanly, and cut the dough into four 4 inch squares. Make four diagonal cuts in each square, each one from a corner almost to the centre. Fold one cut half of a corner to the centre and repeat with alternate halves (shown in photograph), pressing them to secure them. Put the Windmills on a lightly floured baking tray and leave them in a warm place to prove for about 10-15 minutes. Brush them with egg glaze then bake them on the shelf above the centre of a moderately hot oven, *Gas Mark 6 or 400 degrees F.*, for about 15 minutes. While they are still warm, brush them well with sugar glaze. When the Windmills are quite cold place a little glacé icing and a spot of redcurrant jelly in the middle of each.

ALMOND APRICOTS

quarter of the basic dough (see page 126)	little beaten egg
½ oz. ground almonds	8 apricot halves
3 level teaspoons castor sugar	egg glaze (as for Danish Ring, page 129)
2 level teaspoons icing sugar, sifted	

FOR THE SUGAR GLAZE

4 level tablespoons castor sugar	2 level tablespoons milk

Roll out the dough into an 8 inch square, trim the edges, leaving the trimmings aside for the Short Plaits recipe (page 129), and cut the dough into four 4 inch squares.

Mix the ground almonds with the castor sugar and the sifted icing sugar. Add a little of the beaten egg and form the almond paste into a ball. Divide the almond paste into four and roll each quarter into a small roll. Put a roll diagonally across each square of dough with a half of apricot at each end. Egg glaze the opposite corners of pastry, then fold one corner over the almond roll then the other corner over the top (see photograph) allowing the apricot halves still to show at each end. Brush the pastries

Apple turnovers

Above: windmills
Below: almond apricots

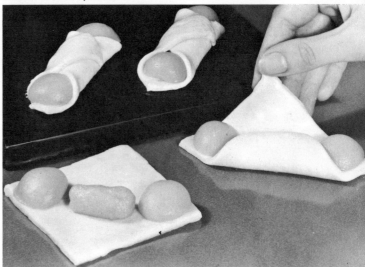

Cheese squares—1   2

with egg glaze, then place them on a lightly floured baking tray and leave them in a warm place to prove for 10-15 minutes. Bake the Almond Apricots on the shelf above the centre of a fairly hot oven, *Gas Mark 6 or 400 degrees F.,* for about 15 minutes until they are golden brown. Brush each pastry well with sugar glaze while it is still warm.

To make the sugar glaze, put the castor sugar and milk into a saucepan and dissolve the sugar over a gentle heat. When it is dissolved, bring the glaze to the boil and allow it to boil rapidly for a minute.

CHEESE SQUARES

quarter of the basic dough (see page 126)	**1 oz. almonds, shredded**
3 oz. cream cheese	**sugar glaze (as for**
1 oz. sultanas	**Almond Apricots,**
egg glaze (as for Danish Ring, page 129)	**page 127)**

Roll out the dough into an oblong 12 inches by 8 inches. Trim the edges and leave the trimmings on one side for the Short Plaits recipe (page 129). Mix the cream cheese with the sultanas and spread this mixture down the middle third of the length of the pastry (see photograph 1). Fold the pastry into three lengthways and egg glaze it all over,

Double cartwheels

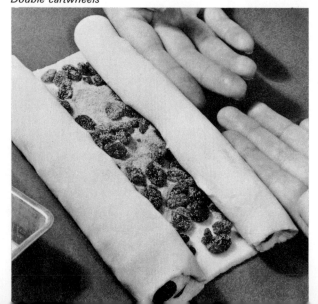

then, using a sharp pointed knife, cut slits into the pastry at 1 inch intervals, only cutting through the top two-thirds of the dough as far as the filling. Sprinkle the pastry with the shredded almonds then cut it into 5 even pieces (see photograph 2).

Put the squares on to a lightly floured baking tray and leave in a warm place to prove for 10-15 minutes. Bake the pastries, on the shelf above the centre of a moderately hot oven, *Gas Mark 6 or 400 degrees F.,* for 15-20 minutes. While the Cheese Squares are still warm, brush them well with sugar glaze.

DOUBLE CARTWHEELS

quarter of the basic dough (see page 126)	**sugar glaze (as for Almond Apricots,**
1 oz. castor sugar	**page 127)**
1 level teaspoon ground cinnamon	**a 7½ inch square tin, lightly greased**
1 oz. currants or sultanas	

Roll the pastry into an oblong 12 inches by 8 inches. Trim the edges and leave the trimmings for the Short Plaits recipe (page 129). Mix the castor sugar, cinnamon and currants together and sprinkle over the surface of the pastry, leaving a ½ inch border all the way round.

Roll up the two 8 inch sides of dough to meet in the middle (see photograph), then cut the dough into 7 equal pieces. Lay the pieces flat-side down in the tin and leave them in a warm place to prove for about 10 minutes.

Bake the double cartwheels in the shelf above the centre of a fairly hot oven, *Gas Mark 6 or 400 degrees F.,* for about 15 minutes. Brush them well with sugar glaze immediately they come out of the oven.

CARTWHEELS

dough and ingredients as for the Double Cartwheels (see above)

Roll the dough out into a long strip about 16 inches by 3 inches, making one end slightly thicker. Mix the sugar with the cinnamon and sultanas and sprinkle this over the length of the dough, leaving a ½ inch border down each side. Then, starting from the thicker end, roll the pastry up.

Cut the roll carefully into 8 even pieces and lay each piece on a lightly floured baking tray. Leave the tray in a warm place for about 10 minutes to prove, then cook on the shelf above the centre of a moderately hot oven, *Gas Mark 6 or 400 degrees F.*, for about 15 minutes. While the cartwheels are still hot brush them well with the sugar glaze.

DANISH RING

basic dough (see recipe on page 126)	egg glaze (an egg beaten with 1 teaspoon of cold water and a pinch of sugar)
4 tablespoons lemon curd	
1½ oz. cleaned currants	
	sprinkling of castor sugar

FOR THE GLACÉ ICING

3 oz. sifted icing sugar	a ring mould which will hold 3 pints of liquid
little water	
drop of vanilla essence	

Brush the inside of the ring mould with a little melted fat. Cut the dough in half. Roll one half into a round and place it over the greased ring; keep the round covering the edge and do not let it slip into the middle. Cut a hole in the centre and press into the ring until evenly lined.

Spread the lemon curd round the base of the lined ring and sprinkle it with the currants. Cut the rest of the dough into seven equal pieces and roll each piece out into a long strip, then roll up each strip.

Place pieces at equal intervals in the lined ring. Stand the ring in a warm place to prove; this will take 20-30 minutes. The yeast mixture should almost fill the tin. Brush the ring with egg glaze then sprinkle the top with castor sugar.

Bake the ring in a hot oven, at *Gas Mark 7 or 425 degrees F.*, for 15 minutes, then reduce the heat to *Gas Mark 5 or 375 degrees F.* for a further 25-30 minutes. Loosen the edges of the ring with a sharp knife and leave the ring in the tin for about 10 minutes before turning it out carefully on to a wire rack to cool. When the ring is cold, mix the sifted icing sugar to a thick consistency with a little water and the vanilla essence and spoon the icing round the roll.

SHORT PLAITS

quarter of the basic dough or the trimmings from the other shapes	sugar glaze (as for Almond Apricots, page 127)
egg glaze (as for Danish Ring, above)	half the quantity of glacé icing used for the Danish Ring (see above)
½ oz. currants	

Divide the dough into three equal portions and roll each portion into a long roll of about 14 inches (the length depends on the amount of trimmings being used). Secure the three rolls together at one end then plait them together. Brush with egg glaze, sprinkle with currants. Cut into 4 inch lengths and place them on a lightly greased baking tray. Leave the tray in a warm place to prove for about 10 minutes before baking them on the shelf above the centre of a fairly hot oven, *Gas Mark 6 or 400 degrees F.*, for about 15 minutes. While the plaits are still warm, brush them with glaze. When cold, spoon a little icing over each.

TEA BREADS

CURRANT BREAD

1 lb. plain flour	1 level teaspoon castor sugar dissolved in ½ pint warm water
2 oz. currants, cleaned	
2 oz. castor sugar	
1 level teaspoon salt	2 level teaspoons dried yeast
	a 2 lb. loaf tin

Sift the flour and add the currants, castor sugar and salt; put in a warm mixing bowl and leave in a moderately hot place. Sprinkle the dried yeast over the sweetened warm water, stir well and leave in a warm place until frothy.

Add the liquid to the flour and mix, then turn on to a floured board and knead the dough well. Grease the basin and drop the dough into it, cover with greased polythene or a damp cloth and leave to rise until it has doubled in bulk. Turn the dough on to a floured board and knead it into the shape of the tin. Grease the tin and drop the dough in and leave to prove; it should rise to within ½ inch of the top of the tin. Bake in a hot oven, about *Gas Mark 8 or 450 degrees F.*, for 20 minutes. Lower heat to *Gas Mark 6 or 400 degrees F.* and cook for a further 15-20 minutes.

CURRANT WHOLEMEAL

1 lb. wholemeal flour	4 level teaspoons dried yeast
2 oz. currants, cleaned	
2 oz. castor sugar	1 level teaspoon castor sugar, dissolved in ½ pint warm water
1 level teaspoon salt	
	a 2 lb. loaf tin

Sift the flour and add the currants, the castor sugar and salt and leave in a warm place.

Sprinkle the dried yeast over the warm sweetened water, stir and leave in a warm place to dissolve, and until frothy. Add the liquid to the flour and turn the dough on to a floured board and knead well. Grease the basin and put the dough back again, cover with greased polythene or a damp cloth and leave until it has doubled in bulk. Turn it out again and knead lightly into the shape of the tin and drop in. Leave in a warm place until it has risen to within ½ inch of the top of the tin.

Bake in a hot oven, *Gas Mark 8 or 450 degrees F.*, for 25 minutes, then reduce the heat to *Gas Mark 6 or 400 degrees F.*, for a further 20 minutes.

BANANA BREAD

14 oz. plain flour	2 oz. margarine
1 level teaspoon bicarbonate of soda	8 oz. castor sugar
1½ level teaspoons baking powder	4 bananas
	little milk if required
2 oz. lard	a 2 lb. loaf tin

Sift the flour, bicarbonate of soda and baking powder. Rub in the lard and margarine and add the castor sugar.

Mash the bananas thoroughly and stir them into the mixture with enough milk, if required, to make a dropping consistency. Grease the tin and turn the mixture into it. Hollow out the centre slightly; bake in a moderate oven, *Gas Mark 4 or 350 degrees F.*, for ¾ hour. Reduce to *Gas Mark 3 or 325 degrees F.* for a further hour.

RICH FRUIT LOAF

4 level teaspoons dried yeast	3 oz. almonds, finely chopped
1 level teaspoon castor sugar dissolved in ⅜ pint warm milk	1½ oz. chopped mixed peel
1 lb. plain flour	2 oz. seedless raisins
a good pinch of salt	1 oz. angelica, chopped
4 oz. margarine	finely grated rind of ½ lemon
2 oz. castor sugar	2 eggs
1 oz. glacé cherries, cut in quarters	a 2 lb. loaf tin

Sprinkle the yeast on to the warm sweetened milk and leave it in a warm place until frothy.

Sift the flour with the pinch of salt. Rub the margarine into the flour and stir in the sugar, cherries, almonds, mixed peel, raisins, angelica, and lemon rind. Beat the eggs well and add them to the mixture together with the yeast liquid. Beat thoroughly. Leave the dough in the bowl, covered with greased polythene or a damp cloth, and put in a warm place to double in bulk. Turn the dough on to a heavily floured board and cut it into three. Plait these pieces together and drop them into the greased tin. Prove in a warm place; it should rise to within ½ inch of the top. Bake the loaf in a fairly hot oven, about *Gas Mark 6 or 400 degrees F.*, for 35-40 minutes. Turn on to a wire tray.

CHEESE LOAF

1 lb. plain flour	1 level teaspoon castor sugar dissolved in ½ pint warm water
1 level teaspoon salt	
1 level teaspoon dry mustard	4 oz. cheese, grated
½ level teaspoon paprika pepper	a 2 lb. loaf tin
2 level teaspoons dried yeast	

FOR THE TOP OF THE LOAF
little milk	1 oz. cheese, grated
1 teaspoon celery salt	

Sift the flour, salt, mustard and pepper into a warm bowl. Sprinkle the dried yeast over the warm sweetened water and leave it in a warm place until frothy.

Stir the grated cheese into the flour. Add the dissolved yeast and, using your hand, mix the dough until it is firm and it leaves the sides of the basin clean. Turn on to a floured board and knead thoroughly. Grease the bowl and return the dough to it. Cover with a damp cloth and leave in a warm place until it has doubled in bulk. Turn it out again and knead it lightly, shaping it to the size of the tin. Grease the tin and drop the bread into it. Leave the loaf in a warm place to prove; it should rise to within ½ inch of the top of the tin. Brush the top lightly with milk and sprinkle with celery salt and grated cheese, then put loaf into a hot oven, *Gas Mark 8 or 450 degrees F.*, for 20 minutes. Lower to *Gas Mark 6 or 400 degrees F.* for a further 10-15 minutes.

APRICOT AND WALNUT LOAF

2 level teaspoons dried yeast	4 oz. castor sugar
1 level teaspoon castor sugar stirred into ½ pint of warm water	4 oz. dried apricots, finely chopped
	2 oz. walnuts, chopped
1 lb. plain flour	a 2 lb. loaf tin
1 oz. margarine	

Sprinkle the dried yeast over the sweetened warm water. Stir well, leave it in a warm place until frothy.

Sift the flour and rub in the margarine. Add the castor sugar, chopped dried apricots and walnuts.

Add the yeast mixture and beat very well, then turn it on to a floured board and knead thoroughly. Grease the bowl and return the dough to it, covering it with a damp cloth and leaving it in a warm place to rise until it has doubled in bulk. Turn it again on to a floured board and knead it lightly to the shape of the loaf tin. Grease the tin and drop in the dough. Leave the loaf in a warm place to prove until it has risen to within ½ inch of the top of the tin.

Bake the loaf in a moderately hot oven, about *Gas Mark 6 or 400 degrees F.*, for 30 minutes. Slip a piece of paper over the loaf and continue baking for a further 15 minutes.

ORANGE AND RAISIN LOAF

14 oz. plain flour	8 oz. castor sugar
1 level teaspoon bicarbonate of soda	grated rind and juice of 1 orange
1½ level teaspoons baking powder	12 oz. seedless raisins, cleaned
2 oz. lard	little milk
2 oz. margarine	a 2 lb. loaf tin

Sift the flour, bicarbonate of soda and baking powder. Rub in the lard and margarine, then mix in the sugar, grated orange rind, and raisins. Put the orange juice into a measuring jug and make up to scant ½ pint with milk. Stir into mixture to dropping consistency. Grease tin and turn mixture in.

Make a hollow in the centre of the loaf and bake in a moderate oven, about *Gas Mark 4 or 350 degrees F.*, for 45 minutes. Lower the heat to *Gas Mark 3 or 325 degrees F.* for a further hour to 1 hour 15 minutes. Cool the loaf.

SULTANA MALT LOAF

1 lb. self-raising flour	4 level tablespoons malt extract
2 level teaspoons bicarbonate of soda	½ pint milk
8 oz. sultanas	2 eggs
4 level tablespoons golden syrup	a 2 lb. loaf tin

Sift the flour and bicarbonate of soda and add the sultanas. Melt the syrup, malt extract and milk together. Beat the eggs and add them to the mixture with the liquid. Grease tin and pour in mixture. Bake in a moderately hot oven, *Gas Mark 5 or 375 degrees F.*, for an hour.

CAKES AND BISCUITS

Every now and again our lives are punctuated with happy reasons for celebrating—birthdays, family gatherings, exams passed, anniversaries of some kind. This chapter includes several recipes for unusual, attractively decorated celebration cakes to honour these occasions. None of the recipes—even for the impressive Daisy Wedding cake—is too difficult for fledgling cooks. And there are lots of other exciting recipes too for everyday cakes and teatime treats to delight your friends and please your family.

EVERYDAY CAKES

CHERRY CAKE

12 oz. glacé cherries	2¼ level teaspoons
6 oz. butter	baking powder
6 oz. castor sugar	pinch of salt
3 eggs	1 tablespoon
10 oz. plain flour	milk

a cake tin 7 inches in diameter will be required

Brush the cake tin with melted fat then line it with grease-proof paper. To do this, stand the tin on a doubled piece of greaseproof paper and draw round the base. Cut round the circle just inside the line so that each piece will fit the tin exactly. For the sides, cut a strip of doubled grease-proof paper, long enough to go round the inside of the tin and at least an inch more than its depth. Make a 1 inch fold along the edge of the paper and make slanting cuts to the crease, about an inch apart. Fit one of the greaseproof paper rounds into the base of the tin then brush it with melted fat. Insert the side strip with the slit edge neatly fitting round the base of the tin. Put in the second round of paper and brush the paper lining with melted fat.

First rinse the glacé cherries in warm water to remove the stickiness which is apt to make them slip to the bottom of the cake. Dry them very thoroughly in a clean tea towel and cut them in half.

Beat the butter to a soft cream, add the castor sugar and continue beating until the mixture is light in colour and texture. Add an egg to the mixture and beat very thoroughly indeed. Add the other eggs in the same way, beating really well between each addition. Sift the flour with the baking powder and pinch of salt. Toss the cherries in a tablespoon of the flour to coat them thoroughly; this also helps to prevent them from slipping to the bottom. Lightly fold in the flour, glacé cherries and the milk.

Put the mixture into the prepared tin, smooth over the surface and hollow out the centre slightly.

Bake the cake in the centre of a moderate oven, about *Gas Mark 4 or 350 degrees F.*, for 1¾ hours. The cake is ready when a warmed thin skewer pushed into the centre comes out clean.

Turn the cake on to a wire tray to cool, and remove the greaseproof paper.

DUNDEE CAKE

3 oz. raisins, cleaned and stoned	1 level teaspoon baking powder
1 oz. glacé cherries	6 oz. butter
3 oz. currants, cleaned	6 oz. castor sugar
3 oz. sultanas, cleaned	finely grated rind
1½ oz. chopped mixed peel	of 1 orange
1½ oz. ground almonds	2 eggs
7 oz. plain flour	1 tablespoon milk
	7 blanched almonds, halved

a cake tin 6 inches in diameter will be required

Brush the tin with melted fat or cooking oil and line it with greaseproof paper. Brush the paper lining with melted fat or oil also.

Chop the raisins and quarter the cherries and mix them with the rest of the fruit. Add the ground almonds and stir them evenly through the fruit. Sift together the flour and baking powder. Beat the butter to a soft cream and then add the castor sugar and the grated orange rind. Beat them together until they are soft and fluffy. Break the eggs one at a time into a cup to make sure they are fresh, then beat them well together. Add a little egg at a time to the creamed mixture, beating well after each addition. When the egg has been added, lightly stir in the flour with the milk and finally mix in the dried fruit. Put the mixture into the prepared tin and smooth over the surface. Hollow out the centre fairly deeply so that the cake will rise evenly.

Bake the cake in a warm oven, about *Gas Mark 3 or 325 degrees F.*, for $1\frac{1}{2}$ to 2 hours. After 30 minutes open the oven door carefully and arrange the halved almonds round the top of the cake; shut the door slowly to avoid causing a draught. Test the cake after about $1\frac{1}{2}$ hours' cooking, as ovens do vary. Pierce the centre of the cake with a warmed thin skewer or knitting needle; if it comes out clean, the cake is ready, but if any of the mixture adheres to the skewer bake the cake a little longer. Turn the cake on to a wire tray and remove the greaseproof paper.

NOTE: This cake keeps well, and it makes a good choice for a birthday or Christmas cake for those not fond of a dark fruit cake.

SEED AND CITRON CAKE

4 oz. butter	1 level dessertspoon
3 level dessertspoons	caraway seeds
golden syrup	2 oz. citron peel
3 oz. castor sugar	1 tablespoon
2 eggs	lemon juice
6 oz. plain flour	1 tablespoon milk
2 level teaspoons	5 slivers of
baking powder	citron peel
pinch of salt	

a cake tin 6 inches in diameter will be required

Brush the cake tin with melted fat or oil and line it with greaseproof paper, then brush the paper lining with melted fat or oil also.

Beat the butter to a soft cream, then beat in the golden syrup and castor sugar. Break the eggs separately into a cup to make sure they are fresh, then beat them well together. Add a little egg to the creamed mixture and beat it in well, then add the rest in the same way, beating it very thoroughly after each addition.

Sift the flour, baking powder and salt together and stir in the caraway seeds. Chop the citron peel and mix it with the flour. Stir the flour lightly into the cake mixture with the lemon juice and milk. Turn the mixture into the lined tin and smooth it over the surface then hollow out the centre slightly. Arrange the slices of citron round the top.

Bake the cake just above the centre of a warm oven, about *Gas Mark 3 or 325 degrees F.*, for between $1\frac{1}{2}$ hours and 1 hour 40 minutes. Test the cake to see if it is cooked by piercing the centre with a warmed thin skewer; if it comes out clean the cake is ready, but if any of the mixture sticks to the skewer bake the cake a little longer.

Cool the cake on a wire tray and remove the greaseproof paper.

CUT-AND-COME-AGAIN CAKE

12 oz. plain flour	6 oz. sultanas, cleaned
a good pinch of salt	5 oz. stoneless raisins,
$\frac{1}{4}$ level teaspoon	cleaned
ground cinnamon	2 oz. glacé cherries,
$\frac{1}{4}$ level teaspoon	chopped
ground nutmeg	1 oz. finely chopped
$\frac{1}{2}$ level teaspoon	candied peel
mixed spice	grated rind of 1
$2\frac{1}{2}$ oz. margarine	lemon
6 oz. soft brown sugar	$\frac{1}{2}$ pint milk
6 oz. currants,	1 level teaspoon
cleaned	bicarbonate of soda

a cake tin 7 inches square will be required

Brush the cake tin with melted fat or cooking oil, then line it with greaseproof paper. Brush the paper lining with fat. Sift together the flour, pinch of salt, ground cinnamon, ground nutmeg and mixed spice. Rub in the margarine, then mix in the soft brown sugar. Mix all the fruit with the lemon rind, then stir it into the mixture.

Make a hollow in the centre of the dry ingredients, add all but 2 tablespoons of the milk, and stir lightly. Heat the 2 tablespoons of milk to blood heat, pour it on to the bicarbonate of soda, then stir this into the mixture. Now mix all the ingredients very thoroughly *without actually beating*. Turn the mixture into the lined tin, smooth over the surface then hollow out the centre slightly. Bake the cake for 1 hour in a moderate oven, *Gas Mark 4 or 350 degrees F.*, then turn the heat down and bake it for another hour at *Gas Mark 3 or 325 degrees F.* Turn the cake on to a wire tray and remove the greaseproof paper.

SULTANA CAKE

6 oz. butter	6 oz. plain flour
5 oz. castor sugar	pinch of salt
2 large eggs	9 oz. sultanas
finely grated rind of	1 level teaspoon
1 lemon	baking powder

a cake tin 7 inches square will be required

Brush the tin with melted fat or oil. Line the tin with greaseproof paper and brush the paper lining also.

Beat the butter to a soft cream, add the castor sugar and beat again till the mixture is light in texture. Break the eggs one at a time into a cup to make sure they are fresh, then beat them well together. Beat a little of the egg into the mixture. Add the rest of the egg by degrees, beating well after each addition. Beat in the grated lemon rind. Sift the flour, salt and baking powder and fold them lightly into the mixture. Mix in the sultanas. Turn the mixture into the prepared tin and smooth over the surface. Hollow out the centre slightly, then bake in centre of a moderate oven, *Gas Mark 4 or 350 degrees F.*, for about $1\frac{1}{4}$ hours or until the cake is cooked when tested with a skewer. Pierce the centre of the cake with a warmed thin skewer; if it comes out clean the cake is cooked, but if some of the mixture has adhered to the skewer bake the cake a little longer.

Turn the cake on to a wire tray to cool and remove the greaseproof paper.

Cutlet pie (see page 97)

Wholewheat tin loaf, wholewheat plait, flower pot loaves
(see page 120)

Loaves (pages 129–130): cheese, currant wholemeal, banana, currant, rich fruit, wholewheat, orange and raisin, sultana malt, farmhouse, apricot and walnut

SPONGE CAKES

SPONGE FINGERS

MAKES 24

1 egg and 1 egg yolk	few drops of vanilla
2 oz. castor sugar	essence
½ oz. butter, melted	dusting of castor
4 oz. self-raising flour	sugar

a large forcing bag and a ½ inch round pipe

Have ready an oiled and floured baking tray.

Put the egg, egg yolk and castor sugar into a mixing bowl, and suspend it above a pan of hot, not boiling, water. Whisk until the mixture is light, creamy and thick. Take the pan off the heat and beat for a few more seconds. Run the melted butter down the side of the basin, sift in the flour and add the vanilla, then fold these lightly into the mixture. Put the mixture into the piping bag with the ½ inch round pipe attached, and pipe out fingers of sponge mixture about 2½ inches long on to the prepared baking tray. Sprinkle them with castor sugar.

Put the fingers straight into a hot oven, about *Gas Mark 7 or 425 degrees F.*, just above the centre for 7 minutes.

SANDWICH SPONGES

2 large eggs	1 level teaspoon
2 oz. castor sugar	baking powder
2 oz. plain flour	

two sandwich tins each 6½ inches in diameter

Brush the tins with melted fat, then line the base of each with a piece of greaseproof paper. Brush the paper with fat. Heat the oven at *Gas Mark 5 or 375 degrees F.* so it will be moderately hot for the baking of the sponges. It is important that the sponges are baked immediately they are mixed.

Break the eggs, one at a time, into a cup to make sure they are fresh, then put them into a bowl and break them up with a wire whisk. Mix in the castor sugar.

Sift the flour and baking powder on to a piece of paper. Have a large pan ready, half filled with boiling water. Take it off the heat and place the bowl over it so that the base of the bowl is suspended in the steam without actually touching the water. Beat the mixture with a wire or rotary whisk until it leaves a clear thick trail when the whisk is lifted from the bowl. This will take about 8 to 10 minutes with a wire whisk, less with a rotary whisk. Lift the bowl off the heat, stand it on a damp cloth to prevent it from slipping and beat for a further 2 minutes.

Sift the flour again, this time straight into the mixture, and with a metal spoon lightly fold it in, working the mixture as little as possible. As soon as the flour is folded in, divide the mixture evenly between the two prepared tins. Tilt the tins to level the surface and do not disturb the air bubbles. Put straight into the oven and bake for 15 minutes.

When the sponges are ready, take them out of the oven, slide a sharp knife round the inside of the tins and turn them on to a wire tray to cool. Remove the greaseproof paper and fill them with whipped cream or jam.

Danish pastries (see page 126): double cartwheels, almond apricots, cartwheels, short plaits, Danish ring, windmills, cheese squares, apple turnovers

SWISS ROLL

2 large eggs	little extra castor
2 oz. castor sugar	sugar
2 oz. plain flour	8 oz. red jam
1 level teaspoon	
baking powder	

a Swiss roll tin 8 inches by 12 inches

Brush the inside of the tin with melted fat or oil. Cut a rectangle of greaseproof paper an inch larger all the way round than the base of the tin, then centre the tin on the paper and draw round it. Fold the paper up along the pencilled lines and fit it into the tin, making a diagonal cut into each corner and overlapping and creasing the cut edges neatly to make sharp corners. Brush the paper lining with melted fat. Proceed as for Sandwich Sponges, left.

Then as soon as all the flour is folded in, fill the Swiss roll tin so that the mixture is of an even depth all over, including the corners. Put the Swiss roll straight into the preheated oven and bake it for 15 to 20 minutes. When it is ready it should be well risen, firm to touch and only lightly coloured. Meanwhile, sprinkle a piece of greaseproof paper, a little larger than the sponge, with the castor sugar. Warm the jam slightly in a saucepan so that it will spread easily.

Turn the sponge straight on to the sugar-sprinkled paper and peel off the greaseproof paper lining. Trim the edges of the sponge with a sharp knife to allow it to roll more easily. Immediately spread the jam over the sponge to within ½ inch of each edge. With a sharp knife, make a deep score across the sponge ½ inch from one of the short sides; this also makes the sponge easier to roll. With this short end towards you, roll the sponge, using the paper to help shape the roll by bringing it round with the sponge and keeping it on top of the roll. Hold the roll in the paper for a few seconds, then remove the paper and cool the roll.

ORANGE CAKE

FOR THE CAKE

2 large eggs and their	a pinch of salt
weight in butter,	2 level teaspoons
castor sugar and plain	baking powder
flour (this will be	1 tablespoon hot
about 4 oz. of each)	water
finely grated rind of	
1 small orange	

FOR THE FILLING

grated rind of ½ a	2 tablespoons
small orange	apricot jam

FOR THE ICING

thinly peeled rind of	little of the juice
1 orange	from the orange
10 oz. icing sugar, sifted	

2 sandwich tins each 7 inches in diameter

First prepare the sandwich tins. Brush them with melted lard then line the base of each with a round of greaseproof paper cut to fit. Brush the paper linings also with melted fat. Set the oven at *Gas Mark 6 or 400 degrees F.*

Put the butter into a warmed mixing bowl and beat it to a soft cream. Add the castor sugar and beat again until the mixture is light and creamy. Beat in the grated orange rind. Break the eggs, one at a time, into a cup to make sure they are fresh, then beat them well together. Beat the egg, a tablespoon at a time, into the creamed mixture, beating very thoroughly after each addition.

Sift the flour, salt and baking powder together, and lightly stir half of the flour into the mixture. Add the hot water, and stir the rest of the flour into the mixture. Divide the mixture between the tins, smooth over the surface and hollow out the centre of each slightly so that the cakes will rise evenly.

Bake the cakes just above the centre of the preheated oven, for about 20 minutes. When the cakes are ready they should be well and evenly risen, golden brown and slightly shrinking away from the sides of the tins.

Take the cakes out of the oven, turn them on to a wire tray to cool and peel off the greaseproof paper.

THE FILLING

Mix the grated orange rind into the apricot jam and sandwich the cakes together with this mixture.

THE ICING

Peel the rind very thinly off the orange; a potato peeler is the best tool to use for this. Cut the rind into fine shreds, cutting across the rind. Put the shreds of orange rind into a pan, cover them with cold water and bring to the boil. Simmer for 5 minutes then drain the orange shreds through a rounded strainer.

Stir the shreds into the icing sugar and add enough orange juice to make the icing a thick coating consistency. Add only a little orange juice at a time as it is very easy to add too much. The icing should run slowly off the back of a wooden spoon.

Pour all the icing on top of the cake and guide it down the sides with a palette knife. When the icing has set, transfer the cake to a pretty plate.

A QUICK CHOCOLATE SANDWICH

5 oz. plain flour	4 dessertspoons
1½ oz. cocoa powder	milk
6 oz. castor sugar	3 eggs
6 oz. margarine	3 level teaspoons
(this must be softened	baking powder
at warm kitchen	
temperature)	

FOR THE FILLING
2 tablespoons apricot jam

FOR THE ICING AND THE SIDES OF THE CAKE

6 oz. icing sugar, sifted	2 oz. grated
1 oz. cocoa powder	chocolate (2 crushed
2 rounded tablespoons	chocolate flake
chocolate spread	bars could be used)
	a few chocolate
	buttons

2 sandwich tins 7½ inches in diameter

Grease the sandwich tins and line the base of each with a circle of greaseproof paper cut to fit. Brush the paper linings with melted fat also.

Sift the flour and cocoa into a mixing bowl and add the sugar, margarine, milk and eggs. Beat all the ingredients together very thoroughly until they are well blended, then stir in the baking powder thoroughly. Divide the mixture between the tins, and smooth over the surface.

Bake the cakes just above the centre of a moderately hot oven, about *Gas Mark 5 or 375 degrees F.*, for 10 minutes, then reduce the heat to *Gas Mark 4 or 350 degrees F.* for a further 15 to 20 minutes. Turn the cakes on to a wire tray to cool. Remove the greaseproof paper.

FILLING AND ICING THE CAKE

Sandwich the cakes with apricot jam. Mix the sifted icing sugar and cocoa with enough cold water to make a thick coating consistency; beat 1 tablespoon into chocolate spread. Turn rest on to the cake and guide over the top with a palette knife. Spread the sides with chocolate spread, working in any drips of icing. Form the grated chocolate into a wide circle on a piece of greaseproof paper, lift the cake into the middle and, using a palette knife, lift the chocolate on to the sides of the cake. Transfer the cake to a plate and surround the base with chocolate buttons.

CHOCOLATE AND BANANA CREAM ROLL

FOR THE CHOCOLATE SPONGE SQUARE

2 eggs	4 oz. castor sugar
2 oz. plain flour	3 tablespoons
1 oz. cocoa powder	water

FOR THE FILLING AND DECORATION

½ pint double cream	3 bananas
2 level dessertspoons	few drops of lemon
castor sugar	juice
1 teaspoon vanilla	
essence	

7½ inch square cake tin will be required

Brush the inside of the tin with melted fat and line it with greaseproof paper. Brush the paper lining with fat also.

Break the eggs into a fairly large mixing bowl and beat them with a wire whisk, just enough to mix them lightly. Sift the flour and cocoa on to a piece of kitchen paper.

Dissolve the sugar in the water over a very gentle heat, without allowing the mixture to boil. Stir until the sugar is dissolved then bring the syrup to a rapid boil. Pour it on to the beaten eggs, whisking all the time. Whisk the mixture for 7 to 10 minutes until it is cooled and of a creamy consistency. Sift the flour and cocoa into the mixture and fold in lightly. Pour the mixture into the prepared tin and put it straight into a moderate oven, about *Gas Mark 4 or 350 degrees F.*, for about 30 minutes.

Turn the sponge out on to a cloth. Remove the greaseproof paper, then with the help of the cloth turn the sponge lengthways round a rolling pin. Cool the sponge round the rolling pin, resting it on the table with the sponge over the top and the cloth over the sponge.

THE FILLING AND DECORATION

Whisk the cream lightly until it will just hold its shape. Stir in the castor sugar and vanilla essence. Put a little of the cream into a forcing bag with a star pipe attached.

Cut five smallish slices from one of the bananas and sprinkle with lemon juice. Cut the rest of that banana and the other two in half lengthways, then cut each half in two.

Turn the roll over and rest one side of it against the rolling pin; hold the other side with your left hand. Put in half of the cream. Add half the banana pieces then cover them with cream. Put in the rest of the banana and cover with the remaining cream. Again using the cloth, turn the roll over on to the serving plate. Decorate the top with piped cream and the slices of banana (see the colour photograph on page 166).

MERINGUES

CREAM MERINGUES

few drops of salad oil and a dusting of flour for the baking tray 2 egg whites 4 oz. castor sugar

FOR THE FILLING
½ pint double cream (this is a very generous filling; half this amount is actually sufficient to sandwich the meringues together)

a piping bag and a large star pipe

First prepare the tray on which the meringues are to be baked: rub a few drops of salad oil over the upturned surface of a baking tray, then dust it with flour. Tip the tray and knock it sharply on the edge so that only a light dusting of flour is left on the surface.

Put the egg whites into a large clean bowl and beat them. Beat slowly at first, then faster as they begin to thicken. A large wire whisk is best for this, though a rotary beater can be used and, of course, if you have an electric mixer it is ideal. Remember it is the egg whites you are beating; a lot of energy can be used up on the bowl!

The main secret of success in making meringues is to get the egg whites stiff enough, so test carefully as you beat (photograph 1 shows the egg whites insufficiently beaten). Keep lifting the whisk out of the mixture, and when the egg white which clings to it stands in a straight peak with no bend (photograph 2), then the egg whites are ready for the addition of the sugar.

Cream meringues

Add 2 dessertspoons of the measured sugar and beat this thoroughly into the egg whites until the original stiff consistency is reached. Using a metal spoon, lightly fold in the rest of the sugar.

Fill a piping bag with a large star pipe attached with the meringue mixture. Hold the bag in the right hand, and keeping the mixture below the pressure of the hand, pipe out meringues on to the tray (photograph 3). The mixture will make about 28 single meringues or 14 filled meringues. Put the meringues into a very slow oven, set at the *lowest Gas Mark or about, 180 degrees F.* Bake them for about 4 hours. If they start to become tinged with colour, open the oven door very slightly. After this time, the meringues should have become firm, dry and crisp to the centre. Take them out of the oven and lift them off the trays.

1 Curved peak—meringue mixture not ready *2 Straight peak—meringue mixture ready* 3 4

TO FILL THE MERINGUES

Put the meringues in pairs in paper cases; this is the easiest way to fill them. Whip the cream until it will just hold its shape then put it into the piping bag and pipe the cream between the meringues (photograph 4).

MERINGUES FOR THE STORE CUPBOARD

If you have space in the oven and egg whites to spare it is most useful to make a batch of meringues to keep in a tin in the store cupboard. They keep very well before they are filled with cream.

COLOURED MERINGUES

A drop of pink or green colouring or a dusting of instant coffee powder can be added to the meringue mixture just before it is piped on to the baking tray.

HAZEL MERINGUE GÂTEAU (p. 177)

This is a large gâteau for a party of 10 or 12 people. It can be made smaller very easily by omitting a meringue layer or simply by making the rounds smaller.

TO MAKE FOUR MERINGUE ROUNDS
(each 8 inches in diameter)

4 oz. hazelnuts	8 egg whites
little tasteless salad oil for the baking tray	1 lb. castor sugar

FOR THE FILLINGS

first layer	*second and third layers and the top*
3 level tablespoons cocoa powder	½ pint double cream
4 level tablespoons cornflour	small packet frozen raspberries or 4 oz. fresh raspberries
3 level tablespoons castor sugar	16 whole hazelnuts
1 pint milk	
1 tablespoon tasteless salad oil	

a piping bag and a large star pipe

THE NUT MERINGUE ROUNDS

It is probably best to make one round at a time, using two egg whites and 1 oz. nuts per round.

First toast all the nuts. Put them on a baking tray and toast them under a moderate grill, rolling them round on the tray so that they brown lightly and evenly. The skins will shrink and crack. Tip them on to a clean cloth and rub off the skins. Grind the nuts and divide into four ready to add to each lot of meringue mixture.

Cover an upturned baking tray with kitchen foil then put a flan ring or dinner plate, 8 inches in diameter, in the centre and draw round it. Brush the round with oil.

Whisk 2 of the egg whites stiffly and add 4 oz. castor sugar in the same way as described for the cream meringues on page 139. When the mixture is ready, lightly fold in one portion of grated nuts and put it into the piping bag with the large star pipe attached. Then, starting at the centre of the circle and working outwards, pipe rounds of meringue. Bake the meringue in a very cool oven, at the *lowest gas setting or about 180 degrees F.,* for about 4 hours. Slip the meringue round off the foil and leave it to cool.

Make the other three meringue rounds in the same way; they can be stored in an airtight tin at this stage.

THE CHOCOLATE FILLING

Mix the cocoa and cornflour and sugar together. Add just enough of the measured cold milk to make a thin cream. Put the rest of the milk into a pan, add the blended ingredients and stir the mixture over a gentle heat until it thickens and comes to the boil. Simmer the mixture for a few minutes. Pour it into a tall jug so that the area of the surface of the mixture is fairly small. Run over the surface a tablespoon of tasteless salad oil; this prevents a skin forming while the mixture cools. When the mixture is cold beat it up well to incorporate the oil and give the filling a shine.

TO ASSEMBLE THE GÂTEAU

Choose the best-shaped meringue round for the gâteau top and put aside. Place one of the other rounds on the plate from which the gâteau is to be served, cover it with the chocolate filling and place another meringue round on top. Whip the cream lightly so that it will just hold its shape, put a little of it into the piping bag and pipe small stars round the edge of the reserved top layer. Use the rest of the cream to sandwich the remaining layers together, dotting the top layer of cream with the raspberries. Top each cream star with a hazelnut.

This gâteau should be assembled only 30 minutes or so before it is served.

NOTE: If you like, custard cream can be spread between the top two layers. Make a custard, using 4 level teaspoons of custard powder and ¼ pint milk. When the custard is cold, fold in ¼ pint of whipped double cream.

MERINGUE MELBAS

MAKES 8

FOR THE MERINGUE CASES

4 egg whites	8 oz. castor sugar

FOR THE FILLING

1 family block of vanilla ice cream	1 tin cranberry sauce (7 oz.)
1 tin peach halves (1 lb. 13 oz.), drained	

a piping bag and a large star pipe will be required

Prepare the baking tray: rub a few drops of salad oil over the upturned surface of the tray, then dust it with flour. Tip the tray and knock it sharply on the edge so that only a light dusting of flour is left on the surface. Mark 8 circles on the tray, using a ring 3¾ inches in diameter as a guide.

Make the meringue as described on page 139, and put it in a piping bag with a large star pipe attached. Then pipe 8 melba cases, starting at the centre of a circle and working outwards in rings. Pipe three circles, on top of each other, round the outer edge of each case for the sides.

Bake the cases for about 4 hours in a very slow oven, at the *lowest gas setting or 180 degrees F.* Use a sharp knife to slip the cases off the tray; at this stage they will keep well in an airtight tin.

FILLING THE CASES

Put a spoonful of ice cream into each case and top it with half a peach. Sieve the cranberry sauce and coat each peach half with it.

PAVLOVA GÂTEAU

3 egg whites
6 oz. castor sugar
½ level teaspoon
  vanilla essence

1 level dessertspoon
  cornflour
1 teaspoon distilled
  white vinegar

FOR THE FILLING
8 oz. fresh raspberries
few stalks of ripe
  redcurrants

½ pint double cream
1 level dessertspoon
  icing sugar, sifted

a piping bag and a large star pipe

Brush a baking tray with melted fat and cover it with kitchen foil. Using a plate or flan ring 8 inches in diameter as a guide, mark a circle on the foil, brush with fat.

Put the egg whites into a large mixing bowl and beat them stiffly. Very gradually add the sugar, beating well all the time. Fold in the vanilla essence, cornflour and vinegar.

Spread 2 tablespoons of the meringue mixture over the centre of the foil circle and put the rest into a piping bag, with a star pipe attached. Pipe a rim of small, overlapping circles, then top with a second rim of meringue circles. Bake the meringue in a very cool oven, about *200 degrees F. or the lowest gas setting,* for about 3 hours. As soon as the meringue is firm enough to be lifted off the foil, take it out of the oven and peel off the foil from underneath.

Keep aside a handful of the best raspberries and heap the rest into the meringue case. String 2 stalks of redcurrants and scatter them over the raspberries.

Whip the cream very lightly and sweeten it with the sifted icing sugar. Turn the cream on to the fruit. Arrange the remaining stalks of redcurrants on one side of the gâteau and encircle the cream above the meringue with raspberries, with a redcurrant tucked into the centre of alternate ones.

CELEBRATION CAKES

CHOCOLATE AND CHESTNUT CAKE

FOR THE CAKES
3 oz. plain dessert
  chocolate
2 oz. plain flour
1 level teaspoon
  baking powder
3 eggs

3 oz. castor sugar
half an 8½ oz. tin
  sweetened
  chestnut purée (the
  other half is used in
  the filling)

FOR THE FILLING
half the tin sweetened
  chestnut purée
few drops of vanilla
  essence or 1 teaspoon
  rum

4 tablespoons
  double cream

FOR THE ICING
2 tablespoons water
4 oz. plain dessert
  chocolate
2 teaspoons salad oil

1 oz. castor sugar
Spanish chestnut, if
  available, for the
  decoration

two sandwich tins each 7½ inches in diameter

Brush the sandwich tins with melted fat and line the base of each with a piece of greaseproof paper cut to fit. Brush the paper lining with fat also.

Break the chocolate on to a plate and put it in a warm place or over a pan of hot water to melt. Work it with a palette knife to make it smooth. Leave it in a warm place ready to add to the mixture.

Sift the flour and baking powder and leave it ready to add to the mixture. Separate the whites from the yolks of the eggs and put the yolks into a mixing bowl with the castor sugar. Suspend the bowl over a pan half full of hot (not boiling) water and beat them with a wire whisk or rotary beater until they are thick and creamy and light in colour. Take the basin off the heat and stir in the chocolate and the chestnut purée. Whisk the egg whites fairly stiffly; stir in a tablespoon to soften the mixture then lightly fold in the rest alternately with the flour. Turn the mixture into the prepared tins, dividing it evenly.

Bake the cakes just above the centre of a moderately hot oven, about *Gas Mark 5 or 375 degrees F.,* for 40 to 45 minutes. Turn the cakes on to a wire tray to cool and remove the greaseproof paper.

Mix the chestnut purée with a little vanilla essence or rum to flavour it lightly. Whip the cream and fold it into the purée. Sandwich the cakes with the chestnut cream.

Put the water, the chocolate broken into pieces, the oil and castor sugar into a saucepan and stir over a very gentle heat until the castor sugar has completely dissolved. On no account allow the mixture to boil. Take off the heat and allow to cool. When the mixture is almost cold and thick enough to coat the cake, pour it over the cake and, using a palette knife, guide it over the edges into nice generous drips. Decorate with a Spanish chestnut, as in the photograph on page 166.

RICH CHOCOLATE CAKE

FOR THE CHOCOLATE RECTANGLES
6 oz. plain dessert
  chocolate
3 bars (about 6 oz.)
  white chocolate

waxed paper

FOR THE CAKE
4 oz. plain dessert
  chocolate
5 tablespoons milk
2 oz. cocoa powder
few drops of vanilla
  essence
8 oz. margarine

6 oz. castor sugar
4 eggs
4 oz. plain flour
2 oz. ground rice
2 level teaspoons
  baking powder

FOR THE BUTTERCREAM
8 oz. butter
8 oz. castor sugar
¼ pint water

4 egg yolks
4 oz. plain dessert
  chocolate

FOR THE FILLING
2 tablespoons apricot jam

FOR THE DECORATION
a sprinkling of
  chocolate
  vermicelli

7 small pieces of
  glacé or crystallised
  cherry

a cake tin 7½ inches in diameter

Before making the cake, make the chocolate rectangles so that any left-over trimmings of dark chocolate can be added to the cake mixture.

MAKING THE CHOCOLATE RECTANGLES

Draw two rectangles 10½ inches by 3 inches, each on a separate piece of waxed paper. Never use greaseproof paper as the chocolate may stick to it.

Start with the dark chocolate. Break the chocolate on to a plate and leave it in a warm place (the warming drawer of your cooker is ideal). Only a very gentle heat is required; too strong a heat will give the chocolate a streaky white appearance when it is set. The plate can be placed on a saucepan of hot water, but great care must be taken to dry the base of the plate because the smallest drip of water will spoil the consistency of the chocolate. To help the chocolate melt, beat it with a palette knife and, when it is smooth, spread it evenly over one of the waxed paper rectangles. The chocolate will be fairly thick. If it is thinner it is more economical but the rectangles are more easily broken.

Melt and spread the white chocolate over the other rectangle in exactly the same way, as seen in photograph 1. Leave the chocolate in a cool place on a perfectly flat surface to set. When it is set, using a ruler and a sharp knife, trim the dark and light chocolate to the rectangle outlines. If the chocolate sets very quickly, as it may do in cold weather, warm the knife to make it easier. Cut each chocolate rectangle into seven equal sized pieces, each 1½ inches wide. Bend the waxed paper from under the pieces of chocolate and they will come away easily. At this stage the chocolate pieces can be stored for a little while, layered with greaseproof paper and packed into a tin.

LINING THE CAKE TIN

Brush the cake tin with melted fat. Cut two circles of greaseproof paper, using the base of the tin for a guide. Cut a double strip of paper long enough to go round the inside of the tin and overlap an inch, and wide enough to come an inch above the top of the tin. Put one of the circles into the base of the tin and brush it with melted fat. Make an inch fold along one long side of the strip and make slanting cuts, about an inch apart, up to the fold on the narrow side. Fit this slit edge neatly round the base of the tin; the rest lines the sides. Brush the lining with melted fat and put the second circle on top of the first; grease this also.

MAKING THE CAKE

Chop the chocolate roughly and put it into a pan with any trimmings from the dark rectangle, milk, cocoa and vanilla essence. Melt the chocolate over a *very gentle* heat. Beat the margarine and sugar to a soft cream, light in colour and texture. Separate the egg yolks from the whites and beat one yolk at a time into this mixture. Sift the flour, ground rice and baking powder and stir them into the mixture together with the melted chocolate. Beat the egg whites fairly stiffly and stir in 2 tablespoons of these to soften the mixture. Fold in the rest very lightly. Turn the mixture into the prepared tin and put it just above the centre of a slow oven, about *Gas Mark 3 or 325 degrees F.,* for about 1½ hours, or until the cake is cooked. To test if the cake is cooked, push a warmed thin skewer into the centre, and if it comes out clean, the cake is ready. If any mixture sticks to the skewer, bake the cake a little longer. Turn the cake on to a wire tray to cool and remove the greaseproof paper.

THE BUTTERCREAM

Beat the butter to a very soft creamy consistency and leave it at room temperature ready to add to the sugar syrup and egg yolks.

Dissolve the sugar in the water over a very gentle heat, stirring occasionally; *do not allow the syrup to boil before all the sugar has dissolved.* When every grain of sugar has dissolved bring the syrup to the boil, stop stirring and boil rapidly until the "short thread" stage is reached. To test, lift a little syrup in a spoon, touch the surface of it with the third finger, press it to the thumb, then separate the finger and thumb quickly. If the syrup is ready it should form a short thread, at least an inch long, before breaking. Take it off the heat.

Put the egg yolks into a medium sized bowl, and stand it on a damp cloth to prevent it from slipping. Beat the egg yolks well with a wire whisk then very gradually pour the syrup on to them, whisking all the time. As the mixture cools it will become thick and creamy. While it is still slightly warm, beat in the creamed butter, a teaspoon at a time. Take out about four tablespoons of the buttercream for the top.

Break the chocolate into pieces. Put them on a plate and melt them in a warm place, beating with a palette knife to make the chocolate really smooth. Beat the chocolate into the remaining buttercream, which should not be quite cold (if it is cold, the chocolate will set in lumps which will prevent the icing piping smoothly). Leave both the buttercreams in a cool place for an hour to thicken slightly.

DECORATING THE CAKE

Slit the cake in half and sandwich it together with apricot jam. Spread the top and sides of the cake, not too thickly, with the chocolate buttercream, leaving some for piping up the sides. Surround the cake with alternate rectangles of light and dark chocolate as seen in photograph 2, spacing

1

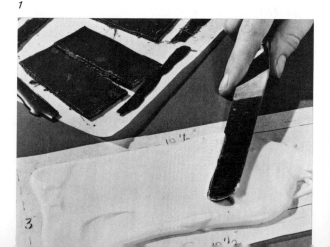

2

them evenly and sticking them to the buttercream round the cake. Put the cake on to a plate or board for serving.

Fill a forcing bag, with a small star pipe attached, with chocolate buttercream and pipe up the joins of chocolate, finishing with a star inside the top of the cake. Using the back of a knife, mark lines from the centre of each white rectangle to the centre of the cake as seen in photograph 3. Fill a forcing bag, again with a star pipe, with the white icing and pipe a scroll along each line.

Dust the centre with chocolate vermicelli. Place small pieces of cherry round the top of the cake on the white buttercream.

NOTE: Baked in two 7½ inch sandwich tins, the mixture takes 40 to 45 minutes to bake just above the centre of the oven at Gas Mark 4 or 350 degrees F.

BRANDY SCROLL CAKE

FOR THE SPONGE

3 eggs	3 oz. plain flour
3 oz. castor sugar	1 level teaspoon
grated rind of ½ orange	baking powder

FOR THE FILLING

1 egg white	¼ pint double cream
2 level teaspoons icing sugar, sifted	

FOR THE TOP OF THE CAKE

13 or 14 brandy snaps (see page 153)	about ⅛ pint whipped cream

2 sandwich tins 7¾ or 8 inches in diameter

First prepare the sandwich tins. Brush them with melted fat, then line the base of each with a round of greaseproof paper cut to fit. Brush the paper lining also with melted fat. Heat the oven at *Gas Mark 5 or 375 degrees F.*

Break the eggs, one at a time, into a cup to make sure they are fresh, then put them into a large mixing bowl and break them up with a wire whisk. Mix in the castor sugar and the orange rind.

Sift the flour and the baking powder on to a piece of grease-proof paper, ready to add to the mixture.

Have ready a large pan half filled with boiling water. Take it off the heat and place the bowl over it, so that the base of the bowl is suspended in the steam without actually touching the water. Beat the mixture with a wire or rotary whisk until it leaves a clear thick trail when the whisk is lifted from the bowl. This will take about 8 to 10 minutes

with a wire whisk, less with a rotary whisk. (If you are using an electric mixer, there is no need to heat the bowl in any way. It will take less time—about 3 or 4 minutes—to reach the same consistency.) Lift the bowl off the heat, stand it on a damp cloth to prevent it from slipping, and beat for a further 2 minutes.

Sift the flour again, this time straight into the mixture, and fold it in lightly with a metal spoon, working the mixture as little as possible. As soon as the flour is folded in, divide the mixture evenly between the prepared tins. Tilt the tins to level the mixture; in this way air bubbles beaten into the mixture are not disturbed. Put the sponges straight into the oven for 20 minutes or until cooked.

When the sponges are ready, turn them out on to a wire tray and remove the greaseproof paper.

Whisk the egg white very stiffly. Add the sifted icing sugar and whisk again until the mixture retains its former stiffness. Whip the cream until it will hold its shape then fold in the egg white and sugar mixture. Spread one of the sponges with about two-thirds of the cream mixture. Put the other sponge on top and spread with remaining cream. Crush 4 or 5 brandy snaps and sprinkle on top of the cake. Fill a forcing bag with a star pipe attached with the whipped cream and pipe a star of cream into each end of 9 brandy snaps. Arrange the scrolls on top of the cake.

CHRISTMAS CAKE

FOR THE CAKE

10 oz. plain flour	6 oz. soft brown sugar
½ level teaspoon bicarbonate of soda	2 oz. chopped candied peel
¼ level teaspoon each of ground mace, ground ginger, ground cloves and cinnamon	3 oz. quartered glacé cherries
	1 lb. cleaned sultanas
2 oz. ground almonds	8 oz. cleaned currants
4 eggs	1 oz. shelled chopped walnuts
4 oz. golden syrup	2 tablespoons brandy or orange juice
7 oz. butter	
finely grated rind of 1 small orange	

FOR THE ALMOND ICING

5 oz. icing sugar, sifted	a little lemon juice
5 oz. castor sugar	a sprinkling of cornflour for dusting the icing
10 oz. ground almonds	
1 egg or 3 or 4 yolks (if yolks are used, the whites can be kept in a screw-topped jar and used for the royal icing)	8 oz. sieved apricot jam

FOR THE ROYAL ICING

4 egg whites (saved from the almond icing if you used yolks)	1 tablespoon glycerine
about 2 lb. icing sugar, sifted	a few drops of bright red colouring

a cake tin 7½ inches in diameter, a cake board 10 inches in diameter, 2 yards self-sticking rayon red ribbon ¾ inch wide, a No. 2 writing pipe and 2 greaseproof paper icing bags, and a Christmas spray will be required

3

Brush the cake tin with melted lard then line it with greaseproof paper. To do this, pencil round the base of the tin on to a doubled sheet of greaseproof paper. Cut out the two rounds just inside the pencil line. Then cut a doubled strip, this time to go round the inside of the tin and to come 2 inches above the rim; make a 1 inch fold along the length of the strip and snip diagonally up to the fold at 1 inch intervals. Fit one greaseproof circle into the bottom of the tin then curve the long strip round the inside of the tin with the snipped edge resting on the bottom circle. Brush the paper with melted fat. Put the second circle of paper into the tin and brush this with melted fat also.

Sift together the flour, bicarbonate of soda and spices, and stir in the ground almonds.

Whisk the eggs together. Warm the golden syrup and stir it into the eggs. Beat the butter to a soft cream with the finely grated orange rind; add the soft brown sugar and beat again. Beat in the eggs and golden syrup mixture a little at a time; then fold in the sifted ingredients, prepared fruit, walnuts, and either the brandy or the orange juice.

Turn the mixture into the prepared tin, smooth over the surface and hollow out the centre slightly. Bake the cake in the centre of a moderate oven about *Gas Mark 4 or 350 degrees F.* for 30 minutes then lower the heat to *Gas Mark 3 or 325 degrees F.* for a further 2 to 2½ hours or until cooked. To test when the cake is ready, pierce the centre with a warmed thin skewer or knitting needle and if it comes out clean the cake is cooked. If any of the mixture adheres to the skewer, bake the cake a little longer.

Turn the cake on to a wire tray to cool and remove the greaseproof paper.

At this stage, the cake can be stored in a polythene bag, or covered with almond icing next day.

THE ALMOND ICING

Thoroughly mix together the icing sugar, castor sugar and ground almonds. Beat the egg, or the egg yolks, and add them to the mixture with enough lemon juice to make a stiff paste; it should have the firm consistency of short crust pastry—not sticky, but firm enough to handle without crumbling.

Turn the cake upside down and use the flat base of the cake for the top. Brush it all over to remove any loose crumbs. Cut the almond icing in half. Using the lightest dusting of cornflour to prevent the icing from sticking, roll one half into a round to fit the top of the cake. (The base of the tin in which the cake was baked can be used for a guide.) Brush the top of the cake with sieved apricot jam and put the round of almond icing on top.

Roll the rest of the almond icing, plus any scraps, into a long sausage shape between the palms of the hands and the board. Cut a piece of string the right length to encircle the cake and use it as a guide for measuring the length of the roll. With a rolling pin, flatten the roll as evenly as possible to the depth of the cake. Use a ruler to trim the edges of the strip to the right depth. Brush the sides of the cake with sieved apricot jam. Turn the cake, very carefully, on to its side, and place it at one end of the almond strip. Roll the cake along it and the strip will stick to the sides of the cake. Press the almond icing firmly to the cake, especially round the top and down the side where the almond icing is joined. Leave the cake in a cool airy place for a day or two before coating it with royal icing.

THE ROYAL ICING

Beat the egg whites in a large bowl, then gradually beat in enough sifted icing sugar to make a thick coating consistency. Take out about 3 tablespoons of the icing and place on one side for the piping; put it in a small bowl and cover the surface directly with polythene. Beat the glycerine into the rest of the icing and test the consistency by lifting some of the icing on the back of the wooden spoon; it should flow off slowly and leave the spoon well coated. Put the cake on an upturned plate on a clean surface. Turn two-thirds of the icing on to the top of the cake and allow it to coat the cake completely, guiding it where necessary with a palette knife. When the icing has stopped flowing, lift the cake still on the plate and scrape up all the drips of icing (without, of course, any cake crumbs), and put it back in the large bowl with the remaining coating icing and cover the surface directly with polythene.

Next day, transfer the cake to the cake board, sticking it firmly to the centre of the board with a good smear of icing. Make the greaseproof paper icing bags. Fold a 10 inch square of greaseproof paper in half diagonally then roll it into a cone. Repeat with another piece of greaseproof paper. Thicken the small amount of icing, which was kept for the piping, to a piping consistency with a little extra sifted icing sugar. Cut the tip off a paper icing bag and drop in a No. 2 plain writing pipe, then put in a teaspoon of icing and fold the top of the bag over it. Always keep the rest of the icing covered when not in use. Tip the cake board, holding it up with a weight or other firm prop, so that it is at a convenient angle for piping the sides. Pipe an uneven zigzag round the sides of the cake, approximately a third of the way down the sides. This will form the edge of the drip shapes on the second coating of icing (see the colour photograph on page 164). After use, put the icing bag and pipe into a small polythene bag to keep the icing moist for the trellis.

Add a little extra sifted icing sugar to the icing in the large bowl so that it will form good thick drips, and turn it on to the top of the cake. Use a palette knife to guide the icing over the top and down the sides of the cake. The piped zigzag will hold it. Leave the cake until it is touch dry.

THE FINAL TOUCHES

Fix a band of ribbon round the base of the cake and another round the edge of the board. Using the icing in the pipe and bag, pipe diagonal lines from just above the cake ribbon to the edge of the cake board, then cross this with piped lines in the other direction (see the colour photograph on page 164). Again it is easier to do if you tip the cake, by placing a weight under the board. Dot the ends of the trellis where the lines meet with the white icing.

Colour the remaining piping icing with a drop of bright red colouring and, using a new bag filled with red icing and a clean pipe, pipe a mass of dots between the drips and the trellis.

Place a Christmas spray just to one side of the centre of the cake.

NOTE: The trellis is not really difficult, but should you prefer, you can finish the cake with dots of white icing above and below the ribbon instead.

Daisy wedding cake (see page 147)

Dundee cake (page 131), seed and citron cake (page 132),
cut-and-come-again cake (page 132), sultana cake
(page 132), cherry cake (page 131)

DAISY WEDDING CAKE

While the baking of a wedding cake is simple and straight-forward, many people are diffident about embarking on the piped icing decoration. It is not really difficult if you follow these instructions carefully because the cake has been designed with a daisy pattern and the petals for the daisies can be made in advance and will keep indefinitely in an airtight tin. They are arranged on the cake after it has been iced all over. To make the sides easy and pretty they have been banded with ribbon and white braid. The small amount of piping on the cake itself gives it dignity.

The recipe is for a three-tier cake but the top two tiers on their own make a splendid cake for a small wedding. The mixture can be made all at once or each cake separately; a lot of time can be saved if it is all mixed together.

Remember the cakes are best stored, wrapped in foil, for at least a month before being iced—to allow the flavour to mellow. Time must also be allowed for the almond and royal icing to harden sufficiently to bear the weight of the upper tiers. The almond icing will take a week and the royal icing a further week, so start in good time.

FOR THE CAKES	12 INCH CAKE	9 INCH CAKE	6 INCH CAKE
currants, cleaned	1½ lb.	12 oz.	6 oz.
raisins, seedless	12 oz.	6 oz.	3 oz.
sultanas, cleaned	1 lb.	8 oz.	4 oz.
glacé cherries	1¼ lb.	10 oz.	5 oz.
mixed chopped peel	4 oz.	2 oz.	1 oz.
walnuts, shelled	6 oz.	3 oz.	1½ oz.
ground almonds	6 oz.	3 oz.	1½ oz.
finely grated lemon rind	4	2	1
plain flour	1¾ lb.	14 oz.	7 oz.
salt	1½ level teaspoons	¾ level teaspoon	⅓ level teaspoon
baking powder	4½ level teaspoons	2¼ level teaspoons	1¼ level teaspoons
mixed spice	4½ level teaspoons	2¼ level teaspoons	1¼ level teaspoons
butter	1½ lb.	12 oz.	6 oz.
soft brown sugar	1½ lb.	12 oz.	6 oz.
eggs	9 large	5 standard	3 standard
black treacle	4 level dessertspoons	2 level dessertspoons	1 level dessertspoon
rum	9 level tablespoons	5 level tablespoons	3 level tablespoons

3 round cake tins, 12, 9 and 6 inches in diameter

FOR THE ALMOND ICING	12 INCH CAKE	9 INCH CAKE	6 INCH CAKE
ground almonds	1½ lb.	1 lb.	8 oz.
icing sugar, sifted	12 oz.	8 oz.	4 oz.
castor sugar	12 oz.	8 oz.	4 oz.
egg yolks, large (keep the whites in a screw-topped jar for the royal icing)	8	5	2
lemon juice (approx.)	5 level tablespoons	3 level tablespoons	2 level tablespoons
sieved apricot jam	8 oz.	4 oz.	4 level tablespoons
a dusting of cornflour			

FOR THE ROYAL ICING	12 INCH CAKE	9 INCH CAKE	6 INCH CAKE
egg whites, large	7	6	4
glycerine	3 level teaspoons	2 level teaspoons	1 level teaspoon
lemon juice	1 level tablespoon	3 level teaspoons	2 level teaspoons
icing sugar, sifted	3 lb.	2½ lb.	1½ lb.

THE DAISY PETALS

2 large egg whites
about 12 oz. sifted
  icing sugar plus 2 oz.
  to thicken a quarter
  of the icing
two No. 2 plain
  round writing pipes
waxed paper

4 greaseproof paper
  icing bags (each
  made by folding a
  10 inch square of
  greaseproof paper
  in half diagonally
  then rolling it into a
  cone)

These are made in three sizes—2 in. long, 1½ in. and 1 in. You will need 40 of each size for each cake. Allow an extra 5 petals in each size in case any break.

The icing for the outline and for filling the centres is made together, a little of it being thickened with extra icing sugar to make it firm enough for the outline. The petals are all piped on to waxed paper; it is most important to use waxed paper so the petals will come off easily when they are dry—they tend to stick to greaseproof paper.

Beat the egg whites lightly to break them, then beat in enough sifted icing sugar to make a thick pouring consistency. Take out a quarter of the icing and cover the rest

1   2   3   4

5   6   7   8

directly over the surface with polythene, or put it into a screw-topped jar, to prevent the air forming a skin on the surface. Beat enough extra sifted icing sugar into the smaller quantity of icing to make a piping consistency; the icing should hold its shape (it is always worth getting the consistency just right for piping even if this means filling another icing bag). Cover whenever it is not being used.

Take an icing bag, cut off the tip and insert a No. 2 plain round writing pipe. Put a spoonful of the thicker icing into the bag and fold over the paper to keep it inside. Put some of the thinner icing into the other bag, with the other pipe attached. Never have more icing in a bag at a time than will half fill it. Shave a matchstick and put it in the point of the pipe from the outside to hold in the icing until it is required. Start with 5 large petals for 1 daisy. Draw the largest petal shape 5 times on to a piece of white paper, making a fairly thick outline. Cut a piece of waxed paper to fit over the white paper and stick it down with four dabs of icing from the thicker icing bag, then pipe the outline of each petal, which shows clearly through the waxed paper (photograph 1). Lift the waxed paper off the paper pattern, place it on a tray and, using the softer icing, pipe the centres of the petals full of icing. The outline should disappear into the flooding (this is also seen in photograph 1). Make the rest of the daisy petal sets for the large cake and leave them on the tray for 2 days to dry undisturbed. Make the other two sets of petals for the middle and top tiers.

When the petals are dry, peel them off the waxed paper and store them in a dry place in an airtight tin.

LINING THE CAKE TINS

Start with the largest tin. Place the tin on a doubled piece of greaseproof paper, draw round it with a pencil and cut out two rounds just inside the line. Cut a double strip 2 inches deeper than the tin and long enough to go round the inside. Make an inch fold along the length of the strip and cut diagonal snips to the fold, 1 inch apart. Brush the inside of the tin with melted fat and fit one paper circle into the base of the tin, brushing it with melted fat. Fit the

paper strip round the sides of the tin with the snipped edge fitting neatly round the base. Finally, insert the other paper circle and brush the whole lining with fat.

For extra protection for large cakes it is a good idea to wrap a doubled band of brown paper round the outside of the tin and tie it firmly with string.

Line the other two tins in the same way; it should not be necessary to wrap them in brown paper.

THE MIXTURE

Put the currants into a large mixing bowl, chop the seedless raisins and add these to the currants with the sultanas. Wash the cherries in warm water and dry them very thoroughly in a clean towel. Quarter them and add them to the fruit, then stir in the mixed chopped peel. Chop the walnuts fairly finely and add them with the ground almonds, and grated lemon rind.

Sift the plain flour, salt, baking powder, and mixed spice, and mix a third of these with the dried fruit mixture.

Beat the butter to a soft cream with your hand, add the soft brown sugar and continue beating until the mixture is soft and light. Break the eggs into a cup, one at a time, to make sure they are fresh, then beat them well together. Add them gradually to the creamed mixture, beating very well between each addition. Slowly beat in the black treacle and stir in the sieved dry ingredients alternately with the dried fruit and rum. Mix well.

Turn the mixture into the prepared tins. If you are making all three together, put about half the mixture into the largest tin then proportion out the remaining mixture between the other two. Smooth over the surface of the mixture and hollow out the centre of each cake fairly deeply with the back of a wooden spoon. This is to help them rise as evenly as possible.

Bake the large cake first; the smaller cakes can be baked together or separately. It will do no harm to keep the mixture in a cool place overnight.

Bake the cakes in the centre of a very moderate oven, about *Gas Mark 2 or about 300 degrees F*. The large cake should

148

take $5\frac{1}{4}$ to $5\frac{1}{2}$ hours, the middle cake $4\frac{1}{4}$ to $4\frac{1}{2}$ hours, and the top tier between $2\frac{1}{2}$ hours and $2\frac{3}{4}$ hours. It will do no harm to look at the cakes if the oven is opened and closed gently. Warm a thin skewer or metal knitting needle and push it into the centre of the cake. If it comes out clean the cake is ready; if there is any stickiness on the skewer, bake the cake a little longer and test again. When the cake is firm in the centre and shrinks away slightly from the edge of the tin it is usually ready. Leave the cakes in the tins overnight. They can then be stored well-wrapped in kitchen foil; to help the flavour a little rum or brandy can be sprinkled over the base of each cake. Storage will improve the flavour.

MAKING THE ALMOND ICING

This is very quick to make. Mix for each cake separately as smaller amounts are easier to manage. Mix the ground almonds with the sifted icing sugar and castor sugar. Beat the egg yolks and add them to the mixture with enough lemon juice to make a stiff dough. The consistency should be just a little softer than short crust pastry. To prevent the surface hardening keep any almond icing in a polythene bag when not in use.

COATING THE LARGE CAKE WITH ALMOND ICING

Cut off the top of the cake to get the depth of the side even all the way round and to get a nice, level top (photograph 2). Cut the almond icing in half. Roll half of it into a circle a fraction bigger than the cake, using a little cornflour to prevent the almond icing from sticking to the board or rolling pin. Using the tin in which the cake was baked for a guide, trim round with a sharp knife (photograph 3). Add the scraps to the rest of the almond icing. Bring the sieved apricot jam to the boil and brush the bottom of the cake with it; a paint brush 1 inch wide is ideal. The base of the cake has now become the top; turn the cake on to the almond icing, jam side downwards.

Using a small palette knife, work the edge of the almond icing into a nice square shape (photograph 4). Turn the cake almond icing upwards.

With a piece of string measure round the sides of the cake to get the length required for the almond icing strip which is to be wrapped round it (photograph 5).

Roll the remaining almond icing into a sausage shape the length of the string and cut it into three (it is easier to put on the cake in sections). Flatten one piece with the rolling pin and trim it to the exact depth of the cake (including the top almond coating). Cut the ends straight. Brush round a third of the side of the cake, very liberally, with sieved jam, then lift the first section of almond icing on to the side of the cake (photograph 6). Complete the side with the other two pieces of almond icing, joining them carefully.

Coat the smaller cakes with almond icing in the same way; the sides can be coated in one or two pieces. Leave the cakes in a cool airy place for at least a week.

THE ROYAL ICING

It is best to mix the icing for each cake separately. Start with the large cake.

Beat the egg whites, glycerine and lemon juice in a large mixing bowl. The glycerine helps to prevent the icing becoming chip hard. When well blended together, gradually beat in the sifted icing sugar to make a fairly thick coating consistency. The icing should coat the back of a wooden spoon smoothly but thickly (photograph 7). An electric mixer is very good for this but it should be used on the slowest speed; although the icing should be well beaten and smooth, whipping it would incorporate too much air and make the icing bubbly. In any case some bubbles form in the icing and it is best to cover it with polythene and leave it overnight. Next day stir it well and adjust the consistency if necessary with a little extra sifted icing sugar or sieved egg white.

Put the cake on to a wire tray placed over a clean surface. Have a palette knife ready to help guide the icing. Turn all the icing on to the top of the cake, guiding it evenly to the sides with the palette knife, then leave it to find its way down the sides, again using the palette knife if necessary. While the icing is still creeping over the cake, prick out any large air bubbles with a skewer.

Coat the other cakes in the same way; the smallest one can be put on an upturned plate instead of a wire tray. Leave all the cakes for 2 or 3 days to dry. The decoration can be finished as soon as the icing is firm enough to touch although the cakes should not be assembled for a week as the bottom ones have to hold quite a lot of weight.

THE DECORATION—FOR ALL THE CAKES

2 egg whites	1 yard medium pink
about 1½ lb. icing sugar, sifted	2 inch wide satin ribbon (9 inch cake)
8 sets of icing petals for each cake	⅔ yard pale pink 2 inch wide satin ribbon (6 inch cake)
very small silver balls	
3 cake boards, 14 inches 10 inches and 7 inches in diameter	sticky tape
	3 yards white cotton daisy braid 1 inch wide
6 greaseproof paper icing bags (each made by folding a 10 inch square of greaseproof paper diagonally in half, then rolling it into a cone)	2 yards medium pink ¼ inch wide satin ribbon
	4 pillars each 3½ inches high
	4 pillars each 3 inches high
No. 2 icing pipe	2 bunches of pink velvet forget-me-nots
small tweezers	
1¼ yards deep pink 2 inch wide satin ribbon (12 inch cake)	a small wineglass of fresh flowers arranged in Florapak

Mix the egg whites with enough sifted icing sugar to make a piping consistency, as described for making the petals. Smear a little icing on the centre of each board and put the cakes in position. Using a small palette knife, fill in any little cracks and crevices round the base of each cake. Start with the large cake and mark the top edge into eight. The easiest way to do this is to cut a paper circle the size of the top of the cake (again using the cake tin as a guide). Crease the circle into four then into half again, open it out and place it on top of the cake and mark the end of each fold boldly on the cake with the point of a skewer, then lift off the paper. Using a ruler, measure an inch towards the centre from each marked point; mark with a skewer.

Work round the cake, arranging the petals of each daisy round its marked centre; there is no need to stick them on. Fill an icing bag, with a No. 2 plain round writing pipe attached, with icing and pipe a cushion of icing into the centre of each daisy, also covering the ends of the petals; immediately flick this with small silver balls, and fill any odd spaces by placing the silver balls in them with a pair of tweezers. The balls must go on to the icing while it is wet so that they stick. Remove any stray balls with a small clean paint brush or tweezers. At this stage the petals can be moved to get between them more easily. Before going on to the second flower make sure the petals are correctly positioned round the centre, as they will be held by it when it sets. Work round the cake, a daisy at a time. Band the cake with ribbon, fixing it at the join with sticky tape. Cover the centre with cotton braid and fix this.

Still using the No. 2 pipe, pipe little spots of icing on to the ribbon above and below the braid (photograph 8).

Fill a piping bag without a pipe, flatten the tip and cut a small V-shape off. Try out a few icing leaves (photograph 8 shows the leaves being piped on to the cake) to make sure the sides of the leaves come out evenly; a little more may have to be trimmed off one side of the V to make the leaves symmetrical. Pipe little leaves round the top.

Encircle the base of the cake with leaves, making them a little larger than those round the top by cutting a wider V from the tip of the bag.

Finish the other cakes in the same way, marking the centre of the daisies on the middle cake ¾ inch from the edge and on the small cake ½ inch from the edge markings.

Wrap spirals of the narrow ribbon round the pillars and fix the ends with sticky tape.

TO ASSEMBLE THE CAKE

Do this on the table where it is to be cut. Stand the base cake on a tray or stand, or put the board directly on the table. Arrange the taller pillars in the centre of the largest cake and put the middle tier on top. Check that it is level otherwise a tiny square of thin white card under the base of the necessary pillars will correct it. Put the top tier on in the same way. Cut the stalks off the velvet forget-me-nots, to about an inch long and arrange a few sprays round the base of each pillar. Put the glass of flowers on top.

SHOE CAKE

FOR THE CAKES
8 oz. margarine
8 oz. castor sugar
5 eggs
10 oz. plain flour
5 level teaspoons baking powder
3½ oz. cocoa powder

a good pinch of salt
5 level tablespoons black treacle
1 teaspoon vanilla essence
4 tablespoons milk
two 1 lb. cocoa tins

FOR THE CHOCOLATE ICING
1 lb. sieved apricot jam
2 oz. cocoa powder
2 lb. icing sugar, sifted
3 oz. powdered glucose
1 teaspoon glycerine

6 tablespoons boiling water
a little drinking chocolate

FOR FINISHING THE SHOE
1 yard red silk cord
4 oz. icing sugar, sifted
2 shredded wheat biscuits
a greaseproof paper icing bag (made by folding in half diagonally a 10 inch square of greaseproof paper then rolling it into a cone) and a No. 2 plain round writing pipe
spills and glue to make the ladders and television aerial
a length of thread for the washing line

2-inch and 6-inch thin sticks to support the washing line
paper clothes, coloured with paints or chalks, cut out of fairly stiff paper and with tabs on the shoulders to hook over the line
demerara sugar to sprinkle round the shoe

One chocolate cake is required for the foot and a second for the upright part of the shoe. This mixture is enough for both cakes, but if you do not have two 1 lb. cocoa tins bake

1

2

3

half the mixture at a time. Keep the uncooked mixture in a cool place until the tin is free to bake it.

Brush the cocoa tins with melted fat and line the bases with greaseproof paper cut to fit. Brush the paper linings with melted fat also.

Heat the oven at *Gas Mark 5 or 375 degrees F.* so that it will be moderately hot for baking the cakes.

Beat the margarine to a soft cream, then beat in the castor sugar. Separate the yolks from the whites of the eggs and beat the yolks gradually into the creamed mixture. Sift the flour, baking powder, cocoa and salt together and stir gradually into the mixture with the black treacle, vanilla essence and milk. Whisk the egg whites until they are really stiff and fold them lightly into the mixture.

Divide the mixture between the prepared tins and bake the cakes for 50 minutes to 1 hour. To test if the cakes are ready, push a long thin warmed skewer into the centre of each cake in turn. If the skewer comes out clean the cakes are baked, but if any of the mixture sticks to it bake the cakes a little longer. Turn the cakes out of the tins and leave to cool.

SHAPING THE SHOE

Cut two wedges of cake diagonally from the top of one of the cakes, thus forming it into a roof shape, as seen on the left of photograph 1.

Cut a slice off the length of the other cake, to make a flat top surface. Cut a piece off one end of the slice and taper the slice on both long sides to make a wedge to build up the instep of the shoe (also photograph 1).

Assemble the two cakes on the board from which the shoe is to be served, turning the second cake flat side downwards for the foot. Brush the whole surface very thoroughly with sieved apricot jam, then put the small wedge of cake in position with the widest end towards the upright cake, and brush with apricot jam also (photograph 2).

THE ICING

Now make the icing. Sift the cocoa, icing sugar and powdered glucose together. Add the glycerine, then the boiling water, and mix the icing to a mouldable paste with

your hand; the texture should be like pliable short crust pastry. Cut the icing in half and put one half in a polythene bag to keep it moist.

Using a dusting of drinking chocolate to prevent the icing from sticking to the rolling pin and board, roll the icing into a rectangle big enough to wrap round the upright of the shoe. Lift the upright piece of jammed cake on to the icing and wrap it up completely, moulding in the joins. Put the cake back.

Cut off a quarter of the remaining icing and roll it into a sausage shape for the tongue of the shoe. Flatten the tongue a little with the rolling pin, then put it in position with one end curled over as seen in photograph 3. Roll the rest of the icing into a strip long enough and wide enough to go along the two sides and round the toe of the shoe. Lift one end of the icing on to the side of the shoe as seen in photograph 3, and carefully work the other end of the icing round to the other side of the shoe. Take a small piece of greaseproof paper and press it round the toe of the shoe with both hands to make a good shape.

FINISHING THE SHOE

When the shoe is completely coated, mark a crease for the sole all the way round the base of the shoe with the side of a wooden spoon, as seen in photograph 4. Pinch the joins in the icing between the main foot and the tongue into wavy lines and prick round the toe-cap with a skewer to represent stitching. With a skewer pierce four holes down either side of the shoe large enough to thread through the cord shoe-lace (see the colour photograph of the finished cake on page 163). Criss-cross the lace and tie it in a bow.

Mix the sifted icing sugar with a very little water to make a piping consistency. Split one shredded wheat biscuit in half along the join and stick a half either side of the shoe-top with a dab of icing. Split the remaining shredded wheat biscuit in half then cut in half lengthwise, and fix one piece with a little icing to make the apex of the roof.

Put the rest of the icing into the greaseproof paper icing bag, with the No. 2 writing pipe attached, and pipe a door under the tongue of the shoe, a round window with curtains in the toe, a diamond-shaped window just below

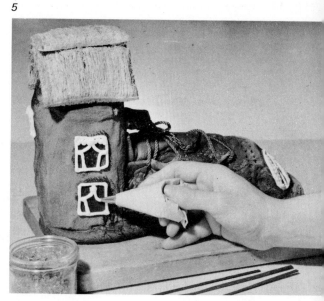

the apex of the roof, and three square windows with curtains on each side of the shoe as seen in photograph 5 and the colour photograph of the finished cake on page 163. Make the ladders and television aerial with spills, joining them with dabs of glue. Rest one ladder against one side of the shoe leading to the door and a smaller ladder on the tongue of the shoe and leading to the roof window. Tie one end of the cotton to the short stick and press it into the cake just below the apex of the roof. Press the other stick into the toe of the shoe and tie the other end of the washing line to it. Hook the clothes over the line. Surround the shoe with demerara sugar.

BISCUITS

DATE PINWHEEL BISCUITS

MAKES ABOUT 20

2 oz. butter	$\frac{1}{4}$ level teaspoon
2 oz. castor sugar	baking powder
1 egg	pinch of salt
6 oz. plain flour	

FOR THE FILLING

4 oz. cooking dates	$\frac{1}{4}$ pint water
2 oz. soft brown sugar	1 oz. walnuts,
grated rind of 1 lemon	finely chopped

Cream the butter and sugar, then beat in the egg. Sift the flour with the baking powder and the pinch of salt and stir them into the mixture. Wrap the mixture in greaseproof paper and leave it in a cool place while making the filling. Chop the dates and put them in a saucepan with the soft brown sugar, lemon rind and water. Simmer the mixture until it is a thick, spreading consistency, then stir in the chopped walnuts. Leave the mixture until it is cold.
Roll the pastry into an oblong about $\frac{1}{8}$ inch thick and spread it with the filling. Roll it up lengthways, wrap it and leave the roll to chill for at least 1 hour. Cut off $\frac{1}{4}$ inch slices with a sharp knife and bake them on a greased baking tray in a moderate oven, about *Gas Mark 4 or 350 degrees F.*, for 10 to 15 minutes.

CHOCOLATE BALLS

MAKES 12

10 digestive biscuits	2 oz. margarine
5 level tablespoons	1 small tin
drinking chocolate	sweetened
powder	condensed milk
5 level tablespoons	
desiccated coconut	

FOR THE COATING

chocolate vermicelli,	desiccated coconut
in a polythene bag	in a polythene bag

Crush the biscuits into fine crumbs; add the drinking chocolate powder and coconut.
Melt the margarine and add it to the mixture with the tinned milk. Divide the mixture into 12 small balls. Toss half in the bag of vermicelli and half in the coconut.

CHOCOLATE SHORTIES

MAKES ABOUT 24 SHORTIES

2½ oz. margarine	1 oz. cocoa powder
2½ oz. lard or vegetable	1½ oz. digestive
shortening	biscuit crumbs or
2 oz. castor sugar	browned
6 oz. plain flour	breadcrumbs

FOR THE ICING

12 oz. icing sugar	water to mix
1 oz. cocoa powder	

a Swiss roll tin 8 inches by 12 inches will be required

Beat the margarine and lard together to make a soft cream, then beat in the castor sugar. When the mixture is light and well beaten sift the flour and the cocoa together and gradually work them into the mixture with the crumbs.
Brush the Swiss roll tin with melted fat, then spread the mixture over the tin and flatten it evenly. Bake the mixture in a moderate oven, about *Gas Mark 4 or 350 degrees F.*, for 25 minutes. Cut it into 2 inch squares in the tin as soon as it comes out of the oven, but leave it in the tin until it is cold.

TO ICE THE SHORTIES

Sift the icing sugar with the cocoa. Beat in just enough cold water to make a coating consistency. Arrange the shorties closely together on a wire tray and ice them altogether—but separate them at once, before the icing has time to harden.

TENNIS TRIANGLES

MAKES ABOUT 40

12 oz. rolled oats	6 oz. margarine
grated rind of 1 large	3 level tablespoons
orange	golden syrup
6 oz. soft brown sugar	

FOR THE ICING

4 oz. icing sugar	grated rind of
6 oz. butter	1 lemon
3 level dessertspoons	
golden syrup	

a rectangular tin 12 inches long and 8 inches wide will be required

Brush the inside of the tin thoroughly with melted fat. Mix the rolled oats, orange rind and brown sugar together. Put the margarine and syrup into a pan and stir them over a gentle heat until the margarine has melted; then mix this into the dry ingredients. Pack the mixture into the tin and press the surface level. Bake in a moderate oven, about *Gas Mark 4 or 350 degrees F.*, for 20 to 25 minutes.
Put the icing sugar into a pan with the butter and golden syrup. Stir over a gentle heat until the butter has melted and the syrup is runny; add the grated lemon rind. Pour this icing over the top of the rolled oat mixture and leave it until it is set (the rolled oats need not be cold when you ice them). Mark the top with a fork. Cut into squares then into triangles; lift them out of the tray.

ALMOND SHORTCAKES

MAKES 20

5 oz. butter	20 halved, blanched
2 oz. castor sugar	almonds
1 egg yolk	icing sugar, sifted
3 oz. ground almonds	a fluted cutter
1 dessertspoon brandy	2 inches in diameter
10 oz. self-raising flour	will be required

Beat the butter to a soft cream and beat in the castor sugar really well. Beat the egg yolk into the mixture then add the ground almonds and the brandy. Sift in the flour and knead the mixture well to form a dough.

Turn the dough on to a floured board, roll it to about ½ inch in thickness and cut out the shortcakes with the fluted cutter. Roll out the scraps to make more biscuits; the mixture should make about 20. Put a halved, blanched almond in the centre of each biscuit. Dust two baking trays with flour, put the shortcakes on them and bake them just above the centre of a moderate oven, about *Gas Mark 4 or 350 degrees F*. They will take about 20 minutes. Take the biscuits out of the oven, slip them on to a wire tray, close together, and sift them thickly with icing sugar while they are hot.

BRANDY SNAPS

MAKES ABOUT 40

6 oz. margarine	6 level tablespoons
4½ oz. castor sugar	golden syrup (this must be very carefully measured)
1 level teaspoon finely grated lemon rind	4½ oz. plain flour
	3 level teaspoons ground ginger

If time permits make up the mixture one day and bake the brandy snaps the next; this seems to make them easier to handle.

Put the margarine, sugar, lemon rind and golden syrup into a pan and melt them over a low heat. Sift the flour and ground ginger together then mix in the melted ingredients. Put the mixture in teaspoons on to well oiled baking trays. Put 6 on each tray, spacing them well to allow room for them to spread. You will have to bake them in batches. Put the brandy snaps into a slow oven, about *Gas Mark 2 or 3, or 300 to 325 degrees F.*, for 8 to 10 minutes.

While they are baking, oil two wooden spoon handles ready for rolling the brandy snaps while they are still hot and flexible. Lift the brandy snaps out of the oven, run a sharp knife under each to loosen it, then turn the first one over and roll it round the handle of a spoon. Leave it while you roll the second, then slip off the first to make room for the third. If you have three wooden spoon handles it will be easier. If the brandy snaps get too cold and start to crack put them back in the oven for a second or two before attempting to roll them, as the heat will make them flexible again. Bake and roll the remainder in the same way.

These keep well in an airtight tin or a polythene bag.

GINGER SNAPS

MAKES 15

4 oz. plain flour	2 oz. golden syrup
1½ level teaspoons baking powder	2 oz. castor sugar
2 level teaspoons ground ginger	2 teaspoons lemon juice
finely grated rind of ½ lemon	1 oz. margarine

Sift the flour, baking powder and ground ginger together then lightly mix in the lemon rind.

Weigh the syrup into a saucepan. The easiest way to do this is to weigh the empty pan and a spoon, then spoon syrup into the pan to increase the weight by 2 oz. It is important for this type of recipe to use the correct amount of syrup, but 3 level tablespoons, carefully measured, should be about right.

Add the castor sugar, lemon juice and margarine to the syrup and melt the ingredients together over a gentle heat. Then stir into the sifted mixture. Roll the mixture into 15 small balls and place them on greased baking trays, well spaced to allow them to spread.

Bake the snaps in a rather slow oven, about *Gas Mark 3 or 325 degrees F.*, for 15 to 20 minutes until they are golden brown. Cool the snaps for a few seconds to allow them to firm slightly, then lift them with a palette knife on to a wire tray to cool. Store in an airtight container.

MELTING MOMENTS

MAKES 30

3 oz. butter	10 oz. self-raising flour
3 oz. lard or vegetable shortening	1 egg
5 oz. castor sugar	1 breakfastcup of cornflakes
1 teaspoon vanilla essence	

Beat the butter and lard or vegetable shortening to a soft cream, then add the castor sugar and vanilla essence, and beat the mixture again until it is light in texture and colour. Sift the flour. Beat the egg and add it to the creamed ingredients with the flour; the mixture should be a fairly firm consistency. Roll the mixture into 30 little balls. Crush the cornflakes lightly, and roll the balls in them. Arrange the balls on greased baking trays, well spaced to allow them to spread. Flatten the tops slightly with a wooden spoon.

Bake the Melting Moments in a moderate oven, about *Gas Mark 4 or 350 degrees F.*, for 15 to 20 minutes. Cool them on a wire tray.

PARTY FARE

The aim in giving a dinner party—or any other kind of party—is to create an enjoyable occasion for your guests and yourselves. The reason for giving it may be simply to offer hospitality to your friends, or it may verge on the side of duty. Whichever it is, first thoughts must be for your guests. A carefully presented meal or buffet makes a terrific impact (and so it should as it is none too easy to achieve with every detail perfect) but remember that the meal you plan is only part of the occasion—so be careful not to get over-enthusiastic about it; an exhausted hostess cannot be at her best!

With the table-laying details complete and the meal cooked, serve the food attractively. If a garnish is necessary, make it enhance the food in both colour and flavour. A garnish usually indicates or complements the main flavour. For instance, fish stuffed with prawns can be decorated also with prawns; duck served with orange sauce can have slices of orange as a garnish. Complementary garnishes include watercress with grills; grapes or cucumber with fish; lemon is a particularly useful garnish with all fried fish or meat dishes.

Finally, have really hot plates for hot courses, and use a napkin to hold them with. The food will keep so much hotter and it's unlikely your guests will really want to start before their host and hostess, so serve the food quickly and neatly so that you can rejoin them and enjoy the party. This delay can sometimes be solved by asking your guests to help themselves.

Certainly entertaining requires more advance planning and thought than everyday family meals, but a successful party—with you as the popular hostess—is well worth the trouble!

154

SUN-UP BREAKFAST

AN EARLY IN THE DAY PARTY
THE MENU
FOR 6-8 PEOPLE
**Grapefruit and Prunes
Orange Juice
Cereal**

**Kedgeree
Bacon, Fried Bananas
and Tomatoes
Sausage Cakes and
Fried Eggs
Kippers**

Breakfast Baps

**Tea
Chocolate
Coffee**

A breakfast party at the weekend is a splendidly original way of entertaining your friends—maybe after church or an early walk or before a day in the country. Even the busiest people are likely to be free at nine or ten in the morning!

GRAPEFRUIT AND PRUNES

$\frac{1}{2}$ lb. prunes	2 oz. castor sugar
$\frac{1}{2}$ pint cold tea	1 tin grapefruit
a small piece of lemon	(1 lb. 3 oz.)
rind	

Soak the prunes overnight in the tea. Cook them gently with the lemon rind and sugar until they are tender. Add the grapefruit when the prunes are cold.

KEDGEREE

1 large packet frozen skinless and boneless cod or haddock	salt and pepper
	8 oz. Patna rice
$\frac{1}{4}$ pint milk	4 hard-boiled eggs
2 oz. butter	chopped parsley

Put the fish into a fairly large pan with the milk and butter. Sprinkle it with salt and pepper, put on a lid, and cook the fish very slowly. Meanwhile put the rice into plenty of boiling salted water and boil it rapidly until it is tender, about 10 to 12 minutes. Drain the rice and run a little boiling water through it to separate the grains. Stir the rice straight into the cooked fish; this will break it up sufficiently. Season the kedgeree carefully. Shell the hard-boiled eggs; chop one of them and add it to the mixture. Heap the kedgeree into a hot dish, halve the other eggs and arrange them round the dish. Sprinkle parsley down the centre.

BACON, FRIED BANANAS AND TOMATOES

6 rashers of streaky bacon, cut thinly	browned breadcrumbs
	6 tomatoes
6 rashers back bacon	salt and pepper
a little fat for frying	a pinch of castor
6 bananas	sugar

Cut the rind off the bacon, melt the fat and fry the bacon gently. Put it into a hot dish and keep it warm. Peel and toss the bananas in browned crumbs and fry them gently in the remaining fat. Cook them on both sides until they are tender. Heap them in the centre of the dish.

Halve the tomatoes and fry them for a few minutes, face downwards, then turn them the other way up, season them with salt and pepper and a pinch of sugar. Cook them for a few seconds longer, then transfer them to the hot dish, beside the bacon and bananas.

SAUSAGE CAKES AND FRIED EGGS

1 lb. sausagemeat	a little fat for frying
a dusting of flour	8 eggs

Cut the sausagemeat into eight and form each piece into a flat circle. Dust with flour.

Fry the sausage cakes on both sides and stack them up round the edge of the pan or in a hot dish while you fry the eggs. Fry these in the remaining fat then put one on each sausage cake; they are easy to serve in this way.

KIPPERS

There are four quick and easy ways of cooking kippers. First cut off the heads.

FRIED KIPPERS

Put a little fat in the frying pan and fry the kippers, first bone side downwards. After a few minutes turn the fish and finish off the frying skin side downwards; they can be lifted on to the plate without further turning. Dot with butter.

GRILLED KIPPERS

Put the kippers, bone side upwards, under a moderate grill and grill them for 2 or 3 minutes until the bones lift easily.

OVEN COOKED KIPPERS

Bake the kippers in a moderate oven, about *Gas Mark 4 or 350 degrees F.*, for about 15 minutes until the bones lift easily. Alternatively, they can be put into a roasting tin, covered with boiling water and baked for 5 minutes.

KIPPERS IN A JUG

Spear a skewer through the tails and drop the kippers into a jug, keeping them suspended across the top by the skewer. Pour boiling water to the top of the jug; after 5 minutes, the kippers will be done. Lift out and serve with butter.

BREAKFAST BAPS

1 lb. plain flour	$\frac{1}{4}$ pint milk
2 level teaspoons salt	$\frac{1}{4}$ pint water
2 oz. lard	a little milk and
$\frac{1}{4}$ oz. dried yeast	flour for the
1 teaspoon castor sugar	tops

Make the dough the day before, keep it in a cool place overnight and bake the baps in the morning. If you want to make them the same day, use a little more yeast, and allow the dough to rise for an hour before shaping the baps.

Sift the flour and salt into a mixing bowl and rub in the lard. Put the dried yeast and sugar into a jug, heat the milk and water until it feels warm to the touch then pour it on to the yeast and sugar. Stir occasionally to help the yeast to dissolve; it will take about 20 minutes in a warm place. Add the yeast to the flour and mix to a soft dough, beating well. Cover the bowl with polythene and leave it at cool room temperature overnight.

Turn the dough on to a board and knead it lightly. Divide it into eight pieces and form each into a ball. With a rolling pin flatten each ball of dough into a round. Place the baps on a greased, floured baking tray, brush them with milk, then dust them with flour. Cover with a cloth and put the baps in a warm place to prove for 15 minutes or until they are well risen. Just before baking the baps, dust them again with flour and press a finger into the centre of each to release air bubbles. Bake the baps in a hot oven, about *Gas Mark 7 or 425 degrees F.*, for 15 to 20 minutes.

HARVEST SUPPER

THE MENU
FOR ABOUT 24 PEOPLE
Cottage Pie
Apple and Bramble Tart
Cheese, Bread and Biscuits
Hereford Spiced Punch
Glühwein

Simple food is best: Cottage Pie baked in a roasting tin followed by Apple and Bramble Tart. Home-made bread (see page 120), butter and English cheese with a good selection of home grown apples should be served too.

COTTAGE PIE

4 lb. brisket of beef, boned and rolled	2 tablespoons tomato ketchup
salt and pepper	1 tablespoon Worcester sauce
½ lb. turnip, diced	1½ pints stock (from the cooked meat)
½ lb. carrots, diced	
½ lb. onions, diced	

FOR THE TOP OF THE PIE

5 lb. potatoes	1 egg
4 oz. butter	a forcing bag and large star pipe
¼ to ½ pint hot milk	a roasting tin 18 inches by 12 inches
salt and pepper	
a little grated nutmeg	

Put the brisket into a large pan with salt and pepper and just cover it with cold water. Bring it to the boil then skim the top, cover the pan with a lid and simmer the meat for 2 hours. Halfway through the cooking add the turnip, carrots and onions, bring the meat quickly back to the boil, turn it down to simmer for the rest of the time.

Leave the meat until it is cool enough to handle. Drain off the vegetables and mince the meat. Mix the meat, vegetables, tomato ketchup and Worcester sauce with the stock and season carefully, then turn into tin.

FOR THE TOP OF THE PIE

Peel the potatoes and boil them until they are absolutely tender. Drain off the liquid. It will probably be easiest to cream them in two batches. Add the butter in small dots and as much of the milk as you require to make a soft creamy consistency, season it well with salt and pepper and a little grated nutmeg. Fill the forcing bag with the star pipe attached and pipe the potato first in the centre of the dish then round the sides and finish by covering the centre again so that the surface is slightly raised in the centre. Leave the potato to become quite cold then beat the egg with a few drops of water and brush it over the potato.

To heat the pie bake it in a moderately hot oven at *Gas Mark 5 or 375 degrees F.* for about 1 hour. As this is a large quantity, it must have time to heat thoroughly. Turn up the heat for 10 minutes if surface requires browning.

APPLE AND BRAMBLE TART

TWO OF THESE TARTS WILL BE REQUIRED FOR 24 PEOPLE

FOR THE PASTRY OR PÂTÉ SUCRÉE

8 oz. plain flour	2 egg yolks
4 oz. castor sugar	2 dessertspoons cold water
2 oz. lard, softened	
2 oz. butter, softened	a drop of vanilla essence

a shallow tart tin 11 inches in diameter will be required

FOR THE FILLING

1 oz. plain flour	2 oz. butter
2 oz. castor sugar	½ lb. brambles
2 eggs	2 oz. granulated sugar
¼ pint plus 4 tablespoons milk	2 oz. icing sugar, sifted
1 lb. cooking apples	

1   2

First make the pastry. Sift the flour on to a clean kitchen surface, form it into a circle. Put the sugar, lard, butter and egg yolks, water and vanilla into the centre and squeeze them together with the tips of the fingers using one hand only until they are evenly mixed (see photograph 1). Then, holding a palette knife in the other hand, flick the flour into the ingredients. Knead the flour into the mixture as you do to make a soft pastry consistency (see photograph 2). Wrap the pastry in greaseproof paper and put it in the refrigerator, or a cold place, for 10-15 minutes. Roll out the pastry and lift it into the tin over the rolling pin. Line the tin neatly and trim the edges.

THE FILLING

Beat the flour, castor sugar and eggs together, gradually beat in the milk, keep this ready to pour over the fruit. Peel and core the apples, then cut them into fairly thick slices. Melt the butter in a frying pan and simmer the apples and brambles for a few minutes, shaking the pan continuously until the juice from the brambles flows a little and pinks the apples, sprinkle over the granulated sugar. Turn the fruit into the pie and pour over the filling.

Bake the pie in a moderate oven, about *Gas Mark 4 or 350 degrees F.,* for 45 minutes.

Mix the icing sugar to a thick consistency with a little water and pour it in a zigzag pattern over the surface of the tart; this is most easily done from a jug.

Serve the tart hot or cold, if it is to be used cold it is best to run the icing sugar over the tart when it is cold.

HEREFORD SPICED PUNCH

12 cloves	1 lemon, thinly peeled
two 4-inch sticks of cinnamon	1 orange, thinly peeled
	½ pint water
4 blades of mace	2 oz. demerara sugar
¼ grated nutmeg	2 quarts cider

Put the cloves, cinnamon sticks, mace, nutmeg, lemon and orange peel, water and demerara sugar into a saucepan. Bring the spices slowly to the boil and simmer them for 15 minutes. Strain the spiced liquid into a large pan and add the cider. Heat until almost boiling.

Warm the glasses before serving; small glasses are best. If there is fear of the punch cracking the glasses, put a teaspoon in the glass before pouring out the punch.

GLÜHWEIN OR MULLED WINE

2 bottles inexpensive red wine	6 cloves
1 pint water	12 oz. granulated sugar
½ level teaspoon grated nutmeg	thinly peeled rind and juice of 4 lemons
stick of cinnamon, 2 inches long	

Put all the ingredients into a large pan and bring very slowly to the boil, stirring occasionally. Reduce the heat so that the *glühwein* remains hot, without boiling, for 15 minutes. Strain and serve as hot as possible. Wrap paper napkins round the glasses.

CELEBRATION PARTY

THE MENU
FOR 12 PEOPLE
**Pâté with Melba Toast
and Butter Balls**
or
Tomato and Shrimp Soup
or
**Surprise Grapefruit
Cocktail**

Roast Saddle of Lamb
*glazed and garnished with
oranges and prunes*
**Baked Lemon Potatoes
and Green Peas**
to accompany the saddle served hot
**Mint Potatoes
and Spring Salad**
to accompany the saddle served cold

Mocha Meringue
or
Marquise Alice

**Normandy Pear Tart with
Cranberry Tartlets**

**A Selection of Cheeses
A Basket of Fruit
Sangria
Coffee**

PÂTÉ AND MELBA TOAST

12 oz. pâté, sliced (you could use a selection of pâtés—see the recipes on pages 15 and 16)	24 slices Melba toast (see page 18) or a 4 oz. packet
24 butter balls, chilled	sprigs of parsley

Arrange the pâté, the butter balls and the toast on two plates so that it will be easy to serve. It is best to cut the pâté just before it is used. Arrange the portions with sprigs of parsley between them. Be sure the butter balls are ice cold.

If you use a tin of pâté put it in the refrigerator for several hours to firm it before it is opened. Hold the tin under hot water 2 or 3 seconds before opening, and shake out the pâté which should then slide out easily and in one piece. Cut into slices or wedges.

TOMATO AND SHRIMP SOUP

1 oz. butter	4 tins cream of tomato soup
1 onion, very finely chopped	about ¾ pint milk
1 level tablespoon plain flour	8 oz. shrimps (fresh, frozen or tinned)

Melt the butter in a large pan, add the onion and cook it very gently in the butter so that the onion cooks but remains uncoloured. Take the pan off the heat and stir in the flour. Add all the soups. Fill one of the empty soup tins with milk and add. Stir the soup over a gentle heat until it comes to the boil. Take it off the heat and add the shrimps, together with any liquid. Reheat when required but be careful not to boil the shrimps or they will toughen.

SURPRISE GRAPEFRUIT COCKTAIL

6 large grapefruit	sugar
6 tomatoes	2 ripe avocado pears
1 large melon	

Cut each grapefruit in half. Scoop out the fruit with a pointed spoon and put it in a bowl. Scrape away the white skin from the walls of the grapefruit, then put the cases into individual grapefruit glasses or dishes.

Skin the tomatoes, cut them in quarters, remove the pips then cut the quarters into neat strips and stir them into the grapefruit.

Cut the melon in half lengthways and remove the seeds. Cut out balls of melon with a ball cutter, or with the tip of a teaspoon, and add these to the grapefruit.

Mix the fruit well and sweeten it carefully with sugar. It can be left overnight at this stage. Peel the avocado pears as you would a dessert pear, and remove the stones. Cut the fruit into cubes and add it to the grapefruit. Heap the fruit into the grapefruit cases and serve cold but not chilled.

ROAST SADDLE OF LAMB

a saddle of lamb, prepared by the butcher (between 10 and 11 lb.)	kitchen salt 3 oz. lard

FOR THE GLAZE

4 tablespoons orange juice	4 tablespoons prune syrup

FOR THE GRAVY

the natural gravy from the roast	a little boiling water, if necessary

FOR THE GARNISH

3 medium sized oranges 1 small tin (7½ oz.) prunes in syrup; the syrup is used for the glaze	2 bunches of watercress, washed

Check the weight of the joint and calculate the roasting time. Allow 20 minutes for every pound in weight and add 20 minutes to the total time. After it is cooked the saddle should be allowed to "rest" in a warm place or on a plate warmer for at least 20 minutes as this makes it easier to carve. This time is convenient for making the gravy and serving the first course. It also frees the oven for the potatoes.

The joint is a large one, so line the roasting tin, if necessary, with kitchen foil, extending it over the sides of the tin to go under any overhang and catch all the juices. Rub the joint very thoroughly with salt, to give it a good crisp surface. Place the joint in the tin; melt the lard and pour it over the joint.

Have a fairly hot oven ready, about *Gas Mark 6 or 400 degrees F.*, and put the joint just above the centre. After 30 minutes baste the joint and lower the heat to *Gas Mark 4 or 350 degrees F.* for the rest of the time. It needs to be basted once or twice.

30 minutes before the meat is cooked, mix the orange and prune juice and pour over the joint. Baste twice during the last 30 minutes.

Lift the saddle on to a hot serving dish and put it in a warm place for about 20 minutes.

NOTE: To serve the saddle cold cook it the day before the party. Keep it in a cool larder, not a refrigerator, overnight.

THE GRAVY

Slip the foil out of the tin and allow the gravy to settle; then skim off all the fat. Taste the gravy and add a little boiling water if necessary. Pour it into a pan, where it is easier to keep hot than in the roasting tin.

THE GARNISH

This can be made the day before if the oranges are kept in a polythene bag.

Cut each orange into eight sections taking the cuts from the top to just below half way down, leaving the sections firmly attached at the base. Slip a prune between the tips of each pair of sections.

SERVING

Arrange the oranges on and around the roast with bunches of watercress between them.

BAKED LEMON POTATOES

4 lb. potatoes, weighed before peeling 3 oz. butter 1 large onion, finely diced	grated rind and juice of 1½ lemons 4 level tablespoons chopped parsley salt and pepper

Peel the potatoes and cut them into inch cubes. Put them into a large pan, cover with cold water and bring to the boil. Boil for 3 minutes, then drain them. Put the butter into the empty pan, add the diced onion and fry it very slowly until it is transparent without being brown. Add the lemon rind and juice, chopped parsley, salt and pepper. Return the potatoes to the pan and toss them gently so that they are evenly coated by the mixture. They can be kept in a bowl overnight at this stage.

About 20 minutes before joint is ready, turn potatoes into a roasting tin and put them into the oven below the saddle of lamb at *Gas Mark 4 or 350 degrees F.* When the joint is taken out, increase the heat and cook the potatoes in a moderately hot oven, about *Gas Mark 6 or 400 degrees F.*, until they are cooked and golden brown on top; they will take a further 20-25 minutes.

GREEN PEAS

1 level teaspoon sugar 2 sprigs of mint 2 lb. green peas (buy frozen peas in large bag by weight)	2 oz. butter salt and pepper

Half fill a large pan with boiling salted water; add the sugar and the mint and tip in the peas. Bring to the boil and boil the peas just long enough for them to become tender; 5 minutes is usually enough. Drain them. Melt the butter in the pan, then return the peas, adding salt and pepper if necessary, and toss them over the heat for a second. Turn them into a hot dish for serving.

NEW MINT POTATOES

TO SERVE IF THE JOINT IS COLD

3 lb. new potatoes 3 oz. butter salt and freshly ground black pepper	3 sprigs of mint a large double sheet of greaseproof paper

Scrape the skins off the new potatoes, wash and dry them. Spread the sheet of greaseproof paper over the base of a roasting tin and turn the potatoes on to it. Dot them over with the butter and season with salt and pepper and the sprigs of mint. Fold the greaseproof paper up like a parcel to enclose the potatoes completely.

Cook the potatoes just above the centre of a fairly hot oven, about *Gas Mark 6 or 400 degrees F.*, for about an hour (the time varies a little with the kind of potato). It may seem a long time but this large quantity of potatoes has to heat through before they start cooking.

When the potatoes are ready, slit open the bag and tip the potatoes into a serving dish.

SPRING SALAD

TO SERVE WITH THE COLD JOINT

Choose a selection of three from the following green salad vegetables: lettuce, endive, chicory, celery, watercress, small cress, cucumber, green pepper, spring onions.
Allow three large lettuce or endive for the main bulk of the salad. Toss the washed and dried salad lightly in French Dressing just before serving.

FRENCH DRESSING

Mix 4 tablespoons of white vinegar very thoroughly with 1 level teaspoon of French mustard. Add salt and pepper, then pour the mixture into an empty bottle. Add 4 tablespoons of salad oil, cork the bottle and shake well to mix the ingredients thoroughly. French dressing keeps well if made in this way and kept in the bottle.

MOCHA MERINGUE

CHOCOLATE BUTTERCREAM

8 oz. unsalted butter	4 egg yolks
8 oz. castor sugar	6 oz. plain dessert
$\frac{1}{4}$ pint water	chocolate

FOR THE MERINGUES

6 egg whites	3 level tablespoons
12 oz. castor sugar	instant coffee
	powder

a forcing bag with a large star pipe will be required

TO TOP THE MERINGUES
4 oz. plain dessert chocolate

This sweet can be made up to two days beforehand. It is best to make the chocolate buttercream first, as the egg whites keep well in a screw-topped jar and can be used for the meringues later.

CHOCOLATE BUTTERCREAM

Beat the butter to a very soft creamy consistency and leave it at room temperature.
Put the sugar into a pan together with the water and dissolve over a very gentle heat. Stir occasionally but *do not allow the syrup to boil before every grain has dissolved.* When every grain of sugar has dissolved stop stirring and bring the syrup to the boil. Boil it rapidly until the short thread stage is reached. To test for this, lift a little syrup with a spoon, touch the surface of it with the third finger, press it to the thumb, then separate the finger and thumb quickly. If the syrup is ready it should form a short thread between the fingers before breaking.
Put the egg yolks into a medium sized bowl and stand it on a damp cloth to prevent it from slipping. Beat the egg yolks well with a wire whisk then, very gradually, pour on the syrup, whisking all the time. As the mixture cools it will become thick and creamy. While it is still slightly warm beat in the creamed butter, a teaspoon at a time. Break the chocolate into pieces and put it on a plate in a warm place to melt and, when it is soft, beat it into the mixture. Leave the buttercream in a cool place to firm slightly, though it is easiest to use when it is soft so avoid using it too cold.

This buttercream will keep well for up to two weeks in a covered container in the refrigerator.

MERINGUES
Make the white meringues first; for these you will require 2 egg whites and 4 oz. sugar. Rub a large baking tray, or two smaller ones, with tasteless salad oil and then dust them with flour. Put 2 egg whites into a mixing bowl and beat them very stiffly indeed until they will stand up in sharp peaks. Add 2 dessertspoons of the castor sugar and beat again until the same stiff consistency is reached. Very lightly fold in all that remains of the 4 oz. sugar. Fill the piping bag, with a star pipe attached, with the meringue mixture and pipe small whirls of meringue on the baking tray.
Bake the meringues in a very cool oven, about *Gas Mark 0 or 175 degrees F.* They will take up to 4 hours to become quite crisp to the centre. The slow oven is essential to keep them white. It is possible that gas oven heat will not be low enough, so keep the door just ajar.
When the meringues are ready they will lift easily off the trays. Cool them and store them in an airtight tin. They will keep for weeks.
Make the coffee meringues in the same way but they will make twice the amount and you may have to do them in two batches. Mix in the instant coffee with the egg whites before starting to beat.

TO ASSEMBLE THE SWEETS
Beat the buttercream until it is nice and soft and heap up the meringues, spreading the buttercream between.
Melt the chocolate and trickle it over the top of the meringues.
This sweet is nicer when assembled the day before the party to allow the buttercream to soften the meringues slightly. If you like, it can be made two days beforehand. Keep in a cool, dry atmosphere. Serve it at room temperature.

MARQUISE ALICE

FOR THE PRALINE

1 oz. castor sugar	1 oz. unblanched
4 tablespoons water	almonds

FOR THE SET CREAM

1 pint milk	4 tablespoons water
$2\frac{1}{2}$ oz. castor sugar	$\frac{1}{4}$ pint double cream
4 egg yolks	2 egg whites
$\frac{1}{2}$ oz. gelatine	

a tin mould which holds 2 pints of liquid, or a cake tin 8 inches in diameter, or a china dish, in which to set the cream

FOR THE CHOCOLATE CONES

seven 4 inch squares	14 paperclips
of waxed paper, cut	3 oz. plain dessert
from corner to corner	chocolate
to make 14 triangles	

TO DECORATE THE SWEET AND FILL THE CONES

$\frac{1}{2}$ pint double cream	2 piping bags
2 tablespoons	a small star pipe
redcurrant jelly,	a No. 2 plain writing
sieved	pipe

TO MAKE THE PRALINE

Put the sugar and water into a small pan and *without allowing it to boil*, dissolve the sugar over a very gentle heat. Bring the syrup to the boil and boil it rapidly until it is a mid-golden brown. Stir in the almonds then pour the mixture on to a well-oiled laminated plastic surface. Leave to set, then crush the praline with a rolling pin.

TO MAKE THE SET CREAM

Rub the inside of the mould with tasteless salad oil. Heat the milk slowly in a saucepan. Put the sugar and egg yolks into a bowl and beat them well together. Pour the hot milk slowly on to the egg yolks and sugar, stirring all the time. Strain the mixture back into the pan and stir the custard over a gentle heat without allowing it to boil, until it thinly coats the back of a wooden spoon. Stir in the praline crumbs. Pour the mixture into a bowl and leave it until it is lukewarm.

Put the gelatine and water into a small pan and dissolve the gelatine over a gentle heat then stir it into the lukewarm mixture and leave it until it is cold but not set. Whip the cream until it is fluffy without being stiff and fold it into the mixture.

Beat the egg whites stiffly, carefully mix a dessertspoon into the mixture then fold in the rest. Pour the mixture into the oiled mould. Leave it to set.

TO MAKE THE CHOCOLATE CONES

Curl the triangles of waxed paper into cone shapes and fasten with paper clips. Stand them between the wires of a wire cooling tray to keep them upright.

Break the chocolate on to a plate and put it in a warm place to melt; do not overheat it but beat it with a palette knife until it is melted. Using a small teaspoon, drop a small spoonful of chocolate into a wax cone and tip the cone round to coat the sides with chocolate for about an inch and a half.

Make the other cones in the same way and then leave them standing upright in the wire tray to set. When the chocolate is set, peel off the waxed paper.

TO DECORATE THE SWEET AND FILL THE CONES

Turn the set cream on to a pretty plate. Whip the rest of the double cream very lightly, just to a spreading consistency, and cover the top and sides thinly with about half the cream. Fill a piping bag, with a No. 2 plain writing pipe attached, with sieved redcurrant jelly and pipe straight lines about an inch apart over the top of the cream. Draw the back of a knife across the lines, alternately from each side, at the same distance apart, making a feather pattern. Pipe a little redcurrant jelly into the base of each cone. Whip the remainder of the cream a little more stiffly so that it will just hold its shape and with it fill a piping bag with a star pipe attached. Pipe a whirl of cream into each cone and tip it with a spot of redcurrant jelly. Arrange the chocolate cones round the cream.

This sweet must be decorated the same day as the party, though the set cream and the chocolate cones can be made the day beforehand. The cones keep well in an airtight tin, so they can be made even earlier.

NORMANDY PEAR TART

FOR THE WALNUT PASTRY

12 oz. plain flour	3 oz. lard
a good pinch of salt	6 oz. castor sugar
½ level teaspoon ground cinnamon	2 oz. walnuts, finely chopped
3 oz. margarine	3 egg yolks
half a lightly beaten egg white and a little castor sugar for the glaze	

a large flan ring 9 inches in diameter will be required

FOR THE FILLING

1 large tin (1 lb. 13 oz.) halved pears or lightly poached fresh pears can be used	¼ pint clotted cream or lightly whipped double cream
	a few chopped pistachio nuts or walnuts

Sift the flour, salt and cinnamon into a bowl and rub in the fats, then stir in the sugar and chopped walnuts. Mix the pastry to a firm but not stiff dough with the egg yolks and a very little cold water. Wrap the pastry in greaseproof paper and leave it in a cold place for at least 30 minutes.

Drain the juice off the pears. Roll half the pastry into a circle 2 inches larger than the flan ring. Place the ring on an upturned baking tray and lift the pastry, over a rolling pin, into the ring and line it carefully and fairly thickly. Trim round the top, leaving a ¼ inch overlap. Place the pears in a circle round the flan, points to the centre. Cut off half the remaining pastry and roll it into a circle to fit the top. Moisten round the pastry beneath, lift on the top and press the pastry edges together. Trim round the edge, keeping the trimmings for the Cranberry Tartlets (see below). Using a round cutter, 3 inches in diameter, cut a circle from the centre of the top; brush the beaten egg white over the top and dust with castor sugar.

Bake the tart just above the centre of a hot oven, about *Gas Mark 7 or 425 degrees F.*, for 20 minutes then reduce the heat to *Gas Mark 6 or 400 degrees F.* for a further 15-20 minutes. Leave the tart on the tray until it is cold. Loosen round the ring with a sharp knife then lift it off. Using a palette knife, slip the flan on to a serving dish.

Heap the centre of the tart with clotted cream or whipped cream and sprinkle over the pistachio nuts.

CRANBERRY TARTLETS

the trimmings of walnut pastry from Normandy Tart (see above)	a forcing bag and a fairly large star pipe
1 tin (8 oz.) whole cranberry sauce	very small paper cases
¼ pint double cream, whipped and lightly sweetened with castor sugar	small tartlet tins each measuring 2 inches in diameter

Roll out the pastry fairly thinly and carefully line the tartlet tins (the number will depend on how thick the flan pastry is, but it will probably be about nine or ten).

Line each tartlet with kitchen paper filled with baking beans. Bake the tartlets in a hot oven, about *Gas Mark 7 or 425 degrees F.*, for 7 minutes, then remove the beans and paper and return them to the oven for a further 3 or 4 minutes. Cool the tartlets on a wire tray. (They will keep well in an airtight tin.)

To fill the tarts fill a forcing bag with whipped cream and pipe a star of cream into the base of each tartlet. Fill the cases with whole cranberry sauce and pipe a collar of whipped cream round each. Put into paper cases.

SANGRIA

2 oranges	2 bottles inexpensive
2 lemons	red Spanish wine
cinnamon stick,	6 tablespoons brandy
3 inches long	1 pint soda water
12 oz. castor sugar	a tray of ice cubes
1½ pints water	

Slice the orange and lemon into a large bowl; add the cinnamon stick. Put the castor sugar into a large pan with the water and dissolve it slowly over a very gentle heat. When it is dissolved, bring it to the boil and boil for 2 minutes. Pour the syrup over the fruit and cinnamon and leave it for 4 hours.

Just before serving, add the wine, brandy and soda water and lastly, the ice cubes.

CHILDREN'S PARTY

THE MENU
FOR 12 CHILDREN
Sandwiches
Sausage Centipede
Sausage and Cheese Savouries
Star Cake
Cat Cakes
Shortbread Biscuits
Cherry Kisses
Chocolate Crunchies
Jam and Fruit Salad Tarts
Jelly Folk
Lemon Squash
Orange and Grapefruit Squash

THE SANDWICHES

Choose the popular fillings for the biggest success, such as peanut butter; grated apple and raisin; and yeast extract; but you can add any of the following:—jam, banana, cream cheese and tomato, lettuce and fish or meat paste.

There are about 22 slices in a sandwich loaf, which will require about ½ lb. butter.

SAUSAGE CENTIPEDE

1 lb. beef chipolata	2 red or green
sausages	cocktail onions
1 French loaf about	about 30 cocktail
18 inches long	sticks

Twist each sausage in the centre to make twice the number of sausages. Prick them lightly with a skewer. Snip between the sausages with a pair of scissors. Put the sausages into a cold frying pan and cook them gently, rolling them round in the pan so that they brown evenly. Leave them to cool. Turn the loaf upside down and press a row of cocktail sticks down each side for legs. Spear a little sausage on the end of each, then turn the "centipede" on to his feet. Spike each cocktail onion on to half a cocktail stick and press the sticks into the "head" end of the loaf. Put the centipede on to a long dish or use a washable mat.

SAUSAGE AND CHEESE SAVOURIES

16 slices of fairly	16 slices of
thickly cut white	processed cheese
bread, spread with	about 4 tomatoes
butter	sprigs of
16 (1 lb.) chipolata	watercress
sausages, cooked	

Cover each slice of bread and butter with cheese. Cut off the crusts and halve each slice diagonally. Slit the sausages in half and then cut them crossways; making four from each sausage. Slice the tomatoes and put a slice in the centre of each triangle of bread and butter and flank it on each side with pieces of sausage. Top the tomato slices with a sprig of watercress.

STAR CAKE

FOR THE CAKE

6 oz. margarine	6 oz. plain flour
6 oz. castor sugar	3 level teaspoons
3 eggs	baking powder
finely grated rind of	2 tablespoons water
1 small orange	
a rectangular tin 10 inches long and 6 inches	
wide will be required	

FOR THE ICING

6 oz. butter	about 2 tablespoons
9 oz. icing sugar,	hundreds and
sifted	thousands
juice of an orange	9 glacé cherries

Brush the cake tin with melted fat and line it with greaseproof paper. Brush the paper lining with melted fat also. Beat the margarine to a soft cream, then gradually beat in the castor sugar. Break an egg into a cup and add it to the creamed mixture and beat very thoroughly. Add the rest of the eggs in the same way. Beat in the grated orange rind. Sift the flour and baking powder and fold them lightly into the mixture with the water.

Turn the mixture into the tin. Smooth over the surface and hollow out the centre slightly so that the cake rises as evenly as possible. Bake the cake, just above the centre of a moderately hot oven, about *Gas Mark 5 or 375 degrees F.*, for 35 to 40 minutes.

Turn the cake on to a wire tray and remove paper.

TO SHAPE THE STAR

Cut a wide V from each short end of cake. Take one V shape and lay it against one long edge of the cake then trim off a little cake from either side to make the points of the star in correct proportion. Complete the star shape with the other V-shaped slice of cake.

Transfer the cake to the board from which it will be served.

THE BUTTER ICING

Beat the butter to a very soft cream then gradually beat in the sifted icing sugar. Gradually beat in the orange juice. First spread butter icing between the edges of the two loose star points. Spread the top of the cake with just over half the butter icing. Sprinkle the points with hundreds and thousands. This is most easily done if you lay a ruler across the wide end of each point while the tip is sprinkled. Brush away any odd hundreds and thousands from round the board and spread the remainder of the butter icing round the edge of the cake.

Decorate the tip of each point with a whole glacé cherry and the inside points with half a cherry as shown in the photograph on page 188.

CAT CAKES

2 chocolate Swiss rolls	a very little
4 individual chocolate	butter icing or
Swiss rolls	softened butter
24 shortbread crescents	12 paper cases
(see below)	3 oz. icing sugar,
12 pairs shortbread ears	sifted
(see below)	a drop of red
	colouring

Cut each chocolate Swiss roll into 6 slices and stand each slice on end in a paper case. Cut each individual roll into three pieces and with butter icing stick a piece on top of each large slice to represent the head. For a tail, stick a shortbread crescent into the side of each large Swiss roll slice. Give each cat a pair of ears, stuck on with butter icing. (See the photograph on page 188.)

TO PIPE THE NAMES

Mix the sifted icing sugar with a very little water and a drop of red colouring to a thick consistency. Fill a piping bag with this mixture, and with a No. 2 plain round pipe attached, pipe the children's names on the remaining crescents.

TO MAKE THE SHORTBREAD CRESCENTS

6 oz. plain flour	1 oz. castor sugar
4 oz. butter, softened at	
room temperature	

Knead all the ingredients together. Using a sprinkling of flour, roll out the mixture so that it is just under a $\frac{1}{4}$ inch thick. Cut out circles from the mixture with a cutter $2\frac{3}{4}$ inches in diameter. From these circles cut fairly wide crescents. Roll up the scraps and make more crescent biscuits. After the second rolling use the scraps to make little triangles for the ears of the cats (see recipe above). Bake the biscuits in a slow oven, about *Gas Mark 3 or 325 degrees F.* for about 30 minutes. The ears, being smaller, will be ready sooner.

CHERRY KISSES

6 oz. margarine	1 level teaspoon
2 oz. icing sugar,	baking powder
sifted	$4\frac{1}{2}$ oz. plain flour
vanilla essence	25 glacé cherries
$1\frac{1}{2}$ oz. cornflour	50 paper sweet cases

Put the margarine into a warm basin, break it up into pieces and beat it until it is really soft. Add the icing sugar gradually, beating really well; the mixture should be very soft and creamy. Beat in a few drops of vanilla essence. Sift the flour with the cornflour and baking powder, and stir them into the creamed ingredients.

Put the mixture into a forcing bag with a fairly large star pipe attached, and pipe the mixture into the paper cases. Top each with half a cherry. Bake in a moderately hot oven, about *Gas Mark 5 or 375 degrees F.,* for 10 minutes.

CHOCOLATE CRUNCHIES

3 oz. margarine	3 oz. sultanas,
3 level tablespoons	cleaned
golden syrup	3 oz. cornflakes
2 oz. icing sugar	17 paper cake
3 level tablespoons	cases
cocoa powder	

Slowly melt the margarine, syrup, icing sugar and cocoa together in a fairly large pan. Take the pan off the heat and stir in the sultanas and cornflakes. Heap the mixture into the cases and leave them to set.

JAM AND FRUIT SALAD TARTS

8 oz. plain flour	a fluted cutter $2\frac{3}{4}$
2 oz. margarine	inches in diameter
2 oz. lard	tartlet tins $2\frac{1}{2}$ inches
cold water to mix	in diameter

FOR THE JAM TARTS
preferably a small amount of a variety of different jams, and lemon curd

FOR THE FRUIT SALAD TARTS

1 tin (15$\frac{1}{2}$ oz.) fruit	2 level teaspoons
cocktail	arrowroot

First make the pastry. Sift the flour and rub in the fats. Mix the pastry to a stiff dough with a little cold water. Roll the pastry thinly and cut out circles with the fluted cutter. Line the tartlet tins with the pastry.

Put a little jam or lemon curd in each of twelve tartlets and bake them in a moderately hot oven, about *Gas Mark 5 or 375 degrees F.,* for about 20 minutes. Slip them out of the tins to cool.

For the fruit salad tartlets prick the pastry cases with a fork and bake them at the same temperature as the jam tarts until they are ready; they will take about the same time.

Drain the juice off the fruit cocktail and measure $\frac{1}{4}$ pint. Blend the arrowroot with just enough water to make a thin cream and stir it into the measured fruit juice. Put this glaze in a small pan over a gentle heat and stir until it comes to the boil. Fill the tartlets with fruit then coat the tops with the shiny arrowroot glaze.

Shoe cake (see page 150)

Above: Christmas cake; right: brandy scroll cake
(see page 143 for both recipes)

Rich chocolate cake (see page 141), chocolate and banana cream roll (see page 138),
chocolate and chestnut cake (see page 141), chocolate balls (see page 152)

JELLY FOLK

2 packets strawberry jelly	12 paper sweet cases
1 large tin unsweetened evaporated milk	12 small glasses each holding about 4 tablespoons liquid
little pieces of glacé cherry for mouths	12 coffee cups or containers with the same top measure-ment as the glasses
currants for eyes	
12 marshmallows	

Make up the 2 jellies using 1½ pints of boiling water. Let it cool then beat in the evaporated milk. Rinse the cups with cold water and fill both the cups and glasses with the jelly. Leave them to set.

Turn the cups out on to the jelly in the glasses, making the domed tops as in colour picture on page 188. Make each a mouth of a sliver of cherry and use two currants for eyes. Lastly put a marshmallow in each paper case and rest it on top at a slight angle to represent a hat.

LEMON SQUASH

This recipe makes 2¾ pints of concentrated lemon squash, which will make up into about 11 pints of diluted squash.

1 lb. 10 oz. granulated sugar	1½ pints boiling water
1½ oz. tartaric acid (8 level teaspoons)	finely grated rind and juice of 2 large lemons
¼ oz. Epsom salts (3 level teaspoons)	

A ¼ pint of concentrated squash made up to a pint with water suits most tastes.

Put the sugar, tartaric acid and Epsom salts into a large bowl. Pour the boiling water over and stir until the sugar is dissolved. Cool the liquid, then add the grated lemon rind and the juice. Leave overnight, or until the squash is quite cold, then pour it into bottles and cork or cover with screw caps. The squash will keep quite well in a cool place for two or three weeks.

ORANGE AND GRAPEFRUIT SQUASH

This recipe makes 3¾ pints of concentrated squash which can be diluted to make 17 pints.

2 lb. granulated sugar	finely grated rind and juice of 2 large oranges
1½ pints water	
¾ oz. tartaric acid (4 level teaspoons)	finely grated rind and juice of 1 grapefruit

Put the sugar and water into a pan and stir over a gentle heat until the sugar has dissolved. Bring the syrup to the boil and simmer for 10 minutes. Pour the hot syrup over the tartaric acid and the grated rinds. Leave the squash over-night then stir in the orange and grapefruit juice. Pour the squash into bottles and cork them.

The squash will keep well in a cool place for about 3 weeks.

FONDUE BOURGUIGNONNE

At the party your guests help themselves to small cubes of raw steak with a fondue skewer, and proceed to fry the cubes in a dish of hot fat. While the steak is cooking, every-one helps himself to an assortment of accompanying side dishes of sauces and pickles arranged round the fondue pan. Served with new bread and fresh butter and bottles of red wine, the fondue makes a satisfying meal that everyone will enjoy. Round it off with plenty of freshly made coffee.

Unless you have a round table, it is a good idea to limit your guests to five or six people as more are inclined to get in each other's way. It can also be a bit difficult to keep the fat hot enough for frying the steak if too many people are dipping into it at once.

THE STEAK
allow ½ lb. rump steak per person—this is liberal weight. Ask your butcher to cut the steak into slices ¼ inch thick
1 lb. lard

THE MAYONNAISE
the following quantities make ¾ pint which is divided into four portions: one for each of the sauces mentioned below

3 egg yolks (2 whole eggs if using the blender method)	salt
	¾ pint salad oil (the eggs and the oil should be at room temperature)
3 level teaspoons French mustard	
a good pinch castor sugar	about 2 tablespoons distilled white vinegar
a good sprinkling of freshly ground pepper	

First make the mayonnaise.

Mix the egg yolks with the mustard, sugar, pepper and a good pinch of salt. Measure the oil into a jug and add a drop at a time to the yolks, beating all the time with a wooden spoon. When the mayonnaise starts to thicken the oil can be added a little more quickly. When it is really thick, add a little vinegar to thin it again to the right consistency. Season carefully. The mayonnaise keeps well in a screw-topped jar stored in a cool place.

BLENDER METHOD
A blender is most useful for making mayonnaise though if it is a small blender, you may have to make the mayon-naise in batches. For this method use the whole eggs, instead of only the yolks as you would if you were making the mayonnaise by hand. Put the eggs into the liquidiser with the seasoning and the vinegar, blend them together for a second, then add the oil in a steady thin stream. It can be added more quickly when it starts to thicken.

Divide the mayonnaise into four portions—one for each of the following sauces. They can be prepared well in advance and covered with polythene to prevent a skin forming on the surface.

TOMATO SAUCE
¼ of the mayonnaise

2 tablespoons
tomato ketchup

CURRY SAUCE
¼ of the mayonnaise

2 level teaspoons
curry powder, or to
taste

MUSTARD SAUCE
¼ of the mayonnaise
2 level teaspoons
French mustard

1 tablespoon chopped
vegetable
piccalilli

HERB SAUCE
¼ of the mayonnaise
1 rounded dessertspoon
chopped chives

1 rounded
tablespoon chopped
parsley

Mix together the ingredients for each sauce and put the sauces into small dishes.

THE OTHER ACCOMPANIMENTS
1 small tin anchovies
stuffed olives
gherkins
pickled onions
1 tin button mushrooms
½ bottle brown steak
sauce
1 small tin whole
cranberry sauce

1 small tin pineapple
chunks
1 tin cherry pie
filling
2 bananas
juice of ½ lemon
brown bread and
butter

Open the tin of anchovies and tip them into a small dish. The olives, gherkins and pickled onions can be arranged on one plate. Tip the tinned mushrooms into a shallow bowl and pour over the brown steak sauce. Fill three separate dishes with the cranberry sauce, the pineapple chunks and the cherry pie filling. Slice the bananas into a dish and sprinkle with the lemon juice.

ARRANGING THE FONDUE
Trim any fat off the meat and cut it into cubes. Heap the meat on to a large platter or wooden chopping board.
Arrange the meat and all the other dishes on the table round the fondue pan so they are within easy reach of your guests. Or place them on a tray which can be handed round.
Just before you plan to start eating, heat the lard on the kitchen stove—it should just over half fill the pan. When a faint haze rises from it, transfer the pan to the spirit heater on the serving table and the party can begin.
If you don't possess a fondue pan and spirit heater, use a picnic spirit cooker and an ordinary kitchen saucepan which will work just as well—very efficiently in fact.

WEDDING BUFFET

A wedding reception is, in the truest sense, a movable feast so it is difficult to lay down exact amounts of food to allow. Four savouries (including sandwiches) and three cakes should be enough for each person, plus the sausages and bacon on sticks for good measure. These proportions can be changed according to the time of day of the reception. You may want to include favourites such as sausage rolls, asparagus and brown bread rolls and cheese straws, so add them to the list and allow for them when you make your

selection. You will find a recipe for The Daisy Wedding Cake on page 145.
Many hands make light work, but make sure that any friends helping you know exactly the results you wish. To make serving easy, arrange selections on trays. Provided plenty of napkins are available, plates are not necessary. It is particularly difficult for the lady guests to hold plate, glass, handbag and gloves and eat at the same time.

THE MENU

Sandwiches
Ham and Chutney
Grated Apple, Sultanas and Mayonnaise
Lettuce and Lemon

Savoury Boats
Haddock and Prawn
Mushroom
Sweetcorn and Bacon
Cheese

Savouries
Cheese Whirls
Tuna Fish Squares
Egg Savouries
Sausages and Prune and
Bacon Rolls

Cakes
Chocolate Cakes
Cherry Shortbread Horseshoes
Cherry Gateau
Raspberry Cream Tartlets
Daisy Wedding Cake

Rosé Wine Cup

SANDWICHES

One sliced sandwich loaf has about 26 slices. 6 oz. of butter will be required to spread on it. This will make 13 rounds of sandwiches, and each round is cut into four. The following fillings are together just sufficient for one loaf. All the sandwiches can be made the day before the wedding, arranged on trays or plates ready for serving and covered tightly with polythene. Slip off the polythene covers at the last possible moment. If the sandwiches are kept in a cool place overnight they will be moist and fresh.

GRATED APPLE, SULTANAS AND MAYONNAISE
1 grated apple (there
is no need to peel
the apple)
2 oz. sultanas

3 level tablespoons
mayonnaise

Mix the ingredients together. They are enough for 4 rounds.

Wedding buffet

HAM AND CHUTNEY

4 oz. ham, chopped	made up mustard,
1 level dessertspoon	if liked
chutney	

Mix the ingredients together. They are enough for 4 rounds.

LETTUCE AND LEMON

1 large lettuce	salt and freshly
finely grated rind of	ground black
1 lemon	pepper

Wash, dry and shred the lettuce. Make 5 rounds liberally filled with lettuce and sprinkled with salt, pepper and grated lemon rind.

THE SAVOURY BOATS

THE PASTRY BOATS

The pastry boats can be made up to a week beforehand and kept in airtight tins, or stacked and put into polythene bags. Early on the day they can be crisped in a hot oven for a few minutes. This amount makes about 48 boats.

Those with less time to spare can use the alternative recipes for baking these savouries, complete with fillings, in large trays and cutting them into fingers.

1 lb. plain flour	4 oz. lard
1 level teaspoon salt	cold water to mix
4 oz. margarine	

boat-shaped tartlet tins, 4 inches long

Sift the flour and salt and rub in the fats. Mix the pastry to a stiff dough with just a little water. Roll about half of the pastry fairly thinly. Line as many tins as you can and add the scraps of the pastry to the other half. Prick the base of the tartlets with a fork. Bake them in a fairly hot oven, *Gas Mark 6 or 400 degrees F.*, for 15-20 minutes. Lift them out of the tins and leave them to cool on a wire tray before stacking them together. Make the rest of the tartlets.

THE BASIC SAUCE FOR THE PASTRY BOATS

The basic sauce for the haddock, mushroom and sweetcorn tarts can all be made together by an easy method, then divided into three and the other ingredients added. In each case a pint of sauce (with the extra ingredients added) fills the 48 boats made from one batch of pastry.

4½ oz. plain flour	4½ oz. margarine
3 pints milk	

Put the flour into a bowl and blend it to a smooth cream with a little of the milk. Put the rest of the milk and the margarine into a large pan on a gentle heat. When the margarine has melted, whisk in the blended mixture. Continue whisking while the sauce is coming to the boil over a moderate heat. Boil the sauce for 1 minute then pour it into a bowl, cover it closely with damp greaseproof paper, pressing it firmly to the surface, and cover the bowl with a plate. The sauce will keep in the refrigerator for two days.

HADDOCK AND PRAWN BOATS

48 baked pastry boats	salt and pepper
third of the basic sauce	good pinch of
as given in previous	mace
recipe (1 pint)	5 oz. tin of prawns
1½ lb. smoked haddock	

Put the haddock into a pan with enough water to cover it and cook it gently until it will flake easily. Flake the fish and remove all the skin and bones. Beat the fish into the sauce and season it with salt and pepper and a pinch of ground mace. Fill the tartlets and put a prawn on top of each.

HADDOCK FINGERS

¾ of the pastry	sauce with the
2 eggs	haddock mixed
	into it (see above)

a rectangular tray 14 inches long and 8 inches wide

Line the tray with the pastry and trim the edges. Beat the eggs and add them to the sauce. Pour the sauce into the pastry case and bake it in a moderately hot oven, about *Gas Mark 6 or 400 degrees F.*, for 20 minutes, then reduce the heat to *Gas Mark 5 or 375 degrees F.* for a further 20 minutes. Cut into fingers and serve hot or cold.

MUSHROOM BOATS

½ lb. mushrooms	salt and pepper
½ lb. mushroom stalks	48 baked pastry boats
juice of 1 lemon	1 tin (7½ oz.) of
third of the basic sauce	button
(1 pint)	mushrooms

Wash and chop the fresh mushrooms and stalks roughly. Put them into a pan with the lemon juice and enough water to cover them. Simmer them for 2 or 3 minutes until they are tender, then drain them and beat them into the sauce with salt and pepper to season it. Fill the boats and top each with a button mushroom.

MUSHROOM FINGERS

¾ of the pastry	sauce with the
2 eggs	mushrooms added
	(see page 169)

a rectangular tin 14 inches long and 8 inches wide

Line the tray with pastry and trim the edges. Beat the eggs into the sauce and pour it into the pastry case. Bake and serve as for Haddock Fingers (see page 169).

SWEETCORN AND BACON BOATS

48 baked pastry boats	1 tin sweetcorn
third of the basic sauce	kernels (7 oz. tin)
(1 pint)	salt and pepper
4 oz. chopped fried	
bacon	

Add the cooked bacon and sweetcorn to the sauce and season it with salt and pepper. Fill the boats.

SWEETCORN AND BACON FINGERS

¾ of the pastry	sauce with the
2 eggs	sweetcorn and
	bacon added
	(see above)

a rectangular tin 14 inches long and 8 inches wide

Line the tray with the pastry and trim the edges. Beat the eggs and add them to the sweetcorn and bacon mixture. Pour it into the pastry-lined tin and bake and serve as for Haddock Fingers (see page 169).

CHEESE BOATS

48 baked pastry boats	2 level teaspoons
12 oz. Cheddar cheese,	made English
grated	mustard
4 oz. butter	a little extra grated
¼ pint milk	cheese for the tops

Put the 12 oz. of grated cheese into a bowl. Melt the butter in the milk over a gentle heat and when it is quite hot beat it into the grated cheese. Flavour the mixture with the mustard. Fill each boat and level the top. Sprinkle the tops with grated cheese and put them under a hot grill for just a few seconds to melt the cheese.
These are really nicer hot.

SAVOURIES

CHEESE WHIRLS

These can be made and the tops piped on the day beforehand.

1 lb. self-raising flour	the mixture as for the
1 level teaspoon salt	filling for Cheese
1 level teaspoon dry	Boats (see above)
mustard	slices of stuffed olive
3 oz. margarine	a round cutter about
3 oz. cheese, finely	1½ inches in
grated	diameter
about ½ pint milk	

Sift the flour, salt and mustard. Rub in the margarine, then mix in the grated cheese. Add the milk carefully and mix to a soft but not sticky dough. Using a floured board and rolling pin, roll the dough to about ½ inch thick. Cut out rounds with a cutter 1½ inches in diameter. Bake the savoury bases on floured baking trays in a hot oven, about *Gas Mark 7 or 425 degrees F.,* for 10 to 12 minutes.
Fill a forcing bag, with a large star pipe attached, with the cheese mixture and pipe generous whirls on top of each savoury. Decorate each one with a slice of stuffed olive.

TUNA FISH SQUARES

1 tin tuna fish (7 oz.)	2 level tablespoons
3½ oz. butter	chopped parsley
juice of ½ lemon	1 packet small square
1 dessertspoon	crisp biscuits
tomato ketchup	(60 biscuits)
1 dessertspoon milk	

Tip the tuna fish into a bowl. Melt the butter and beat it into the tuna fish with the lemon juice, tomato ketchup, milk and parsley. Spread this on the biscuits and mark them with a fork.

EGG SAVOURIES

21 round savoury	1 small jar caviar-
biscuits each about	style lump fish roe
2 inches in diameter	(1¾ oz. jar)
3 oz. butter, softened	3 hard-boiled eggs

Spread the biscuits with the softened butter. Turn the caviar-style lump fish roe on a plate and spread out. Turn the buttered biscuits on to it so that it clings to the butter. Place on a serving dish, right side up. Shell and slice the eggs and put a slice in the centre of each biscuit.

SAUSAGES AND PRUNE AND BACON ROLLS ON STICKS

These can be made the day beforehand and speared on to the loaf. If they are preferred hot, put the whole loaf, ready skewered with the savouries, into the oven and heat it for a few minutes before serving.

1 lb. chipolata sausages	8 oz. thinly cut
a little fat for frying	streaky bacon
8 oz. cooked prunes	1 round brown loaf
	wooden cocktail
	sticks

Twist the chipolata sausages in half and snip between them. This will make about thirty-two sausages. Fry them gently in the fat, or put them in a roasting tin with the fat and cook them in a moderate oven.
Cut the prunes in half and remove the stones. Cut the rinds off the bacon rashers with a pair of scissors and cut them in half. Wrap a half prune in a piece of bacon and thread it on to a meat skewer. Wrap the rest in the same way, threading them on to the skewer as they are ready. Cook them under a moderate grill or in a roasting tin in the oven, turning them on the skewer halfway through the cooking. Spear a sausage and bacon roll on to each cocktail stick, and stick them into a loaf of brown bread.

THE CAKES

CHOCOLATE CAKES (makes 34)

These can be made, iced and decorated the day beforehand.

6 oz. margarine	1 oz. cocoa powder
6 oz. castor sugar	3 level dessertspoons
3 eggs	ground almonds
5 oz. plain flour	1 tablespoon milk
3 level teaspoons	greaseproof paper
baking powder	cake cases
a pinch of salt	

Cream the margarine and castor sugar. Break an egg and add it to the creamed mixture and beat well. Add the rest of the eggs in the same way, beating well after each addition. Sift the flour, baking powder, salt and cocoa and stir them lightly into the mixture with the ground almonds and milk. Put a little mixture into each paper case. Much the quickest way is to fill a forcing bag, with a plain round pipe $\frac{1}{2}$ inch in diameter attached, with the mixture and pipe it into the cases, making them about a third full.

Bake the cakes in a moderately hot oven, about *Gas Mark 5 or 375 degrees F.,* for 10 to 15 minutes.

For the icing

1 oz. cocoa powder	12 oz. icing sugar, sifted

For the decoration

2 oz. butter	9 wafer mints, cut
4 oz. icing sugar,	diagonally in
sifted	quarters to make
	triangles

Ice the cakes when they are cold. Sift the cocoa and icing sugar and mix them to a thick coating consistency with water. Spoon a little icing on top of each cake and leave it to set.

Beat the butter to a soft cream, then beat in the 4 oz. of icing sugar. Pipe this mixture into a star on top of each cake and top with a triangle of wafer mint.

SHORTBREAD HORSESHOES

These can be made up to a fortnight before they are required. The amount makes 66 horseshoes.

1$\frac{1}{2}$ lb. plain flour	8 oz. glacé cherries,
a good pinch of	chopped
salt	4 oz. finely chopped
1 lb. butter	mixed peel
4 oz. castor sugar	a dusting of icing
	sugar, sifted

Sift the flour and salt into a basin. Rub in the butter. Add the sugar and chopped fruit and knead the mixture into a ball. Take a good handful of mixture at a time and roll it into a long sausage shape on a floured board. Cut off 5 inch lengths and shape these into horseshoes. Put them on baking trays and bake them in a very moderate oven, about *Gas Mark 3 or 325 degrees F.,* for 20 to 25 minutes. Cool the biscuits on a wire tray.

Just before they are required dust the biscuits with icing sugar rubbed through a rounded strainer.

CHERRY GÂTEAU

For the genoese sponge

5 oz. butter	6 oz. castor sugar
6 eggs	6 oz. plain flour

a Swiss roll tin 14 inches long and 9 inches wide will be required

For the cherry top

2 packets of cream	2 tins of cherry pie filling
topping	milk to mix

Line the tin carefully with greaseproof paper so that it will hold the mixture in place. Cut a rectangle of greaseproof paper, 2 inches all round larger than the base of the tin. Draw round the base of the tin in the centre of the paper and snip up to the corners with a pair of scissors. Brush the tin with melted fat and line it with the greaseproof paper. Brush the paper lining also with melted fat.

Beat the butter to a very soft cream without actually melting it. Keep it in a slightly warm temperature.

Put the eggs and sugar into a bowl and suspend it over a bowl of hot, not boiling, water. Whisk it really well until the mixture is thick and fluffy; it is most important to get it thick enough (if you have an electric mixer there is no need to suspend the bowl over hot water; just whisk it to the correct consistency). Take the bowl off the heat and sift half the flour on top of the mixture. Quickly dot over the butter and sift the rest of the flour over the butter. Lightly fold the flour and butter into the mixture, working it as little as possible, and turn it into the prepared tin.

Bake the sponge in a moderate oven, about *Gas Mark 4 or 350 degrees F.,* for 40 minutes. Turn it on to a wire tray.

Turn the packets of cream topping into a bowl and gradually add the milk, whisking the mixture with a rotary beater to make a piping consistency. Fill a forcing bag, with a large star pipe attached, with the topping and pipe a diagonal line from corner to corner. Pipe parallel lines at either side and at the corners, leaving a space between each for the cherry filling.

Open the tin of cherry filling and take out half the thickened syrup and keep it.

Spoon the cherry filling between the cream. Cut the gâteau in fingers.

RASPBERRY CREAM TARTLETS (makes 48)

The pastry tartlets can be made in advance and stored.

short crust pastry as	thickened syrup from
for savoury boats	the cherry filling
(see page 169)	used for Cherry
3 packets of cream	Gâteau
topping	small round tartlet
milk to mix	tins, each holding
$\frac{1}{2}$ lb. redcurrant jelly,	2 tablespoons of
sieved	liquid, will be
about 2 lb. raspberries	required

Line the tartlet tins with the pastry and bake as for the savoury boats.

Turn the cream topping into a bowl and gradually add the milk, whisking the mixture with a rotary beater to make a piping consistency. Fill a piping bag, with a large star pipe attached, with the redcurrant jelly and pipe a little into the base of each tartlet. Wash and refill the bag with the cream and pipe a whirl into each tartlet. Arrange three raspberries on the top of each and spoon over a dot of the cherry glaze.

ROSÉ WINE CUP

MAKES ABOUT 35 MEDIUM SIZED GLASSES

½ gallon Rosé wine
(this is equal to
3 bottles but is
bought more
cheaply in one
large jar)
1 orange
4 tablespoons cherry
brandy

3 large bottles
lemonade (1 pint
bottles
ice cubes
cocktail sticks
skewered with slices
of orange, and green
and black grapes to
serve across the
glasses

Pour the wine into a large bowl. Peel the orange very thinly with a potato peeler and put the peel into the wine for at least 30 minutes (longer will do no harm). Strain and add the cherry brandy, and, just before serving, the lemonade. Float some ice cubes or crushed ice on the surface. Decorate with the skewered orange slices and green and black grapes.

COCKTAIL PARTY

THE MENU

**Savoury Bites
Orange Pincushion
Devilled Chestnuts
Cheese Puffs
Eastern Creams
Carolines
Smoked Haddock Balls
Baked Bacon and Egg Fingers
Onion Dip
Devil Dip
Curry Mayonnaise Dip
Piquant Ring
Ruby Wine Cup**

A cocktail party is a wonderful way to entertain large numbers and, if it is planned carefully, it can be fun for both the hostess and guests. If you follow these suggestions, and plan everything in advance, you will find that it is all much less effort than you might have expected.

Invite the number of people your room will hold in comfort, allowing for some refusals. Arrange the flowers where they cannot be knocked over and make sure that your vases are fairly heavy and stable.

Try to invite people with varied interests and backgrounds and introduce them carefully, giving each little group an interesting topic of conversation. Keep a look out for anyone who may be miserably clutching a glass and feeling shy and awkward, but don't spend the whole evening shuffling people around like a pack of cards just when they're beginning a good discussion.

Have a varied selection of food and a smaller choice of drink—too many different drinks mean a complicated array of glasses and bottles and makes refills difficult. Red

or white wine and perhaps a punch would make a good, simple choice of drinks, or you could have a choice of punch, sherry and a gin-based cocktail. Remember to include some soft drinks as well. It is a good idea to have some drinks ready poured out before your visitors arrive. Cocktail party food must be easy to handle and either be small enough to eat at one bite or, if it is bigger, it should not break easily into pieces. Allow seven canapés for each person as well as a selection of nuts and savoury biscuits. Serve ones which have a definite flavour and display them attractively with plenty of colour. You can choose from the recipes I give and add your own special favourites—I am sure your party will be a great success.

SAVOURY BITES

THESE AMOUNTS MAKE ABOUT 50

4 oz. lean ham, cooked
and finely chopped
salt and pepper

the choux pastry as
given in recipe for
Carolines (see
page 173)
fat for deep frying

Beat the chopped ham and seasoning into the choux pastry and fill a forcing bag, with a plain round pipe attached, with the mixture. Heat the fat and when it is hot press out an inch of the mixture and cut it off into the fat. The "bites" should puff up and fry crisply in just a few seconds. Serve hot or cold.

ORANGE PINCUSHION

1 orange
large tin of pineapple
chunks
4 oz. Cheddar cheese,
cut into ½ inch cubes

cucumber, thinly
sliced
stuffed olives
cocktail sticks

Spear the cocktail sticks with an assortment of the ingredients and spike them into the orange.

DEVILLED CHESTNUTS

1½ lb. chestnuts
½ pint stock or water
4 oz. butter
6 oz. cheese, grated
¼ teaspoon ground
pepper

a pinch of cayenne
pepper
4 oz. browned
breadcrumbs
paper sweet cases

Take the shells and inner skins off the chestnuts. To make this easier, cut a fairly large cross in the centre of each and put them all in an ovenproof dish in a very hot oven, *Gas Mark 8 or 450 degrees F.*, for 10 to 15 minutes. Now the outer and inner skins should come off quite easily.

Put the skinned chestnuts into a saucepan with the stock or water, put on the lid and cook them gently until they are tender. Drain off the liquid.

Melt the butter and mix the cheese, ground pepper and cayenne pepper together on a plate. Brush the chestnuts with butter and roll them in the cheese mixture so that they are completely coated. Brush with the remaining butter and roll the chestnuts in browned breadcrumbs.

These preparations can be done well in advance and the chestnuts will only have to be heated for the party.

Put the coated chestnuts into an ovenproof dish, or roasting tin, and bake them in a hot oven, *Gas Mark 6 or 400 degrees F.*, for about 10 minutes until they are brown and hot. Transfer them to paper sweet cases to make them easier to handle.

CHEESE PUFFS

1 small packet (7 oz. size) frozen puff pastry, thawed overnight	2 triangular portions Camembert cheese
	6 stuffed green olives
1 egg yolk mixed with 1 tablespoon water	salt and pepper

Roll out the puff pastry into a rectangle measuring 9 inches by 6 inches and cut it into 3 inch strips $\frac{3}{4}$ inch wide. Cut each strip into $1\frac{1}{2}$ inch lengths and brush them with egg glaze. Put the pastry on to a baking tray and bake it in a hot oven, about *Gas Mark 7 or 425 degrees F.*, for about 10 minutes or until the cheese puffs are nicely browned. Cool them on a wire tray.

Cut the outer skin off the Camembert cheese sections, chop the olives and beat them into the cheese with salt and pepper to flavour. Slit the cheese puffs in half lengthways and sandwich them with the filling.

EASTERN CREAMS

1 jar lumpfish roe ($3\frac{1}{2}$ oz. jar)	little freshly ground pepper
$\frac{1}{4}$ pint double cream (whipped)	small round cheese biscuits
juice of $\frac{1}{2}$ a lemon	few shreds of tomato

Mix $\frac{3}{4}$ of the lumpfish into the cream, stir in the lemon juice and season with a little freshly ground pepper. Heap the mixture on to the cheese biscuits and decorate the tops with the rest of the lumpfish and shreds of tomato.

CAROLINES (Savoury Eclairs)

THESE AMOUNTS MAKE ABOUT 36

FOR THE CHOUX PASTRY

5 oz. plain flour	$\frac{1}{2}$ pint water
4 oz. margarine	4 eggs

a forcing bag with a plain round pipe $\frac{1}{2}$ inch in diameter attached

FOR THE FILLING

6 oz. liver sausage	chopped whites of 2 hard-boiled eggs
$\frac{1}{2}$ lb. cream cheese	
2 oz. margarine, melted	

FOR THE DECORATION

paprika pepper	chopped parsley
2 hard-boiled egg yolks, sieved	1 lightly beaten egg white

First make the choux pastry. Weigh the flour carefully and sift it on to a piece of kitchen paper. Using a fairly large saucepan melt the margarine in the water over a gentle heat, then bring the mixture to a rapid boil. Take the pan off the heat, and immediately shoot in the flour from the paper. Using a wooden spoon, beat the mixture sharply just until it is smooth and leaves the sides of the pan. Leave to cool slightly, then beat in one egg at a time making the mixture smooth and shiny.

Fill with choux pastry a forcing bag with a plain round pipe half an inch in diameter attached. Pipe éclairs about 2 inches long on to lightly greased baking trays. To ensure a straight shape, let the mixture fall from the pipe on to the tray and cut it off with a knife.

Bake the éclairs in a moderate oven, about *Gas Mark 4 or 350 degrees F.*, for 10 minutes, then increase to about *Gas Mark 5 or 375 degrees F.* for another 10 minutes; then increase the heat again to *Gas Mark 6 or 400 degrees F.* for a further 5 or 10 minutes. Take the éclairs out of the oven and cool them on a wire tray; they should be used the day they are baked.

THE FILLING

Beat the liver sausage and cream cheese together and gradually add the melted margarine. Beat in the chopped egg white. Put this mixture into a forcing bag with the same plain round pipe attached. Slit down the side of each éclair and pipe filling into the centre of each.

Have the paprika, sieved egg yolk and chopped parsley on separate plates. Dip the top of each éclair into the lightly beaten egg white then into the paprika, the chopped parsley or the sieved egg yolk, making equal numbers of each.

SMOKED HADDOCK BALLS

THESE AMOUNTS MAKE ABOUT 30

$\frac{1}{2}$ lb. smoked filleted haddock	pinch of grated nutmeg
$\frac{1}{2}$ pint milk	salt and pepper if required
1 oz. margarine	
1 oz. plain flour	1 egg
4 oz. freshly made white breadcrumbs	dried white breadcrumbs for coating
	fat for deep frying

Simmer the fish very gently in the milk until it will flake easily. Strain off the liquid and flake the fish, removing any skin and bone.

Melt the margarine in a saucepan, take it off the heat and stir in the flour. Whisk in the liquid in which the fish was cooked and stir the sauce over a gentle heat until it thickens and comes to the boil. Stir in the fish, freshly made breadcrumbs, nutmeg and seasoning. Form teaspoons of the mixture into small balls.

Beat the egg well and put it on a deep plate. Coat the balls with egg then transfer them to the dry crumbs, tossing them to coat evenly.

Heat the deep fat, test with one ball, it should brown almost at once, then fry the rest in batches, reheating the fat between each batch.

The balls can be served hot or cold.

Serve these with tartare sauce (see page 86).

BAKED BACON AND EGG FINGERS

THESE AMOUNTS MAKE 24 FINGERS

FOR THE PASTRY
½ lb. plain flour
a pinch of salt
2 oz. margarine
2 oz. lard
cold water to mix

FOR THE FILLING AND GARNISH
½ large onion
4 oz. streaky bacon
3 eggs
salt and pepper
½ pint of milk
4 oz. cheese, grated
5 long rashers of
streaky bacon for
garnish

a Swiss roll tin 8 inches by 12 inches will be required

First make the pastry. Sift the flour with a pinch of salt, then rub in the fats and mix to a stiff dough with cold water. Roll out the pastry as near to the size of the tin as possible, allowing an extra inch all round to line the sides of the tin. Line the tin with the pastry, trim the edges and prick base with a fork. Leave it in a cold place.

THE FILLING

First dice the onion finely. Cut the rinds off the 4 oz. of bacon, then chop the rashers into small squares. Fry the bacon squares gently until some of the fat melts from them, then add the onion and fry it with the bacon, again very gently, until it is tender but not brown.

Beat the eggs, add the milk, onion, bacon and ¾ of the grated cheese, then season the mixture with salt and pepper. Be careful not to add too much salt because some will come from the bacon.

Pour the mixture into the pastry-lined tin and sprinkle over the rest of the cheese.

Bake in a moderately hot oven, about *Gas Mark 5 or 375 degrees F.*, for 30 minutes, then reduce the heat to *Gas Mark 4 or 350 degrees F.* for a further 5 minutes. The filling should be set and nicely browned.

When the filling is cold, cut it into 24 fingers and garnish each one with a little bacon roll.

THE GARNISH

Cut the rinds off the five rashers of bacon and elongate them on a board under a heavy knife. Cut each rasher across into four and roll up each little piece, not too tightly. Thread the rolls on a skewer and place them under a moderately hot grill, turning when one side is cooked.

DIPS

to serve with sausages, potato crisps or cheese biscuits

DEVIL DIP
½ pint thick mayonnaise
2 tablespoons
Worcester sauce
2 level dessertspoons
concentrated
tomato purée
1 tablespoon
chutney
1 teaspoon Tabasco
sauce
salt and pepper

Mix all the ingredients together and leave the dip in a covered container overnight.

ONION DIP
1 packet onion soup mix   ½ pint soured cream

Mix together and leave overnight in a covered container.

CURRY MAYONNAISE DIP

¼ pint mayonnaise
2 level teaspoons
curry powder
2-inch pieces of celery
raw carrots,
quartered
flowerettes of raw
cauliflower

Mix the mayonnaise and curry powder together and put it into a bowl. Put the bowl on a tray and surround it with heaps of the raw vegetables.

PIQUANT RING

2 tins (each 14 oz. size)
of tomatoes
a good pinch of dried
marjoram
salt and pepper
1 lb. self-raising flour
½ level teaspoon salt
1 level teaspoon dry
mustard
3 oz. margarine
about ½ pint milk
8 slices processed
Cheddar cheese
2 tins (each 2½ oz.
size) anchovies
16 black olives,
halved and stoned

Put the tomatoes, marjoram, salt and pepper into a thick saucepan and boil for about 20 minutes until the mixture has reduced by one third.

Sift the flour, salt and mustard into a mixing bowl and rub in the margarine. Add enough milk to make a soft, though not sticky, dough. Divide this in half, put each piece on to a baking tray and press them out into 8-inch rounds. Make the edges come slightly higher than the centres to prevent the filling from overflowing.

Divide the tomato mixture between the two rounds. Cover this with the cheese slices, cutting them to fit if necessary. Criss-cross the top with anchovy fillets and arrange a half olive symmetrically between the squares.

Bake the rounds one underneath the other just above the centre of a fairly hot oven, *Gas Mark 6 or 400 degrees F.*, for 25 to 30 minutes. Transfer the two rounds halfway through the cooking time. Serve hot or cold, each sliced into sixteen pieces.

RUBY WINE CUP

These quantities are enough for 12 fairly large glasses. The cup is quick and easy to mix and is best made just before serving—this quantity is quite enough to make at one time.

1 bottle inexpensive
burgundy
juice of 2 oranges
juice of 1 lemon
sugar, if required,
to taste
1 wineglass port
2 pints lemonade

TO GARNISH
slices of orange and lemon

Mix all the ingredients together, adding the lemonade last. Float sliced oranges and lemons on top of the jug.

Opposite: sun-up breakfast (see page 154) with kidneys, mushrooms and toast (see page 69), brioches (see page 122). Overleaf: hazel meringue gâteau (see page 140), lemon meringue pie (see page 101), meringue melbas (see page 140)

DISHES FROM ABROAD

With more of us venturing further afield every year on holiday, and restaurants of every nationality being opened in most big towns, it is not surprising we want to recreate the exciting dishes from other parts of the world in our own kitchens. Making and eating a colourful Paella, for instance, can help to bring back happy memories of a holiday in the sun, and a Chinese spread, with lots of different dishes, will be doubly delicious if you prepare it yourself. Invite friends in to share it, and your party will be the talk of the district for months!

Foreign cooking need not be more difficult than any other sort, in fact it is often very simple. The ingredients for all the dishes I suggest here should be available from most good grocers and stores.

CHINESE RECIPES

Chinese cookery is one of the most ancient culinary arts still practised today. It excels not only in preserving food values but in being economical, too.

This and the fact that the selection of dishes is so varied may account for its present popularity. A meal may consist of any number of different dishes, served individually or together. In a restaurant, for a number of people it is best to order a different dish for each person, then everyone can choose an assortment. Most dishes should be very tender and easy to manipulate so that the food can be eaten with chopsticks, the traditional eating implements.

A meal may be made up of soup, then a series of main dishes using vegetables, pork, beef, mutton, poultry and fish as basic ingredients, followed by fruit for dessert and China tea.

We give recipes using some of these ingredients, with their various accompaniments, including boiled and fried rice and noodles.

BOILED NOODLES

The home-made noodle pastry, as given in the recipe for Chinese Savoury Pancakes (see page 180), can be cut into strips while it is still pliable, dried and used as required. If preferred, dried egg noodles can be bought in most continental food shops.

To cook the noodles, put them into plenty of boiling salted water and simmer for 5 to 7 minutes or until tender. Drain them and rinse with boiling water to separate the noodles and remove the excess starch.

CRISPY NOODLES

Parboil the noodles for 2 minutes then drain them, and rinse under boiling water to separate them; this will also dry them, as they will make the fat splutter if they are too damp. Heat a saucepan of the deep fat, put a few noodles at a time into the deep fat basket and plunge them into the hot fat until they are crisp and lightly browned. Keep them hot while frying the next batch. Don't try to fry too many at the same time.

TO PREPARE IN ADVANCE
The noodles can be fried well beforehand and kept crisp in a warm oven.

PLAIN BOILED RICE

Allow 2 oz. of Patna rice per person and wash it well. Put the rice (with a slice of lemon, which helps to keep it white when cooked) into a large saucepan with enough boiling salted water to cover it completely. Boil the rice rapidly until it is just tender when a grain is rubbed between the fingers. This will take about 10 to 12 minutes. Drain the rice and remove the lemon slice, then run a little boiling water through the rice to separate the grains and remove the excess starch. Serve heaped in a hot dish.

TO PREPARE IN ADVANCE
The rice will come to no harm if it is cooked well beforehand, heaped on to greased trays or tins and kept in a warm oven; turn over the surface with a fork occasionally.

Harvest supper (see page 155)

FRIED RICE

1 tablespoon cooking oil	½ pint stock
8 oz. chopped onion	1 dessertspoon Soy sauce
6 oz. Patna rice	

Put the oil into a large frying pan, add the chopped onion and fry it over a gentle heat until it is tender. Add the rice and cook over a moderate heat for a few minutes, stirring all the time. Add the stock and Soy sauce gradually then leave the rice to simmer and absorb all the liquid. After 15 to 20 minutes, the rice should be dry, soft and tender.

CHINESE SAVOURY PANCAKES

These are made with noodle paste, which can easily be prepared at home.

FOR THE NOODLE PASTE

8 oz. plain flour	2 egg yolks
1 level teaspoon salt	cold water to mix
2 eggs	

FOR THE FILLING

2 rings of tinned pineapple, drained and cut in fairly small pieces	1 dessertspoon Soy sauce
	8 oz. cooked chicken, diced
8 almonds, blanched and halved	fat for deep frying
10 oz. tin bean sprouts	

First mix the noodle paste. Sieve the flour and the salt together. Mix the eggs and the egg yolks well together, then work them into the flour with a very little cold water to make a smooth elastic dough. Turn the dough on to a floured board and knead it thoroughly. Turn the outside edge of the dough in towards the centre, and press the dough out again with the knuckles as seen in photograph 1, bottom right.

Roll the paste out very thinly, then fold it in four and roll it out again. When it is as thin as you can get it, put your hands under the edges of the paste and carefully pull it out even more thinly. Cover the paste with a very slightly damp cloth and leave it for 2 hours; this will take out all the elasticity.

Meanwhile, mix together all the ingredients for the filling. Cut the paste into rectangles about 6 inches long by 5½ inches wide, and place a spoonful of filling in the centre of each of them. Brush round the edge of the paste with water then fold the sides of the paste in towards the centre, as if wrapping a parcel. Fold in the ends and stick them with a drop of water (photograph 2).

Heat the fat and when it is hot enough to turn a cube of white bread slowly brown, fry the pancakes, one or two at a time, remembering to reheat the fat after each batch. Drain the pancakes and serve them stacked on a hot plate.

CHINA TEA

This is always made very weak; 2 scant level teaspoons of tea leaves are enough for 1½ pints of water. Warm the pot, put in the tea and immediately pour freshly boiled water over the leaves. Allow 5 minutes for the tea to infuse. Serve piping hot in small cups, without sugar or milk.

Melon fruit salad, Chinese meatballs, chicken and almonds, sweet and sour pork, crab and sweetcorn soup

The following are a selection of dishes to serve at a large party—quantities are enough to serve up to 20 people. For a smaller party, make only a few of the dishes.

SWEETCORN AND CRAB SOUP with SHREDDED PANCAKES

FOR THE PANCAKES

4 oz. plain flour	¼ pint milk
pinch of salt	little oil for frying
1 large egg	

FOR THE SOUP

6 pints chicken stock (this can be made from stock cubes)	2 level tablespoons sherry (optional)
two 15 oz. tins sweetcorn	1 level tablespoon cornflour
salt and pepper if required	2 tablespoons water
	6½ oz. tin of crabmeat

Chinese savoury pancakes—1   2

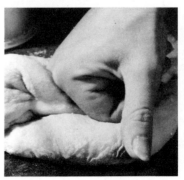

FOR THE PANCAKES

Beat the flour, salt, egg and milk to a smooth batter. Heat a little oil in a 7 inch frying pan and pour it off, then pour a little batter into the pan, and swirl it round to cover the base. Fry the pancake briskly on the first side, then turn it and fry briskly on the other side. The mixture will make about 5 pancakes and the pan should not require any more oil.

FOR THE SOUP

Put the stock into a large saucepan with the drained sweet-corn and place the pan over the heat until it boils. Add the seasoning and sherry, if used. Blend the cornflour to a smooth paste with the water and a little of the hot liquid then add it to the saucepan, stirring all the time until the soup comes to the boil. Boil it for a few minutes to cook the cornflour then add the shredded crabmeat. Cut the pancake into ¼ inch strips with a pair of scissors and serve a few strips floating on top of each bowl of soup.

TO PREPARE IN ADVANCE

The pancakes can be made well in advance and kept in a polythene bag in the refrigerator; the strips will reheat when placed in the soup. There is no reason why the soup should not be made the day beforehand, adding the crabmeat just before using.

CHINESE MEATBALLS

MAKES 20 BALLS

5 hard-boiled eggs	2 tablespoons oil
little flour seasoned with salt and pepper	2 level tablespoons cornflour
2 lb. minced beef	½ pint stock or water
4 tablespoons Soy sauce	2 tablespoons sherry (optional)
4 tablespoons tomato sauce	
4 large onions, finely chopped	

Shell the eggs and cut them into quarters, cutting first lengthways then widthways, then dust them with the seasoned flour. Put the minced beef into a bowl with 2 tablespoons of the Soy sauce, 2 tablespoons tomato sauce, and half the chopped onions (the rest of these ingredients are used in the sauce), and mix them together well. Put a little of the meat on to the palm of the left hand and flatten it well, place a piece of dusted egg in the centre and, using the right hand, mould the meat around the egg until it is completely covered (see photograph). Repeat this process with the other pieces of egg.

TO MAKE THE SAUCE

Put the oil into a frying pan and fry the rest of the onions until they are golden brown. Add the rest of the Soy sauce, tomato sauce and sherry, if used, then blend the cornflour with a little of the stock and stir it into the mixture in the frying pan with the remainder of the stock. Cook the sauce and stir until it comes to the boil then put it into an oven-proof dish and place the meatballs on top.

Cover the dish and place it in the centre of a moderate oven, *Gas Mark 4 or 350 degrees F.*, for 1 hour or until the meatballs are cooked. Serve with bean sprouts (see above right).

Chinese meatballs—moulding meat round egg

BEAN SPROUTS

Wash 2 lb. of bean sprouts (they can be bought fresh from some delicatessens or greengrocers), remove their jackets and roots; it is best to wash them several times. Cook the bean sprouts in boiling salted water for about 3 to 5 minutes; they should still be crispy to eat. Drain them well before serving.

NOTE: Bean sprouts can be bought in tins and the instructions on the tin for cooking them should be followed.

CHICKEN AND ALMONDS

1 boiling fowl, about 7 lb. trussed weight	4 tablespoons Soy sauce
6 peppercorns	6 level tablespoons cornflour
1 bay leaf	1½ pints chicken stock (from cooking the chicken)
salt	
4 large onions, finely chopped	
12 oz. mushrooms, sliced	1 level teaspoon monosodium glutamate (optional)
8 oz. celery, diced	
10 oz. tin water chestnuts, drained and chopped	3 oz. toasted almonds, shredded

Wipe the chicken with a damp cloth, and wash the giblets in cold water. Place the chicken, breast uppermost, in a large pan with the giblets, peppercorns, bay leaf and salt; add enough water to come above the legs of the bird then bring it slowly to the boil over a gentle heat. Skim the surface then put the lid on and simmer the bird slowly for 2½ to 3 hours or until it is tender. Alternatively the bird can be cooked in a pressure cooker; allow 8 to 10 minutes to every pound of meat and cook it at 15 lb. pressure.

When the chicken is cooked, strain off the liquid and reserve 1½ pints of it for the sauce; the remainder can be used for soup. Remove the meat from the bone and cut it into fairly large pieces. Put the finely chopped onion, sliced mushroom, diced celery and chopped water chestnuts into a large saucepan with ½ pint of the chicken stock. Cover with a lid and bring it to the boil then reduce the heat and simmer the vegetables for about 5 minutes, shaking them occasionally. Add the chopped chicken with the Soy sauce. Blend the cornflour to a smooth paste with a little of the remaining chicken stock then stir it into the saucepan with the rest of the stock and the monosodium glutamate, if used. Cook the chicken over a gentle heat until it is hot; it will take about 20 minutes.

Serve the chicken in a fairly deep dish (this helps to keep it hot during serving) with the almonds scattered on top.

TO PREPARE IN ADVANCE

The chicken can be cooked the day before and left overnight in a cool place in the stock it was cooked in; this helps to keep the meat moist.

All the vegetables can be prepared in the morning.

SWEET AND SOUR PORK

3 lb. blade of pork, boned	about 1½ level teaspoons salt
3 level tablespoons soft brown sugar	1½ level teaspoons monosodium glutamate (optional)
4 level tablespoons Soy sauce	1 tablespoon sherry (optional)
FOR THE BATTER	
9 oz. plain flour	6 tablespoons milk
3 large eggs	fat for deep frying

FOR THE SWEET AND SOUR SAUCE WITH VEGETABLES

6 onions, sliced fairly finely	6 tablespoons tomato sauce
6 carrots, sliced fairly finely	1 small tin of pineapple pieces
3 green peppers, sliced fairly finely	3 level tablespoons cornflour
¾ pint white vinegar	the pineapple juice made up to 1 pint plus 4 tablespoons of liquid with stock
1½ level teaspoons salt	
4½ oz. soft brown sugar	

Cut the meat into about ¾ inch cubes. Put them into a bowl and add the sugar, Soy sauce, salt, monosodium glutamate and sherry, if used. Stir well and leave for 15 minutes.

Beat the flour, eggs and milk together to make a coating batter. Heat the deep fat, dip each piece of meat in batter and fry them in the hot fat for about 5 minutes. Coat and fry the meat in batches, making sure to reheat the fat in between. Drain the pork on crumpled kitchen paper and keep it hot.

FOR THE SAUCE

Blanch the sliced onions, carrots and green peppers, by putting them into cold salted water and bringing them to the boil, then draining them well. Put the vinegar, salt, brown sugar, and tomato sauce into a pan. Blend the cornflour with a little of the pineapple juice to a thin cream. Add the rest of the juice to the mixture in the pan, bring this to the boil and stir it into the blended cornflour. Return the sauce to the pan and stir it over a gentle heat until it comes to the boil then simmer it for 3 minutes. Add the vegetables and the pineapple cubes to the sauce and gently cook them for 2 to 3 minutes until they are heated through.

Heap the pork diagonally across a dish and serve the sauce with the vegetables on either side of it.

TO PREPARE IN ADVANCE

It is perfectly all right to cut the meat into pieces and make the marinade on the morning of the party, but do not combine them until 15 minutes before you are ready to begin frying. The batter can be made and left in a cool place until required, and the vegetables blanched and left to drain, so that they can be added to the prepared sauce to reheat just before serving.

MELON FRUIT SALAD

FOR THE SYRUP

1 lb. granulated sugar	½ pint water

FOR THE FRUIT

2 melons	4 bananas
6 oranges	little preserved
1 lb. red-skinned apples	ginger, finely
½ lb. each black and white grapes	chopped (optional)

First make the syrup—it is best to do this the day before the party. Put the sugar into a pan with the water and stir the mixture over a gentle heat until all the sugar is dissolved, without allowing the syrup to boil. When all the sugar has dissolved, bring the syrup to the boil and boil it rapidly until it starts to thicken and becomes sticky when tested between the finger and thumb. Pour the syrup into a basin and leave it to become cold.

To prepare the fruit, first cut a large slice out of each melon and scoop out the pips with a dessertspoon. Cut out the flesh from the slices and the melons with a ball-cutter or a teaspoon. Scrape out the inside of the melon thoroughly, leaving only the skin. Put the melon balls and the rest of the melon into the syrup. Using a very sharp knife, cut the skin spirally off the oranges, removing the white pith as well. Then cut the oranges into segments, discarding the membranes, and add the segments to the salad. Quarter the apples, core them and slice them without removing the red skin. Halve both the white and black grapes and pip them, then add them to the salad. Lastly peel and slice the bananas and add them to the salad with the ginger, if used. Stir all the fruit well together then fill the melons with it; keep any left over for refills. Place the melons on plates surrounded by whole, fresh fruit. The melon skins can be refilled as the fruit salad is used up.

TO PREPARE IN ADVANCE

The syrup for the fruit salad can be made the day before the party. The melons can be prepared and the balls added to the salad, with the grapes and oranges, early in the day, but it is better not to add the rest until just before the party.

CURRY DINNER

FOR 4 PEOPLE

The supporting dishes of chutney, rice, coconut, dahl and poppadums are as important as the curry itself. It is in fact a very satisfying meal. Fresh fruit is the natural follow-up, so although there is quite a lot of preparation for the main course, the rest of the meal is very simple. Serve the curry in a large dish and let your guests help themselves to all the accompaniments. A spoon and fork is the correct place setting. Always have ice-cold water or lager to drink.

The curry sauce should be made the previous day and the

main ingredient added; the whole is reheated just before serving. The spices then have time to combine and the curry has a much better flavour. I have chosen meatballs as the main ingredient since they are both economical and excellent.

CURRY SAUCE

(THE MEATBALLS ARE COOKED IN THIS)

$\frac{1}{2}$ pint boiling water	1 level tablespoon
4 level tablespoons	curry powder
desiccated coconut	1 level teaspoon
6 medium sized onions	curry paste
(about 1$\frac{1}{2}$ lb.)	$\frac{1}{4}$ level teaspoon
3 oz. margarine	red chilli powder
1 level tablespoon	1 level teaspoon salt
turmeric	2 bay leaves
$\frac{1}{2}$ level tablespoon	4 fairly large
ground cumin	tomatoes
$\frac{1}{4}$ level teaspoon	$\frac{3}{4}$ pint stock or
ground ginger	water
1 level tablespoon	
ground coriander	

This is a very important sauce recipe because it is the base of any curry. It can be varied as you like to make it stronger or more bland in flavour.

Pour the boiling water on to the coconut and leave for 30 minutes while you collect the other ingredients, then strain the water and keep it to add to the curry. Ideally, coconut milk should be used.

Peel and slice the onions, melt the margarine in a fairly large pan and fry them gently in the margarine until they start to soften and colour lightly. While the onions are still frying stir in the turmeric, cumin, ground ginger, ground coriander, curry powder, curry paste, red chilli powder, salt and bay leaves. Allow them to fry gently for 10 minutes. Meanwhile, pour boiling water over the tomatoes and leave them for just a few seconds until the skins will peel off easily, then pour off the water and skin and chop the tomatoes. Add the tomatoes to the mixture and fry them over a slightly increased heat for about 8 minutes, until the liquid which forms is well reduced. Stir in the stock or water and the water drained from the coconut. Bring the sauce to the boil and simmer very gently for 30 minutes.

NOTE: If all these spices are not available, use another level tablespoon of curry powder instead of the coriander, cumin and red chilli.
To increase the sharpness of a curry sauce, add a few drops of lemon; for extra sweetness add a pinch of sugar.

MEATBALLS

(MAKE THESE WHILE THE CURRY SAUCE IS COOKING)

1$\frac{1}{2}$ lb. minced steak,	salt and pepper
uncooked	2 oz. flour well
1 egg	seasoned with salt
2 oz. shredded suet	and pepper
$\frac{1}{2}$ medium sized onion,	2 oz. fat for frying the
finely chopped	meatballs

Break up the mince, beat the egg and work it into the mince with the suet, chopped onion, and salt and pepper. Form the mixture into 16 small balls and roll them in the seasoned flour.

Heat the fat in a large frying pan and fry the meatballs, rolling them round the pan to brown them evenly. When they are well browned transfer them to the curry sauce and simmer them gently for about 20 minutes.

If the sauce should become too thick when the meatballs are reheated on the following day, add a little extra stock.

NOTE: Chicken, fish, hard-boiled eggs, prawns or root vegetables all make good curries; if they are cooked they should only be reheated in the sauce. If the chicken, meat or vegetables are cooked entirely in the sauce add a little extra stock at the beginning, as it will evaporate during the cooking. Always remember to cook a curry slowly.

DAHL

1 large onion	1 level teaspoon salt
1 level tablespoon	$\frac{1}{2}$ pint hot water
curry powder	$\frac{1}{2}$ lb. red lentils
3 oz. butter	

Chop the onion finely. Melt 2 oz. only of the butter and fry the onion very slowly to soften it. Add the curry powder and salt and fry them lightly together. Stir in the hot water then wash and add the red lentils. Simmer very slowly for 35 minutes or until the lentils are soft and all the water has been absorbed. Sieve the mixture and beat in the remaining ounce of butter. Serve the dahl in a separate dish from the curry, garnished with a few fried onion rings (see below).

FRIED ONION RINGS

Slice an onion crossways and break the slices into rings. Dust the rings with seasoned flour, and fry them in a little hot fat.

POPPADUMS

Poppadums can be bought in tins. Fry one at a time, just for a second or two, in a little hot fat, which makes them crisp and curly. Keep them in a warm oven to serve with the curry. Allow about two per person.

RICE

Always use the long-grained Patna rice for curry, as the grains separate easily, making light fluffy rice. Plain boiled rice or saffron rice can be served with curry. There should always be plenty of rice—at least 2 oz. per person—as of course there are no potatoes or any other cooked vegetables.

BOILED RICE

8 oz. Patna rice	1 pint water
1$\frac{1}{2}$ level teaspoons salt	1 teaspoon lemon
	juice

Wash the rice by putting it into a rounded strainer and running cold water through it. Put the rice into a pan with the salt and lemon juice and add the cold water. Bring the rice to the boil and allow it to boil slowly until a grain rubbed between the fingers is firm but without a hard core, about 10 to 12 minutes. By this time all the water should have been absorbed by the rice. If the rice is not ready and there is no water left add a little more water. It is best not to stir the rice. When the rice is cooked turn it into a strainer and pour a little boiling water through it to separate the grains and remove the excess starch. Heap it into a hot dish to serve.

SAFFRON RICE

1 level dessertspoon saffron	$\frac{3}{4}$ pint cold water
$\frac{1}{4}$ pint boiling water	8 oz. Patna rice

Put the saffron into a small bowl, pour on the boiling water and leave it to infuse for 10 minutes. The water will turn bright yellow. Strain the liquid and add it to the rest of the water for cooking the rice, following the method described in the previous recipe.

Choose several accompaniments from the following list of suggestions—the more the merrier; each should be served in a separate dish, except Bombay Duck which is scattered over the curry.

MANGO CHUTNEY

Most grocery shops stock this.

DESICCATED COCONUT

Fresh grated coconut is nice if you can get it.

FRESH TOMATO AND ONION CHUTNEY

Peel 4 medium sized tomatoes and chop them finely. Chop an onion finely, and mix together with a little salt and fresh ground pepper.

ALMONDS AND SULTANAS

Put 8 oz. almonds into boiling water; when the skins loosen pour off the water, slip the skins off the almonds, and spread them on a baking tray. Bake them in a moderate oven, about *Gas Mark 4 or 350 degrees F.*, for a few minutes to brown lightly. Clean 8 oz. sultanas and mix them with the almonds. A little chopped tinned or fresh pineapple is a good addition (if tinned, use about two rings).

SLICED BANANAS

Slice two bananas and sprinkle them with lemon juice to prevent them discolouring.

APPLE, RAISIN AND PEPPER CHUTNEY

Slice half a green pepper and mix it with 3 oz. seedless raisins. Thinly slice a rosy dessert apple without peeling it and add it to the other ingredients.

YOGHOURT

Season a jar of yoghourt with a few caraway seeds and add a little finely shredded red pepper.

BOMBAY DUCK

This is a dried tropical fish, which can be bought in tins. Lightly brush a few pieces with oil and heat them for a few seconds under a hot grill. Serve them on top of the curry.

DUTCH RECIPES

ERWTENSOEP (Pea Soup)

FOR 5 TO 6 PEOPLE

$\frac{1}{2}$ lb. green or dried yellow split peas	3 medium onions
3 pints water	3 leeks
2 pigs' trotters	3 sticks of celery
1 marrow bone	2 level tablespoons chopped parsley
$\frac{1}{2}$ lb. potatoes, peeled	4 oz. tin or 6 small frankfurter sausages, sliced
salt and pepper	

Wash the peas then soak them in $1\frac{1}{2}$ pints of the water overnight. Simmer the trotters and the marrow bone in the remaining $1\frac{1}{2}$ pints of water for 1 hour, then add to this the peas and the water they were soaked in. Cook for about 1 hour, until soft, and season well. Peel the onions and wash the leeks well then slice all the vegetables and add them to the soup 40 minutes before serving.

When the soup is cooked, remove the trotters and the marrow bone and scrape out the meat, then put this back into the soup which can be thinned if necessary with a little stock. Check the seasoning then stir in the chopped parsley and sliced frankfurter sausages. Allow the soup to heat through again before serving.

NOTE: In Holland this soup is often served as a complete meal on its own with hunks of crisp, fresh bread.

BLINDE VIRKEN (Stuffed Veal Fillets)

FOR 4 PEOPLE

4 veal escalopes, about 1 lb. in all	4 oz. Gouda cheese, thinly sliced
8 slices of streaky bacon	

FOR THE COATING AND DECORATION

1 egg	4 slices lemon
3 oz. breadcrumbs	watercress sprigs
fat for deep frying	

Place each veal escalope between damp greaseproof paper and beat it flat with a rolling pin or the back of a wooden spoon, then remove the greaseproof paper. Cut the rind off the bacon and place two slices on each escalope and then a slice of the Gouda cheese. Roll up the veal, beat the egg for the coating and pour it into a fairly deep plate. Have the crumbs ready on a piece of kitchen paper.

Stand each escalope in the beaten egg, brush the egg over it and lift on to a plate. Coat the other 3 in the same way. Then coat them all with the breadcrumbs, using the edge of the paper to flick the crumbs over the surface.

Heat the fat until it is hot enough (about *360 degrees F.*) to brown a cube of bread fairly slowly. Lower the escalopes into the fat in the deep fat basket (the pan should hold all 4 at once) and fry them for about 15 minutes to cook them right through. Lift them out on to a piece of absorbent paper to drain.

TO SERVE THE ESCALOPES

Cut each escalope in half and arrange the halves down either side of a serving dish with the cut sides outwards; on every alternate half place a twist of lemon and fill the centre of the dish with the watercress.

These are excellent served cold at picnics.

YOGHOURT PUDDING

FOR 5 PEOPLE

8 oz. tin raspberries	few drops of pink
½ oz. powdered gelatine	colouring
2 oz. castor sugar	¼ pint double cream
1 pint natural	few fresh raspberries
yoghourt	jelly mould holding
juice of 1 lemon	1½ pints of liquid

Drain the raspberries and reserve the juice. Melt the gelatine in the fruit juice, in a small pan over a gentle heat, then add the sugar. Blend the yoghourt and the lemon juice together and gradually stir in the gelatine mixture, adding a few drops of pink colouring if necessary. Allow the mixture to cool, and just before it sets stir in the raspberries.

Rub the inside of the jelly mould with a drop of tasteless salad oil and pour in the mixture. Leave to set.

Turn out the yoghourt pudding on to a serving dish, lightly whip the cream and pour just over half of it on top of the pudding; it will slightly coat the sides. Serve the remaining cream separately. The few fresh raspberries are used to decorate the top and the base of the pudding.

GINGER BOTERKOEK
(Ginger Butter Cake)

9 oz. plain flour	1 large egg, lightly
pinch of salt	beaten
7 oz. castor sugar	a sandwich tin
7 oz. Dutch butter	8½ inches in
3 oz. crystallised ginger,	diameter
finely chopped	

Sieve the flour and salt into a large bowl, and add the castor sugar and the butter cut into pieces. Rub in the butter, then add the chopped ginger and almost all the beaten egg, reserving a little for the glaze. Knead all these ingredients to a smooth dough with your hands.

Put the dough into the tin and pat it down well; smooth the surface with a palette knife and mark round the side with the back of a fork. Brush the surface with the rest of the beaten egg, then cook the cake just above the centre of a moderate oven, *Gas Mark 4 or 350 degrees F.*, for 40 minutes or until the cake is fairly firm to the touch.

Leave the cake in the tin to cool slightly before turning it out.

JANHAGEL (Cinnamon Biscuits)

MAKES 24 BISCUITS

4 oz. Dutch butter	1 oz. almonds,
2 oz. castor sugar	chopped or flaked
6 oz. plain flour	1 oz. granulated sugar
½ teaspoon ground	a lightly greased
cinnamon	Swiss roll tin
beaten egg for glazing	8 inches by 12
	inches

Beat the butter to a soft cream, add the sugar and continue beating until the mixture is light in colour and texture. Sieve the flour and cinnamon together then stir them into the mixture. Press the mixture into the prepared tin and flatten it with a knife, glaze with the beaten egg and then prick with a fork. Mix the almonds and the granulated sugar together and sprinkle them over the surface.

Bake the biscuits just above the centre of a moderate oven, *Gas Mark 4 or 350 degrees F.*, for about 20 minutes or until it is golden brown. Cut the mixture into 2 inch squares while it is still warm.

RECIPES FROM OTHER COUNTRIES

CHICKEN PILAU

FOR 6 PEOPLE

1 roasting chicken,	two 2 inch pieces of
3½ lb. trussed weight	cinnamon stick
2 oz. dripping	8 allspice berries
1 level tablespoon	½ level teaspoon
curry powder	turmeric
3 medium sized onions	1 lb. Patna rice
4 oz. margarine	2 pints stock or water
1 clove of garlic	4 oz. seedless raisins
salt and pepper	2 oz. shelled cashew
1 bay leaf	nuts
12 cardamom seeds	3 hard-boiled
6 cloves	eggs

Put the giblets inside the chicken carcass to add to the flavour. Put the bird in a roasting tin with the dripping and sprinkle it with the curry powder. Roast it in a fairly hot oven, about *Gas Mark 6 or 400 degrees F.*, for 1 hour. Baste the chicken occasionally during roasting with the curry-flavoured dripping.

Peel and slice the onions into rings. Melt the margarine in a large pan and fry the onions in the margarine until they are golden brown, turning them continually. Take a third of the onions out of the pan and keep them hot for the garnish. Peel the papery skin off the clove of garlic, slice it, sprinkle it with salt and crush it to a cream under the blade of a heavy knife. Add the garlic to the onions in the pan with the bay leaf, cardamom seeds, cloves, cinnamon sticks, allspice berries and turmeric. Rinse the rice in cold water and stir it into the onion and spice mixture. Toss the rice and spices over a moderate heat for a few minutes to absorb the fat, then add the stock, salt and pepper and cook the rice very gently, stirring it as little as possible, until all the liquid is absorbed. It will take about 15 minutes and the rice should then be tender though the grains still separate. Add the raisins.

When the chicken is ready, add the curry-flavoured dripping to the rice. Joint the chicken, cutting the legs and the breast in half, and stir the joints into the rice. Heap the pilau into a brass or copper dish if possible, and scatter the top with cashew nuts and the fried onion rings. Shell and quarter the hard-boiled eggs and arrange them round the dish.

PIZZA

FOR 5/6 PEOPLE

FOR THE YEAST BASE

½ lb. plain flour	2 oz. margarine
1 level teaspoon salt	½ oz. fresh yeast
¼ pint mixed milk and and water	1 level teaspoon castor sugar

FOR THE TOPPING

1 lb. tomatoes	1 small tin anchovy
6 spring or small onions	fillets
	3 oz. sliced
1 dessertspoon olive oil	processed cheese
	5 Spanish stuffed
1 level dessertspoon chopped marjoram	manzanilla olives

Sift the flour with the salt into a large bowl. Put the milk and water into a saucepan with the margarine and melt the margarine over a gentle heat, then cool the liquid to blood heat. Meanwhile, mix the yeast with the castor sugar to make a thin cream, then stir in the warm liquid. Make a hollow in the centre of the flour, pour in the liquid, and mix the ingredients to a dough. Beat the dough well, then turn it on to a floured board and knead it for 5 minutes. Grease the bowl to prevent the dough from sticking and put the dough into it; cover it with a damp cloth and leave it to rise for 1-1½ hours or until it has doubled in bulk. When it has risen, turn the dough out again on to a floured board and form it into a round about 11 inches across. Transfer the dough to a greased baking tray. Wash, peel and chop spring onions and fry them gently for a few minutes in the olive oil. Simmer until well reduced. Peel, quarter and add tomatoes with the marjoram.

Spread this mixture to within an inch of the edge of the dough mixture. Cut the sliced cheese into strips and form a trellis of cheese strips crossed with anchovy fillets on top of the tomato mixture. Arrange the halved stuffed olives round the edge of the tomato mixture. Put the pizza in a warm place for about 20 minutes before baking.

Bake the pizza in a fairly hot oven, about *Gas Mark 6 or 400 degrees F.*, for 30 minutes. Slip it on to a tray or board for serving and cut it into slices.

INDIVIDUAL PIZZAS

Divide the dough into five small rounds to make individual pizzas. They will take only about 15 minutes to bake.
NOTE: As dried yeast is sometimes more convenient use it instead of fresh yeast. Use half the quantity given for fresh yeast, and mix it with the castor sugar and the warm liquid. Leave it to soak in the warm liquid, stirring it occasionally, until the liquid starts to froth.

AUSTRIAN CHEESECAKE

MAKES 6 SLICES

FOR THE SHORTCRUST PASTRY BASE

6 oz. plain flour	1½ oz. margarine
good pinch of salt	1½ oz. lard

FOR THE FILLING

½ lb. curd cheese (home-made, or cottage cheese)	3 oz. stoned raisins, chopped
	2 tablespoons top milk
2 oz. demi-sel cheese	3 eggs
1¾ oz. butter	a flan ring 8 inches in diameter
1¾ oz. castor sugar	
1 oz. plain flour	

Sift the flour with the pinch of salt, then rub in the fats, and add just enough cold water to make a firm short crust pastry.

Roll out the pastry, put the flan ring on an upturned baking tray and line it with the pastry. Make a ledge round the top, just inside the ring, then roll off the scraps of surplus pastry.

Sieve the cheeses together. Beat the butter and sugar to a soft cream then lightly mix in the flour, raisins and top milk. Separate the yolks from the whites of the eggs. Beat yolks, then add to mixture with the cheeses. Whisk whites until they are stiff and fold them in lightly. Pour the mixture into the pastry case.

Bake the cheesecake in a fairly hot oven, about *Gas Mark 6 or 400 degrees F.*, for 30 minutes. Serve it hot or cold.

CINNAMON CHEESECAKE

MAKES 5/6 SLICES

4 oz. margarine	2 eggs
4 oz. soft brown sugar	8 oz. self-raising flour
½ teaspoon vanilla essence	3 tablespoons milk

FOR THE TOPPING

6 oz. cream cheese	1 level teaspoon
2 level tablespoons castor sugar	ground cinnamon
	a 7 inch square cake tin

Brush the cake tin with melted fat and line it with greaseproof paper. Brush the paper lining with melted fat also. Beat the margarine to a soft cream then beat in the soft brown sugar with the vanilla essence. Beat the eggs together then add a little egg at a time to the mixture, beating well after each addition. Sift the flour and stir it lightly into the mixture with the milk. Turn the mixture into the prepared tin and smooth over the surface. Hollow out the centre slightly. Beat the cream cheese until it is a really soft spreading consistency, add the castor sugar and then spread it evenly over the cake mixture. Sprinkle the top with the ground cinnamon.

Bake the cake in a moderate oven, about *Gas Mark 4 or 350 degrees F.*, for about 1 hour. The cheese on the surface will still be soft but the cake mixture beneath should be cooked.

Fondue bourguignonne (see page 167)

Children's party (see page 161)

PAELLA

FOR 6 PEOPLE

1 pint live mussels	$\frac{1}{2}$ lb. filleted haddock
1 pint cooked prawns	$\frac{3}{4}$ lb. Patna rice
6 tablespoons olive oil	$\frac{1}{2}$ pint water
2 onions, sliced	6 oz. tin lobster
1 green pepper	4 tomatoes, peeled
1 red pepper	and quartered
4 oz. chicken's liver	salt and pepper
1 clove of garlic	8 black olives

First wash the mussels thoroughly. Use only live mussels which will either be tightly shut or close when tapped. Put the mussels into cold salted water to cover them and bring slowly to the boil. Simmer them for 5 minutes; by this time they will have opened. Remove the beards from the mussels; this is a small fibre attached to each mussel and must be removed.

Shell all but five or six of the prawns, and keep these aside for the decoration.

Make the paella in a large shallow flameproof pan from which it can be served.

Heat the oil in the pan, add the sliced onions and cook them gently. Meanwhile cut the peppers in $\frac{1}{4}$ inch rings and remove the seeds. Add the pepper rings to the onions with the chicken's liver and continue frying the mixture gently. Peel the outer papery skin off the clove of garlic, chop the garlic, then sprinkle it with salt and crush it to a cream under the blade of a knife.

Skin the fillet of haddock and cut it into 1 inch strips. Add these to the mixture with the rice and fry the ingredients until the oil is absorbed. Pour in the water, cover the pan and cook the rice very gently until the water has been absorbed, by which time the rice should be tender. Lightly stir in the lobster, shelled prawns, cooked mussels and quartered tomatoes. Cook very gently for a few minutes to heat thoroughly, and season with salt and pepper. Add the black olives and whole prawns and serve the paella at once.

MADELKAKE

3 eggs	5 rings tinned
8 oz. ground almonds	pineapple
10 oz. icing sugar, sifted	few glacé cherries
$\frac{1}{2}$ pint double cream,	a cake tin 10 inches
lightly whipped	in diameter

Brush the tin with melted fat, then line the base with a piece of greaseproof paper cut to fit. Brush the paper lining with fat also.

Set the oven at about *Gas Mark 6 or 400 degrees F.*, so that it is ready for baking the cake—it must be fairly hot. Break the eggs into a mixing bowl, and stand it over a pan of hot, not boiling, water—if the water boils the eggs become solid and cooked, but gentle heat speeds the whisking. Using a rotary or wire whisk, beat the eggs until they are really stiff. A spoon drawn through the centre should leave a deep groove remaining in the mixture. This will take about 20 minutes. Take the eggs off the heat, and whisk for a further 5 minutes till cool.

Mix the ground almonds and sifted icing sugar together,

and using a metal spoon fold them into the mixture with a light, flicking movement. Immediately turn the mixture into the prepared tin, tip the tin to level it, and put it at once into the pre-heated oven, for 20 to 25 minutes. Turn the oven off. With an electric cooker leave the door open until the cake is cool. With a gas cooker leave cake in closed oven until it is cool. Turn out and remove the greaseproof paper.

At least 1 hour before serving, spread the top of the cake with whipped cream, and decorate it with a whirl of halved pineapple rings and glacé cherries.

NOTE: If you have an electric mixer it is, of course, ideal for beating the eggs and there is no need to stand them over hot water. But it is important that the consistency of the beaten mixture is the same.

NASI GORENG

FOR 6 PEOPLE

1 lb. Patna rice	2 oz. peeled prawns
2 pints water	4 oz. shelled peanuts
2 chicken joints,	2 dessertspoons Soy
uncooked	sauce
4 oz. rump steak	salt and pepper
2 meduim sized onions	1 egg
1 clove of garlic	$\frac{1}{4}$ oz. margarine
4 tablespoons cooking oil	

FOR THE ACCOMPANIMENT
cucumber, cut in chunks
quartered tomatoes

Wash and drain the rice. Put it into a pan with the water and simmer gently until all the water has been absorbed and the rice is cooked.

Meanwhile, take the chicken meat off the bones and cut it into 1 inch pieces. Cut the rump steak into pieces the same size, removing any fat and gristle. Peel and slice the onions. Peel the outer skin off the clove of garlic, sprinkle the garlic with salt, chop it then crush it under the blade of a knife until it becomes a cream.

Heat the oil in a large pan, add the onions and fry them slowly until they are tender, then briskly fry the chicken and steak. Add the creamed clove of garlic, the prawns and the peanuts. When the rice is tender, add it to the mixture and heat it all together with the Soy sauce. Season carefully with salt and pepper.

Break the egg into a bowl and beat it with salt and pepper. Melt the margarine in a small frying pan, pour in the egg and stir it round for a second then leave it to set. Turn the omelet on to a board and cut it into strips. Heap the Nasi Goreng on to a hot dish and garnish the top with strips of egg omelet. Serve the cucumber and tomato separately.

RECIPES FOR YOUNG COOKS

When the children are on holiday, why not let them try their hands at a little simple baking and cooking? They will love it—and the results of their work can be surprisingly tasty too! So dress them up in aprons, turn them loose in the kitchen, and await results.

All the recipes in this chapter can be made by boys and girls from about the age of nine upwards on their own—but even if they tire of being cooks, you'll find the recipes just as useful for you to use for normal family cooking.

Kidney, bacon and banana kebabs

KIDNEY, BACON AND BANANA KEBABS

FOR 4 PEOPLE

2 slices of white bread	2 bananas
4 lamb's kidneys	2 oz. butter, melted
6 rashers of streaky bacon	4 small sprigs of rosemary

Toast the bread lightly on one side then remove the crusts and cut each slice into two. Remove the skin from the kidneys and cut them in half, then cut out the core. Cut the rind off the bacon and, using the back of a knife, stretch each rasher to about double its length before cutting it into two.

Wrap a piece of bacon around each half of kidney, then peel and halve the bananas and wrap a piece of bacon round each half of these as well.

Place two pieces of kidney and one piece of banana on the untoasted side of each piece of bread, skewer them together, then brush the kebabs with the melted butter and place a small sprig of rosemary on top of each.

Grill the kebabs slowly for about 10 minutes on one side, then turn them over, brush the other side with the melted butter, and cook them for another 10 minutes or until the kidneys are cooked.

BURGER BITES

FOR 4 PEOPLE

1 small French loaf	1 tomato, cut into three slices
a little butter	
1 level teaspoon French mustard	3 triangular sections of cheese
4 frozen beefburgers	

Slit the French loaf in half lengthwise. Spread the lower half with butter and smear it with French mustard.

Grill the beefburgers on both sides and arrange them along the loaf, putting a slice of tomato and a section of

Burger bites

Sausage toasts and cocoa for supper

cheese between each. Put them back under the grill for a few seconds to soften the tomato slices and cheese. Serve the loaf on a long dish or a breadboard. Cut the top in four, and cut between the beefburgers so that you can make four sandwiches.

AN ALTERNATIVE FILLING

Spread the French bread with mayonnaise. Top with rings of pineapple. Cover with grated cheese and cross with rashers of bacon. Grill slowly.

COD AU GRATIN

FOR 4 PEOPLE

4 frozen cod steaks	salt and pepper
¾ pint milk	6 oz. cheese, grated
1½ oz. margarine	1 large packet frozen
1½ oz. plain flour	peas to serve with it

Put the cod, which can be still frozen, into a heatproof dish. Put the milk, margarine and flour into a saucepan and stir the sauce over a gentle heat until it is smooth. Increase the heat and continue to stir until the sauce thickens, then boil it for a minute or two. Season with salt and pepper and beat in three-quarters of the cheese. Coat the fish with the sauce and sprinkle the rest of the grated cheese on top.
Bake the fish in a moderate oven, about *Gas Mark 4 or 350 degrees F.*, for about 30 minutes or a little longer; if the fish is frozen when you start cooking, you will need to cook it for an extra 5 to 10 minutes.
Serve with frozen peas, cooked as directed on the packet.

SAUSAGE TOASTS AND COCOA FOR SUPPER

FOR 2 PEOPLE

4 rounds of white bread	tomato ketchup
4 oz. sausagemeat	

Toast both sides of the bread lightly and then spread sausagemeat fairly thinly over each slice; grill slowly to cook the sausagemeat. Cut the crusts off the toast and cut the toast into fingers. Top each with a small teaspoon of tomato ketchup.

MAKING A JUG OF COCOA

1 pint milk (this can be half milk and half water)	3 level dessertspoons sugar
2 level dessertspoons cocoa powder (3 if you like it stronger)	

Put the milk into a pan and stir in the dry cocoa powder and sugar. Continue stirring over a low heat and as the milk heats the cocoa will blend with it. Bring the cocoa to the boil, taking care to watch it all the time. Pour it into a jug.
For a special cocoa drink, put a few marshmallows into the jug then pour the cocoa on to them.

ORANGE ICE CREAM JELLIES

FOR 6 PEOPLE

1 small tin mandarin oranges	1 small block of ice cream
1 packet orange jelly	3 glacé cherries, halved

Strain the juice off the mandarin oranges and make it up to ¾ pint with water. Bring this to the boil, cut up the jelly block and pour the hot liquid over it. Stir until the jelly has dissolved and leave it to cool slightly. Stir in the ice cream, pour the mixture into individual dishes and leave to set. When they are set, decorate the top of each with mandarin orange sections and half a glacé cherry.

BANANA SPLITS

FOR 2 PEOPLE

2 bananas	little double cream
2 slices chocolate ripple ice cream	2 glacé cherries
	2 ice cream wafers

Peel the bananas, slit them in half, and lay one half at each side of two oval or other long-shaped dishes. Put a slice of ice cream on each split banana. Whip the cream until it will hold its shape and put a little on top of the ice cream. Top with a glacé cherry and an ice cream wafer.

191

ROCK BUNS

MAKES 13 BUNS

8 oz. self-raising flour
pinch of salt
good pinch mixed spice
1½ oz. margarine,
   softened at room
   temperature
2 oz. lard or white
   cooking fat, softened
   at room temperature
3 oz. granulated sugar

3 oz. cleaned currants
1 oz. chopped mixed
   peel (optional)
finely grated rind
   of 1 lemon
1 large egg
about 1 tablespoon
   milk
little extra granulated
   sugar

Grease two baking trays ready for baking the buns. If you haven't two trays the buns will have to be baked in batches. Set the oven at *Gas Mark 6 or 400 degrees F.*
Sift the flour, salt and mixed spice into a mixing bowl. Add the margarine and lard or cooking fat and cut them into small pieces with a knife. Rub the fat into the flour with the tips of your fingers then stir in the sugar, currants, mixed peel and grated lemon rind. Lightly beat the egg and add it to the mixture with the milk and stir well to a stiff consistency. Heap the mixture in small mounds on the baking tray, leaving a space between each for the buns to rise. Sprinkle a little sugar over each bun.
Bake the buns near the top of the oven for 10 to 15 minutes. Slip a palette knife under the buns to lift them from the tray. Cool them on a wire tray.

CHERRY BUNS

MAKES 16 BUNS

3 oz. butter
3 oz. castor sugar
1 egg
4 oz. self-raising flour

pinch of salt
1½ oz. glacé cherries
1½ tablespoons milk

FOR THE ICING
2-3 tablespoons water
5 oz. icing sugar,
   sifted

8 glacé cherries,
   halved
16 paper cake cases

Set the oven at *Gas Mark 6 or 400 degrees F.* so that it will be hot for baking the cakes.
Put the butter into a warmed mixing bowl and beat it to a soft cream. Add the castor sugar and beat again until the mixture is soft and light. Break the egg into a cup and beat well, then add it to the creamed mixture a little at a time, beating very thoroughly after each addition. Sift together the flour and salt.
Cut the cherries into quarters and mix with 2 tablespoons of the dry ingredients. Lightly stir the dry ingredients into the creamed mixture; do not beat. Stir in the cherries, then add the milk. Divide the mixture between the paper cases and bake the buns for 12 to 15 minutes.
When the cakes are cool, make the icing. Add the water very gradually to the sifted icing sugar to make a very stiff, almost coating, consistency. Put a small teaspoon of icing in the centre of each little cake and spread it round with the back of the spoon until it completely coats the top of the cake. Decorate each cake with half a glacé cherry.

CHILDREN'S FRUIT CAKE

1 oz. glacé cherries,
   chopped
4 oz. currants, cleaned
4 oz. raisins, cleaned
2 oz. mixed peel
5 oz. margarine
¼ pint water
1 small tin sweetened
   condensed milk

5 oz. plain flour
½ level teaspoon
   bicarbonate of soda
pinch of salt
a cake tin
   6 inches in diameter
   will be required

First brush the inside of the cake tin with melted fat or cooking oil and line the base with a circle of greaseproof paper, cut to fit. Grease the paper.
Set the oven, so that it will be ready for baking the cake, at *Gas Mark 3 or 325 degrees F.*
Put the chopped glacé cherries into a fairly large saucepan with the currants, raisins, chopped mixed peel, margarine, water and condensed milk. Heat the ingredients slowly, stirring all the time, until the mixture comes to the boil, and then simmer gently for 3 minutes. Take the pan off the heat and allow the mixture to cool while measuring out the other ingredients.
Sift the flour, bicarbonate of soda and salt together and stir them into the melted mixture. Make sure all the ingredients are thoroughly mixed then turn them into the prepared tin. Bake the cake, just above the centre of the oven, for about 1¼ hours. The mixture should still be warm when it goes into the oven; if, however, it has cooled, the cake will take a little longer to cook. To test if the cake is cooked, push a warmed skewer into the centre and if it comes out clean the cake is ready; if any mixture sticks to it then bake for a little longer. Turn the cake on to a wire tray to cool and remove the greaseproof paper when it is cold.

ICED GINGER OATIE

8 oz. rolled oats
2 level teaspoons
   ground ginger
4 oz. soft brown sugar

4 oz. margarine
2 level teaspoons
   golden syrup

FOR THE TOP
6 level teaspoons
   icing sugar
3 oz. butter
1 level teaspoon
   ground ginger

3 level teaspoons
   golden syrup

a round sandwich tin 8 inches in diameter will be required

Brush the inside of the tin thoroughly with melted fat or cooking oil.
Set the oven at about *Gas Mark 4 or 350 degrees F.* so that it will be ready for baking.
Mix together the rolled oats, ground ginger and soft brown sugar. Put the margarine into a pan with the golden syrup and stir them over a gentle heat until the margarine is melted. Pour this into the dry ingredients and mix thoroughly. Pack this mixture into the tin, pressing the surface level.
Bake the oatie for 20 to 25 minutes.

THE TOP

Put all the ingredients for the top into a pan and stir them over a gentle heat until they have melted together. Pour this on top of the baked oatie, which need not be cold. Leave it to set, then mark the top with a fork. Cut into slices when cold.

CHOCOLATE CHRISTMAS TREE CAKE

3 oz. plain flour	4 tablespoons milk
1 oz. cocoa powder	1 small egg
2 oz. golden syrup	¾ level teaspoon
2 oz. soft brown sugar	bicarbonate of soda
2 oz. margarine	

FOR THE CHOCOLATE BUTTERCREAM

3 oz. butter	little cocoa powder
6 oz. icing sugar,	1 packet chocolate
sifted	drops
1 small egg	2 oz. sugar beans

a sandwich tin 7½ inches in diameter will be required

Cut a circle of greaseproof paper to fit inside the base of the tin. Rub the inside surface of the tin with a few drops of cooking oil then slip the paper into position and grease this too. Put the tin on a baking tray.

Set the oven at *Gas Mark 5 or 375 degrees F.*, so that it will be moderately hot for baking the cake. Make sure the shelf inside the oven is just above the centre.

Sift the flour and cocoa into a bowl. Weigh a medium sized pan and a tablespoon and, leaving the pan on the scales, add enough syrup in the spoon to increase the weight by 2 ounces; this saves having a messy scale pan, and the spoon can be used for stirring the ingredients. Add the brown sugar and margarine and stir the mixture over a gentle heat until they are melted, then pour these into the bowl with the flour. Break the egg into another bowl, beat it and stir in the milk and the bicarbonate of soda; add these to the rest of the ingredients and stir very thoroughly. Tip the mixture into the tin and smooth over the surface to make sure it is level. Bake the cake in the pre-heated oven for 20 or 25 minutes. When baked, loosen round the edge of the cake with a sharp knife and tip it on to a wire tray. Peel off the greaseproof paper and leave the cake to cool.

Meanwhile wash up and then make the buttercream. Put the butter into a bowl and beat it really well to a soft cream. Gradually beat in the sifted sugar, then break the egg into the mixture and beat it in well. Add just enough cocoa powder to make the icing a good chocolate colour.

When the cake has cooled, spread the icing over the top and arrange the chocolate drops in the shape of a tree. Add the sugar beans for candles and shape some into a tub. Clear up and wash up.

JOLLY JELLIES

MAKES ABOUT 12

½ packet jelly	12 sweet moulds or
2 tablespoons water	a 6 inch square tin
1 oz. castor sugar for	will be required
coating	

Dissolve the jelly square in the water over a gentle heat, taking care not to boil it.

Grease the moulds or tin with a little oil then pour the jelly in and leave to set.

When the jelly is set, remove it from the moulds or, if you used a tin, cut the jelly into squares. Toss each jelly in a bag of castor sugar.

NOTE: Use raspberry, lemon or lime-flavoured jelly.

GOLDEN FUDGE

MAKES ABOUT 30

3 oz. butter	few drops of vanilla
1½ lb. granulated sugar	essence
1 large tin	about 12 glacé cherries
unsweetened	an 8 inch square tin
evaporated milk	will be required

Melt the butter in a large, strong pan, but not an enamel one. Add the sugar and evaporated milk, and stir occasionally over a very gentle heat—do not allow the mixture to boil before every grain of sugar has dissolved. Meanwhile rub the tin with a little tasteless salad oil.

When the sugar has dissolved, boil the mixture steadily for about 45 minutes, stirring occasionally, especially during the last 20 minutes.

As the mixture cooks, it thickens and darkens. To test when it is ready, take the pan off the heat, drop a small spoonful of the mixture into a cup of cold water, leave it for a second then roll it between the fingers into a ball, which should be firm though soft. The colour will have darkened considerably to a deep straw colour. If the fudge is cooked, beat in the vanilla essence and continue beating with a wooden spoon as it cools and thickens. Whilst it is still soft enough to pour turn it into the prepared tin.

When the fudge is almost cold and set, cut it into squares with an oiled knife and decorate each square with several slivers of cherry. Leave it to set completely before turning it out.

TOFFEE TRIOS

MAKES ABOUT 18

6 oz. caramels	2 oz. chopped walnuts
1 dessertspoon milk	1½ oz. plain chocolate

Put the caramels and milk into a basin over a saucepan of hot water and allow the caramels to dissolve. Stir the mixture occasionally to mix in the milk.

When the mixture is smooth and creamy remove the basin from the heat and mix in the chopped walnuts. Place teaspoonfuls of the walnut caramel on to waxed paper and allow to set.

Place the chocolate on a plate over the pan of hot water and allow it to melt; do not boil the water or the chocolate will be dull when it is set. Put a little melted chocolate on top of each caramel and allow the chocolate to set before removing the Toffee Trios from the paper.

HOME PRESERVES

Jam and jelly making must surely give more satisfaction than almost any other type of cooking. It is a wonderful feeling to look proudly at rows of sparkling, neatly labelled jars, and know you have captured the best of the summer fruits to last you right through the year. As well as traditional jams, jellies and marmalades, I have included in this chapter recipes for some not-so-traditional preserves which I am sure you will enjoy.

A deep freeze is today's answer to preserving food. Although this may seem an expensive luxury, if you can invest in one, you'll find it will soon repay you in convenience, economy and saving of time. Fresh foods can be bought when they are at their best and cheapest and preserved for the rest of the year. Just think how extra-delicious fresh garden raspberries would be served in midwinter!

JAMS

The family will always welcome home-made jams and jellies. If you use a lot of jam you will probably want to make large quantities from the most economical fruits, such as plum and blackcurrant. If you don't use much, a small boiling of as many kinds as possible will be your aim.

If the fresh fruit months really pass you by, and sadly there is often too much fruit to cope with all at one time, there is no need to despair because you can still make the kind of home-made jam you prefer from tinned fruit specially prepared for jam-making.

THE PAN

A large preserving pan is most useful but certainly not essential. If you don't possess a preserving pan it is important to use instead your largest and strongest aluminium pan, even for small quantities, as jam must boil hard and room must be allowed for it to rise. Also, boiling jam reaches a very high temperature and would burn easily in a thin or enamel pan.

GENERAL JAM-MAKING

First rub the base of the pan with a little butter to help to prevent the jam from sticking, then put in the prepared fruit, with the water and lemon juice if required.

Simmer the fruit until the skins are tender. The time this takes varies with each kind of fruit but it is important that the skins are tender before the sugar is added, as they are apt to harden afterwards. While the jam is simmering, press out the juice from the fruit against the sides of the pan with the back of a wooden spoon. The fruit will swell up again once the sugar is added. If you want to break down the fruit while it is cooking, use a potato masher for speedy results.

Warm the measured sugar in the oven, then add it to the fruit and stir over a gentle heat until it has dissolved. Never allow the jam to boil before all the sugar has dissolved.

Bring the jam to a "rolling boil"; it should bubble all over the surface, and any timing given in the recipe should be started from this point. Stir the jam frequently with a long-handled wooden spoon until the setting point is reached. This varies with different recipes and fruit.

To remove the scum from the surface of the jam, either skim it carefully or drop in a knob of butter just before the jam is removed from the heat; this gives the jam a shine and makes most of the scum disappear.

TO TEST FOR SETTING

Draw the pan off the heat, spoon a little jam on to a cold plate and cool it. Draw your finger through the jam on the plate, and if it is ready the surface should wrinkle quite thickly.

When you are an experienced jam-maker, a quicker way to test for setting is to dip the wooden spoon into the jam then hold it sideways well above the pan; the jam should slip down and off the spoon in a heavy, clinging drop.

FILLING THE JARS

After the setting stage is reached, leave the jam to cool slightly. This is especially important with large-berried fruit, such as strawberries, as it helps to keep the fruit or the peel evenly suspended. Warm the jars and hold them over a tray to catch any drips, as you fill them with a ladle. Fill the jars well up to the necks, as jam shrinks slightly when it is cold. As they are filled stand the jars on a tray covered with folded newspaper. (A hard, cold surface might cause the jars to crack). Wipe any drips off the sides with a damp cloth while still warm.

COVERING AND LABELLING THE JARS

Jam may be covered immediately or when it is cold. Place a round of waxed paper—supplied with packets of jam-pot covers—directly on to the jam, making sure it touches the surface all over. Moisten one side of the transparent cover and stretch it over the top of the jar, damp side upwards. When it dries it contracts and makes a seal. Fix the cover with an elastic band or a piece of thin string; string is really better as bands are apt to perish in time.

STORING THE JAM

If the jam is to keep well, it is important to store it in a cool, dry, dark cupboard. Avoid a cupboard which might get overheated from cooking as this is often the cause of mould forming on the surface of jam. A slightly damp larder has the same effect.

RED CHERRY AND REDCURRANT JAM

MAKES ABOUT 8 LB.

2 lb. redcurrants
4 lb. red cherries

5 lb. granulated sugar

Put the redcurrants into a pan—there is no need to remove the stalks—and cook them gently to a pulp. Strain off the juice, measure it, and add water to bring it up to a pint.
Stone the cherries; this is really worthwhile. Slip the tip of a potato peeler into the cherry where the stalk has been removed. Twist out the stone, leaving the cherry whole.
Simmer the cherries and redcurrant juice in the preserving pan until the fruit is absolutely tender, pressing the juice out of the cherries. Add sugar and dissolve over gentle heat. Boil for 15 minutes, or until the setting stage is reached. Allow the jam to cool for 10 minutes before pouring it into the jars and covering them.

PLUM AND RUM CONSERVE

MAKES 3½ LB.

2 lb. plums
juice of 3 lemons

2 lb. demerara sugar
6 tablespoons rum

Stone and chop the plums and put them into a pan. Add the lemon juice, removing any pips; there should be just under ¼ pint of juice. Add the sugar and stir frequently until it has dissolved; this will take about 10 minutes. Boil the conserve hard for three minutes, stirring continuously. Add the rum and continue to boil, but a little less rapidly, for a further 7 or 8 minutes, stirring occasionally. Remove from the heat. Put a little conserve on to a saucer, leave to cool, and test to see if it is set. Pot in warm jars, place waxed paper circles directly on to the conserve, then cover the jars with cellophane and label them.
NOTE: Plum and Rum Conserve makes an unusual tea-time treat.

DAMSON JAM

MAKES ABOUT 9 LB.

4½ lb. damsons
1½ pints water

5 lb. granulated sugar

Remove the stalks from the damsons, then cut the fruit in half and remove the stones. Simmer the fruit in the water until it is tender. Add the sugar and boil the jam rapidly until the setting stage is reached. This will take about 10 minutes.
Pour the jam into jars and cover them.
NOTE: If you like, the stones may be left in the fruit and skimmed off after the sugar has been added, when most of them will float to the surface.

MELON AND LEMON CONSERVE

MAKES ABOUT 3½ LB.

3½ lb. melon (weighed after peeling and pipping

3½ lemons
2¾ lb. granulated sugar

With a sharp knife peel the rind off the melon. Cut a square of butter muslin, remove the melon pips and pulp and put them on the muslin square. Cut the melon flesh into cubes and put it into the preserving pan.
Peel the lemons thinly with a vegetable peeler, taking care not to remove any of the bitter white skin. Squeeze the lemons and strain the juice into a bowl.
Put the lemon rind and pips on the muslin square with the melon pips and pulp, tie it into a bag with a piece of string and add it to the melon in the preserving pan.
Bring the melon slowly to the boil over a gentle heat and boil gently for about 40 minutes until the melon is soft and transparent. Take the pan off the heat, remove the muslin bag and squeeze it over the pan.
Add the sugar and lemon juice to the melon and stir well, making sure that every grain of sugar dissolves. Bring the jam to the boil, and boil fast for about 20 minutes, until it reaches the setting stage.
Ladle the jam into the jars and cover them.

MARROW AND GINGER JAM

MAKES ABOUT 4 LB.

4 lb. diced marrow, weighed after removing the seeds and skin

3½ lb. sugar
juice of 2 lemons
4 oz. root ginger

Cut the marrow into 1 inch cubes, then steam it until it is tender; this will take about 20 minutes.
Put the marrow into a basin in layers with the sugar and lemon juice and leave overnight.
Put the marrow and sugar into a preserving pan. Bruise the ginger with a weight or hammer, so that the flavour will come out, and tie it in a square of muslin. Add the ginger to the marrow. Stir the marrow and sugar over a low heat until all the sugar has dissolved—most of it will have dissolved overnight. Boil the jam rapidly until the setting stage is reached. This will take between 20 and 30 minutes. Remove the bag of ginger. Test for setting, and pot and cover.

Sweetheart conserve

SWEETHEART CONSERVE

MAKES 3 LB. OF CONSERVE

1 lb. plums
3 medium sized
   cooking apples
   (1 to 1½ lb.)

3 cooking pears
   (1 to 1½ lb.)
granulated sugar

Cut the plums in half and remove the stones. Chop the plums roughly. Peel and quarter the apples and pears and cut out the cores. Chop the apples and pears roughly. Weigh all the prepared fruit and allow three-quarters of a pound of sugar for each pound of prepared fruit.
Put the fruit and sugar together into a preserving pan or a large saucepan and stir the fruit over a gentle heat. When the sugar has completely dissolved bring the fruit to the boil and boil rapidly for about 15 to 20 minutes until a little dropped on to a saucer will set when it is cooled. Pour into jars and cover. This makes about 3 lb. of conserve. The pieces of fruit will remain whole in the conserve.

DRIED APRICOT JAM

MAKES 12 LB. OF JAM

2 lb. dried apricots
3 good-sized lemons
5½ pints water

4 oz. almonds
6 lb. granulated sugar

Wash the apricots and, if they are large, cut them in half and put in a very large bowl, such as a clean washing-up bowl. Peel the rind off the lemons very thinly (a potato peeler is the best thing to use for this), then shred the peel finely and add it to the apricots.
Squeeze the lemons. Tie the pips in a piece of muslin and add both the bag of pips and the lemon juice to the apricots. Pour the water over the fruit and leave to soak for 24 hours.

Meanwhile blanch the almonds and slip the skins off. Dry them in a clean cloth, then split each one in half.
Put the soaked apricots and the liquid into a preserving pan with the lemon pips and bring to the boil. Boil rapidly for about 5 to 10 minutes, or until the apricots are tender. The time required will depend on the kind of apricot.
Take the bag of pips out of the jam; add all the sugar and dissolve it gradually. Bring the jam to the boil again, stirring frequently, then allow it to boil rapidly for about 30 minutes or until the setting stage is reached. Skim the jam and stir in the halved blanched almonds. Allow to cool for 5 or 10 minutes before potting the jam and covering.

LEMON CURD

MAKES JUST OVER 1 LB.

2 lemons
2 eggs

4 oz. butter
6 oz. castor sugar

Grate the rind very finely off the lemons. Squeeze out the juice. Break the eggs into a bowl and beat them to break them. Put the butter, sugar, lemon juice and rind into a double saucepan; the water in the pan beneath should be simmering. Stir until the sugar has dissolved. Stir half a cupful of this into the eggs. Add the egg mixture to the liquid in the saucepan and stir continuously until it thickens. It should lightly coat the back of a wooden spoon. Pour the curd into small warmed jars and cover.

MINCEMEAT

MAKES 5½ LB. MINCEMEAT

8 oz. stoned raisins,
   cleaned
4 oz. mixed peel
8 oz. sultanas,
   cleaned
12 oz. currants,
   cleaned
4 oz. blanched
   almonds, chopped
1 lb. cooking apples,
   peeled, cored and
   chopped
1 lb. soft brown sugar
8 oz. shredded suet

1½ level teaspoons
   ground nutmeg
1 level teaspoon
   ground allspice
¼ level teaspoon
   ground cinnamon
finely grated rind
   and juice of
   1 small orange
finely grated
   rind and juice
   of 1 lemon
6 tablespoons rum

Prepare mincemeat at least two weeks before you wish to use it to give the fruit time to mellow and improve the flavour. If you wish to keep it for several months, store it in a cool, dry place, preferably away from direct light.
Chop the raisins, mixed peel and sultanas and mix them with the currants. Add to the fruit the chopped almonds, chopped apple, sugar, suet and spices. Stir all the ingredients thoroughly together. Add the grated orange and lemon rinds and mix again. Lastly stir in the orange and lemon juice and the rum. Pack the mincemeat into jars and cover them with squares of polythene, tied down with string or an elastic band; polythene will keep the mincemeat more moist than jam-pot covers.

Celebration party (see page 157)

Baked gammon and Madeira sauce (see page 48) and profiteroles (see page 107)

Curry dinner (see page 182)

Rosé wine cup (see page 172)

JELLIES

Fruit for jelly-making should have a good pectin content, and any of the following fruits are suitable: redcurrants, blackcurrants, blackberries and apples, gooseberries, crab apples and raspberries.

Currants need not have their stalks removed. Apples need not be cored and peeled but should be roughly sliced after washing. All the stalks and skins will be kept back in the jellybag. You can squeeze the extra juice out of the pulp if you wish, though it tends to make the jelly cloudy.

REDCURRANT JELLY

MAKES ABOUT 5 LB.

4 lb. redcurrants	granulated sugar
about 2 pints of water, or just enough to come level with the top of the fruit in the pan	

Wash the currants gently but leave the stalks on. Put the currants into a preserving pan with the water and simmer for about 30 minutes, until all the juice is extracted from it. Pour the fruit into a jelly-bag or a large square of doubled muslin. For the latter, put the muslin square into a large basin and ask someone to hold it over the sides of the bowl while you ladle the pulp into the centre. Gather the edges together and tie them securely with string. Lift the muslin bag, tie it up, and hang it over a bowl so that the juice can drip through. Leave overnight.

Measure the clear juice and weigh out the required sugar, estimating 1 lb. of sugar to 1 pint of juice. Put the juice and sugar into a preserving pan and heat it slowly until the sugar is dissolved. Then bring the jam to a rapid boil, and boil until the setting stage is reached. This will only take 4 or 5 minutes, as redcurrants are rich in pectin and therefore set quickly.

Pour the jelly into jars and cover when cold.

BLACKBERRY AND APPLE JELLY

MAKES ABOUT 5½ LB.

2 lb. cooking apples	3 pints water
2 lb. blackberries	granulated sugar

Cut the apples in slices—it is not necessary to peel them or remove the cores. Put the sliced apples, blackberries and water into a preserving pan and simmer steadily until they are a soft pulp. Strain the pulp through a jelly-bag or doubled muslin as described in the recipe for redcurrant jelly (see above). Leave to drip overnight.

Next day measure the juice and allow 1 lb. sugar to every pint of juice. You can squeeze the extra juice out of the pulp if you wish, though it tends to make the jelly cloudy. Pour the juice into the pan, add the sugar, and dissolve it over a gentle heat. Bring the jam to the boil, and boil it very rapidly until the setting stage is reached, in about 20 to 30 minutes.

Pour the jelly into jars and cover when cold.

ROWAN JELLY

MAKES ABOUT 3½ LB.

2 lb. rowan berries	1¾ lb. granulated
1¾ pints water	sugar

Take all the stalks off the berries, put the berries into a colander and wash them under cold water. Transfer the berries to a large pan, add the water, and cook them for about 1 hour. As they simmer, squash out the juice with a potato masher.

Strain the pulp through a square of muslin or a jelly-bag and leave it to drip overnight. Next day stir the juice and sugar together over a gentle heat until the sugar is dissolved, then bring the jelly to the boil, and boil rapidly until the setting stage is reached (see Crab Apple Jelly below). Pour it into small jars and cover when cold.

This jelly is nice with cold meat, rabbit dishes or game.

CRAB APPLE JELLY

MAKES ABOUT 7 LB.

6 lb. crab apples	a little red colouring
6 pints water	if liked
granulated sugar	

Wash the crab apples and cut them in quarters. Put them into a preserving pan with the water and cook gently to a soft pulp. This will take about 30 minutes. It is most important that the crab apples are really soft.

Strain the pulp through a jelly-bag or a large square of muslin, and leave it to drip overnight.

Next day, measure the juice and allow 1 lb. of sugar to every pint of juice. Pour the juice into the preserving pan, add the sugar and stir over a gentle heat until the sugar has dissolved. Bring the jelly to the boil, and boil rapidly until the setting stage is reached in about 10 minutes. To test for setting put a little jelly in a saucer. If a firm skin forms over the surface when it is cold then the jelly is ready. At this stage you may add a few drops of red colouring if you think the jelly is rather pale.

Pour the jelly into jars and cover and label them when cold.

APPLE MINT JELLY

MAKES ABOUT 2¾ LB.

2 lb. cooking apples	2 heaped tablespoons
thinly peeled rind and juice of 1 lemon	chopped mint
2 pints of water	few drops of green colouring
2 lb. sugar	

Wash the apples but do not peel or skin them. Cut them into rough chunks and put them into a fairly large pan with the lemon rind and water. Simmer the apples for about 30 minutes until they are absolutely tender. Turn the pulp into a jelly bag or large piece of muslin; suspend it above a bowl and allow the juice to drip overnight.

Put the juice into a pan with the sugar and lemon juice, and boil the jelly for about 30 minutes or until the setting stage is reached. To test this, put a teaspoonful on a cold plate—when cold it should have a skin across the surface. Add the mint, bring it back to the boil, colour the jelly a pale green and pour it into small jars.

The jelly should be only lightly set; serve it traditionally with roast lamb. It is also good with bread and butter or used as a cake filling.

MARMALADES

A TRADITIONAL RECIPE

MAKES ABOUT 18 LB.

4 lb. fruit (2 sweet oranges, 4 small or 3 large lemons, and the weight made up with Seville oranges)	10 pints water 10 lb. preserving or granulated sugar

1. Wipe the fruit with a damp cloth, and cut them in half. Cut round the flesh, using a sharp serrated knife, preferably a curved grapefruit knife. Scoop out the centre of the fruit with a spoon and put it into a bowl (photograph 1, see opposite page).
2. Shred the peel—as finely or as coarsely as you like. It is easiest to shred the peel with the rind upwards, using a very sharp knife and keeping your fingers upright to avoid cutting them (photograph 2).
3. Chop the pulp of the oranges and lemons roughly, removing the pips. Tie the pips in a square of muslin, loosely so that the juice can boil through the pips.
4. Put the shredded peel, the pulp of the oranges and the lemons, the bag of pips and the water into a large china bowl and leave them to soak overnight.
5. Next day turn the contents of the bowl into a large preserving pan, put the pan on a slow heat and gently bring to the boil. This will take nearly 1 hour. Put the lid on the pan to prevent excess evaporation.
6. Simmer the fruit until it is quite tender. The time required will depend on how finely the peel is chopped, but it should take 1 to 1½ hours.
7. Take out the bag of pips, cool it on a plate, then squeeze all the juice from the pips back into the marmalade.
8. Add the sugar (photograph 3). Stir the marmalade over a gentle heat until the sugar has dissolved, then bring to a rapid boil. Let it continue boiling rapidly; the surface should "roll" all over the pan. Stir the marmalade occasionally, and at the same time move the pan slightly so that a different part of the base comes in contact with the heat.
9. After the marmalade has boiled for 30 minutes, test it to see if it has reached setting stage. Put a spoonful of the marmalade on to a saucer or plate and let it cool. When it is cold, run your finger through it and if a wrinkle forms on the surface the marmalade is ready (photograph 4). You may have to make several tests—the time will vary between 30 and 50 minutes, depending on how fast the marmalade is boiling. When you think the marmalade is nearly ready, turn off the heat while you are testing so that the marmalade does not over-boil.
10. When the marmalade has reached setting point, turn off the heat and leave it for 15 to 20 minutes so that the peel will be evenly distributed when it is poured into the jars.

11. Have ready some dry, clean, warmed jars. Ladle the marmalade into the jars, then stand them on a wooden board or folded newspaper, but not on metal, enamel or marble in case the jars crack. Wipe each jar carefully with a damp cloth to remove any stickiness. Cover the marmalade immediately or when it is quite cold (photograph 5). Label the jars and store them in a dry cupboard. You may find the marmalade thickens slightly on keeping.
NOTE: This recipe can be halved if a smaller amount of marmalade is required. The only difference in the method is that the final boiling will take less time—nearer 30 than 50 minutes.

FOUR SEASONS MARMALADE

MAKES ABOUT 14 LB.

4 good sized sweet oranges 1 large lemon 2 medium sized grapefruit	8 pints water 10 lb. preserving or granulated sugar an extra pint of water

Make in the same way as Traditional Marmalade (see left). Simmer the fruit for 2 hours or even longer to make sure the peel is absolutely tender. It should be transparent. Add the extra pint of water before adding the sugar. Make the first test to see if the marmalade is ready after it has boiled for 40 minutes—it will probably take between 50 minutes and 1 hour.

JELLY MARMALADE

MAKES ABOUT 8 LB.

3 lemons and enough Seville oranges to make a total weight of 4 lb.	10 pints water about 5 lb. sugar

Wipe the fruit with a damp cloth, then chop it or mince it through a coarse cutter. Put the fruit into a pan with the water and bring it to the boil, then cover the pan and simmer the fruit until it is tender—this will take about 2 hours. Pour the marmalade into a jelly-bag and leave the juice to drip into a basin overnight.

Next day, measure the juice and allow 1 lb. of sugar to 1 pint of juice. Put the juice and the sugar into the preserving pan and stir it over a gentle heat until the sugar has dissolved. Bring the marmalade to the boil and boil it rapidly until the setting stage is reached. Test in the way described in the Traditional Marmalade recipe, left, then pot, label, and cover the jelly.

TANGERINE MARMALADE

MAKES ABOUT 7 LB.

1 lemon 3 Seville oranges, made up to 2 lb. with tangerines	5 pints water 5 lb. preserving sugar

Make this in the same way as the Traditional Marmalade, left. The fruit may need to be simmered a little longer to make sure the peel is tender.

Traditional marmalade—1

2

3

LEMON MARMALADE

MAKES ABOUT 8 LB.

2 lb. lemons
5 pints water

5 lb. preserving sugar

Make this by the method used for the Traditional Marmalade on page 202—the fruit will take about $1\frac{3}{4}$ hours to tenderise. Test the marmalade to see if it has reached setting stage after it has been boiling rapidly for 15 minutes.

GRAPEFRUIT MARMALADE

MAKES ABOUT 8 LB.

3 large grapefruit (the total weight should be as near 2 lb. as possible)

1 lemon
5 pints water
5 lb. granulated sugar

Make this by the method used in the Traditional Marmalade recipe on page 202.

4

PRESSURE COOKER MARMALADE

MAKES JUST UNDER 8 LB.

2 lb. marmalade oranges
1 lemon

2 pints water
5 lb. granulated sugar

5

Wash the fruit and put it whole into a pressure cooker with the water. Cook the fruit with the water at 15 lb. pressure, for 12 minutes; by this time it should be tender. When it is cool enough to handle, halve the fruit, scoop out the inside of the oranges and lemon, and sieve the pulp. Shred the peel, finely or coarsely according to taste, then return it to the pan with the pulp and sugar.
Dissolve the sugar slowly, stirring all the time, then bring the marmalade to a rapid boil for about 20 minutes or until the setting stage is reached. If there is any danger of the marmalade boiling over, boil it a little more slowly—it will then take slightly longer to reach the setting stage.
Remove the pan from the heat. Allow it to cool for 15 minutes, then pour the marmalade into warm jars and cover it when it is cold.

INDEX

Colour photograph on page 134 by courtesy of Allinson Ltd.